THE
GENESIS
OF
GEORGES SOREL

*AN ACCOUNT OF HIS FORMATIVE PERIOD
FOLLOWED BY A STUDY OF HIS INFLUENCE*

by
JAMES H. MEISEL
UNIVERSITY OF MICHIGAN

The George Wahr Publishing Company
Ann Arbor, Michigan
1 9 5 1

LITHOPRINTED IN THE UNITED STATES OF AMERICA BY
CUSHING - MALLOY, INC., ANN ARBOR, MICHIGAN, 1951

Dedicated to my wife,

MARIANNE

whose consistent loathing of the subject

did much to speed up my work.

PREFACE

Dis manibus Europae?

To treat of the complete but — alas! — uncollected works of Georges Sorel is in itself an act of gross temerity; the fact that this is the first full-length study of Sorel to appear in this country is only one more cause for trepidation. For the subject is as immense as it is disquieting. As there was, for Sorel, no end of the quest ever, likewise there can be no end of him, unless it be the end of Europe and her great traditions, all of which were very much Sorel's concern. The fragmentary character of the Sorelian work may not explain, but possibly excuse its fragmentary treatment here. The accent will be placed on Sorel's politics; his physics, metaphysics, ethics and aesthetics could, of course, not be eliminated from the survey, but they could be treated only incidentally. The philosopher Sorel still remains to be discovered by this country.

But even the political writer Sorel is far less known than fame (or ill fame) would have it. His prestige is still based on a single book, the only one so far translated out of the multitude of his French and Italian publications. If this essay has any raison d'être, it may be found in the attempt to put the **Reflections on Violence** back into the context of Sorel's vast oeuvre, by indicating his slow evolution toward that climactic product of his versatile and yet persistent mind. Beyond that point, this study tries to let Sorel speak for himself, rather than to speak for or against Sorel (who seems to have a fatal attraction for writers eager to **interpret** and to paraphrase his thought — not always with fidelity).

To be sure, the impact of Sorel on his contemporaries is a subject not less worthy of attention than the exegesis of his writings. Accordingly, his influence has been made the subject of the second part, treating the dubious affiliations of our author with such movements as French Royalism, Italian Fascism and Russian Communism.

Both studies were made possible by the encouragement I received from my colleagues, Professors A. W. Bromage, E. S. Brown, H. W. Nordmeyer, J. K. Pollock and L. Preuss, as well as from the Horace Rackham School of Graduate Studies, University of Michigan, which, by two generous grants, enabled this writer, first, to unearth precious source materials in Sorel's Paris, and, later, to complete the manuscript unencumbered by teaching obligations.

For valuable information I am grateful to Professor Benedetto Croce (Naples); to Doctors Daniel Halévy, Pierre Andreu and Maximilien Rubel, to Mlle. Gaston-Chérau of the Bibliotheque Nationale, M. Robert Abranson, Director of Marcel Rivière, Publishers, and Mr. Ian Forbes Fraser, Director of the American Library (all in Paris);

in this country: to Director Warner G. Rice and Mr. Rolland C. Stewart
of the General Library, University of Michigan; to Dr. Franz L. Neumann of Columbia University for helpful criticism.

   For permission to reproduce several articles which reappear — in
amended form — as chapters of this book, I wish to thank the editors
of the following journals: **Michigan Alumnus Quarterly Review** (Vol.
LV, No. 20, May 7, 1949: "A Much-Maligned Man — Georges Sorel,"
now Introductory i); **The Western Political Quarterly** (Vol. III, No. 1,
March, 1950: "A Premature Fascist? — Sorel and Mussolini," now
chapter 9); **The Journal of Politics** (Vol. XII, No. 1, February, 1950:
"Georges Sorel's Last Myth," now chapter 10); **The South Atlantic
Quarterly** (Vol. IXL, No. 2, April, 1950: "Disciples and Dissenters,"
now chapter 11); **University of Toronto Quarterly** (Vol. XIX, No. 1,
October, 1949: "Sorel Revisited," now chapter 12).

   The index has been compiled by Milton Feder.

Ann Arbor, January, 1951.   James H. Meisel

TABLE OF CONTENTS

PART ONE

THE WORK

Introductory i:

A MUCH-MALIGNED MAN

Some time in the nineteen-twenties, Whittaker Chambers, a man who has been in the news in the past years, "read Georges Sorel's **Reflections on Violence** and was converted to an acceptance of the evil thing," communism.[1]

This succinct statement is a fair example of the great confusion that has been the curse of the old French engineer (retired), Georges Sorel, ever since his **Reflections**, one out of a dozen published books, and the only one translated into English, made him relatively famous.[2] In that work, he had been trying to do with Marx what Marx had done with Hegel; as the German philosopher of "dialectical materialism" had put his teacher's idealistic system "on its feet," so the Frenchman thought that he could put Marxism on a strictly proletarian footing. Whereas most Marxists saw in the working class at best the agent, at worst the mere instrument of a historical process that would, in the end, abolish the proletariat together with capitalism, Sorel wanted labor to retain its class identity, to increase its proletarian character and to develop its particular morality into an austere creed; it was to give birth to an élite of autonomous producers reviving "the old hero-isms" — which were none other than the old, decaying middle class virtues of thrift, hard work, and the "chastity" of family life. (Sorel felt very strongly about this point.)[3]

In short, the proletariat according to Sorel would fulfill its historic mission not by destroying class society but by strictly "minding its own business," in building up juridical and cultural institutions apart from bourgeois society, very much as the early Christians had created their own world in the catacombs of the Roman cosmopolis. And as the

---

[1]Time, Vol. L11, No. 25 (December 20, 1948), p. 17.

[2]First edition, Paris, 1908. Italian edition, Bari, 1909. Second French edition, with an additional chapter on "Unity and Multiplicity," Paris, 1910. Third edition, including an "Apology of Violence," Paris, 1913. First English edition (translation by T. E. Hulme), London, 1914. Spanish edition, Madrid, 1915. Fourth French edition, with the "Plea for Lenin" (the final text), Paris, 1919. By 1950 the work had reached its eleventh French printing. German and Japanese editions in 1928. American editions (using T. E. Hulme's translation) New York, 1914 (Ben Huebsch), New York 1941 (P. Smith), 1950 (Free Press, Glencoe, Illinois, adding appendices i and iii, not included in the earlier English and American editions).

[3]"Mankind will become more just only to the extent that it becomes more chaste." Sorel, Preface to N. Colajanni, Le Socialisme, in Matériaux d'une théorie du prolétariat, 2. edition, (Paris, 1921), p. 199.

early Christians had been fortified in their perseverence by a great
religious myth, by their belief in the Lord's Second Coming, so the
proletarians were to be inspired by their faith in the ultimate, "Napoleonic" battle of the general strike. Whether that day of judgment
would ever come did not matter as long as the workers believed in it
and lived accordingly, that is, in a state of permanent alertness and
preparedness. Their task was to keep themselves in perfect fighting
trim for the supreme test, and that was possible only if they resisted
all offers to call off the class war, if they refused all compromise with
a frightened bourgeoisie gone soft. It was proletarian duty to keep the
ruling class always at arms length, to prod it into resistance by frequent acts of class violence. If in that contest the bourgeoisie should
prove the stronger part, that would be bad news for the Sorel who was
the partisan of labor, but quite all right with the Sorel who was concerned with the survival of Western civilization.

After his death in 1922, when certain European dictatorships
seemed to spell out what eager, but perhaps not at all too careful,
readers thought Sorel had written, the confusion grew to the point
where he was credited with having fathered fascism. Still later, it became the fashion to say: "No Hitler without Nietzche, no Mussolini
without Georges Sorel." The case of the latter seemed to be especially
bad, since he had also endorsed Russian communism by adding a brief
laudatory chapter called "For Lenin" to the fourth edition of his
Reflections. The uninitiated reader who never heard of Marx or Lenin
might well get the idea that here was an author who not only had anticipated the violent political explosions following World War I but had
supplied both the leader of the Russian revolution and the Duce of the
Italian counter-revolution with intellectual ammunition, if not a detailed design for action.[4]

Nietzsche and Sorel

It is no accident that their names have been linked together. Insistence on the instinctive, volitional element in human nature, disparagement of rationalism, and, in politics, contempt of democratic,
egalitarian principles — these tendencies are indeed to be found in the
work of the former university professor of Germany and the former
civil servant of France. And it is perfectly legitimate to point out the
recurrence of those notions in Fascist and National-Socialist "philosophy." But to deduce from that fact the intellectual and moral "responsibility" of the two thinkers, to declare that they made twentieth
century barbarism possible, that is quite another matter.

---

[4] A typical example of this "Vulgar Sorelianism" is Julien Benda's statement: "It is current knowledge that Italian Fascism and Russian Bolshevism
both derive from the author of the Reflections on Violence." (The Great Betrayal [La trahison des clercs], London, 1928, p. 72, note 1.)

Was it really the iconoclast of **The Will to Power** who made the Nazis behave as they did? Would there have been no Buchenwald had the author of **Thus Spake Zarathustra** never divulged his vision of "superman"? It seems hardly necessary to restate the historic evidence showing that the general social and economic breakdown of European civilization preceded rather than followed the influence of a coarsened, perverted Nietzscheanism. As long as nineteenth-century society was a "going concern," Nietzsche's "philosophy of the hammer" remained the possession of an esoteric minority with no practical influence whatsoever. When the storm broke, it came from quite a different quarter. The great revolt was the logical outcome of that long leveling process described by Nietzsche as the decadence and death of all values; but at the same time the revolt was a protest against that very loss; the masses wanted to be reassured, they were content with substitutes. No wonder the new leaders were eager to annex to their hastily improvised doctrines those teachings of the old élite which were an indictment of the recent past as well as a restatement of the lost, the "nobler" heritage. And so it happened that the very "slave revolt" which Friedrich Nietzsche had been decrying so passionately was carried out with his aristocratic slogans.

The same thing happened to Sorel, who was Nietzsche's lesser contemporary. They were born only three years apart, but Sorel did not commence his career as a writer until the very year in which the world learned that the author of **Ecce Homo** had lost his mind. Contrary to a widespread belief, Sorel owed Nietzsche nothing. Daniel Halévy, author of two books on Nietzsche, and Sorel's friend, informs us that Sorel had not heard of Nietzsche when he wrote his **Trial of Socrates**, a book in which he branded Plato's teacher as "the first rationalist and decadent," exactly as Nietzsche had done in his **Birth of Tragedy**.

Indeed, their agreement is coincidental rather than fundamental. Sorel shares with Nietzsche the anti-intellectual bias as well as the vision of an aristocratic élite destined to restore to civilization its lost vigor. But Nietzsche's "creative minority," to use Arnold Toynbee's term, was not Sorel's, namely, the industrial proletariat; and Sorel's aversion to the intelligentsia was, unlike Nietzsche's, based on economic categories: the distinction between producers and parasites. By narrowing the concept of creative work to manual labor, Sorel wanted to express his conviction that the labor class, if it was to be more than an object of politics, ought to cut itself loose from nonproletarian interlopers and rely exclusively on its own strength.

In that hope, Sorel was disappointed. In the history of social movements before the great catastrophe, Sorel never was a first-rate influence — he remained unknown for the greater part of his long life, and his present reputation is based on hearsay rather than on sound information. He has founded no school; the few disciples he had, are dead; there exists, at present, no living Sorelian tradition in France or anywhere else. And yet his political influence, if not more import- ant than that of Nietzsche, is at least more direct: if Nietzsche was a philosopher and psychologist first, with only an incidental interest in politics, Sorel, who also started out as a philosopher and psychologist (at the age of forty, after a long career in the highway department), nevertheless wrote with a political intent — with an immediate interest in social action. The trouble is that he cannot be identified with any particular current of thought or action: he learned from Marx, but he was not a Marxist; he admired Proudhon but was quite critical of him; he was associated for some years with French organized labor, but he cannot be labeled a syndicalist; he studied the nationalist movement and agreed with some of its objectives, but it would be unfair to speak of him as a nationalist. He sampled many ideas and adhered to none.

One could call him a marginal figure, but again, it is possible to study the entire history of political and social ideas by just reading Sorel. It would not be quite correct to call his work a clearing house of political currencies because the business it did was rather limited in scope, but future generations may well decide that Sorel's signifi- cant contribution was his ability to reflect the powerful forces of his time rather than to shape them. The reputation of Sorel, the migratory student of our period of transition, may well survive the present fame of Sorel, the author of some distinct theories of rather dubious value.

Even these celebrated theories, developed in what Sorel used to call, ruefully, his "standard work," did not escape the fate of travesty that seemed to haunt him in all his undertakings. If we are to believe common gossip, forty years ago mankind had finally evolved from barbarism; civil society had achieved peace and order; social dis- putes were being settled according to a sensible procedure that made violent means unnecessary. Into this charmed circle of decency stepped a malcontent scribbler who, mistaking the enlightened benevolence of the governing classes for weakness, began to whisper evil advice into the ears of the workers.

If his conclusions came as a shock to his nonproletarian con- temporaries, that was only because they were living in a fool's para- dise of peace. They had forgotten that violence, if not continually practiced, was continually present, forever waiting in the wings of the social scene. They had forgotten that all their rules, all their judicial safeguards, were only sublimated violence. As economic competition went on furiously even in the age of monopolies and market regulation, so violence was still society's supreme political law, only it operated silently, more subtly, by indirection: exerting pressure as effectively as it had done in times more primitive, even though its sanctions did not lead to physical extermination quite as frequently as before.

But violence, as it became more refined, grew to be more vicious — Nietzsche had made that discovery before Sorel. Only, people did not realize it, and this lack of consciousness became a social fact which Sorel happened to consider dangerous. He lamented the dominant tendency to smooth over the fact of class antagonism; he was afraid class reconciliation as practiced by all interested parties, abetted by the general humanitarian spirit of the times and institutionalized by the modern welfare state, was detrimental to social morality. Sorel despised the bourgeoisie gone soft and philanthropic only slightly less than the proletariat looking for assistance from the state rather than standing on its own feet.

As a historian, he had found that a civilization will decay unless its leaders maintain high standards of morality and exact the last ounce of effort from their people. Modern industrial civilization particularly, Sorel believed, meant increasingly more work, not less — and what did he behold? A general weakening of effort; a general willingness to compromise, to bribe and to be bribed. In the past the classes had been forced to struggle against heavy odds for their vision of social justice; social rights had to be conquered or defended inch by inch. Sorel was afraid freedom would be lost whenever the martial instinct of the social groups became extinct. He was no totalitarian. His theory — pitting the two main classes of industrial society against each other — was certainly influenced by Marx, but it was equally indebted to the old Aristotelian and Polybian concept of governments as the resultant of conflicting power claims. And in contradistinction to Marx, who saw in the proletariat the last class bound to destroy itself, as a class, together with capitalism, Sorel urged the workers not only to remain but to become more proletarian: he assured them that their historic role consisted in minding their own, and not the capitalist's, business.

It was the capitalist's business, however, to "ensnare" the workers, to win them over to his way of thinking at least, if not to his way of life. Against this danger to the "integrity" of the proletariat, Sorel saw only one protection: violence. It was to him a class weapon of defense rather than of offense, a means for labor to retain its class identity and class morality rather than an instrument of conquest. Least of all Sorel wanted the proletarians to conquer the government. Sorel did not believe in any need for the workers to possess the state; he was no power-worshipping Marxist.

The Scope and the Style

If this is known so little and misunderstood so vastly, if the man who introduced the term of the "myth" into the language of political science has himself become the object of mythification, if not mystification, that is partly his own fault. He cannot be blamed for the fact that his total oeuvre is scattered in many little magazines long since defunct and hardly accessible, even in France; but also in his known

works Sorel did his worst to confuse the reader. The organization of
the materials is often misleading — reprints of older writings are
jumbled together with recent pronouncements; chapters that have little if any connections with the main topic are tagged on as "annexes"
or "supplements" under the flimsiest of pretexts.

Anyone interested in tracing the line of Sorel's intellectual development is forced to tear apart his dozen volumes and regroup the
parts according to the many themes that occupied the writer's catholic
curiosity at one time or another. Those who are wont to see in Sorel
only the theorist of revolutionary syndicalism, will be surprised to
learn that he was, first, and last, a student of philosophy.[5] Years before turning to the social field, he published articles on psychophysics
and an essay — which later filled a book — dealing with "The Old and
New Metaphysics," meaning Aristotle and Marx.[6] In that early work
he already discovered for himself Henri Bergson, as he later would
discover William James. And even at the height of his preoccupation
with the Russian and Italian revolutions Sorel went on treating questions of aesthetics or epistemology as matters of the first importance.[7]

The long list of his readings easily yields the list of those whom
Sorel considered as his masters. To those already mentioned must
be added, first of all, Renan who vies with Proudhon, Marx and Giambattista Vico for the place of the authority most-cited by Sorel.[8] But
there is always Taine, and there are Frédéric Le Play,[9] Gustave Le
Bon,[10] and Emile Durkheim; there are Alfred Fouillée and Gabriel
Tarde, Edouard Le Roy, Cournot and Renouvier — they all left traces

---

[5]"What was the aim and what was the accomplishment of G. Sorel? To be
a philosopher." Fernand Rossignol, La Pensée de G. Sorel (Paris, 1948), p. 57.

[6]L'Ancienne et la nouvelle métaphysique in L'Ere nouvelle, March-June,
1894. Published in book form as D'Aristote à Marx, with an introduction by
Edouard Berth (Paris, 1935). See chapter 4.

[7]The readers of Sorel's correspondence with Benedetto Croce will be impressed by the extent to which the non-political interests prevail. See chapters 1 and 7.

[8]Renan's influence on Sorel is treated in chapter 6 and in the supplement,
part 1; for Vico, see chapter 3; Proudhon and Marx are discussed in chapter 4.

[9]For Le Play, see especially Sorel, Introduction a l'économie moderne
(1st edition, Paris, 1903, 2nd edition, Paris, 1922), Part I, chapters iv-vi.

[10]The author of The Crowd, who in turn was influenced by Taine, anticipated
Sorel's definition of the Myth when he wrote: "Whatever strikes the imagination of crowds presents itself under the shape of a startling and very clear
image, freed from all accessory explanation . . . a great victory, a great miracle, a great crime, or a great hope. Things must be laid before the crowd
as a whole, and their genesis must never be indicated." (Chapter 3 § 3).
Sorel had reviewed Le Bon's work in Le Devenir Social, November, 1895.

in his work.[11] And there is, last, but not least, Eduard von Hartmann, the philosopher of the Unconscious, whose mark is to be found in the **Reflections.** The catalogue of influences contains names from such heterogenuous camps as the physician, Georges Castex,[12] the syndicalist leader, Fernand Pelloutier,[13] and Ferdinand Brunetière, the idealist and catholic apologist, — the last-named representative of Sorel's habit to learn even from those he loved to hate and ridicule.[14]

Is it necessary to insist that a servant of so many masters is most likely to be the servant of none? There still remains, of course, the possibility that Georges Sorel, while able to digest his immense erudition, still did not succeed in giving his own work the unity on which we insist in an author even if we grant him the right to mercurial changes and protean restlessness. Now, the diffusion of interests and the difficulty of streamlining the evidence are not the only obstacles that make it so hard to penetrate through the crowd of Sorels to Sorel. The truth will out: he was not a good writer.

Sorel himself was very conscious of his defect, and he was clearly thinking of himself when he quoted a remark made by Daniel Halévy about their common master, Proudhon:

"In order to understand his thought one must search with him, grope with him. Let us not forget that he began to write rather late . . . that he had to compose under stress and in haste, incessantly improving

---

[11]Sorel, "Les théories de M. Durkheim" in Le Devenir Social, April, May, 1895; "Les théories pénales de MM. Durkheim et Tarde" in Archivio di Psichiatria, scienze penali, Vol. XVI, 1895. On Fouillée: "Le mouvement idéaliste et la réaction contre la science positive" in Le Devenir Social, July, 1896; "Le mouvement positiviste et la conception sociologique du monde" in Le Devenir Social, February, 1897. Fouillée's concept of the ideé-force, developed in his work, La psychologie des ideés-forces (Paris, 1893) probably influences Sorel's conception of the "myth." Cf. Serbos, Une philosophie nouvelle de la production (Aix et Paris, 1913), p. 94.

[12]Sorel wrote a preface to that author's La douleur physique (Paris, 1905), an essay which, as "L'humanité contre la douleur," became the supplement to the second edition of Sorel's Introduction à l'économie moderne (Paris, 1922), pp. 399-419. Sorel expressed his indebtedness to Castex in a personal inscription, "Hommage d'un auditeur du Collège de France au maître," to be found in a copy of Castex's work which he presented to the author (in the possession of the present writer.)

[13]Sorel wrote a preface for Pelloutier's L'histoire des bourses du travail (Paris, 1902).

[14]Cf. especially Sorel, "Léon XIII" and "Nouveaux réquisitoires de M. Brunetière" in Etudes Socialistes (Paris, 1903). Cf. chapter 3, section on Church and State.

upon his ideas; what we have to consider above all is the direction of his work, its ultimate goal."[15]

It is hardly an accident that the only one of Sorel's books that came close to being a best seller and was translated into other languages, the Reflections on Violence, had received the benefit of Daniel Halévy's editorial touch. Not that Sorel lacked the gift of expression —the same Halévy, a writer of great musical sensitivity, numbers him among the masters of French prose.[16] But over long, all too long, stretches, Sorel's writing is fuzzy, oblivious for whole pages — in themselves always rewarding — of the task at hand. His most loyal disciple, Édouard Berth could not help exclaiming:

"Surely, the first impression is disconcerting. The line of development seems to be ragged, much too abrupt; one has the feeling of being a traveller . . . guided by a Cicerone of bizarre and malicious humor; at each turn magnificent vistas seem to open but they pass away as quickly as a stroke of lightning; the curtain falls abruptly and we have to continue on our obscure and difficult pilgrimage over roads forever rutted and washed out."[17]

This is a grave indictment; no writer, particularly no French writer, can afford to shrug it off, and if the saying that le style, c'est l'homme is true, the conclusion would be that Sorel wrote a fuzzy style because his thought was fuzzy.

The more charitable explanation would be to think of Sorel as a mere commentator who never intended to be a writer in his own right. Not at all impressed with "original sources," he drew his information from secondary writings, compiling quotes of quotes and justifying this procedure with mock modesty: "I thought my readers would have more confidence if the selection was the work of a member of the Institute rather than my own." But his fondness for "authorities" is that of the Grand Inquisitor playing with his victim. It is fair to say that Sorel's scholarly instinct is in the main that of an irate reader filling page after page of his text with angry marginal exclamations. Sorel's passion for polemics forever gets in the way of the writer. One can almost visualize the old retired civil servant hibernating in the National Library of Paris, buried behind a wall of heavy tomes, taking notes upon notes until the pile grows into what looks like another book. But Sorel, although sincerely humble about his accomplishment, has something to say for the notorious vagueness of his writing:

---

[15]"Mes raisons du syndicalisme" in Matériaux d'une théorie du prolétariat (2nd edition, Paris, 1921), p. 242, note 2.

[16]Oral statement, made to this writer in August 1948. Sorel expressed his gratitude to the friend in the long and important "Letter to Daniel Halévy" which served as an introduction to the Reflections.

[17]Berth made this comment in his review of Sorel's book, Le système historique de Renan in Le Mouvement Socialiste, Nos. 189 and 190 (August 15 and September 15, 1907), p. 179.

"We must beware of too much strictness in our language because it would then be at odds with the fluid character of reality; the result would be deceptive."[18]

A truly Bergsonian argument: language is an intellectual attempt to freeze the flux of life into intelligible patterns; a device as necessary as it is dangerous because truth is accessible only to the intuitive mind; the rational element of all expression, if it predominates, obscures the real image, which needs, in order to shine brightly, an aura of obscurity.

The Bergsonian writer, obviously, will be at his best when the artist in him keeps reason under control. Sorel, unfortunately, although he took a very lively interest in the arts, was not an artist. His recipe of linguistic vagueness was an intellectual insight only; it could not help him to write good books. But Sorel had other outlets to express his spontaneous self: in the letters to his friends or when he talked to a group of attentive youngsters (there was nothing he loved better), when his style was not cramped by the requirements of composition, his language was inspired, most pungent and felicitous in form as well as content.

It is in his correspondence and in the protocols of his famous soliloquies that we will have to look for information not found in his books. Especially if we want to find out what Sorel thought of the two great upheavals of our time, the Russian revolution and its Central European sequence, we will do well to consult the intimate Sorel rather than the author of the Reflections.

A Double Disclaimer

There is, on the surface of it, no reason why one and the same man should not have inspired both Lenin and Il Duce. The precedent of Hegel, who "fathered" both Marxism and modern nationalism, suggests the possibility. As far as Sorel himself is concerned, he vigorously disclaimed all "credit" for both Lenin's and Mussolini's ideas.

Why did he endorse Lenin?

When the chief of the Bolsheviks made himself master of Russia in 1917, Sorel was a lonely old man who had given up all hope of the coming of Giambattista Vico's ricorso, the barbaric rejuvenation of an aging civilization. Socialism, Sorel had declared, was dead. Nor had the French working class taken to Sorel's myth of the General Strike, which was to be something like the second coming of the early Christians.

---

[18]L'Avenir socialiste des syndicats, preface of 1905, in Matériaux d'une théorie du prolétariat, 2nd edition, 1921, p. 58. Cf. also Reflections (1950 ed.) pp. 31-33.

And in Italy, where Sorel had been more honored than in his own country,[19] such left wingers as Benito Mussolini had turned rabidly against the master when he had shown a passing interest in the French nationalist movement, calling Sorel the clown of reaction.[20]

No wonder that the Russian revolution kindled a new fire in the heart of the ailing, lonely philosopher of the small Paris suburb Boulogne sur Seine, from which he undertook less and less frequent sallies into the city in order to browse in the library or to buttonhole the few remaining loyal friends.

He had always been curious about Russia. As a European, Sorel sensed long before the war that the czarist regime was a menace to the peace of Europe; as a socialist, he hated its system of social oppression. In 1916, he predicted the revolution; "The Czar will end on the gallows."[21] But when the prophecy came true (although the gallows was replaced by guns), Sorel, like the rest of his contemporaries, was slow to understand what had really happened in distant Russia. At first it seemed to him that the small band of revolutionaries that had wrested power from the Russian liberals was bound to lose in the uneven struggle against the counter-revolution encouraged by the Western world. Having always taken the part of the underdog, Sorel could not help feeling sympathetic with the man who claimed to be the liberator of the Russian working class. Too bad Lenin had to put up with such helpmates as Trotsky, intellectuals the whole lot of them, Jacobins, would-be Napoleons suspect of sidetracking the revolution from its goal.

To Sorel, Lenin and his proletarian parliaments, the Soviets, represented the idea of the free, self-governing producers. Sorel was unable to see the reality behind the Soviets: Lenin's dictatorial rule based on his party. There was terror in Russia, Red terror? Agreed, but Sorel passionately refused to see the similarity between Lenin's Cheka and Robespierre's guillotine. The author of the Reflections was caught in his own terminology: Lenin stood for proletarian violence while the French Jacobins had relied on the oppressive power of the state, on "force." The terror had been forced on Lenin's "Dictatorship of the Proletariat": the responsibility for that rests with the Western democracies! Sorel sounded in 1919 like a typical fellow traveller of 1949.[22]

---

[19]And "some of his books were published in Italian before they appeared in French." Benedetto Croce, "Cristianesimo, socialismo e metodo storico" in La Critica, Vol. V (1907), p. 317. This essay, written apropos of Sorel's study of Renan (see note 14) later became the introduction to the Italian edition of the Reflections (see note 1) and the subject of a controversy between Sorel and Croce (see chapters 1, 6, and Supplement 1).

[20]About Sorel's "nationalistic phase" consult chapter 8.

[21]René Johannet, "L'évolution de Georges Sorel" in Itinéraires d'intellectuels (Paris, 1921), p. 230. About Sorel's "prophecies," cf. Introductory ii.

[22]See chapter 10.

Did he really believe that Lenin was no longer a Marxist believer? Did Bolshevist rule mean that the workers had shaken off the yoke of the intelligentsia? Had they succeeded in organizing industry along syndicalist lines of proletarian autonomy? Had they turned from being objects of state policy into free agents, sovereign within their own social and economic sphere? In one word, had Lenin become a Sorelian?

Sorel may have been slow to find out the truth about the new Russia, but when he finally did, he was still far ahead of his time. When he discovered that Lenin had destroyed the czarist state only to replace it by a state incomparably stronger, and one that was intensely Russian at that, he anticipated by almost two decades the interpretation of the Soviet regime that has become commonplace today. In contrast, however, to the many socialists who felt that Lenin had "betrayed" socialism, Sorel remained to the end true to belief that the Russian revolution was a step in the right direction: a decisive blow for the freedom of mankind. He utterly failed to see that there might be a contradiction between the Bolshevist power of the Party and the proletarian freedom of the workers.

If Sorel ever had any difficulty in reconciling the two concepts: the Communist and the syndicalist view of society, he did not say so. For if Lenin was master of a strong and ever stronger state, he also was, Sorel insisted, that exceptional ruler who wanted nothing that was not also to the interest of the people. Lenin was that rare event: the idea become action. He was the modern Moses leading his Russian people from the desert of medievalism directly into the Canaan of the industrial age, saving them the detour over Egypt with its capitalist fleshpots. Lenin was, for Sorel, as later for Toynbee, above all the great colonizer, who brought the slavic East, and with it most of Asia, into the orbit of Western civilization, presenting the West at the same time with revolutionary challenge. From now on (Sorel could say, with Stalin, whose name was unknown to him) the West, if it chose to remain the bourgeois West, will have to meet the competition of the Soviet Union constituting, as a nation, the united proletarian front which the workers of the West had failed to organize internally, as a united class.

With that result, Sorel, the historian, was as satisfied as Sorel, the socialist: the national revival of Russian power coincided with worldwide social progress; the industrialization of one sixth of the world would be the signal for the emancipation of the "producers" everywhere. Or so he thought. And that is why he prayed for Lenin's triumph and excoriated his detractors at home and abroad with the vociferous ferocity of an Old Testament prophet.

Meanwhile another national leader in socialist clothing had emerged out of the turmoil of postwar Europe; a man who, unlike Lenin, had gone on record that he was indeed indebted to Sorel. And ever since,

Sorel's reputation has been under a cloud. How could he, the "disinterested servant of the proletariat," as he called himself, condone, or even praise, the Duce of Fascism, as tradition has it that he did? What seems excusable in the case of Lenin, or at any rate understandable, will not find us equally disposed in the case of Mussolini and his squads of terrorists let loose against Sorel's best friends and comrades.

In all fairness to Sorel it must be stated that he never officially endorsed fascism. Never did he feel for Mussolini what he felt for Lenin. It is hardly necessary to point out that Sorel never saw fascism in power, since he died two months before Victor Emmanuel III made the chief of the Fascist party prime minister of Italy. Sorel, as his correspondence with Benedetto Croce and others bears witness, observed the ascendancy of the new movement with trepidation: "It seems we are entering a new Dark Age!" he exclaimed. He had thought highly of young Mussolini, the socialist firebrand who in his writings echoed Sorel's theory of violence and his contempt of parliamentary pussyfooting. But when Mussolini in 1914 began to clamor for Italian participation in the war, when he adopted Nietzsche's slogan of "living dangerously," Sorel, who had predicted the war and loathed it, shook his head. And when Mussolini, after the war, entered the civil war raging in Italy on the opposite side of labor, when his henchmen indulged in wholesale incendiarism and murder, Sorel grew more and more desperate.

But there remained at the bottom of Sorel's despair an element of confusion. As a socialist he could not but view the turncoat Mussolini with contempt and anguish in his heart; as far as fascism was a radical movement out to destroy the rule of the parliamentary cliques, it looked good to Sorel. Indeed, the confusing thing about Mussolini was that he fought, or seemed to be fighting, a two-front war: against both socialism (and Sorel despised the tame political socialism of the Second International as much as Lenin did) and liberalism (Sorel's old enemy). If Mussolini hankered after power, if he eulogized the strong state, that was distasteful to Sorel, as the disciple of Proudhon, the libertarian. But the destruction of the liberal state, Sorel was ready to accept as a partial blessing.

It must also be remembered that Mussolini, in his Fascist prime, still voiced many notions of his syndicalist past: when he proposed to liberate the economy from as much state interference as possible, that must have been agreeable to Sorel, believing as he did in the autonomous organization of production as opposed to the modern idea of the welfare state. Sorel could, if he tried hard, make himself believe that the Fascist onslaught was not really directed against the working-class institutions proper but only against their hapless, cowardly leadership; he could have pointed to the Fascist labor unions that were making headway, especially among the rural proletariat (prodded as it was by Blackshirt terror).

Once more Sorel was fascinated by the spectacle of a backward nation being forced to join the family of the industrial nations. In believing Mussolini to be the man capable of modernizing Italy, Sorel found himself in the best company. What impressed him particularly was the mixture of national and social elements in the Duce's power formula. Mussolini's new nationalism, unlike the nationalism of old, claimed to be social revolutionary. Sorel had speculated along the same lines but, as he confessed, without real conviction. He was too firmly anchored at his internationalist, laborist moorings to ride the tide of the new nationalism, but he could watch the historical phenomenon with a speculative, semi-appreciative eye. In his heart, he felt nothing but sorrow, but his mind was ready to appraise fascism as part of the barbaric ricorso that has to precede any cultural revival.[23]

It is not necessary to bracket Russian communism and the fascism of the Italian and German variety under the common heading of "totalitarianism" in order to understand how, in popular parlance, both Lenin and Mussolini could become associated with Sorel. The truth is that both Lenin and Sorel came "out of Karl Marx's mantle," both taking a part of Karl Marx's doctrine and elevating it into their ruling principle: Lenin developing the concept of the "vanguard of the proletariat," the party, and its dictatorship, while Sorel relied on the proletariat to free itself even from its vanguard. And with Mussolini, both Sorel and Lenin shared one thing, and that thing only: all three were agreed in the belief that the bourgeoisie, with its nineteenth-century political and social institutions, was unable to consummate the next stage of the industrial revolution. Lenin was convinced that in Russia his party, and his party alone, could achieve the job at hand. The Italian Mussolini appealed to a national cross section of all the classes to perform the task which he felt the proletariat was not yet — or no longer — able to accomplish; so he based his dictatorship on a "classless" élite standing, like Lenin's party, behind and above the officially responsible managers of bureaucratic government.

And Sorel? Were he alive today, he would, most probably, not feel any regret over the liquidation of the nineteenth century which we are witnessing. But would he go on praising communism; would he write another plea, this time "For Stalin"; would he still consider Mussolini to have been a figure of first rank? Judging from the total record which the old rebel left behind, we may well doubt that he would care to set a date for his "Napoleonic battle" of Man's liberation. His proletarian myth has faded beyond recognition, and the great Viconian renaissance seems more remote than ever.

---

[23]See chapter 9.

1. A LIFE IN LETTERS i

(1895-1908)

Sorel's correspondence with Benedetto Croce[1], covering a period of over twenty-five years or almost the entire life span of the writer Sorel, — that correspondence is much more than a document of friendship and intellectual crossfertilization. The 343 letters which went from Paris to Naples between 1895 and 1921 in a hardly ever interrupted flow, do not add very much to the information we possess about the personal life of Sorel, in which outward commotion was so singularly absent.[2] But they do permit us, in conjunction with the letters Sorel wrote to other friends[3], to reconstruct his vita intellectualis, the stupendous scope and everchanging variety of his interests. Nothing less than the entire evolution of Sorel's mind can be traced through those casual ramblings which never betray the self-consciousness so often on display in the exchange between two Great Ones. Sorel's letters were never meant for posterity[4]; we must be grateful to the recipients for having disregarded his injunction, for those writings of the moment show us Sorel at his best; as the omnivorous reader who might have evoked the jealousy of a Gamaliel Bradford; a reader who would never fail to draw creative sparks even from his dullest texts; a correspondent always eager for new information, anxious to have others share the sorrows and joys of his intellectual growing pains. Above all, the letters reveal Sorel as the passionate man he was, with pet preferences and aversions which, in the view of some readers, often overshot the

---

[1]Published by Croce in his review, La Critica, Vols. XXV-XXVIII (1927-1930), altogether 343 letters written between 1895 and 1921. In the following identified by the date of the letter cited and by the year and pages of the volume in which they appeared. Quoted by permission of Benedetto Croce.

[2]For Sorel's life, see Part II, Introduction.

[3]Paul Delesalle, Daniel Halévy, Hubert Lagardelle, Agostino Lanzillo and Edouard Dolleans. The letters which Sorel wrote to his foremost disciple, Edouard Berth, are being readied for publication by Sorel's present publisher, Marcel Riviere, Paris.

[4]"Georges Sorel had been strictly opposed to the publication of his correspondence after his death. He had taken pains to destroy all the copies of his own letters and those which he had received. He had expressed his wish to his friends, in particular to P. Delesalle and M. Rivière, who obeyed it to the letter. Did he forget to communicate it to B. Croce? The latter does not express himself upon that point." Boris Souvarine, introducing a selection of Sorel's correspondence with Croce, appearing in La Critique Sociale, No. 1 (March, 1931).

mark.[5] Yet a thousand trivia and asides do not obscure the inner continuity and general consistency of Sorel's thought; the great themes of
the richly orchestrated Sinfonia Soreliana emerge with a clarity that is
sorely lacking in his published works.

It all begins, on December 20, 1895, with the widely unknown G.
Sorel soliciting a contribution for the newly-founded revue Le Devenir
Social.[6] Though the recipient of the request was already a man with
an established reputation, both as a historian of his native Naples and
as an important critic of Marxism, Sorel shows no sign of awe: his
tone is modest without being subservient.[7] Croce complies, but the
new relationship at once hits a snag when the contribution threatens to
offend the sensitivities of the revue's co-founder, Paul Lafargue, Karl
Marx's son-in-law and one of the "authoritative" interpreters of
Marxism in France. Sorel is forced to do what an editor hates to do
most: he has to tell the new contributor for whom he is himself responsible, "that M. Lafargue and you could not very well write for the same
revue...."[8]

But the momentary embarrassment does not seem to affect the
fast growth of cordial relations. While the first letter is still formally
headed "Monsieur," the third missile already begins with "Cher monsieur," and the seventh tentatively introduces a "Cher monsieur et
ami," only to retract it again in the eighth to return to the more distant
"Cher monsieur." But the tenth message finally establishes the en-
dearing term of "Cher ami," which is to stay until the end.

Already the long second letter plunges in medias res. Sorel confesses to a steadfast dislike of utopian, intellectual constructions: "I
am not as convinced as you are of Morus' Utopia being intended as a
serious political work." Sorel regards it, like Plato's Republic, as a
persiflage of social conditions then existent, rather than as a program of action. This, to Sorel, would seem to be "the more respectful
interpretation."[9]

A Marginal Marxist

The third letter sounds the leitmotif that is to remain the main
topic of conversation for both Sorel and Croce in many years to come:
their mutual interest in the work of Karl Marx and his disciples. Of
these, Antonio Labriola comes first, he who had written Croce about
Sorel, and to whom Sorel owes his initiation into the Marxist cult, the
same Labriola who would become Sorel's bête noire and the butt of

---

[5]See Supplement.

[6]To Croce (1927, p. 38-39), December 20, 1895. This is the first letter
Sorel wrote.

[7]Ibid. (p. 39), January 14, 1896. — "Enclosed with the letter was a calling
card: Georges Sorel Ancien ingenieur en chef des ponts et chaussees, 25 rue
Denfert-Rochareau [sic], Boulogne, s/S (Seine)." Ibid., Croce's note.

[8]Ibid.   [9]Ibid.

much ridicule and scorn in the progressing correspondence. In connection with a book by Lenin's teacher, George Plekhanov, to which Croce had devoted a critique, Sorel remarks that "Marxism is still precious little known in France." A few lines later, the name of Babeuf occurs, and Sorel expresses his doubt whether the unfortunate leader of the "Conspiracy of Equals" really deserves the fame of being the first truly modern communist. After all, the struggle of the lean against the fat ones had been at the root of all the revolutions since antiquity: "I don't believe Babeuf surpassed that conception. . . ." Sorel's distinction between the perennial revolt of the poor and the revolution of the industrial workers is clearly stated at this early date: "The modern proletariat finds itself in the position of the organized producers representing the elements of scientific industrial progress: it has no resemblance with the populo minuto of the medieval Italian communes."10

Between letters number 4 and 5, there intervenes a longer pause. We learn the reasons: Benedetto Croce has been sick and Georges Sorel has lost his wife. We know how much he was in love with her, but not more than four lines are given over to the sad news: "Since then, I lost my dear, devoted wife who has shared with me twenty-two years of labors, and to whom I have been tied by la forza del primo amore. Her memory, I hope, will remain the best part of my self and the true soul of my life."11

After this brief confession, Sorel returns to literary gossip, discussing half a dozen authors, among them the leading Italian Marxist, Achille Loria, with whom Croce had a critical fracas; he shares Croce's opinion that there is considerable similarity of views between Marx and Pareto, although, Sorel adds, the latter had no knowledge of Marx when he wrote and was highly surprised by some of Friedrich Engel's letters which were published in Sorel's revue.12 The collaborator of Karl Marx is so little appreciated in France, that Sorel's attempts to find a publisher for a French Engels edition got nowhere. He prods Croce to pursue his critical analysis of the Marxian theory of surplus

---

10 Ibid. (p. 42), October 9, 1896. — Sorel was referring to the German edition of Plekhanov's In Defense of Materialism, and Croce adds in a note: "Sorel did not know any German; that fact indicates the difficulties which he encountered in his study of Marxism." Ibid.

11 Ibid. (p. 44), About Madame Sorel see also, chapter 6, section "Sorel's Rousseau" and Part II, Introduction.

12 Ibid. For Croce's critique of Loria, see Croce, Pagine Sparse, series I, 273-4. — Engels' letters had been published in Der Sozialistische Akademiker, 1895; the French translation in Le Devenir Social, 1897, 228-61. (Croce's notes) — Sorel had reviewed Pareto's Cours d'économie politique in Le Devenir Social, May, 1896 and May, 1897.

value:[13] the famous contradiction between Volume I and III of Capital. Sorel informs his correspondent that Charles Andler[14] plans to bring out a slim volume with the title The Decomposition of Marxism in Germany.[15] The author told Sorel that "the main theses of the Marxist school may be considered as abandoned now." Eager as Sorel is to discover the weak spots in Marx, this summary dismissal is too much for him: he insists on a distinction between Marx and his disciples who made a caricature of their master's work. "Let us return to Marx," Sorel exclaims, "that is my slogan, and I think it is the right approach."[16]

Next, Sorel turns to the question of nationalism. Taking as his text a work by Croce[17], Sorel finds that the 1799 uprising of the Neapolitans against the French "furnished the first example of patriotism in the modern sense." Spain and Germany soon followed suit. Napoleon never understood the lesson. It is utterly erroneous, Sorel holds, to see in movements of that sort a replica of the French revolution and to say that France was vanquished by its own ideas. Modern patriotism, on the contrary, is of a "popular, sentimental, altogether impulsive nature, utterly devoid of all idealism; like everything nascent, it takes on barbaric forms," only to become self-conscious later on "through a process of intellectualization, thereby losing its strength."[18]

We are confronted here with another of Sorel's key notions: his discrimination between the rational, "idealistic" element in human thought; and the irrational, or as he would put it later on, the "mythical" component, both often coexisting, but always at odds with one another in the social movements of all times. We also may note the influence of Giambattista Vico and his theory of cultural cycles which Sorel had already studied.[19]

---

[13]Sorel had treated the same subject under the title, "Sur la theorie marxiste de la valeur" in Le Journal des Economistes, May, 1897; the same article appeared as "Ueber die Marx'sche Werttheorie" in Sozialistische Monatshefte, June, 1897.

[14]Author of Les origines du socialisme en Allemagne (1897). Cf. also chapter 4, p. 114.

[15]Sorel later used the same title (minus the two last words) for a work of his own: La décomposition du Marxisme (Paris, 1908).

[16]To Croce (1927, p. 45). — Cf. also chapter 4, p. 114.

[17]Ibid. (p. 46), August 7, 1897. — "The second edition (Rome, 1897) of my youthful studies of The Neapolitan Revolution of 1799." Croce's note.

[18]Ibid. This is not to be understood as a defense of idealism, for, as Sorel will say later, "the work of the idealists is . . . a lie and dupery." Introduction à l'économie moderne (Paris, 1903; cited from the 2. edition, Paris, 1922, p. 392). But he agrees that "there is a force which always leads the mind toward idealism" (Ibid.); cf. chapter 11, p. 266.

[19]Sorel, "Etude sur Vico," in Le Devenir Social, October — December, 1896. See Chapter 3.

After two years of correspondence, Sorel informs his friend in a long letter[20] that he is no longer an editor of Le Devenir Social. It is the first installment of a story that will repeat itself monotonously: Sorel announcing that he, at last, found the ideal literary outlet for himself and his friends; Sorel soliciting the contributions of his friends; Sorel announcing that he is "through" with his review and on the look-out for another organ. Having found it, he will impress his friends with the necessity of joining his Hegira: they are exhorted to cease writing for the old and wicked publication. Occasionally those Sorelian walkouts are caused by purely personal considerations: Sorel would take a fierce dislike to a co-worker who impressed him as an intriguer or careerist; but in the majority of cases, the secession coincided with a turning point in Sorel's intellectual development. His sudden refusals to go on with a project considered to be of vital importance only a few weeks earlier; his frequent announcements that he is tired, ill, washed-out, — all that is only Sorel signaling to Sorel, warning himself against complacency, impressing on himself the need for a new orientation. Like Socrates, he always listened to the promptings of his "demon," even if that meant breaking off relations that had become dear to him. It would be wrong to attribute the many bitter remarks about people that appear in these letters, to a cantankerous disposition on Sorel's part; more correctly, he may be said to be the type of man who will dislike a person if he feels obliged to disapprove of his opinions. If Sorel was a great hater, it was only so because he had a powerful, if repressed, urge for friendship.

Always returning to "the" topic, Sorel pleads with Croce to continue his attack on the Marxian fortress. He passes on the information, received from Charles Andler that the 'early Marx of The Holy Family, The Misery of Philosophy and the Manifesto (1844 — 1847) had been influenced by Lorenz von Stein. A study of that period, Sorel is convinced, would complete, in the most fortunate manner, Croce's previous studies of historical materialism and its "obscure theses on which, I am happy to state, we found ourselves so often in agreement." For the first time, Friedrich Engels comes in for an unfriendly remark: he is called a deviationist, straying from the path of Karl Marx' "truly scientific thought." It is the beginning of a hostility which will become increasingly accentuated, as Sorel attempts to break the Marxist spell. Quite likely, he was not at all aware that his thrusts at the minor of the Dioscuri were but feints aimed at the forbidding figure of Karl Marx himself, whom he was not yet prepared to attack openly. So it has to be Engels who "contributed much to launch historic materialism on the road to evolutionism, elevating it to an absolute dogma." The future philosopher of violence accuses Engels of "employing forensic tricks to deny [the efficacy of] direct action."

But as Sorel warms to his subject, he discloses the real target of

---

[20]To Croce (1927, pp. 50-52), December 27, 1897.

his criticism: The more one studies Marx, the less one understands the true relationship between him, Hegel and Feuerbach. "The formulas which Marx used to indicate his position, are very obscure, most of all his dialectic." And he repeats: "The more I try, the less I understand it." A blasphemous thought occurs to him: The best thing would be to dispense with the dialectic altogether: "That would be a great advance because for us moderns all that Hegelian apparatus no longer makes any sense." The real Marx, Sorel seems to suggest, is the one who is purged of Hegel-Engels: "Marx ought to be translated into modern idiom," or else his work will become the source of "a mythology founded on the maladies of language. . . ."

Whether Sorel's habit to defer to others and to credit them with his own insights was mere modesty or an autodidact's way of reassuring himself, — the letters of that period extoll Croce's triumphs over Marx, while saying very little about the by no means meager output of the Marx critic Sorel. If he shows any pride at all, it is of his connections. It must have given him some satisfaction to point out to Croce new publication outlets for his Marxist studies, such as the new, "independent revue" in Berlin, which "could print your memoir".[21] We gather that the official organs of Marxism had become suspicious of the innovators, and apparently with good reason. Sorel relates, with obvious glee: "M. Pareto writes me that you and M. Labriola are the 'rationalists' of Marxism and almost heretics. Professor Gide of Montpellier writes me the same thing."[22] Labriola is already anathema to the German organ of social democratic orthodoxy, Die Neue Zeit. Sorel reports that his own view of Marx's theory of value could not have been less of a shock to that revue's editor, Karl Kautsky: "It seems to me that these questions no longer excite anybody. I wonder whether Marx himself was not the first to suspect that much, and whether he had not already come to the conclusion that all those theories

---

[21]Ibid. (p. 105), February 26, 1898. — Sorel refers to the Sozialistische Monatshefte, to which he had contributed, in addition to the essay mentioned in note 13, two more on "Die Entwicklung des Kapitalismus" (October, 1897) and on "Der Ursprung des Staatssozialismus in Deutschland" (November, 1897). In the following years he published in the same periodical: "Was Man Von Vico Lernt" (June, 1898, a sequence to his 1896 essay on the same author; see chapter 3), "Betrachtungen über die Materialistische Geschichtsauffassung" (July — September, 1898), "Der Amerikanische Kapitalismus," based on Paul de Rousier's study, Les industries monopolisees aux Etats-Unis (December, 1898), "Über die Kapitalistische Konzentration" (February — March, 1900), "Soziale Ideen and Organisation der Arbeit" (June, 1902), "Die Ethik des Sozialismus" (May, 1904). Many of these contributions, but by no means all of them, are translations of essays published previously or simultaneously in French or Italian journals.

[22]To Croce (1927, p. 103), January 20, 1898. Professor Gide: the famous economist, co-author of the well-known "Gide-Rist" history of economics.

are a bit useless. That could well be the reason why he never finished
Capital."23

The main deficiency of Marxism, Sorel decides, is its neglect of
morals and religion. They take their revenge on socialism by continuously re-entering the system in the disguise of idealist utopias taking
the place left empty. "I have the impression that Marx and Engels believed that place ought to be left empty, that religion and morality had
been valuable only for the ancient world and would evaporate like phan-
toms the very day man entered the realm of the Free Spirit. How could
they tell! How could they be sure the realm of freedom can be fully
realized?" And Sorel adds the sacrilegious words: "In Marx, a great
deal more idealism has survived than one would be lead to believe, and
in the case of Engels it is even worse...."24

Does that amount to an outright rejection of the Marxian doctrine
on the part of Sorel? Not yet: "I would like...to complete and improve Marxism in accordance with Marx's principles, but following
the method rather than the letter."25 He flatly rejects all attempts to
strengthen the deterministic element in Marxist thought. Plekhanov's
notion of utopian socialism having shown the method whereby "the
future may be easily deduced from a past well observed," — that notion
makes Sorel quite angry: "I should like to be shown a single authentic
instance" that would bear out St. Simon's method of prediction. Neither
does Sorel believe that Marx himself has been much happier in that respect, and he concludes that "history is not susceptible of being foreseen, since the facts never arrange themselves in such a way as to
make rational what the contemporary mind experiences as contradictory
relationships. The unpredictability of coming things is to my mind essential to historical materialism, while it would be a scandal for the
idealist."26

Arturo and Antonio

The angry mood demands a victim less intimidating than Karl
Marx, or even Engels. Throughout the spring of 1898, Sorel concen-
trates all his fury on one author mercifully sheltered by the editor behind the cipher "X". Our curiosity is aroused. Who is the noted Marxist writer for whom no insult in Sorel's ample vocabulary is strong
enough? And why did Croce see fit to withhold the name? Harsh things
are said about so many people in these letters, that the precaution used
in this one case, strikes a mysterious note. Was it a man who must
not be offended by the editor,27 a former Socialist turned Fascist?

23Ibid. (p. 105), February 26, 1898.
24Ibid. (p. 107), April 1, 1898.   25Ibid.
26Ibid. (p. 169), April 23, 1898.
27The reader is reminded of the fact that this Sorel correspondence was
published under the Fascist regime.

Was it perhaps — the Duce himself? After all, Benito Mussolini too
had taken part, at one time, in the Marxist controversies, as an editorial
writer.... But the solution is as disappointing as it is amusing. Unfortunately, for his purpose, Croce had not been too careful in covering
the tracks, for "Monsieur X" is attacked by Sorel as the author of a
wretched Ph. D. thesis on Quesnay in the letter of April 1, 1898,[28] and
it takes no detective to discover an earlier reference to the same work
with the author given as Arturo Labriola.[29]

The answer is now very easy: It is not Labriola whom the editor
intended to protect, but Georges Sorel, because the latter happened to
change his mind about "X" so radically that he deemed him worthy of
a preface of his own.[30] Sic transit ignominia mundi.

The May of 1898 finds Sorel, as he indicates with his usual restraint, too ill to accomplish any writing. Yet, he seems to be as fever-
ishly at work as ever. Also, he has finally taken his stand in the grand
debate then raging all over Europe between orthodox and revisionist
Marxists. "Socialism will either take the road taken by Bernstein, or
else it will end up in mere scholasticism."[31] Marx's theory of value
now has become for Sorel a metaphysical law helpful to throw light —
an indirect light — on a state of affairs that existed at the beginning of
the 19th century: "For those who understand, Marx's method cannot
have more than historical interest."[32]

These strictures find a summary expression in the preface Sorel
contributes to Saverio Merlino's book, Form and Essence of Socialism[33]
— an introduction which he calls, with unusual boastfulness, "interesting".[34] He is, naturally, pleased when Croce likes the piece, and he
shrugs off the attacks of sundry outraged socialists: "The asses." But
there is such a thing as going too far in the opposite direction and throwing Marx completely over board: Those people "give up all of Marxism

---

[28]To Croce (p. 106).

[29]Ibid. (p. 49), November 30, 1897. — N.B.: Arturo, not Antonio, Labriola.

[30]Arturo Labriola, Karl Marx: L'économiste, Le socialiste (Paris, 1910),
pp. i-xxxviii.

[31]To Croce (1927, p. 170), May 8, 1898.

[32]Ibid. (p. 171), May 17, 1898. — On July 25th of the same year Sorel writes
to Hubert Lagardelle: Marx' originality consists in having suggested a mechanism of social transformation...whether he saw the facts more or less correctly matters very little: his successors who see these facts more clearly
are in a position to use a counter-mechanism constructed along his general
indications (class struggle). But that struggle needs interpretation; it has to
be understood above all as a struggle for justice and not as a struggle for the
belly...." Reproduced by Lagardelle in his revue, L'Homme Réel, No. 2 (February, 1934), p. 121.

[33]Formes et essence du socialisme (Paris, 1898), pp. i-xlv. — See chapter
4, p.

[34]To Croce (1927, p. 172), October 10, 1898.

and do not know what to put in its stead."[35] Sorel will never disown
his indebtedness to Marx. He sees his task in "purging Marxism of
all the leftovers of the old Socialism and of all the nonsense which the
politicians added.... It is true, a Marxism thus expurgated would disappear as a system, but Marx's own work would still remain, and it is
that rest which will constitute a scientific deposit."[36] The inveterate
hater of "the intellectuals" in politics raises his voice: "The reform
of Socialism would prevent the exploitation of the masses by the charlatans who, whether they preach Communism or state Socialism, are
as unscrupulous in their means to gain power as the clergy."[37]

It is precisely because the old church is losing ground, that the
morality of the new church becomes a crucial issue. Sorel treats it in
an article[38] and comments: "Maybe I moralized Marx and Engels a
bit; I don't think they ever pondered these questions very deeply. But
I still believe I developed my theses in a Marxian spirit."[39]

In the meantime, he has found another editorial home, though not
for long. It is Le Mouvement Socialiste, the revue, directed by his
friend, Hubert Lagardelle, which is eventually to publish the original
French version of the Reflections on Violence.[40] The general tendency
of the new organ is revisionist, and this leads to an exchange of letters
between Sorel and the great heresiarch, Eduard Bernstein, who informs
him that his own thought had been inspired, to a certain extent, by
Croce's Marx critique. Relaying that remark to the Italian friend,
Sorel adds: "Very interesting, because Germans are not in the habit
of acknowledging a foreign influence."[41] He declares to have learned
a great deal about German socialism from Bernstein's letters: "There
you have a labor movement in its infancy." This remark may have
sounded slightly preposterous at the time, when the German Social
Democratic organization was the envy of all other European Socialists;
today, Sorel's evaluation no longer sounds so much off key.

Bernstein's famous book finds in Sorel a sympathetic reader, although "the lack of a broad philosophical culture makes itself felt on a

---

[35]Ibid. (p. 174), October 29, 1898. His examples are Jules Guesde, the leader
of Marx orthodoxy, and the Dutch socialist, Van Kol, whom he will however,
quote approvingly a few years later in his Introduction à l'économie moderne
(Paris, 1903) on p. 395.

[36]To Croce (1927, p. 175), December 12, 1898.

[37]Ibid. (p. 300), June 3, 1899.

[38]"L'éthique du socialisme" in La Revue de Métaphysique et Morale, May,
1899.

[39]To Croce (1927, p. 304), May 27, 1899.

[40]Not without Sorel having broken off relations with that journal in the mean
time (1902-1904).

[41]To Croce (1927, p. 311), September 9, 1899.

good many occasions,"[42] a judgment which is in agreement with that
of the experts. Only four months later, his opinion on the Germans
borders on contempt: Speaking of Marxist publications, he declares
that "Germany has run out of ideas, or almost so; all the world says
that her science is in a stage of marked decadence."[43] In this verdict,
the gradualists à la Bernstein seem to be lumped together with the
guardians of orthodoxy. It is perhaps no accident that at this crucial
point of Sorel's evolution other than Socialist themes begin to assert
themselves in his correspondence. He shies away from a Crocean
treatise on aesthetics,[44] pleading incompetence. But in the very next
sentence he mentions, for the first time[45] a philosopher whom he has
not found too difficult: "I signal to you a book by Bergson on Le Rire
et la signification comique."[46]

In the following letter, Sorel subjects another Italian friend, Vilfredo
Pareto, to a criticism which the latter will reciprocate, together with
high praise.[47] "I believed for a long time." Sorel writes, "that the
school of Pareto ought to discard its method of pseudo-psychological
exposition."[48] Sorel reads everything; the letters read like a bibliography of all the European periodicals available at the Paris National
Library. And all the time the old man is in search of fresh, young
talent: "Who hides behind the signature Rerum Scriptor in La Critica
Sociale?" he inquires. It is Gaetano Salvemini. "And what of Labriola?
Is he still mad at me?"[49] He is, and thereon hangs a tale. The Labriola
in question is Antonio, who came long before Arturo into Sorel's life.
The story of their quarrel will be told elsewhere;[50] the letters faithfully reflect the changing attitudes of Sorel toward the old mentor, from
suspicion of the worst to calm regret. One time, Sorel reaches the

---

[42] Ibid. (p. 312), December 17, 1899. — See also Sorel, "Les dissensions de
la social-democratie allemande à propos des écrits de M. Bernstein" in La
Revue politique et parlementaire, July, 1900, and "Les polemiques pour l'interprétation du marxisme" in La Revue Internationale de Sociologie, April and
May, 1900.

[43] To Croce (p. 361), April 12, 1900.

[44] Ibid. (p. 362), June 5, 1900. — Croce's treatise: "Tesi fondamentali di
un' estetica come scienza dell' espressione e linguistica generale" in Atti
dell' Academia Pontaniana (1900).

[45] For the first time in this correspondence. Sorel had already "discovered"
Bergson as early as 1894. See Chapter 4, p. 104.

[46] Exact title: Le Rire, Essai sur la signification comique (Paris, 1900),
translated as Laughter, An Essay on the Meaning of the Comic (New York, 1911).

[47] Pareto called the Reflections on Violence "one of the most remarkable
works of our epoch." (Manuel d'économie politique, 2. edition, Paris, 1927,
p. 134. The Italian original was published in Milano, 1906, the 1. French edition
in 1909.) — For Pareto's critique of Sorel, see Supplement 2.

[48] To Croce (1927, p. 362), July 27, 1900.

[49] Ibid. (p. 363), December 21, 1900. [50] See chapter 4, p. 105 f.

point where he desires to know if Labriola has sold out to the government, like Millerand;[51] and yet, his steady carping proves one thing:
Sorel is sorry to have lost a friend, almost as sorry as he will be when
Péguy deserts him.[52] Still, when he learns of Labriola's death, he
remarks merely: "He had to suffer terribly because he apparently was
very sick. I am afraid, the scientific luggage which he left behind, is
not too heavy, unless he wrote something during his illness."[53]

Personal Encounter

It is time to consider the relationship between Sorel and Croce.[54]
The fact that their first meeting of the minds had taken place in the
sign of Karl Marx, is perhaps significant: it was something negative
that brought them together: their dissatisfaction with the Marxist
exegesis, their agreement on the points and means of critical attack.
However, whereas Croce ended by dismissing Marx from his work,
turning his mind to other pastures, Sorel was not content with such a
negative solution; he tried to replace it by a positive version, by discovering the "living Marx." He must have felt that Croce would and
could not follow him on the new road; it is therefore not surprising that
the correspondence of the period during which Sorel was finding his
new bearings, should be less rewarding: the interval between the letters
becomes wider, and the content more restrained. However, there was
one exception: After Marx, Sorel and Croce found another subject on
which they agreed, and this time it was love, not criticism, that united
them.

"Thank you for sending me your note on Vico," Sorel writes on
April 30, 1901: "but why don't you do the work about that great philosopher yourself?"[55] It seems that Croce had been urging his French
friend to do the book on Vico, since Sorel was already on record as a
student of that author,[56] but now he seems impressed by Sorel's argument and asks him for a copy of his Vico study. Is Sorel bashful about
his effort of five years ago? For he replies that he has not a single
reprint of his essay left.[57] Still, Croce must have managed to secure
the text. What he thought of Sorel's contribution to the   second

---

[51]To Croce (1927, p. 364), August 21, 1901.
    [52]For Sorel's relationship with Charles Péguy, see below, p. 180, and chapter
8, p. 209.
    [53]To Croce (1928, p. 35), February 6, 1904.
    [54]See also Supplement 1.
    [55]To Croce (1927, p. 363). Croce had sent Sorel G. B. Vico primo scoprit-
ore della scienza estetica (Napoli, 1901), to be found in his Aesthetic.
    [56]"Etude sur Vico" in Le Devenir Social October — December, 1896. See
chapter 3.
    [57]To Croce (1927, p. 366), January 4, 1902.

Vico-Renaissance,[58] we do not know. In his magistral work on The Philosophy of Giambattista Vico, Croce mentions Sorel's Study in the bibliography, but in the text itself he confines himself to stating briefly Vico's influence on Sorel, linking him with Marx.[59] It may well be that Sorel started the new Vico vogue, but to assume that Croce owes Sorel a special debt is unwarranted. If Sorel influenced the other man at all, it was by his encouragement and general enthusiasm for the admired Neapolitan; Sorel's own contribution to the understanding of the first modern historian will be discussed later on; be it said here that it reflects the thoughts of Sorel rather than of Vico.[60]

Still, Sorel might have written more about the subject in his letters, had he not been "extremely busy": a collection of some of his articles on Marx is to come out in Italy,[61] and Sorel is not one to believe in simply compiling old materials without changing them around beyond recognition. But that does not imply he ever changed the content. With the sovereign assurance of a man who can afford to change his mind, he left the old ideas as they were; there was no need to falsify the record.[62]

The announcements of new works begin to crowd each other: the noontide of Sorel's creative life is near. He had not exaggerated when he pleaded overwork. Now he is able to announce "a volume which will interest you; it contains reflections on the fall of the ancient world, from the Marxist point of view. If you could do something to attract public attention to the book, I count on your friendship."[63] Only two months later he reports two newly-published works at once: a preface to a book on Socialism and Agriculture,[64] and another one for a History

---

[58]The first Vico-Renaissance had been inaugurated by Jules Michelet, when he published a French text of the Scienza Nuova in 1841.

[59]See Supplement 1, p. 283, and note 3.

[60]Nor does Croce reflect Giambattista Vico's thought correctly according to Karl Lowith, Meaning in History,(Chicago, 1949), pp. 126-127, 132; see also Morris R. Cohen, Studies in Philosophy and Science (New York, 1949)pp. 205 ff.

[61]To Croce (1927, p. 363-364), April 30, 1901. — Sorel refers to his Saggi di critica del marxismo (Palermo, 1903).

[62]See especially Sorel's Avertissement of his La ruine du monde antique (Paris, 1902): "I did not think I had the right to correct the numerous passages in which I affirmed, in a trenchant manner, the scientific transformation of society by socialism. It is on that question that I take issue today with those who are considered to be the representatives of Marxist orthodoxy in Germany...." (p. xix of the third edition, Paris, 1933). — See also chapter 11, conclusion, p. 268.

[63]To Croce (1927, p. 366),January 4, 1902. The book is La ruine du monde antique; see preceding note.

[64]Ibid. (p. 366),March 6, 1902. For Sorel's preface to G. Gatti, Le socialisme et l'agriculture (Paris, 1901), see chapter 9, p. 222-223.

of the Labor Exchanges.[65] One would expect Sorel to have something
to say about the author of the second work, his good friend, Fernand
Pelloutier, the leading organizer and theorist of revolutionary syndicalism. But, once more, Sorel is uncommunicative; or perhaps he did not
want to waste Croce's time with a restatement of the feelings he had
already expressed in the preface: his great indebtedness to the man
who had helped him to clarify his ideas on the institutions of the proletariat in 1898, and again in 1901.[66]

The correspondence had now gone on for more than five years. In
all that time their friendship, cordial as it was, had remained an intellectual affair, conducted at a distance: Croce and Sorel had never laid
eyes on each other. Sorel, being a Frenchman, did not travel; besides,
he was advanced in age, and ailing. But now Croce had arrived in Paris.
It turned out that his schedule was formidable, and with Sorel living in
a suburb and not too mobile, the difficulties of meeting within one and
the same city seemed quite formidable. One also perceives a touch of
nervousness on the part of Sorel in the brief notes which he sends to
Croce, trying to arrange the entrevue. Not that Sorel minded calling
on the younger man; his pride was not involved. But the encounter
posed some difficulties that must have been bothersome to him, and
even frightening. For one thing, the visit disrupted his routine: his
reading session at the library was likely to be broken up. He would
have to dress up for the occasion, put on a stiff collar and plastron,
as he did when his young friend, Variot, dragged him off to a tense
and fatiguing luncheon with Barrès.[67] He would have to disguise himself as the respectable bourgeois that he was; the result is recorded
in one of the rare photographs we have of the great revolutionary and
friend of the working man, M. Georges Sorel. And then, he was essentially as shy as he was proud: suppose he did not "hit it off" with his
cher Croce? Suppose, he talked too much (as he was likely to do) and
said too little? "In order not to make you waste your time, I could
come tomorrow, Thursday, at one o'clock," Sorel writes; "at that moment you would have finished lunch, since you informed me that the
luncheon will start at noon. If my suggestion should not suit you, pray,
let me know." And he apologizes for the difficulties of communication:
"In Boulogne, we don't have pneumatic letters; in case of urgency, we
have to use the telephone for messages."[68] Sapienti sat.

Whether that meeting, so meticulously arranged, took place at all,
we have no means of saying. The next entry in the correspondence
meaning either that Croce had not been able to see Sorel on that day
after all, or that there was still another call: "With the greatest pleasure shall I visit you at the hotel at one o'clock on Saturday. The weather

---

[65]Fernand Pelloutier, Histoire des bourses du travail (Paris, 1902).

[66]When Sorel wrote and revised his L'Avenir socialiste des syndicats.
See chapter 4, p.

[67]See chapter 8, p. 210. [68]To Croce (1927, p. 368), May 14, 1902.

has been very bad during your stay, and you cannot have enjoyed it very much."[69]

That solicitous remark concludes the episode. The very next letter, sent again to Naples, acknowledges the receipt of "your book on aesthetics which, it seems to me, all but settles the matter. I also received your brochure on the Neapolitan patriots. I am sending you an issue of the Bulletin of the Philosophic Society in which I have exposed what seems to me to be the marrow of historic materialism."[70] Not one word about Paris; the letter reads as if the meeting never happened.

Charles Péguy

The appearance of that name in Sorel's correspondence signals the entry of a new, important figure in his life as well as the beginning of the end of his Marxist period: "I sent you a few copies of Péguy's prospectus (we had a meeting in his Paris office); his work is very interesting, what he writes deserves to be read; besides, he is one of the few Dreyfusards who don't claim freedom exclusively for themselves and for their friends...."[71] Leftist self-righteousness and lack of tolerance suggest to him the urgency of what may be called the revision of the revision; the righting of a wrong became another wrong, Sorel decides: what started out as a movement working for the revision of an unjust verdict, had turned into a disturbing revolution which causes Sorel to revise and reverse his previous sympathetic stand.[72]

He is too busy preparing the Italian collection of his essays to pay more than fleeting attention to a book sent by Croce,[73] but he still finds the time to indicate his general view on the subject: "I don't much fancy those general theories on evolution, but this is probably a fashion which few people dare to buck. I believe you are the only Italian who had the courage to hold up to ridicule Jupiter-Spencer."[74] Sorel's own thought on progress will come to fruition five years later in a book appearing almost simultaneously with the Reflections.[75]

---

[69]Ibid., May 23, 1902.

[70]Ibid., June 9, 1902. — Croce sent Sorel his L'Estetica come scienza dell' espressione R linguistica generale (Milano, Palermo 1902) and his Relazioni dei patrioti napoletani col Direttorio e col Consolato (Napoli, 1902); Sorel sent Croce his essay on "Le matérialisme historique" in Bulletin de la Societe française de Philosophie, May, 1902.

[71]To Croce (1927, p. 370), October 24, 1902. — The prospectus: announcing the Cahiers de la Quinzaine.

[72]See Sorel, La révolution dreyfusienne (Paris, 1909); cf. also chapter 3, section on Church and State.

[73]Sorel's Italian essays: see note 61. — Croce sent him G. Amadori Virgili's L'istituto famigliare nella societa primordiali (Bari, 1903).

[74]To Croce (1927, p. 371), March 30, 1903.

[75]Sorel, Les illusions du progrès (Paris, 1908); see chapter 6, p. 144 f.

An admirer has interpreted Sorel to his Italian public, and Sorel nastens to declare that he does not endorse all the conclusions of the writer.[76] At that occasion he makes a revealing statement which seems to sum up well the most frequently heard criticism of his work: "I never cared to figure out the synthesis of my various writings. I work from one day to the other, led by the needs of the moment."[77]

Sorel does not often generalize in these letters; when he does, it is mostly in a mood of deep discouragement, as when he exclaims, in the midst of a discussion of book contracts: "All your Italian socialists look like buffoons to me, and our French socialists are not a whit better.... In my opinion, Socialism would do well to go to sleep for some time; the working classes are in no way able to rid themselves of the babblers who dominate them. Jaurès, who is proclaiming his communist ideals with so much sound and fury, Jaurès knows his proletarians well." The flames of the Dreyfusian passion are burned out: "In France, nobody cares for anything; it is simply unbelievable how little stir the anticlerical issue makes actually; the defiance of a couple of monks seems to be merely farcical. The Church — like Socialism — will have to descend the slope of decadence even more before it will be able to reorganize."[78] Nobody but Sorel could have mentioned, in 1903, the Church and Socialism in one breath; nobody but Sorel was ready to see that both forces, their official enmity notwithstanding, drew their strength from the same source — a source which, Sorel feared with deep anxiety, was drying up: Socialism losing its revolutionary elan, while the Church, yielding to modernistic tendencies, is in danger of becoming "democratized."

It is, therefore, not a mere coincidence that with his growing disappointment in Marxism, a renewed interest in religious problems begins to assert itself in Sorel's reading and writing. His "Contribution to the Layman's Study of the Bible,"[79] though relegated to the background during the last decade of the 19th century, had really never been interrupted. Thus, Sorel can accept "with great pleasure" the invitation to review a book by Giovanni Rosadi, entitled The Trial of Jesus for Croce's La Critica, although he will not think much of the work itself, and he expresses his eagerness to do more reviewing in that field. A sure sign that Sorel is readying himself to do another book, for it is his peculiar habit to read himself first into a creative rage before committing his own thoughts to paper; — ancient Greek law, medieval archeology, and above all, church history — no book can be so bad as not to furnish Sorel with material to be scrutinized, digested, stored away in his fermenting mind: "Did you read Ferrero's Grandeur and

---

76V. Racca, "Giorgio Sorel e il socialismo" in La Riforma sociale, 1902.

77To Croce (1927, p. 372), April 28, 1903.

78Ibid. (1928, p. 31), May 9, 1903.

79Title of Sorel's first book, Contribution à l'étude profane de la Bible (Paris, 1889); see chapter 2, p. 48.

Decadence of Rome? The first volume is to be translated into French; what do people think of it in Italy?" Sorel will devote three long essays to the work;[80] for the time being, he reads Croce's critical remarks on Fichte's Closed Commercial State and comments: "Is it not a utopia reflecting the same optimistic trend which led Kant to believe in eternal peace?"[81] Sorel himself has meanwhile published a fat volume dealing, almost exclusively, with economic problems; he sends it to Croce with the words: "This volume is, I am convinced, of real interest; I suppose the Socialists will try to give it the silent treatment."[82]

In the final sentence of the same letter, Sorel makes the cryptical remark: "I am engaged in a work which absorbs me very much: a book about the origins of Christianity." This information makes it possible to date Sorel's work on Renan[83] published three years later in the heyday of his "syndicalist period": the item which, in the Sorelian bibliography, seems to indicate a return to earlier preoccupations, actually belongs to Sorel's "religious phase" and owes its present place merely to the accidents of the publishing trade. This least-known of his works will always retain, like a sickly child, Sorel's special affection: it is with marked grief that he registers the mixed reception the book found in Croce's fatherland: "The ideas which I developed in the introduction which you have read, don't please the scholars: they consider it a scandalous thing to treat the esthetical judgment as the hidden law of all historic criticism. I had thought that this thesis would have particularly appealed to the Italians..."[84] He is, of course, most anxious to please one particular Italian: it is the philosopher of "History subsumed under the Concept of Art"[85] to whom Sorel addresses himself quite explicitly when he writes: "Historiography is neither useful nor worth being taken seriously unless it is correctly understood as a constructive art, subordinated to extra-scientific ends, and one in which

---

[80]To Croce (1928, pp. 35 and 38) February 6 and November 28, 1904. — Sorel on Ferrero: "Grandeur et décadence de Rome" in Le Mouvement socialiste, July 15, 1906, February 1907 and July 15, 1908.

[81]To Croce (1928, p. 39), March 21, 1905. — Referring to Croce's review of I. Petrone, Lo stato mercantile chiuso, di G. A. Fichte in La Critica (1905, pp. 148-150).

[82]Ibid. (1928, p. 34), November 27, 1903. The work is Sorel's Introduction à l'économie moderne (see note 18).

[83]Sorel, Le système historique de Renan (Paris, 1906); see chapter 6.

[84]To Croce (1928, p. 93), December 27, 1905.

[85]La storia ridotta sotto il concetto generale dell' arte, (reprinted in Primi Saggi, Bari, 1919), title of Croce's essay published in 1893, the idea of which was further developed in his Aesthetic of 1902. Cf. R. G. Collingwood, The Idea of History (Oxford, 1946), pp. 190-194; cf. also Maurice Mandelbaum, The Problem of Historical Knowledge (New York, 1938), pp. 39-57; Morris R. Cohen, The Meaning of Human History (La Salle, Ill., 1947), pp. 49-50.

the facts are that which matters least."[86] He should be "very happy,"
we read in his next letter, if Croce would find time to review the Renan;
Sorel tries very hard to steer the friend toward the 'correct' interpretations: "The purpose of my work is, in effect, to furnish an example
of historical materialism rather than to solve special problems which
interest only the erudite."[87]

Sorel then, be it noted, still considers himself a practitioner of
what he regards as the correct Marxist method, even though he had
long since departed from the ways of Marxist orthodoxy.

As the Renan continues to fare badly, Sorel himself a critic sans
merci, falls into a brown study. Paolo Orano's review seems to indicate to him, that "I must have expressed myself rather poorly.... My
point was to show that the history of the church fathers is inaccessible
and useless" [for us]. It seems the eternal dilettante, Sorel, feels vic-
timized by professional jealousy: "Do you know the writer?" Sorel
dimly remembers that Orano "wrote me once to tell me that he published a work on the question.... I never heard of the book.... Is it
any good?"[88]

He comforts himself with the thought that the end of the work[89]
will clear up everything: "The fourth fascicle ... presents a new view
of the early Christian period. I believe I have succeeded in giving a
natural explanation of the things at all susceptible of explanation in that
story."[90]

A few months later Sorel has regained his poise: he now knows
why the book has "not yet called forth any reviews worth noticing": it
has been grievously misunderstood by the Catholics. They "don't appreciate the precision [with which] I am throwing into relief the diverse
and contradictory aspects of things." In other words, his method claims
to show up, with precision, imprecision. But he qualifies that statement
instantly by saying that his scientific method, and, as he insists, all
scientific method contains, of necessity, an arbitrary element: to organize facts, means to simplify them by way of selection. Also, we
must face the world as pluralists: "it is impossible to reach a synthesis; one has to be content with distinct, partial views."

A slightly petulant note is introduced when he complains about the
stubborn Catholics who fail to see "that I am in my views as far from
their opponents as I am from them." It is the typical Sorelian situation:
standing upright in the no-man's land between the battle fronts, with
his gun blazing forth, with complete impartiality, in both directions.
How surprised he is when both sides join in taking shots at him!

86To Croce (1928, p. 93), December, 1905.

87Ibid. January 26, 1906.

88Ibid. (p. 95), August 3, 1906, Paolo Orano had published Problemi del
cristianesimo (Rome, 1899).

89Only three of the four parts of Sorel's Renan had been published by that time.

90To Croce (1928, p. 95), August 13, 1906. — Sorel's emphasis.

For once, Sorel does not seem to be sure of Croce, for he makes another attempt at conditioning him for his critical assignment: "if you should write about my latest works...don't use the Italian text of [my essays on] the general strike, but the more elaborate French version."[91]

Three months later, Sorel has, at last, occasion to thank Croce for a "kind and exact review which makes the really important ideas of my book perfectly clear. In particular, you recognized well the abiding preoccupation of my life: the historic genesis of morals."[92] He has all reason to be grateful, for Croce's essay, a general appraisal of Sorel's significance as well as an analysis of the Renan, was, except for one major reservation, highly favorable.[93] But Sorel, being an author, is loath to be damned, if only faintly, with loud praise. His reaction takes the form of a long letter in which he displays an exemplary moderation, while conceding nothing.[94]

To clinch his argument, he introduces a name to conjure with: Henri Bergson is very much on his mind again. He wants Croce to write about him too, and makes some suggestions for that eventuality: "In the view of many, he would seem to be a pantheist," but Sorel believes differently: Bergson's latest book, Creative Evolution, is, in his opinion, an attempt to explain pantheism without succumbing to it. "The thing by which contemporary thought may be identified, seems to be the great effort made to answer questions without falling back on the hypothesis of the prime mover." On the other hand, Bergson "accepts all too readily and without testing, the hypothesis of evolution; but before reasoning about a thing, one should be sure that it exists; I believe the evolutionists are linking truly isolated laws be a thread...." That is, to Sorel pure intellectualism and should have no place in a philosophy like Bergson's, which is fit to reason only about movements verifyable by observation. True to his own pessimistic view, Sorel adds: "The only movement which we really observe, is that of degeneracy, and it is remarkable that, in speaking of acquired characteristics, Bergson should state that the only traits which seem to be hereditary, are of the morbid kind..."[95]

---

[91]Ibid. (p. 98), January 15, 1907. — Sorel refers to his first sketch of the Reflections on Violence which appeared in the Divenire Sociale ("La lotta di Classi e la violenza," October 1 and 15, 1905, "Lo sciopero generale," December, 1905). The French text was published by Le Mouvement Socialiste, January — June, 1906. See below, p. 43 f.

[92]To Croce (1928, p. 100), May 6, 1907.

[93]Croce's essay, "Cristianesimo, socialismo e metodo storico" in La Critica, 1907, pp. 317-330, became the preface of the Italian edition of the Reflections (Considerazioni sulla violenza, Bari, 1909).

[94]Sorel's view is stated in chapter 6, Croce's criticism and Sorel's rejoinder are presented in Supplement 1.

[95]To Croce (1928, p. 101-102), May 6, 1907.

Because he is convinced that there is an affinity between Bergson
and Hegel,[96] Sorel urges Croce to write something about Hegel for the
"French public, which is convinced that Hegel is deader than dead
and safely buried. One would have to show them that there are certain
Hegelian theories which are still very much alive and stirring." In an
aside, Sorel remarks: "The fact that there are Hegelians in England,
is very odd."[97]

Sorel has a hunch that it will not be easy to sell the French on
Hegel: he finds a Paris publisher for Croce's Saggio sullo Hegel (1906)
as well as the ideal translator, a student of one of the rare French
professors who appreciate Hegel. The young man in question is employed at a hospital, and in his spare time a co-editor of Le Mouvement Socialiste; his name is Edouard Berth,[98] soon to become Sorel's
most trusted friend and follower. But then the project has to be abandoned: the publisher reneges, and Sorel has to ask the friend not to
insist on publication for the time being.[99]

Bergson, Hegel, Croce — soon a fourth figure joins the group:
"In the latest issue of La Critica, the pragmatism of W. James, of whom
everyone talks here, has come in for rather severe treatment on your
hands.... There is something frightening in that idea of making success
the touchstone for the legitimacy of a belief! That is very English
[sic], but not very philosophical, in the sense in which that noble term
is commonly employed." Lest we forget: "It was Greek sophism that
had been the signal (or perhaps the cause) of ancient decadence." If
Sorel is to be labelled as a pragmatist, he was a pragmatist with reservations. His remarks on William James are followed, most abruptly,
but perhaps not without some justification, by a sentence — one of the
none-too-frequent sentences in which he places himself squarely on
record on the side of the man who wrote the Genealogy of Morals: "I
relished very much your observation on the moralism of Nietzsche
who has been misunderstood so often by the pedants."[100]

Having another look at the French contemporary scene, he cautions Croce against being overly impressed with the upheaval of the
era Combes: "It seems, our religious war looks more dramatic than
in truth it is; in general our clergy would rather not fight at all and
live a peaceful life instead; it can't make any sense whatever of the
papal policy based on the heroism of a Catholic bourgeoisie which
has infinitely little heroism."[101] ... "The French Catholics are furious
at the Pope who is disturbing them. Slumber is the only watchword of
the day."[102]

But if Sorel scorns the heroic pretenses of the Church, he is equally
opposed to all attempts to transform the Church into a progressive,

---

[96]Ibid. (p. 96), October 1, 1906.   [97]Ibid. (p. 102), June 10, 1907.
[98]Ibid. (p. 96), October 26, 1906. [99]Ibid. (p. 105), December 6, 1907.
[100]Ibid. (p. 107), May 27, 1908. [101]Ibid. (p. 97), December 31, 1906.
[102]Ibid. (p. 99), February 3, 1907.

democratic institution: "I regard Social Catholicism as one of the greatest dangers menacing the Church because the manoeuvre tends to bring the clergy into direct conflict with the Syndicalists. The priests, in general, are aware of the threat resulting from their often indirect and desultory agitation."[103] To Sorel's intense satisfaction, Croce had approved of the papal encyclical Pascendi, which "at this moment is creating such a havoc in the noisy (and, as I believe, sham) world of modernism. I think the Pope is absolutely right when he reminds the Catholics that the church is a historic institution which does not at all depend on the whims of a few modern minds."[104]

Triumph and Retreat

This may be the right moment to remark upon the prevalence of philosophic and religious topics in the correspondence of a man noted, almost exclusively, for his political and social writings. But nothing in the letters from the close of the year 1907 to the middle of May, 1908, reveal that he was during that time anxiously expecting the French publication of his most important work.

Earlier, it is true, he had given hints of some major event impending in his life, as when he comments on a work of Antonio Labriola, published after his death: "It seems he had not the least interest in revolutionary Syndicalism, although that movement had then already begun to cut a figure, in France at any rate."[105] At that time, Sorel was already busy making up for Labriola's lack of interest.

Three months later, May 21, 1906: Sorel to Croce, in a letter which has an unusually officious sound: "I am writing for the purpose of recommending to you a socialist revue for which I am writing articles since the beginning of the year, a revue which represents the syndicalist spirit in France.... I published in it the articles on violence which appeared in the Devenir social [sic]; but they have been expanded. I count on a long collaboration with this revue.... I believe it would give you a clear idea of a movement little known abroad."[106]

The articles on violence were announced here with much less fanfare than the periodical in which they were reprinted. When, a year later, Sorel's friend, Daniel Halévy with some helpers, lifted the series of essays out of their rather quiet surroundings into a book, not without doing some face-lifting in the process, Sorel wrote him: "My dear editor, I saw with great pleasure to what extent we are in agreement on the moral fundamentals with which the contemporary mind concerns itself so little.... Not only does the world refuse to descend to the

---

[103]Ibid. (p. 104), September 10, 1907.

[104]Ibid. October 23, 1907. Cf. chapter 3, section on Church and State.

[105]Ibid. (p. 94), February 15, 1906.

[106]Ibid. (p. 95). — Sorel confused the Italian Divenire Sociale with his old, defunct review, Le Devenir Social. — Cf. above, note 91.

depths, it busily spreads veils over the sacred hole from which the oracles originate...." Of what stuff is true moral greatness made? Sorel inquires, and he replies: It is, "as you said, to be found in man's self-confidence, which foregoes any hope of instant realization; the confidence untainted by utilitarian considerations.... The truly great man reaches for the stars and does not care whether the end will bring him happiness."

At this point, Sorel states, not for the first and not for the last time, but perhaps more lucidly than ever, his hostility against both optimism and intellectualism (interchangeable concepts for him): "The great value of pessimism consists in that the idea of deliverance is strong enough to fill the consciousness completely.... The mystics, who were consummate psychologists, discovered that the love of God was all-sufficient... putting our mind to rest, while at the same time spurring our will into forceful action." That double feat could never be the result of a merely intellectual resolve: "Action is at its most forceful only if the mind is utterly at peace; all unrest stems from intellectualism...."[107]

We may note, in passing, that Sorel seems to equate forceful action and right action in that letter, although such thought was certainly far from the mind of the great moralist. Ten months later, he is ready to announce to Croce:

"I sent you a copy of the Reflections on Violence: even though you did already write about my ideas, you might decide to draw attention to them once more by referring to the volume." Sorel uses the opportunity to tell his friend about his editor: "The Letter to D. Halévy which forms the introduction, contains some additional elucidations of the problem (D. Halévy is the son of the academician Ludovic Halévy who died just now)."[108] Soon Sorel begins to discuss the Italian edition of the work which is to be published by Croce's own Laterza in Bari. "I address myself to you in this matter since you will select the translator.... I should be very happy if you could find the time to write something to introduce the volume to the Italian public."[109]

Croce is too busy or unwilling to write the preface, but he has a happy inspiration: his essay on Renan, since it was not confined to the work only, could well serve the purpose — if that would be agreeable to the author. It is: Sorel thinks the idea "excellent"; but, asks he, since the essay is to preface the Reflections, would it not be wise to condense the part pertaining to Renan?[110] The relationship between that request and Sorel's displeasure with that particular section is, of course, purely coincidental.

———
[107]Letter to Daniel Halévy of July 7, 1907, in Fédération (Paris, November, 1947), p. 2-4. — Not to be confused with the "Letter to Daniel Halévy," which figures as the introduction to the Reflections.

[108]To Croce (1928, p. 106), May 15, 1908.

[109]Ibid. (p. 107), May 31, 1908. [110]Ibid. (p. 190), October 20, 1908.

For many months now the correspondence will be mostly taken up with technical details regarding the translation of the text, with checking and rechecking the exact significance of Italian words which may or may not be quite the precise equivalent of the original. Yet, Sorel still finds time to continue the great conversation: "Certainly, Bergson will never be the philosopher of the contemporary bourgeoisie; he does not make any effort to be adopted by them; whereas the Cartesians strained themselves to be acceptable. Boutroux too could be reproached for having tried too hard to please...."[111] Follows, without a transition, the startling announcement that the author of the Reflections has broken with the revue in which they had been serialized only a year ago:

"I have withdrawn completely from the Mouvement Socialiste; I don't want to become the courtier of any faction whatever, and my friends don't have the courage to reject outright what they accept only with reservations. I am taking advantage of all the disorder which exists today in the organizations [of the Left] to beat my retreat."[112] His old foes, the "intellectuals" and journalists are taking over the Syndicalist unions, we learn from another letter (November 2, 1908), addressed to Paul Delesalle who will become his closest friend:

"As you told me the other day, we must put our trust in the workers; that is also my opinion; I am convinced that all the tricks of the politicians will come to nought; but for the time being it seems to me that we must be neither accomplices nor dupes. It is this sentiment which made me leave the Mouvement Socialiste which is to much at the beck and call of the Action directe (the principal organ of the politicians with a false Syndicalist nose). I am retiring into my hole."[113]

---

[111]Ibid. (p. 108), June 24, 1908. — On the Cartesians: Cf. Sorel's Illusions du progrès (discussed in chapter 6) 4. edition, Paris, 1927, pp. 44-48. — The chapters of that book had been serialized in Le Mouvement Socialiste, August — September, 1906. Boutroux: Emile Boutroux, the famous philosopher of the College de France (1845-1922).

[112]To Croce (1928, p. 108), June 24, 1908. — "My friends": Hubert Lagardelle and his group.

[113]Georges Sorel, Lettres à Paul Delesalle (Paris, 1947), p. 108-109.

2. JUDAEA, ATHENS, ROME

Many writers have expounded the meaning of Sorel's enormous work,[1] while that work itself remained unknown at least in this country. There seems to be a tacit agreement that the bulk of the Sorelian oeuvre is unreadable, that it is merely quotable. But even the greatest amount of quotations will hardly enable us to reconstruct the original. That is partly Sorel's own fault, for none of his books represent a unified whole. He makes a book merely the container for anything that happened to interest him at the time he wrote, which means practically everything. As a result, the commentators, attempting to create at least some semblance of order where there was none, preferred the functional approach: in studying Sorel, they would pursue one of Sorel's interests at a time, tracing it through his many books, essays, book reviews, letters and interviews. Not only were these productions disjointed at their inception, but, as already has been noted,[2] the published editions of Sorel's main works had the tendency to become ever growing ragbags into which sometimes an author himself, sometimes his editors would stuff earlier or subsequently written pieces under the heading of new prefaces or supplements — additions which more often than not reflect an opinion very different from that which Sorel held when he wrote the original book.

The result is violently disconcerting to the uniniated reader. Perusing, for instance, the third edition of **La Ruine du monde antique,** published in 1933, he will ascertain without any trouble from Sorel's introduction that the work had first appeared in 1902, but he will not easily discover the fact that the first chapter as it now stands, was written ten years later,[3] — that is, at the time when Sorel had repudiated most of his earlier allegiance to Marxian historical materialism.

The functional approach taken by most commentators seems, therefore, largely justified. The result of their labors is a much clearer, neater kind of Sorel, eminently quotable and most impressive, if still somewhat elusive. But it is no longer Sorel, the actual writer. That is why he disappoints so many who, made curious by the choice selections of the Sorelian exegesis, are making bold to penetrate the

---

[1]Some of the commentaries are discussed in chapter 11.

[2]See Part I, Introduction, p. 16-18.

[3]First published as **"Hypothèses sur la conquête chrétienne"** in **Revue de métaphysique et de morale,** January, 1912, as Sorel informs the reader of the second edition (Paris, 1925, p. xxviii) in the preface written in 1922.

primeval forest of the **ipsa verba magistri.** The first impression, in
at least one man's opinion, is disastrous. Those landmarks which we
remember so well, are buried in the underbrush of minute, often petty
observations; the forest has become so many trees among which we
feel lost, and when we finally have reached what promises to be a
clearing, all too often we sink into quicksand. And yet, if we want to
understand Sorel, the actual Sorel, we ought not to give up so easily;
we should try to discover his totality in the very diffusion of his authentic outpourings. At the risk of getting entrapped, we must scale
the ever shifting dunes of the Sorelian landscape. To leave the similes
aside, it is imperative to break through to the core of each of Sorel's
works. For, encased as it has become in later accretions and much as
it may stand in need of them, it is that core which represents his genuine experience. With all the characteristics of a fragment, the first
text stands for a very definite stage in the intellectual growth of a man
who, though he never cared to stop at any given point, still made each
point with utmost vigor and finality, with a cavalier disregard for
earlier findings.

A chronological treatment of Sorel's works, tempered by some
concessions to the functional principle, should satisfy two major needs:
to show the growing complexity of Sorel's interests, and to reveal, behind the disunity of composition, the essential unity of purpose that informs the two sets of writings into which Sorel's work conveniently
arranges itself. It is legitimate to begin with the historian Sorel, while
leaving Sorel, the social critic of his time aside for the moment. Although the two Sorels cannot well be separated — his "historic" observations and his contemporary criticism not representing two distinct
phases, but alternating and over-lapping continuously[4] — the advantage
of tracing one type of writings after the other is more than a matter of
expediency. There was in Sorel's make-up a conflict, never to be resolved, between the passionate observer and the diffident partisan. It
is because he inserted his passions of the day into his interpretations
of the past, that his historic studies are so many calls to present action,
agitation in disguise, while, on the other hand, even his most ardent
revolutionary proclamations seem to emit a certain chill: the sober-
ness of a man with three thousand years of dampening memories on his
conscience. It was because Sorel was a great moralist that he turned
historian, trying to sort out, in himself, the scholar from the partisan,
forcing them both to perform alternate tours of duty. He tried in vain,
and his failure is at the same time the stigma and the distinction of
his work.

---

[4] "He looks upon politics with the eyes of the historian, and upon history
with the eyes of a man of politics." René Johannet, **"L'évolution de Georges
Sorel"** in **Itinéraires d'Intellectuels,** (Paris, 1921) p. 231.

The Bible

That work begins — and almost ends — in the sign and name of Ernest Renan. Long before Sorel likened the myth of the Syndicalist revolution to the early Christian belief in the Second Coming, he was, inspired by Renan's work, strongly attracted to religious problems, and in particular to the probings of nineteenth century scholarship into the mysterious origins of Christianity. It was therefore no accident — although the information may be quite a shock to one who knew Sorel only as the author of a book on proletarian violence — that his first full-length work was a **Contribution to the Layman's Study of the Bible.**[5]

The preface is worth quoting because it sets the pattern not merely for this firstling: "Popular education is the great concern of our contemporary society. The people were taught how to read: but they were not given the Book. The Book of the people exists: it is the Bible.... Today, the popularization of the Bible is a social question."[6] The Bible, not **Das Kapital,** which was as yet untranslated into French. Yet the leitmotif of Sorel's revolutionary writing is already clearly sounded: "The Bible is the sole book which could serve to instruct the people, to initiate them into the **heroic life,** to combat the pernicious tendencies of utilitarianism, to arrest the propagation of the revolutionary idea."[7]

If that still sounds like the statement of a worried conservative, the reference to the "heroic life" already suggests the later Sorel who will plead for a spiritual revolution as the only means of reviving a decadent civilization. Already in his early work, Sorel was the "conservative revolutionary."[8] When, later, he became the advocate of proletarian revolution, it was because he decided that the only truly conservative forces were to be found among those who rejected the utilitarian offerings of both bourgeoisie and pseudo-revolutionary intelligentsia.

But will the people, if proffered the Book, want to read it? Formerly, in the times of heresies, the Church had not trusted the people with the Bible, but today the danger is of a different nature: "the people care very little about heresies; they have become anti-Christian."[9] It would be folly to present the Bible to them from a religious viewpoint: "the people would reject it." What is needed, is "to introduce The Book into secular literature, and to introduce it as a classic work."[10]

But Sorel is very far from emulating the example of the "liberal"

---

[5] Contribution à l'étude profane de la Bible (Paris, 1889), viii, 339.

[6] Ibid., p. vii.

[7] Ibid. - Emphasis of the present writer.

[8] Michael Freund gave his German study of **Georges Sorel** (Frankfurt am Main, 1932) the subtitle: "The revolutionary conservativism."

[9] Sorel, op. cit., p. vii.

[10] Ibid., p. viii.

Bible criticism fashionable in his time. He is not out to "debunk" what the Marxists called "fideism," and although much impressed by Renan's lyrical rationalism, he comes to conclusions that are distinctly not "enlightened." The author of the **Contribution** does not believe in a "science of religion" because all religious experience is founded on a fact beyond scientific disputation: upon "a spontaneous metaphysical creation, a **revelation**. The present-day tendency is to dissimulate that primordial fact as much as possible. We try to reduce everything to a slow and obscure process of evolution."[11]

In contradistinction, Sorel's own critical research anticipates, by several decades, the tendency prevailing today, of reassigning to the Bible, after a century of disparagment, its old status as a source of genuinely historic evidence: "My conclusions are, very often, close to those of the orthodoxy."[12] Some of Sorel's interpretations, however, must have surprised, and perhaps even amused, the churchmen of his time. For Sorel, "the question of the fourth gospel is very simple."[13] Not only does he believe that St. John's testimony is "the most authentic document we possess about Jesus Christ,"[14] it is also "the most ancient document of the New Testament."[15] In this belief, Sorel is following Renan, but while Renan revised his opinion in the later editions of his **Life of Jesus**,[16] Sorel never changed his mind about St. John: "The author was the last of the prophets, his place is by the side of Exekiel."[17] As to the synoptics, he believes to have shown conclusively that their authors were no longer, as St. John was, firmly rooted in the local Jewish tradition, but intellectually displaced persons, full of superstitious notions, probably of Greek descent. In their writings, "the facts are, almost always, slightly distorted, be it because of the ignorance of the authors, or because of their dogmatic preoccupations."[18]

These quotations are probably misleading; the bulk of the work is a most thorough socio-political exegesis of religious institutions, which sometimes reads like an anticipation of Max Weber's master work on the same subject.[19] Afterwards, Sorel thought very little of the **Contribution** except as a sketch of his main work on Renan published 16

---

[11]Ibid., p. 1. - Sorel's emphasis.

[12]Ibid., p. 2.   [13]Ibid., p. 3.

[14]Ibid., p. 2.   [15]Ibid., p. 3.

[16]See Madame James Darmesteter (A. Mary F. Robinson), **The Life of Ernest Renan** (London, 1898), p. 163.

[17]Sorel, **op. cit.**, p. 283. — "The fourth gospel was written before Paul's epistles to the Corinthians; at least one part dates from the very first years following the death of Christ." **Ibid.**, p. 284. — Cf. also pp. 261, 270, 280, 281.

[18]Ibid., p. 3. See also pp. 205, 221-222.

[19]Max Weber, **Gesammelte Aufsaetze zur Religionssoziologic** (Tuebingen, 1920-1921), Vol. III.

years later.[20] Some commentators, however, discovered more in it
than Georges Sorel himself had done. One believed that the author was
inspired by Renan's identification of Christianity with the very spirit
of revolution rather than that of authority: "Judaism and Christianity
represent in antiquity what socialism is in modern times."[21]

Perhaps so, but in 1889 Sorel was not yet a revolutionary, nor
even a Socialist.[22]

The Rejection of Socrates

That same year, he published his second book, **The Trial of Socrates,** with Georges Sorel in the role of prosecuting attorney. His
indictment makes for more interesting, although not less exasperating
reading than that of the original accuser, and the new Anytus seems to
be in cordial agreement with his immediate predecessor in that never
vacant role, that is, with Nietzsche. This agreement was, however,
not based on any knowledge on the part of Sorel of Nietzsche's anti-
Socratic writings.[23] All the more startling is the Nietzschean tenor
of Sorel's "faint praise":

"We admire Socrates very much; as a dialectician, he rendered
invaluable services to philosophy. Unfortunately, he also occupied
himself with morals and politics....Socrates has been elevated to one
of the apostles and martyrs of Liberty. Nothing could be more beside
the point." Far from deserving a place in the Prytanneion as a model
patriot and veteran, "Socrates made a great effort to break the chains
which tied the [Athenian] citizen to the polis. These chains were
those of military discipline."[24] Sorel's authority for this severe re-
proach is no less a scholar than Ernst Curtius.[25]

---

[20]"I see in **Voce** that Prezzolini mentions an old book of mine on the Bible
as a bibliographical rarity; what good it contained, was incorporated, with many
corrections, into my book on Renan." Sorel to Croce (1928, p. 439), November
20, 1912. See also below, note 43.

[21]Renan, **Histoire du peuple d'Israel** (Paris, 1894), V. 422. Cited by
Michael Freund, op. cit., p. 25.

[22]In contrast to Freund, Ernst Posse, in his preface to the German edition
of Sorel's **La décomposition du marxisme,** stresses the "antirevolutionary"
element in Sorel's first book, an element that will remain characteristic even
of his later work.... " We know that Sorel at no time in his life ever showed
any sympathy for the French revolution.... Even his Myth of the General Strike
is at the opposite pole from any revolutionary ideology." Sorel, **Die Auflösung
des Marxismus** (Jena, 1930), p. 4.

[23]See Part I, Introduction, p. 13.

[24]Sorel, **Le procès de Socrate** (Paris, 1889), p. 6.

[25]His **Griechische Geschichte,** 3 vols. (Berlin, 1858-1867). A French edition based on the fifth German edition, was published in Paris, 1880-1883.

Martyr of liberty indeed! "In the ideal city of the Socratics, public opinion [l'esprit] would have been supervised, directed, suppressed."[26] To be sure, the Platonic hero of the **Republic** was not the historic Socrates, Sorel knows it, yet: "Plato exaggerated the principles of his master, but he still followed them."[27] Plato has been called the first church father, and Sorel would agree: "The Socratic state is ecclesiastic.... The citizen would have but one liberty, the liberty of [choosing] The Good..." The situation of the Socratics resembled strongly that of the first Protestant: "Calvin demanded the right to teach what he declared to be the truth; but he expected that his opponents would be reduced to silence.... The Socratics would have acted like Calvin, had they been able to attain power somewhere."[28]

Like every true historian, Sorel studies the past in order to understand the present. Thus he discovers a parallelism between the period of Socratic "enlightenment" and the modern age carrying that name: "The disciples of the 18th century **philosophes** had hardly gained the upper hand, when they in turn began to persecute the church, when they started to fabricate and to impose dogmas."[29] Sorel dreads the idea of compulsory mass education: "It is to be hoped that the state will not succeed in suppressing the consciences."[30] Fortunately, the French system of parliamentary government prevents any stability of administrative power: "Otherwise, France would become a branch of the old Jesuit missions of Paraguay, a truly Socratic state."[31] He cannot say it often enough: "The state transformed into a church, the public power placed at the disposal of the sects, such was the idea of the Socratics...." He is reminded of the virtuous terror of the French revolution: "'Fraternity Or Death!' was the cry of the visionaries of '93."[32] Socrates' crime was that he "confounded morality, law, and science, with the result that you get probabilism instead of morality, and arbitrariness in politics."[33]

As always, Sorel is moved to write because he had been reading another man's book. This time it is Fouillée's work on the philosophy of Socrates that starts him off.[34] For all his loathing, Sorel is filled with grudging admiration for the persisting influence of Socratic ideas. Not yet ready to view great men as "symbol carriers rather than originators,"[35] he assumes that the one Socrates **caused** the intellectual development that led to the break-up not only of ancient society but also to our own, contemporary quandaries: while the theses of the Presocratics disappeared long ago, "the same is not the case with the

---

26Sorel, **op. cit.**, p. 7.   27Ibid.
28Ibid., p. 7-8.   29Ibid., p. 8.
30Ibid., p. 9.   31Ibid.
32Ibid.   33Ibid.
34Alfred Fouillée [1838-1912], **La philosophie de Socrate**, 2 vols. (Paris, 1874).
35Sorel, **Le système historique de Renan** (Paris, 1906), p. 5.

ideas of Socrates and his school.... All contemporary questions have their origin in his teachings...." Ever since Socrates, the would-be totalitarian, "the idea of the state remained in suspense.... We pass from one despotism to another without being able to see the end of our ills."[36] Ever since Socrates confused law and morality," penal law hardly made any progress; this confusion continues to corrupt all decisions in criminal matters...." In addition, Socrates "enjoined his disciples not to concern themselves with the sciences. This improvised and negative judgment still weighs heavily on modern philosophy."[37] But the same Socrates who is here made responsible for the subsequent estrangement between physics and metaphysics, furnished the weapons with which to destroy the towers of airy idealism: "Even though Socrates' ethics were detestable, they contained the principle of all future research...full of contradictions as they were...they provided the dialectician with an inexhaustible arsenal to destroy all false moralities."[38] For centuries, philosophy had lost its dominant role. Even today, "The true source of moral instruction is still the Church. Since the triumph of Christianity, the philosophers had to surrender the direction of the consciences.... Their task now is to define Law in a precise manner and to establish its place within the framework of ethics.... This is a truly scientific question which must be treated in a scientific fashion."[39] Sorel notes: "Under law, we naturally comprise political economy. The confusion of moral principles and scientific formulas is the common sin of all socialist schools."[40] Here is an aside of the first importance, probably the very intimation of Sorel's later pluralistic attempt to define the boundaries between science, ethics and economics.[41]

At this point, Sorel feels the need to apologize for "the somewhat boorish form of our exposition."[42] As a matter of fact, the sensationalist aggressiveness noted so far is almost entirely confined to the preface of the work; what follows is a scholarly and utterly respectful study of the moral, religious and political aspects of Socrates' teachings.[43] It seems, Sorel's commentators, inflamed by Nietzsche's

---

[36]Sorel, Le procès de Socrate [In the following called Socrate], p. 14.
[37]Ibid., p. 15   [38]Ibid., p. 16-17.
[39]Ibid., p. 17   [40]Ibid., note.
[41]Cf. Sorel, Le système historique de Renan, p. 84-87 — See chapter 11, p. 266-267.
[42]Socrate, p. 20.
[43]In later years, Sorel all but disavowed his early work: "Those two books [the Contribution and the Socrate] were written under rather unfavorable conditions, without the necessary source materials; I do not think they are worth much." (To Croce, 1928, p. 440, November 25, 1912.) — And of the Socrate in particular: "That book I wrote twenty seven years ago, in provincial surroundings, without sufficient information, and at a time when, in many respects, my ideas were still rather hazy." (To Croce, 1929, p. 119, March 14, 1915.)

much more violent diatribes against the father of European intellectualism, succumbed to the temptation to over-emphasize the anti-Socratic element in the Frenchman's book. The accents are there, but they are occasional apercus rather than the highlights of a sustained argument. Sorel, remembering that there are two Socratic traditions, that of Xenophon as well as that of Plato, does not press the point made in the preface, where he had identified the protagonist of the **Republic** with the historic Socrates. Now, he directs his criticism exclusively against Plato, anticipating most of the strictures made against him before and during the last, anti-fascist war.[44] Plato's testimony of the Socratic **Apology** is rejected: "The disciple developed, excessively, some rather marginal points while neglecting the important questions. This deficiency is absent in Xenophon's [Apology]."[45] The latter "seems to have composed his little book in order to correct the novelistic creation of the co-disciple."[46] Plato's Socrates mocks his judges, but if Plato's philosophical system is accepted, "how can he say, as he does, that Socrates refused to mollify the judges **because he respected the law?**"[47] Plato notoriously disliked the Athenian democracy; "it is likely that he wrote his **Apology** in a milieu that shared his antipathies. The philosopher played courtier to his protectors by narrating how Socrates had defied the Heliastes."[48] Unlike Plato, Xenophon "had no reasons to ridicule justice, so sacred to all ancients, little as his generation may have conserved the old Greek spirit."[49]

According to Sorel's Xenophon, Socrates died because "his dearest illusions had been shattered; he had seen the noblest and most brilliant of his disciples rebel against the mother city; Athen's destiny was rather triste."[50] He wanted "to die nobly."[51] Socrates himself was not guilty of sedition. But he had kept dangerous company, and he towered above his fellow sophists who attacked the democratic tradition, and taught the Athenian youth, part of whom were organized in **hetairias**, secret brotherhoods, a new, revolutionary morality. The political labels have to be reversed: in the civil war raging in Athens,

---

[44]By such writers as K. R. Popper in **The Open Society and Its Enemies** (London, 1945), Vol. I, and R. H. S. Crossman, **Plato To-day** (London, 1937).

[45]Socrate, p. 244.

[46]Ibid., p. 252.

[47]Ibid., p. 257 — Sorel's emphasis. — "Not for an instant did it cross his mind that this place would be subject to other regulations than those of the market place.... Even now [Plato's] Socrates has not got used to the idea that on this occasion he is no longer the teacher, but simply the criminal. "Ludwig Marcuse, **Plato and Dionysius** (New York, 1947), pp. 61, 63.

[48]Socrate, p. 257.

[49]Ibid., p. 258.

[50]Ibid., p. 259.

[51]Ibid., p. 261.

the "old Democrats" were conservatives, while the innovators were
recruited among the **ci-devant** conservative classes.[52]

A new and revolutionary morality, Socrates did teach it: his theory
of the male Eros "alienated men from the home. . . . Socrates committed a veritable crime in giving the world such a perfect and poetic
theory of unisexual love."[53] Sorel cites his teacher, Proudhon, who,
like him, was a fervent advocate of conjugal love, fidelity and chastity:
"once the union of the sexes is eliminated by the logic of the ideal,,
love has lost its basis; we have reached the contradiction, the catastrophe is not far off."[54]

Sorel recognizes that "Socrates did not push his principle of the
Eros to its ultimate conclusions;"[55] he refers to the **Memorabilia**
where Xenophon has Socrates pay tribute to the institution of marriage. But Sorel insists that although "Socrates was not the organizer
of these lodges" — the brotherhoods of male philosophers — "yet he was
the most brilliant and most daring theorist of the new social organization founded on the fictitious family" — united by the loyalty to Truth.[56]
Definitely, his teachings contain an element of erotic mysticism that
was not of **Greek** origin. Socrates' famous **"daimonion"** too suggests
the penetration of "Asiatic ideas" into Athenian, Western civilization.[57]
Socrates was more than just a brilliant Sophist: "he was a **prophet"** [58]
In Asia, that would have been quite normal, nothing shocking, "but in
Greece it was something else again."[59] It is this prophetic personality of Socrates that lent itself to political tendencies hostile to
Athenian democracy. On this point Xenophon, the admirer of Sparta,
agrees with Plato, and "he is certainly the trustworthy interpreter of
the master's notions."[60]

Not that the philosopher directly participated in anti-democratic
activities, yet "from the political point of view, Socrates' influence was
almost as bad as that of the Sophists. The Socratics were all capti-
vated by the theory of the Absolute; they did not acknowledge the importance of historic [customary] law; that is what made them revolutionaries."[61] They confused, as Sorel said before, law with morals.

---

[52]Ibid., p. 206. "In Athens, a return to the old aristocratic regime was
unthinkable; its restoration would have been impossible. The wealthy classes
were largely in sympathy with the new principles; the youth was full of disdain for the heroic past. . . . " **Ibid.**

[53]Ibid., p. 95

[54]Ibid., p. 96. Sorel's note, **Ibid.**, p. 95: "Justice. 10. Etude, § XXIII."
The quotation is to be found in § XXIV, see **Oeuvres complètes de P. J. Proudhon**, Vol. VIII, Pt. 4 (Paris, 1935), p. 61.

[55]Idid., p. 97.   [56]Ibid., p. 236.

[57]Ibid., p. 99. Cf. also p. 145 ff.

[58]Ibid., p. 129. — Sorel's emphasis.

[59]Ibid.   [60]Ibid., p. 193.

[61]Ibid., p. 203, note. — Sorel's emphasis.

That does not make Socrates a partisan of the oligarchic party,[62] while on the other hand, the abstention of the great majority of his disciples from politics "is no proof either that they were completely innocent of the Athenian misfortunes."[63] In his effort, not to be too rude to Socrates, Sorel becomes more and more involved in contradictions: "The tyranny [of the Athenian oligarchs] was not the work of Socrates, but of all philosophers," he exclaims on page 238, only to throw all caution to the winds on the following page: "It seems that Socrates was more revolutionary than all the Sophists together...." For they were merely utilitarians, men of an altogether skeptical and practical bend of mind, whereas Socrates insisted that all action be directed toward a scientifically determined Good and Just. "This conception struck at the very foundations of the constitution." Socrates, the citizen, and Socrates, the philosopher, are at odds: in his practice he accepted the historically grown law of the city as legitimate; "his theory denied that legitimacy and subjected law to scientific control."[64]

Sorel is obviously thinking of the French revolution and Jacobin terror when speaking of Athens: "One had seen those famous dialecticians at work...they had ruined the city, suppressed all citizens and made all decent people loathe the oligarchs."[65] It does not happen often, Sorel observes, that men of science throw themselves into active politics. As a rule, believers of thought and timidity in action go together. And in reverse, "people who resort to violence are generally rather weak as theorists" Sorel concludes,[66] explaining thereby, incidentally, why it is that, twenty years later revolutionary Syndicalism appreciated so little the subtle implications of the Sorelian theory of violence. But it is one thing not to be heard, and another to be misunderstood, to be taken at your word, that is, a word torn from its context and used for ulterior purposes by people in need of a program. Sorel is convinced "that the **philosophes** of the 18th century would have protested against their disciples, had they lived long enough to see them at work."[67] Again by way of anticipation, Sorel tells us a great deal about himself, and, if we wish, accepts his share of guilt for having been misappropriated by the wrong people: "In vain would Rousseau have attempted to convince his admirers that they had failed to understand his ideas; they would have answered him that a book is there to be read and commented upon, and that it was too bad if the author had expressed himself so poorly."[68] Had Rousseau been all too recalcitrant, Sorel adds, he would have been proscribed like Condorcet.

[62]Ibid., p. 205.   [63]Ibid., p. 204.

[64]Ibid., p. 239, note. [65]Ibid., p. 239.

[66]Ibid., p. 204. "M. Taine taught us all about the false great men who masterminded the great European catastrophe." **Ibid.**

[67]**Ibid.**

[68]Ibid., Cf. Sorel, **Reflections on Violence** (Glencoe, Ill., 1950), where he refers to Rousseau again, adding: "The defects of illustrious men do not justify the faults of the obscure." (p. 32).

The relevant fact about the external succession of revolution and reaction is the struggle of minorities relying on "rational" principles against the haphazard regimes of the day. These minorities get their historic chance "when the vices of democracy have become obvious, when the need is felt to create something more scientific." And one of the characteristics of revolution is the creation of dictatorial power placed at the disposal of small groups. "We had a taste of that in '93. The majority of a nation cannot, in general, so easily accept a complete reversal of affairs, based on absolute theories....The innovators will succeed only by bold means: they are a minority, but if they have the **faith** they will sometimes triumph, if the conditions are favorable...."[69] They have faith in reason: "Had man not been endowed with intelligence so as to rise above the miseries of life? Was not intelligence sovereign?"[70] The Jacobins, Sorel feels, were "perfectly logical."[71] One is reminded of Anatole France's dictum: "If you start with the supposition that men are naturally good and virtuous, you invariably end by wanting to kill all who do not agree with you."[72] And the conservative Sorel of 1889, already highly critical of democratic values, still prefers democracy to the pseudo-scientific rationalisations of would-be philosopher kings: "Much as one may deplore the sad results of the electoral system, our regrets will be attenuated somewhat once we ask ourselves what a regime of savants would be like....Could we imagine anything more horrible than a government of academicians?"[73]

Sorel takes pains to defend Socrates and the Sophists against the accusation, frequently directed against Plato nowadays, of having advanced their educational schemes in order to disguise better their claims to absolute power. True, the Socratics believed that "the scholars had a title to **legitimate** rule,"[74] but that is not to say that they wanted to transform science into a class monopoly or that they denied the possibility of "integral," that is, democratic education.[75] But since, for the people, Socrates summed up the "new education," he became the scapegoat: "the people need a symbolic figure upon which to fasten their ideas...."[76]

That there was any mass hostility toward Socrates among the people of Athens, does not necessarily follow.[77] His trial was a political action designed to "spread terror among the Sophist gang" and to restore the ancient principles to their place of honor.[78] "To acquit Socrates would have been tantamount to an amnesty for the oligarchic innovators."[79]

---

[69] Ibid., p. 205.   [70] Ibid., p. 219.   [71] Ibid., p. 206.

[72] "When one would make men good and wise...one is led to the fatal desire of killing them all." Anatole France, The Opinions of Jérôme Coignard (London, 1913), p. 18. - "The most terrible massacres are inspired by the idea that man is fundamentally good and virtuous ..." Nicolas Ségur, The Opinions of Anatole France (London, 1928), p. 21-22.

[73] Socrate, p. 183.   [74] Ibid., p. 238.   [75] Ibid., p. 237.   [76] Ibid., p. 239.
[77] Ibid., p. 240.   [78] Ibid., p. 241.   [79] Ibid., p. 242.

However, the old traditions were already too far gone: "the restoration [of the democratic regime], far from bringing about the triumph of the old morality, saw instead the flowering of philosophy and sophistry."[80] Indeed, the most remarkable phenomenon of that period, in the view of Sorel, was "the abandonment by Socrates' opponents of all attempts at religious reform."[81]

But what about Socrates' disciples? Why did no religious reform issue from his sainted memory? For the martyred prophet was "perfectly equipped to become the founder of a creed: he was enthusiastic, eloquent, and evidently far superior to Mohammed, to Babi, and many other figures who made a strong impression on the peoples of Asia."[82]

Has Sorel forgotten that his Socrates was a supreme rationalist? Like Nietzsche, he is forced to account for that mysterious residue of the irrational in Socrates, his famous "daemon." And Sorel's difficulty is all the greater as he disdains to take Nietzsche's simpler if ingenuous way out of the quandary. In the German's **Birth of Tragedy** which, we repeat, was not known to Sorel when he wrote his **Trial**, the Socratic "voice, whenever it comes, always **dissuades**. In this utterly abnormal nature instinctive wisdom only appears in order to **hinder** . . . the progress of conscious perception. Whereas in all productive men it is instinct that is the creative affirmative force, and consciousness that acts critically; with Socrates it is instinct that becomes critic, and consciousness that becomes creator. . . ." Nietzsche observes here "a monstrous **defectus** of all mystical aptitude, so that Socrates might be called the typical **non-mystic**. . . ." True, even Nietzsche's Socrates has an uneasy feeling about the limitations of logic; evidence: the dream-apparition in prison admonishing him: "Socrates, practice music." And so the dying Socrates who had thought so little of popular, sensuous art, composes a poem in praise of Apollo and versifies some Aesopian fables: "Perhaps," thus Nietzsche has him reason, "there is a realm of wisdom from which the logician is shut out? Perhaps art is even a necessary correlative of, and supplement to, science?"[83]

But Sorel, basing his case not on Plato's but on Xenophon's record, cannot use Nietzsche's argument. For in Xenophon's **Apology** the daemon by no means confines himself to giving merely negative advice: the voice of a God makes known to Socrates "what I should do."[84] These divine commands Socrates translates into intellectually reasoned

---

[80] Ibid., p. 273.

[81] Ibid.

[82] Ibid., p. 274. — Babi: "The Gate," title of Seyed Mohammed Ali, founder of a Persian sect in the 19th century.

[83] Friedrich Nietzsche **"The Birth of Tragedy From The Spirit of Music"** transl. by Clifton P. Fadiman, in **The Philosophy of Nietzsche** (The Modern Library, New York, 1937), pp. 254, 255, 262. — Nietzsche's emphasis.

[84] Socrate, p. 125.

ethical precepts and decisions, but they still are the product of
genuinely religious revelations, and that is the actual reason behind
Socrates' refusal to accept a remuneration for his teaching, because
what is a gift of the gods cannot and must not be sold for money on the
market place.[85] There is no doubt in Sorel's mind as to the mystical
character of Socrates' inspiration; the great intellectual athlete considered himself literally authorized by the Divinity and believed that
"Truth was incarnated in him; his decisions were infallible."[86]

By now we are a far cry from Socrates, the questioner who knew
nothing and hoped, at best, to sift out the more probable from the less
likely. How then does Sorel account for the fact that a "Socratic religion" did not emerge? Since his Socrates has the makings of a Mohammed, the fault must lie with the Greeks who refused to recognize
their prophet. Sorel finds that the Athenian polis morality, while already weakened too much to permit a return to the old tradition, was
still too vigorous for a new religion to succeed. "It took the Roman
conquest to dethrone all the local deities, to destroy the idea of patriotic solidarity, to level all conditions."[87] The elaboration of the
Christian dogma is a Roman accomplishment and, "consequently, not
at all semitic."[88]

Sorel forgets here that the decomposition of the classic polis was
consummated long before the advent of Rome; it had already begun with
Alexander and the ensuing reign of the Diadochs. Because Sorel totally disregards the whole, long period of Hellenism, he deprives himself of the chance of discovering certain authentic religions of great
importance going back to Socrates. It is well known that the Cynics
as well as the Stoics claimed him as their inspiration and hero. Of the
two schools, the Stoa at any rate could claim to call itself a religion as
well as a philosophy; indeed, it developed into a world religion which
has been called the matrix of Christianity. And Sorel's oversight becomes all the more strange as he says that "the great weakness of the

---

[85]Ibid., p. 136.

[86]Ibid., p. 129. — In the Appendix to the book, entitled "Socrates' Ethics,"
Sorel leaves no doubt that he considers Socrates' teachings as essentially religious in character: "Socrates rendered an immense service to philosophy
by showing that, if man is not the measure of all things in the sense which
Protagoras gave to that formula, man is nevertheless the center of all metaphysics...the Socratic conception is supernatural indeed, for nobody would
dare to maintain that [his] theories of deliverance and moral determinism
are reconcilable with the true nature of man, such as experience and science
define it. When noumenal conceptions of this kind are applied to phenomenal
reality, as was done by Socrates and Marcus Aurelius, then one cannot help
concluding that their doctrine was based on the one supernatural hypothesis
which is the strangest and the hardest to find acceptance." Ibid., p. 298-299.
Sorel's emphasis.

[87]Ibid., p. 274.

[88]Ibid., p. 276.

Socratic schools was their optimism; the masses will not be moved
by an appeal to the harmony and rationality of things. All great religious movements had for their basis a pessimistic world outlook."[89]
Socrates himself, Sorel believed, shared the optimistic attitude of the
Sophists, although, being brought up in an artistic tradition, he did not,
as they did, disdain, the **poetic** sadness of the ancients, which, in the
Sophist view, was "an insult to science."[90]

Now, leaving aside the non sequitur in this statement (harmony
and rationality may well be postulated by a pessimist), the Stoic world
religion can hardly be said to have lacked the spirit of pessimistic
resignation, if the testimonials of such spokesmen as Epicurus and
Marcus Aurelius are at all representative. Yet, even if Sorel could
have granted that much, he would insist that the philosophy of Socrates,
being optimistic, made him ineligible for church fatherhood. But then
Sorel was very far from granting the emperor Marcus the noble qualities usually attributed to him; again and again he goes out of his way
to attack the stoic on the throne as a hypocrite if nothing worse: "The
life of Marcus Aurelius is, in our view, the most convincing evidence
of applied Socratics; it shows, in a peremptory manner, that the doctrine of the master was profoundly vicious."[91]

This is a conclusion all the more deplorable as Sorel came very
close to recognizing that what mattered was not the historic Socrates
— historic according to Sorel — but Socrates the legendary figure, the
image as posterity conceived it. For Sorel himself quotes approvingly
Renan's saying about Mohammed: "What does it matter if the admiration of mankind commits historic errors, making the figures it took
to its heart appear more beautiful and more pure than they really
were? ... These sentiments have a value independent of the reality of
the object which provokes them...."[92] And Sorel adds: The source
of Mohammed's influence on people was not, as many believe, his
"hysteria," — the motor of that great movement was "the [popular]
belief in Mohammed's inspiration."[93] A similar religious success
story of our own tradition is that of St. Francis. The people believed
that he had received the stigmata, and this belief, not the exact, scientific character of the phenomenon, is the important factor, as far as
Sorel is concerned: "What interests the philosopher is the idea which
the contemporaries had about it."[94]

One writer discovered in these remarks "a first presentment, or,
if one wishes, the embryo of the Sorelian concept of the Myth."[95] If

[89]Ibid., p. 277.

[90]Ibid., p. 218.

[91]Ibid., p. 299. Cf. also Sorel, Le système historique de Renan, p. 322ff.

[92]Socrate, p. 121 - 122, note 2, cited from Renan, Etudes d'histoire religieuse, page 271, 5. edition.

[93]Socrate, p. 121.

[94]Ibid.

[95]Fernand Rossignol, La Pensée de Georges Sorel (Paris, 1948), p. 47.

true, this would be a happy discovery indeed, for it would add strength
to the thesis that important ideas do not in general occur to their authors over night but are the result of a slow growing process. Professor Rossignol's suggestion, if correct, would date back by seventeen
years the origin of one of the two **"idees maîtresses"** that made the
fame of Sorel's **Reflections on Violence.** It would elevate the **Trial of
Socrates** to the eminence of having established the seminal unity of
Sorel's thought at the very beginning of his writing career.

Unfortunately, this claim will not stand scrutiny. The fact that
Sorel himself dates the birth of his idea of the Myth much later, may
be brushed aside; authors are quite often unaware of their own findings, and they are sincerely startled when informed of their **trou-
vaille.**[96] But Sorel's early notion, derived from Renan, that fictions
may, under certain conditions, become powerful historic facts, is not
yet more than an inspired guess, a random remark that is nowhere
developed into a central argument. Sorel was unable to recognize its
major importance because the main premises of the work precluded
any linking of the myth concept to the central character: since Socrates had to serve as an exponent of rationalist disintegration, he could
not at the same time be interpreted by Sorel as a protagonist of religious integration. The author is, to the exclusion of everything else,
concerned with the negative task of belaboring the "logical faith" of the
Jacobin **emeute,** the faith in reason which produces utopias and their
sequence: terror and catastrophe; later he will contemplate the positive force that conceives social hopes in terms of mythical images as
immune from disillusion as they are from the contagion of harsh facts.

And so Sorel sums up: Socrates was justly put to death because
the application of his principles would have destroyed the polis. It
matters little whether Sorel's criminal was the historic Socrates;
like the Athenian people, Sorel needed a "symbolic figure upon which
to fasten his ideas"[97] about the modern intellectual, the optimistic destroyer of "life." It is the leitmotif of the book, and Sorel holds out
hope that a turning point is soon to come; twenty-five years before the
first world war, he writes: "We think... that the period of optimism in
France is approaching its end: the revival of pessimistic ideas in certain circles seems to announce a revival of morality. Long enough has

---

[96]At a musical matinee, arranged to reintroduce the Berlin opera habitués
to Richard Strauss' early work, **Feuersnot,** the lecturer, a well-known music
critic, asked the composer at the conclusion of his remarks to play (on the
piano) "the remarkable motif from which the entire melodic material of the
opera had been derived." Richard Strauss played several themes, none of
them to the satisfaction of the critic, until he was finally reduced to a state
of blushing perplexity. The lecturer had to come to the rescue and to point
out to the composer the passage which had been, without his knowing so, the
central inspiration of the entire score.... (Source: the present writer who
witnessed the scene some time during the first world war).

[97]See note 76.

the cult of success been predominant among us: the time has come to view life under a more philosophic aspect."[98] It is because he wants to promote a pessimistic view of life that Sorel accepts as a fact of history "the rationalist Socrates," and in that sense, but in that sense only, Sorel may be said to have applied, without being conscious of what he was doing, his theory of the myth to an historic event, the life and teachings of Socrates which, on Sorel's own showing, in no way bore out what he considered to be the Athenian view of the time. Later Sorel will decide that a myth is the affirmation by action of an irrational belief, and not, as the anti-Socratism of Anytus and Meletus, merely the rejection of something disliked. He will distinguish between mass emotions with constructive results, and constructions (or misconceptions) of the intellect that remain barren abstractions. In the Trial the line between myth and utopia, so sharply, perhaps all too sharply, drawn in the Reflections, is still unmarked. It seems Sorel is not yet ready to distinguish clearly between the Robespierres who place their "faith in reason"[99] and the intuitive mind which evolves its reasoning from faith.

Perhaps because he felt the ambiguity of his position, Sorel ends his study on a neutral, almost conventional note. Sensing the miracle of a unique being in whom "inspiration" and logic were ideally fused, he almost seems to regret that the prophet Socrates had to die rejected so that the First Jacobin could enjoy his ghostly triumph through the ages. For if Socrates, the effigy of Sorel's anti-rationalist bias, is merely a counter-myth directed against the true myth of Socrates the mystic, the counter-myth itself assigns to the philosopher a position hardly less endowed with charismatic sanctity than that befitting a religious genius:

"When the war of the cities had completely exhausted the political strength of the Hellenes ... Greece became ... a museum and a university. The memory of the Sophists gradually paled, while Socrates' fame grew to the extent ... [where] the world saluted him as the founder of philosophy. Never has a tribute to a single man been more legitimate. ... The Greek world seemed to date from Socrates."[100]

Decline and Fall

Sorel's preoccupation with the problem of decadence, a preoccupation so marked throughout his entire work as to justify a special study,[101] lead him, quite logically, from Socrates who signalled the end of classical Greece, to a contemplation of the causes responsible

---

[98]Socrate, p. 219.

[99]See text to notes 69 and 70.

[100]Socrate, p. 280.

[101]Cf. Jean Wanner, Georges Sorel et la décadence (Lausanne, 1943), 90 pp.

for the downfall of Rome. The Socratic movement, in Sorel's view, had been an abortive religion not resulting in a renewal of the Hellenic spirit; the end of the Roman empire, however, was the beginning of something new: a seminal period. Sorel, disturbed by contemporary signs of decay, and not yet sure but hopeful that he had discovered the force that would bring about the generation of an aging Western world, turns his attention to the historic "change of the guard," from Paganism to Christianity. He attempts to draw a **parallel** between the role of the early Church and that of modern Socialism, but the influence of historic Materialism, just adopted by Sorel, injects an anticlerical note in his investigation, a note which is not original with him. His attitude toward Christianity thus remains ambiguous, and for the most part negative. Sometimes he will stress the heroic morality of the persecuted Christians, which makes them the worthy predecessors of the modern proletarians; at other occasions he will extoll the juridical and administrative genius of the Romans and denounce the Christians as asocial wreckers and precursors of the Jacobin and other, more recent visionaries. The latter view prevails, and thus the parallel never quite comes off.

In joining the illustrious history club which has been debating, for the last fifteen hundred years, the why, or rather, the whys, of the Decline and Fall,[102] Sorel, as usual, is prompted by a book he had just read. His comments, first published in article form, expanded into a book appearing eight years later,[103] are preceded by a modest disclaimer: Sorel denies any intention of having attempted a Marxist explanation of Christian thought although he adds that such an attempt might be successful.[104] Why, then, did he give his book the subtitle, "Materialistic Conception of History"? Because, if not a study of the economic "substructure" of Christianity, it was at any rate concerned with the effect the new creed had on the economic and juridic institutions of the empire. Even so, there is precious little in Sorel's findings that would not have been acceptable to all the writers who endeavored to **"écraser l'infame."** Like Gibbon, Voltaire, or, to mention a modern, Otto Seeck,[105] Sorel holds that the new religion did weaken the Roman resistance against the barbarian pressure, if only by popularizing the idea that victory does depend on a superior morality rather than on material strength. But "war, like industry, wins its battles with

---

[102]See M. Rostovtzeff, **The Social and Economic History of the Roman Empire** (Oxford, 1926), pp. 480-487.

[103]It was Gaston Boissier's **La fin du Paganisme** (Paris, 1891), which gave Sorel the inspiration and the title for his own study, first published in **L'Ere Nouvelle**, August - October, 1894; as a book, under the title **La ruine du monde antique** (Paris, 1902).

[104]**La ruine,** pp. xvii and xviii. Quotations are from the 3. edition, 1933.

[105]**Geschichte des Untergangs der antiken Welt,** 6 Vols. (Berlin and Stuttgart, 1901-1920).

materials, man-power and organization."[106] Nobody, Sorel remarks contemptuously, would dare to assert that Christianity improved the productive capacities of the ancient world. "It created the Church, and through it, revolutionized civil society."[107] Sorel proposes to show that the new ideology "shattered" the structure of the Roman state "like a mechanical force acting from without. Far from infusing fresh blood into the aged organism, the new religion may be said to have bled it white. It severed the bonds uniting intellectual with social life; everywhere it disseminated the germs of Quietism, discouragement, and death."[108] To be sure, these vicious results are not due to any specific deficiency of the Christian dogma: they are the bane of all ideologies. Utopian socialism would have brought the same disastrous effect, had it exerted a lasting influence on the minds instead of being swept under by the capitalistic flood. And, dotting his i, Sorel asserts that the utopian socialists deliberately "tried to emulate Christianity in everything." In contradistinction, "Marxism presents itself as a doctrine of life, fit for strong nations: it reduces ideology to the role of an artifice, to an abridged exposition of reality...."[109] Follows the whole catechism, recited with all the ardor of the new acolyte.

The blow under which the Roman tradition crumbled did not come from the barbarians: "their invasions, it is known today, were not much of a threat; yet the Roman government found itself in as weakened a condition as the **Ancien Régime** prior to the revolution; Honorius resembles Louis XVI."[110] And the weakness of the state was in turn caused, according to Sorel, by revolution in the hitherto existing property concept.

The principal concern of ancient society had been the defense of the country; "in the fourth century of our era that question had lost a great deal of its importance.... But custom and sometimes the law obliged the well-to-do to defray the costs of what might be called the collectivists shows, that is, to participate at certain public acts which were to bring home to all citizens the political character of human coexistence under one and the same legal regime."[111] When bearing arms for the country no longer was one of the civic duties, those festivals were the only bond left to unite the body politic. The system imposed heavy burdens on the Roman notable; traditional opinion did not consider him to be absolute master of his fortune. "Christianity, without abolishing the old custom altogether, made it possible for its adherents to hold, with a clear conscience, that property was not, by its own nature, liable to such exactions.... From now on the right to property became...the right to dispose of one's net income without any restriction."[112] The effect was momentous: "The emancipation of

[106]La ruine, p. 42.
[107]Ibid., p. 43.   [108]Ibid., p. 44.
[109]Ibid.   [110]Ibid., p. 45.
[111]Ibid., p. 101.   [112]Ibid., p. 102.

property entailed the emancipation of the individual."[113] However, if
this statement has a strangely modern ring, it merely means that
private revenue was flowing into a different but still public channel.
Less tribute went to Caesar, more to God: "The emancipation [of
private property] was relative, for what the State lost, the Church
gained: what took place was only a transfer which did not constitute
liberty of conscience in the modern sense."[114] But the result was that
"more and more people demanded now, in the name of liberty, that the
State surrender all control over wills, endowments, mortmain, that is,
over everything touching upon the material interests of the Church."[115]
These interests are given a vicarious meaning: in the minds of the
faithful, it is God who is the recipient, God from Whom all bounty
flows mysteriously and to Whom it reverts by an act of human will.
An arbitrary element makes its appearance: "Whereas in civic society
everything had been proportionate, each burden being determined by a
general rule, the new world knows of no proportion or rule; the offering is always insufficient, coming as it does from a creature infinitely
small, standing before a creator infinitely powerful."[116]

By thus teaching the Roman world the new concept of individual
property, by "showing up the obligations of the property holder toward
the polis as so many inane fictions" the Church brought about an economic transformation which resulted in the ruin of all social concepts."[117] And once such a clear consciousness exists, seemingly
indestructible institutions fall almost without an effort.[118] The "dis-
association between the metaphysical principles of religious morality
and the rules of practical life"[119] seemed complete and final: "it was
only with a very great effort that modern man was able to restore what
appeared to be dead forever."[120]

Sorel knows, of course, that all this was not the exclusive work of
the Church; he points to the late Stoa and the relationship between the
"smaller" and the "greater commonwealth" in Seneca's philosophy.[121]
But Christianity "delivered the final blow."[122] When St. Augustine
could write: 'what does it matter under what master lives man who
must die, provided that master does not force him to anything contrary
to piety and justice,' the time had come when "the Middle Age could
start; there is no longer any polis, no longer any law."[123]

---

[113]Ibid., p. 142.
[114]Ibid., p. 144.
[115]Ibid., p. 102.
[116]Ibid., p. 103.
[117]Ibid., p. 142.
[118]Ibid., p. 45.
[119]Ibid., p. 63.
[120]Ibid., p. 142.
[121]Ibid., p. 63.
[122]Ibid., p. 102.
[123]Ibid., p. 122-123. — City of God, Book V, chap. xiii (Sorel's note).

In a post-script entitled "Church, Gospel and Socialism,"[124] Sorel once more returns to a problem already discussed in **Contribution a l'étude profane de la Bible.** Answering Renan's question as to the relative influence of the Judaic and Hellenic elements of Christianity, Sorel points to the role which the Hebrew Bible played during the Reformation: it was the old testament rather than the new one that influenced the members of the new churches in the sixteenth and seventeenth centuries. "The [Hebrew] Bible has a great social value because it is the **book of a peasant democracy:** the cultivators of the earth clamored for legal protection from the city people, the magistrates and priests who were oppressing them."[125] Sorel, not usually given to philosemitic utterances,[126] has at this point a good word to say for the Chosen People: the Old Testament "is a book written for workers; the Jews, more than any other nation, had an admiration for work...."[127] They believed, like modern Socialists, "that nothing could be claimed as a matter of Right, that did not correspond to some work [well] performed...."[128] In contrast, "the true Christian recognizes only the sentimental relations existing between rich and poor; he remains a stranger to the relations of production."[129] On this "economic" substructure, the men of the Church erected a juridico-political superstructure marvelously suited to their ends.[130] Sorel flatly denies that Christianity ever developed a proper social morality in the proper meaning of the word: "the gospels are written for man purified, for the anchorite, the saint; when the theologian concerns himself with economic questions, he is forced to borrow his doctrines from laymen, or else he talks as in a dream."[131]

Sorel ends with an unqualified rejection of Christian in favor of pre-Christian or non-Christian social ethics: "Socialism reverts to ancient thought; but the warrior of the **polis** has become the industrial worker; the weapons have been replaced by machines. Socialism is a philosophy of producers; what could it possibly learn from the Gospels which addressed themselves to beggars?"[132]

---

[124]First published as an article in **Rivista critica del socialismo,** April, May, 1899 in reply to an essay which Professor Talamo, "one of the most distinguished representatives of social catholicism in Italy" had published in the January issue, 1899, of **Rivista internazionale di science sociale e discipline ausiliarie.** In that article Talamo defended the thesis that "socialism could realize its aspirations only by adopting the principles of christian morality." Sorel, **La ruine,** p. 287 and note.

[125]Ibid., p. 307.

[126]See chapter 3, pp. 85f., and chapter 7, p. 188.

[127]La ruine, p. 307-308.

[128]Ibid., p. 273.   [129]Ibid., p. 309.

[130]Ibid., p. 309-310.

[131]Ibid., p. 311. — That thesis is further developed in Sorel's essay, "L'église et l'état"; see chapter 3, p. 75f.

[132]Ibid.

This passage, like many others, that seem to belong to the **Reflections on Violence** rather than to an obscure work of his early phase, is evidence of the fact that his most famous work did not spring from his mind like Pallas Athene from the head of Zeus. And long before he wrote it, Sorel had lost his faith in official Socialism: already in the preface to the first edition of **La ruine,** he states his opinion "that the desire to treat everything from a scientific viewpoint ends inevitably either in Utopia or with State Socialism."[133] The announcement that he feels "today much closer to the real spirit of Historic Materialism than in 1894," is remarkable for what it does not say: Sorel, so fond of quoting others, and also himself, for once forgoes his chance to refer to the publication (three years old when he readies **La ruine**) in which "the real spirit" of Sorel's new Socialism is already unmistakable.[134]

[133]Ibid., p. xix. —See also chapter 1, note 62.
[134]In L'avenir socialiste des syndicats; see chapter 4, p.109f.

Life in the Library ii:

3. HISTORY, SACRED AND VERY PROFANE

From Vico to Dreyfus

By way of Marx, Sorel discovered Giambattista Vico.[1] His extended study of the great Neapolitan preceded Benedetto Croce's first essay on the same subject by five years.[2] It was very likely Sorel's prodding that persuaded Croce to write the **magnum opus** with which the modern, second Vico renaissance is usually associated.[3]

For Sorel, the conjuncture of Marx and Vico becomes fruitful beyond the point of which they superficially agree: in their interpretation of history as the supreme science of man. As always, Sorel's "animated reading" of his text impresses us as a model of scholarly self effacement; it is doubtful whether his **Study of Vico** has been surpassed by anyone in its philological concern for detail. But again — and this may be one of the reasons why the essay has so far escaped the attention of the Vico scouts — the sum total is less an analysis and appraisal of the celebrated subject, than it is a document of Georges Sorel's own intellectual growth. His preoccupation with Marx, which started two years earlier,[4] colors the whole essay and adds to it, as it were, a fourth dimension. Marx and Vico are pitted against one another, with Sorel reaping the benefit. Still a revisionist, non-revolutionary Marxist at the time, he uses Vico as an antidote for the dogmatic teachings of the Marxist epigons; and he uses Marx in turn to improve upon Vico and to bring him up to date.

---

[1] "In a note in **Capital** K. Marx notes how very interesting a history of technology would be, and he adds: 'Darwin has drawn attention to the history of **Nature's technology,** that is to say to the formation of the organs of plants and animals considered as means for sustaining life. Would not the history of the productive organs of social man merit similar research? And would not such a history be easier to compile since, as Vico says, human history differs from natural history in this, that we have made the former, but not the latter?'" Sorel, **"Etude sur Vico"** in **Le Devenir Social** (October - December, 1896) p. 786 — He cites as his source **Capital,** French translation, p. 162, col. 1, note. See the American edition, (translated by Samuel Moore and Edward Aveling, edited by Frederick Engels (Chicago, 1915), vol. 1, p. 406, note 2.

[2] See chapter 1, note 55.

[3] See chapter 1, pp. 34 ff.

[4] With **"L'ancienne et la nouvelle métaphysique"** in L'Ere Nouvelle, March - June, 1894, see chapter 4, p. 109.

At the very beginning, Sorel shows that he has little use for Vico's own 'breakdown theory': "If Vico's ideas [his theory of eternal, cyclical recurrence] had a genuine scientific value, one would have to give up all hope of ever seeing the socialist transformation come true."[5] In other words, if Vico was correct, then Capitalism will not change into socialist collectivism, but revert to "barbarism."[6] Vico's conception of an Ideal History implied the belief in a fixed succession of political and social forms within a system forever reproducing itself, although not necessarily on the same cultural level. Why does the cycle never end? Vico replies that its renewal is, as its beginning was, a miracle, the work of divine intervention. The **Scienza Nuova** is, as its author averred, a "civilian theology" — the historic demonstration of Providence. It is the chronicle of the decrees by which mankind is being led out of the cave to build civilization. This providential power may be likened to what later thinkers called the Cunning of the Idea, inasmuch as it uses the very evil instincts and intents of man for good ends. Vico does not believe in chance. He accepts the notion of the unmoved Prime Mover, who establishes and upholds stability, but at the same time, he attributes to the Aristotelian God the platonic quality of active goodness. Men make their own history, but they make it according to the divine plan. It is this element of fixity which, in Sorel's view, removes Vico from modern science, "confining him to the enclosure of Finalism."[7]

However, if the idea of Ideal History "can be of no use whatever,"[8] Vico's "conception of the creation of history by man... still merits investigation."[9] But to fully appreciate the value of that thesis which impressed Karl Marx so strongly, "it is necessary first to rid the way of obstacles and to clear away all superficial parts of the system."[10] Not the cosmic institution of Providence but the sequel of human institutions is the miracle to study. To have done so, to have evolved, about the origin of society, "excellent theories which are still, today, very important," is Giambattista Vico's feat of genius.[11]

In reconstructing the past, as a linguist, as a jurist, or, where the evidence is lacking, by inspired guesses, Vico establishes "an extremely fruitful principle" of succession: "He tells us to look for the origin of our metaphysical constructions in the more or less empirical constructions of social existence, — just as we find the origin of our scientific theses in the observations of technicians in the arts.

---

[5]Sorel, "Etude sur Vico" [in the following called Vico], p. 785. - The translation of passages quoted from that essay is by Theodore V. Liss, University of Michigan.

[6]Which is however not the same barbarism as that posited by Marx as the only possible alternative to communism: a decadent, stagnant capitalism.

[7]Vico, p. 796.   [8]Ibid., p. 785.

[9]Ibid., p. 786.   [10]Ibid.

[11]Ibid.

Again and again, he insists on the pre-existence of vulgar wisdom; he says that 'the founders of nations precede by more than a thousand years the authors of books'".... [12] The engineer, Sorel who has already made the same discovery in his first essay on Karl Marx,[13] tries to enlist Vico in his service: "If the arts precede the sciences and serve as their preamble, it is necessary to recognize that this priority ought to be translated into metaphysics through a law positing technology as the foundation of all conceivable ideologies."[14] Sorel recognizes that "Vico does not draw this consequence," he left this task to Marx.[15] But Vico knew enough to know: that "science was not born yesterday; it has a history behind it....It is not an object which demands belief or personal adhesion; it concerns the life of a man as a **species** and the development of mankind; we would say today that **it is not individual, but social.**"[16]

The polemics which Vico directed against the Cartesians furnish the key for the understanding of his own position: Descartes' skepticism "seemed to Vico a veritable snare...." This pretension of reconstructing by personal effort what previous generations had had so much difficulty building, appeared to Vico to be "the means of destroying all science." Man, Vico countered, does not place himself in the presence of Nature alone. "The scholar works with material which ...belongs to what we call today the **artificial milieu;**"[17] it is the only reality which we can truly know: **vera facta.**

Vico, living in the eighteenth century, assumed that complete knowledge was confined to mathematics; about physics, an inferior science in his view because it could never become entirely the work of man, "Vico had so inexact an idea that he calls it an **imitation of Nature.**"[18] Today, Sorel adds, "we no longer see essential differences between geometry and rational mechanics, nor even between the latter and all mathematical physics....We construct something that is to our advantage, that is our creation, and is, consequently, both truth and fact, as Vico said...."[19] We do not imitate Nature: "we seek to produce movements which are never realized in the cosmic milieu."[20] In passing, Sorel pays homage to Claude Bernard who "has

---

[12]Ibid., p. 801.   [13]See note 4.

[14]Vico, p. 813.

[15]Ibid. — But "we cannot ask Vico to take exactly the same point of view as Marx; economic questions were unfamiliar to him. He lived a long time before the industrial revolution and in a milieu foreign to scientific discussions... " Ibid., p. 810.

[16]Ibid., p. 812. - Sorel's emphasis.

[17]Ibid., p. 811 - 812. Sorel develops this idea in **L'Ancienne et la nouvelle métaphysique** (see **D'Aristote à Marx,** Paris, 1935, p. 200-201) and in his last book, **De l'utilité du pragmatisme** (2. edition, Paris, 1928), pp. 335-351.

[18]Ibid., pp. 815, 816.

[19]Ibid., p. 816.   [20]Ibid.

expressed analogous ideas;"[21] he mentions him merely in order "to
establish how little modern thought has been able to add to Vico's
thesis; it has only clarified his work and made it more precise."[22]

Why, Sorel wonders, would a man as perspicuous as Vico make
"such an abuse of Providence in his expositions?"[23] Sorel refuses
to fall back on the extraneous argument that Vico was a devout Catholic
and had somehow to square his secularist findings with his super-
naturalist conviction. Did Vico retain Providence because his Ideal
History defied scientific proof? Sorel is not satisfied with this explanation: "Vico's delusion is founded on reasons of another kind,
which must have prevented him from seeing the truth and exercising
a rigorous criticism on these theories."[24] Historic judgments are
moral judgments, and Vico only followed tradition by first passing
moral judgments on historic actions and then trying to discover the
reason for the succession of those moral phenomena. Since the scientific method was of no avail in that pursuit, the investigator took
recourse to more or less supernatural explanations. It is "only in
our time," Sorel says, that a new beginning has been made to dispell
these "idealistic fantasies." We understand now that "moral judgments
have no place in a scientific study of institutions: the latter are phenomena; it is the historian's task to comprehend their functioning and
to follow their changes; but his evaluations will needs be entirely
subjective...." His standards cannot possibly be scientific. "Theses
on progress are epiphenomenal."[25]

Today, The Viconian predicament is ignored. Modern historians
have turned their backs on ethical theories: "the necessities of **tech-
nics** have produced the same consequence in the social sciences as in
physics;" the philosophy of history is as dead as the old philosophy of
nature.[26] We do not have to wait very long to be told by Sorel who
those prodiguous modern historians are: "Just as science has done
away with finalism in nature, historic materialism has made disappear
the great antinomy which perplexed Vico: we no longer have to ask
ourselves how order exists in spite of man's propensity for evil, since
order exists only in our imagination "[27] Vico anticipated both Hegel
and Marx-Engels insofar as he resolved the apparent contradiction,
on the human plane, between our aims and our accomplishments, but
Engels went beyond and against Vico by substituting for his Providence
"those forces which set in motion great masses, whole nations, and
within each nation, whole classes."[28]

[21]Ibid., p. 217.   [22]Ibid.
[23]Ibid., p. 796.   [24]Ibid.
[25]Ibid., p. 797.   [26]Ibid., p. 807-808.
[27]Ibid., p. 808.
[28]Ibid. Sorel cites from Engels' **Ludwig Feuerbach and the Outcome of
Classical German Philosophy,** French translation in **L'ere Nouvelle** (April,
1944), p. 16; English translation, International Publishers (New York, n. d.),
p. 58.

But having for once endorsed Engels whom he will soon declare responsible for most of what is "doctrinary" in the Marxist system,[29] Sorel turns around to censure historic materialism: "Ideal History has perished...but the ethical problem...remains unaltered and cannot be discarded like rubbish."[30] Vico's preoccupation with juridical questions becomes Sorel's: "Nor does it appear that it will be easy to give an answer to those people who ask what becomes of law in the materialistic conceptions of history."[31] The idea which will become a leitmotif of Sorel's work, is sounded at the very end of his Study: "Vico made a perfect distinction between the struggle for ... power and the struggle for rights." Sorel remarks in a footnote: "From the viewpoint of historic materialism it would not be quite exact to speak of the struggle for Right." And he concludes his essay with the words: "That distinction is of the greatest importance which we must keep in mind whenever we examine the history of contemporary conflicts in the light of the evolution of juridical ideas."[32]

In a brief summary of his Vico studies, published two years later,[33] Sorel explains himself further: To be sure, "the principle of Ideal History can no longer be understood in the sense Vico ascribed to it. The corsi and ricorsi are nonexistent." But the great Neapolitan philosopher was right in discovering in history a certain unity of substance as well as a consistency of psychological changes: from the instinctive to the intellectual, from the particular notion to the general idea...from sacred formula to enlightened law, from action to science...."

Vico, however, Sorel continues in the same abstract, was mistaken in assuming that these movements could occur only once in any given corso of the Ideal History, and that they could usher in a new period of rejuvenation only after Divine Providence has brought about a catastrophe terminating the cycle. "Modern psychology, better informed in these matters, teaches that these movements go on all the time, that they appear each moment in all phases of development." Therefore, Sorel concludes, "we no longer need the notion of providential catastrophes in order to understand the continuity of history: they are replaced by unconscious interventions which may assure the rejuvenation of mankind for an indefinite time." This process will either be continuous and regular, then we will speak of evolution; or else, due to

---

[29]See chapter 1, p. 28; chapter 4, p. 114.

[30]Vico, p. 808-809.

[31]Ibid., p. 809. Sorel notes: "Cf. the observations with which the curious brochure by M.B. Croce, "Sulla concezione materialistica della storia," ends. (Essay, very critical of Plekhanov; first read to the Academia Pontaniana in 1896; included in Croce's Materialismo storico ed economia Marxista (Bari, 1900).

[32]Vico, p.1046.

[33]"Was Man Von Vico Lernt" in Sozialistische Monatshefte, July - September, 1898, p. 270.

the accumulation of new factors, the change will be sudden: then we call it revolution. But even abrupt renewal will not be a complete break with the past, if it is the right kind of a revolution: if it is a "struggle for rights" and not merely the usurpation of power. The Marxists are correct, according to Sorel, when they speak of "history as a struggle between [social] groups." But Vico realized that these struggles are not all of the same kind; our contemporary Marxists frequently forget that. Only the struggle for rights fits the Marxian concept of class warfare: "To avoid misunderstandings, it might not be bad to speak of class struggles for Right, in order to show that the principle involved in the clash is the conflict of juridical viewpoints." Only in that case, Sorel feels, is it legitimate to say, with Marx, 'that classes have an existence of their own,' and that their struggle is political.

Vico's tabulation of sentiments which informed his Ideal History is of little interest today because sentiments are not simple things, not elements. Marx saw the complexity of the problem much better when he demanded that we investigate human needs, the means of production used to satisfy those needs, and, finally, the returns resulting from production, and that we do all this in order then to ask the natural question: What will the people involved in these relationships be like? We shall conclude that "history cannot be ruled by principles evolving in a logical fashion," rather we will say that "it depends on an infinite variety of circumstances: any determinism is merely one of possibilities; all actual social changes are the result of the sentiments originating with the groups active at any given time."[34]

This is still fairly orthodox Marx, only towards the end of the passage just cited, Sorel seems to veer away from the strict formula, when he traces social action to psychological sources; that sounds more like Gabriel Tarde, whose lectures at the College de France Sorel had attended.

But he can say, and he does say that Marx himself, if not his epigons, did recognize the importance of the voluntaristic element in history; he even allowed, like Vico, for the intervention of strong individuals. In that respect "historic materialism did not contribute anything new;" Marx's "decisive personalities are the inventors while the active groups are the commercial speculators; these affect the economy and the entire social structure, but only like blind forces, accomplishing ends which they never contemplated as their own."

Sorel is not quite ready yet to accuse Marx himself of "finalism," but the negative accent in this statement is unmistakable. And what follows, although on the surface of it, is directed against Vico, is no less a rejection of revolutionary Marxism: "The political transformations by which the foundations of Law are renewed from time to time, never appear in the form of actual catastrophes." They are the results

---

[34]Ibid., p. 271.

of long preparation, and **our power** to influence the change is not altogether insignificant. For "in a certain sense, the society of the future
will wish to do what we prepared it to wish." We shall do well, therefore, not to rely too much on the miracles attributed to the dictatorship
of the proletariat, "that providence of some too literally-minded Marxists. Here, too, Vico may serve us as a leader." He serves Sorel to
remind Marx's followers of the master's own dictum that "men make
their own history;" Vico's providence which knows of no miraculous
intervention of the Christian God is used to disparage the new faith
which leaves everything to the mystical creativeness of a victorious
proletariat. The voice of the later Sorel becomes almost audible at the
conclusion of the essay; the future has to be built here and now, in the
hearts of the proletarian class only, he expresses that thought in the
language which he still speaks, that of the revisionist Marxist;

"The alteration of law has always been the result of agreements,"
Vico believed. And now the Socialists, too, begin to have a change of
heart; they no longer despise small-scale reforms; they make an effort to enter the political life of contemporary society, so as to realize
programs reconcilable with the existence of capitalism. But in doing
so, the Socialists will be forced to reconsider a question long neglected
by them: the problem of juridical reform. "It just will no longer do
to teach that law is merely the codification of the will of the ruling
class," Sorel exclaims. He has committed the supreme sacrilege,
and, apologetically, he hastens to add that Vico too fell short of doing
justice to that problem. Still the Neapolitan philosopher must be credited with the discovery that "all revolutions are juridical transformations which have to be explained in terms of law." Sorel ends on an
urgent note: "This is a principle which the disciples of Marx may have
to accept very soon."[35]

That hope did not come true, at least not insofar as Karl Marx's
most spectacular disciple was concerned, the same Lenin to whom
the aged Sorel will pay his humble tribute. But his Viconian studies
make most admirably clear that even in his stage of intellectual pupa-
tion, Georges Sorel was nobody's disciple. He takes his position between Marx and Vico: neither of the two is altogether wrong or altogether right. Vico's cyclical catastrophes cannot be fitted into Sorel's
— then — gradualist scheme; nor will the proletarian revolution come
true unless the "real Karl Marx" had been restored by Sorel and ethi-
cally strengthened with the help of Vico. A decade later, when Sorel
shed his revisionist skin and turned syndicalist revolutionary, he could
again accept the catastrophic element in Vico without any stricture.
He even did so with a vengeance: eagerly looking forward to the cataclysm that would overtake the bourgeois world, rejoicing in its fearful prospects. No longer does he speak of the slow transmutation of
legality: the **ricorso** now has a destructive character that blots out

---

[35]Ibid., p. 272.

enemy law altogether. In the **Reflections** he will write of the Calvinists
that "they carried out a veritable catastrophic revolution in each conquered locality, changing everything from top to bottom."[36] And in a
somber aside, Sorel adds, in a footnote: "If Socialism should perish,
it will be for the reason...that it has been afraid of its own barbarism."[37] Words like these will continue to haunt the reputation of
Sorel, because he will find readers willing only to retain what appealed
to their own aggressive disposition; these readers could not be expected to supply each of Sorel's "tough" pronouncements with its
proper meaning as expounded by Sorel whenever he happened to be in
an explanatory mood. His "barbarism" was neither the "barbarism of
reflection" of Vico's decadent man, nor the stagnant capitalism of a
society which, insensitive to the counsel of Marx, refused to "shorten
the birthpangs of socialism." Rather, Sorel thinks of the dawn of a
new civilization when he is using the term usually associated with destruction. Writing in 1905, he returns once more to that "great genius"
who analysed the conditions under which the **ricorsi** occur;[38] explicitly
referring to his early study "which had been extremely useful for my
later work," Sorel likens modern Socialism to early Christianity; its
beginnings would be unintelligible unless we assume in the first enthusiastic followers of Christ, a state of mind "altogether analogous
to that of archaic civilizations;" socialism cannot claim to renew the
world unless it has acquired that same mentality. The barbarism of
the socialist **ricorso,** then, would be characterized by qualities typical
of primitive periods, "when all is instinct, creative and poetical in
society."[39] No wonder the socialist **systems of thought** crumble one
after the other, for "the theories are the fruit of bourgeois reflection"
— with the exception, Sorel hurriedly adds again, of "that which is essential in Marxism."[40] Revolutionary socialism is precisely the realization of "what there is truly true in Marxism": it is powerfully
original, superior to all formulas. In due time, this movement will
"undergo the evolution which is imposed on it by the laws of Vico."[41]
Sorel feels bold to say that this process, (during which the proletariat
will "emerge from the state of 'instinct'") has already started; he refers to the "rejuvenated and deepened Marxism as it is upheld in
France by Lagardelle and Berth (he modestly omits his own contribution) and in Italy by the 'brilliant' Arturo Labriola."[42]

---

[36]**Réflexions sur la violence**, 10. edition (Paris, 1946), p. 23.
[37]**Ibid.**, note 1.
[38]**L'Avenir socialiste des syndicats**, Preface of 1905, in **Matériaux d'une
théorie du prolétariat**, 3. edition (Paris, 1929), p. 66.
[39]**Ibid.**
[40]**Ibid.**, p. 66-67.
[41]**Ibid.**, p. 67.
[42]**Ibid.**, p. 67-68 — For Sorel's changing views concerning Arturo Labriola,
see chapter 1, p. 30-31.

This post-instinctive revolutionary creed which Sorel would, however, not call intellectual, absorbs Viconian elements rejected ten
years earlier: the theory of cycles, the concept of a radically new beginning, the violent break with the past. He retains what he had considered to be Vico's great discovery: the notion of juridical continuity — the future legal structure is to arise in the moral consciousness
of, and in the institutions created by the proletariat prior to the breakdown of bourgeois civilization. This would be a legitimate interpretation, and it is borne out by Sorel's mature work, whenever he
speaks of the values of "our Western civilization," values to be preserved and even strengthened by the proletariat as the heir of the "old
heroisms." The principle of discontinuity thus would apply only to
form, with the unity of content preserved: the ruin of the ancient world
need not be duplicated.

There are no indications in Sorel's writings that he was ever conscious of a change of mind concerning Vico. This powerful intellect,
so merciless in exposing the motive forces in others, seldom paused
to reflect upon its own tergiversations, and if it did take notice at all,
it felt pleasure rather than embarrassment. There were many rooms
in the mansion of his mind, and his wish to explore them all naturally
interfered with his duty as housekeeper: what looks like untidiness
was merely another aspect of his unflagging curiosity. In assuming
the right to clean up after him we must be mindful of the fact that he
preceded us on the exploratory path and that he left us to contemplate,
in his own contradictions, the contradictory evidence he was unable
and unwilling to marshall into artificial unity.

The Church and the State

The great event which more than any other affected Sorel's intellectual development, was recorded by him, in retrospect, in a chilly
summary which hardly reflects what an ardent Dreyfusard he had
been at the height of the excitement.[43] At the inception of the affair,
he confesses[44] that he does not know what to make of the case; all he
can see is that the government shows great reluctance to get the evidence, and as to the generals, he is already convinced that they are
responsible for what looks like a mistrial of justice, if they are not actually guilty of foul play. But "one has to know the special mores of
the French army in order not to be surprised by it all." Sorel ends his
letter which is full of allusions to historic cases of injustice (he compares Dreyfus with Voltaire's Calas) on a note of resignation: "it is a
shame; but what can we do?"

---

[43]La révolution dreyfusienne (Paris, 1909), 64 p.

[44]Letter to Hubert Lagardelle, August 10, 1898, in L'homme Réel, February, 1934, p. 188-191.

He will later draw a line between the judicial aspect of the Dreyfus
case and its political consequences, which frightened him. For the
time being, as the popular excitement grows, Sorel tries to keep out of
it. However, it is not escape he is after, but an understanding of the
great historic struggle between church and state. He turns his back
upon the present as he takes up once more his old studies of the Roman
world; but even when he talks about society in the fifth century A. D.,
he has in mind the latest contest between the two institutions which he
called "the Dreyfus revolution."

The very list of his publications during the brief period from 1899
to 1903 — the same period in which he wrote extensively about problems of Marxism and trade-unionism — is evidence of Sorel's vivid interest in the status of the Church in modern society.[45] In the final
analysis he wants to answer the great question which will be, a generation later, Arnold Toynbee's main concern: What is the role of religion in an industrial civilization; has it a future, or is it bound up with
a past irrevocably dead? And Sorel, who has been such a harsh critic
of the church that "destroyed the polis,"[46] answers now: "I, for my
part, do believe, that Christianity will not perish; the mystic faculty is
something very real in man, and experience shows us that its intensity
does not diminish with the ages; it remains as powerful today as ever;
the scientific development did not weaken it."[47] Sorel believes with
Taine[48] that, in the first century of our era, man's mystical faculty,
determined by complex intellectual causes, discovered what Christianity called The Kingdom of God, thereby introducing a new element
(good or bad, according to our lights) which became an integral part
of occidental civilization: "The human spirit always creates and adds
to its domain; I do not think...that it could ever lose what it has once
acquired." Why, then, should Christianity be an exception to the rule?
Had it succeeded, by way of evolution, to another religion, then we
might infer, that it will, in turn, make room for a new creed. However,

---

[45]"Il vangelo, la Chiesa e il socialismo" in Rivista critica del Socialismo,
April, May, 1899 (discussed in chapter 2, p.   ); "L'église et l'état" in La
Revue Socialiste, August - October, 1901, abbreviated as "De l'église et de
l'état" in Cahiers de la Quinzaine (Troisième cahier de la troisième série),
October, 1901; "La crise de la pensée catholique" in Revue de Métaphysique
et de Morale, September, 1902, and the three essays, "A propos de l'anti-
cléricalisme", "Léon XIII", and "Nouveaux réquisitoires de M. Brunetière in
Etudes Socialistes, Paris, 1903.

[46]See chapter 2, p. 64.

[47]"L'église et l'etat" (September, 1901, see above, note 45), p. 337.

[48] Les origines de la France contemporaine, Le régime moderne, Vol.
II, p. 116. (Sorel's note, no edition given; Vol. III, p. 144 of the 26. edition,
Paris, 1912).

that was not the case: Christianity "has been a **discovery**, a true creation. . . . Why should it perish? I cannot see it."[49]

Sorel's passionate refrain, far from being a **credo quia absurdum,** sums up a careful argument. It is, as he proclaims at the outset, a Marxist argument: the moral philosophy of the early Church is to be understood as a reflection of the attitude which the Church fathers had toward the institution of property; that attitude in turn will mirror, by way of critical negation, but still mirror the social mores of the Roman upper classes. For Sorel does not believe in the "mirage of a Church composed of poor working people, triumphing over a corrupt and brutal oligarchy by means of its virtue and gentleness"; there is, he holds, good evidence to show that the powerful Patrician families of Rome took the Christians under their protection as early as in the last third of the first century.[50] It is the contact with this oligarchy and its mode of acquisition, characteristic of the time of decadence and despotism, which decisively influenced the formulation of Christian social theory. The sources of enrichment are commercial speculation and fraudulent abuse of public power, and while these methods are typical of pagan and Christian society alike, the church fathers are hostile to commerce as the old philosophers had been before them. But fraud and favoritism are both dominated by the element of chance; it is by chance alone that wealth may still be gained, only to be lost in the same, haphazard way to a State whose normal fiscal practice is confiscation.[51] The disjunction of production and consumption, of work and reward, was described by the ecclesiastics, but, — and this is the point Sorel wants to make — the parasitical character of late Roman economics nevertheless permeated the very core of Christian social ethics. Sorel also cautions us against taking the precept of evangelical poverty too seriously: "it is addressed to a very limited category of believers only, namely, to . . . those who are to form the church hierarchy."[52] They form the privileged group exempted from work, who may for their subsistence depend on the liberality of the masses: "the ecclesiastical economy is founded on alms rather than on poverty." Living on charity does not necessarily mean frugality, and, indeed, "being in contact with the wealthy classes, the church too was wealthy." The vigorous protests of St. Jerome and St. John Chrysostomus were of no avail; the Church accommodated itself to the living conditions of its benefactors, and the clergy would "preserve, through the centuries to come, the liking for the capricious bounties bequeathed to

---

[49]"L'église et l'état," p. 337. Sorel's emphasis. In his **Système historique de Renan,** (Paris, 1906), Sorel repeats: "One cannot enough stress the novel character of Christianity. It was not a reform, nor an improvement upon Judaism; neither was it a synthesis of Jewish monotheism and Greek polytheism; the Christian era was a truly new beginning." (p. 459-460.)

[50]"L'église et l'état" (August, 1901), p. 131.

[51]Ibid., p. 133.   [52]Ibid., p. 134-135.

them by the Roman oligarchy." The element of arbitrariness thus becomes for Sorel the key to an understanding of the evolving economic
system of the church. It lacks all rationality: "The existence of the
ecclesiastic body depends entirely on chance."[53]

By relating the bounty of the rich to its heavenly source, the
Church not only justifies its own acceptance of donations, — it also en-
nobles the gift of chance for the donors themselves: the arbitrary becomes "the manifestation of the divine power."[54] Thus the Christian
economy is placed outside science: its basis being "supernatural," one
might speak of a "magic" conception of civil society, were it not for
the fact that "magic" is usually employed in an unfriendly sense. Sorel
is, therefore, satisfied to call the factor determining Christian political philosophy, "a mystical rapport."[55] The notion of existence by the
grace of God, without productive labor, originally confined to the
Church exclusively, was presently projected, by the Church, into a
general theory of society.

A "mystical economy," however, has no use for the classic tradition of law; "How could its logical rigidity be made to apply to phenomena which completely defy the law of causality?"[56] Roman civil law
does not know people, but only "mechanical figures determined by the
play of certain economic forms: the litigants are abstract beings...."
Whereas the Church has to do with concrete people, because its job is
"the reconciliation of souls." We must not be taken in, Sorel warns us,
by "the appearances of ... the **corpus juris canonici;**" it was not really
a system of jurisprudence in the classical and modern meaning of
the word. As soon as a genuine legal renaissance becomes possible,
the power of the Church is threatened. What a "strange drama," Sorel
exclaims, "that destruction of the Christian culture which seemed
to have destroyed the ancient world for good; even today, the men of
the Church cannot recall the **reception of Roman law** without outbursts
of rage...."[57] How could the Christian doctors possibly comprehend
the old Roman formula, 'to each his own,' when for them "everything
is mingled together," so that distribution comes to depend on good will
alone, on the imitation of Christ, on inspiration rather than on legal
guidance...."[58]

With imperturable patience Sorel builds up a crushing load of
historic evidence, until at last he is prepared to apply his thesis to
the situation of the day: The Church really never considered, nor
could it have considered, itself as a proprietor. All it ever wanted
was the power "to administer and **defend** the sources of the revenues
it needed to meet its obligations."[59] Which means, Sorel continues
tersely, that the State, once it takes over some of the traditional social

---

[53]Ibid., p. 135.   [54]Ibid.
[55]Ibid., p. 136.   [56]Ibid., p. 137.
[57]Ibid., p. 138.   [58]Ibid., p. 139.
[59]Ibid., pp. 143, 144.

tasks of the clergy, has a just claim to the Church holdings. If that case occurs, the sanctity of private property cannot well be invoked, since the Church had never held its property in private ownership.[60] Thus the French government of Waldeck-Rousseau which was using confiscatory laws to break the grip of certain religious associations on the school system, finds for once an apologist in Georges Sorel who otherwise, considering himself a Socialist, views the new bourgeois regime of the "counter-church" with utmost diffidence if not with frank hostility.[61]

The conflict between the two powers is, in the last sense, a clash between two radically opposed ideas about property. The new notion of private, exclusive and isolated property "engendered the modern conceptions of the free individual opposed to the State."[62] The parliamentary regime is nothing but the logical consequence of the capitalist principle of private enterprise; it can flourish only in countries where "the modern industrial spirit is strongly developed and where the industrial classes play a preponderant role in parliament." One aspect of that regime is that "everything is provisional": with power changing hands incessantly, the law becomes pliable, a handy tool in the hands of whoever happens to have gotten hold of the public power. This resulted in "sharply reducing the respect for political authority"; again, Sorel is impressed by the analogy between political and industrial life: exactly as all technical procedures are brought up to date continuously, so the revision of legal technique is the modern "order of the day."[63]

Such a regime is incomprehensible to the Church to which it must seem like "the negation of all reason."[64] All that "feverish activity," that "rage of destruction," that trust in the unknown to be explored by chance discoveries, all that "Promethean audacity" cannot be but repulsive to Catholic writers who usually blame the political and economic anarchy of our times on the sixteenth century Protestant revolt, whereas to Sorel "the reverse seems to be the truth; Protestantism gained its freedom [from Rome] when it penetrated those classes which practised industrial liberty," the same classes which transformed the representative system of the medieval constitutions into modern parliamentarism.[65]

The Church, on the other hand, never freed itself from the social suppositions of the Diocletian Servile State, which recognized social duties only, tying every citizen to his place and work, reducing him to

[60]Ibid., p. 144.

[61]Ibid., p. 146. "Counter-church": see below, p. 83.

[62]Ibid., p. 147.   [63]Ibid., p. 148.

[64]Ibid.

[65]Ibid., p. 148-149. — It would be interesting to compare Sorel's thesis with that developed by Max Weber in **The Protestant Ethic and the Spirit of Capitalism** (New York, 1930).

a mere object of administrative considerations. This system in which
justice in the proper meaning of the word was reduced to a secondary
role, was adopted by the Church.[66] The modern notion of a separation
between administrative and legal relationships remain alien to the ecclesiastical mind: the Church, like the Caesarian state, does not understand how a subject could presume to contest authority, the representative of the common weal.[67] "Church law is organized in such a
way as to permit authority to do more or less what it deems to be
convenient...."[68] The spiritual power considers itself above rules;
"the Church replaces the rule of law by the rule of decrees."[69] The
reception of Roman law in the modern world helped to obviate somewhat the arbitrary power, technically unlimited, of parliament. But
this was not enough to endow authoritarian rule with the dignity of
law, and so the critical spirit accustomed itself to looking at the commands of the state as mere reflections of the real, Natural Law, which
was adopted by the Church, since it was based, like science, on the
idea of man's sharing to a limited extent, in Divine reason.[70] Now
the jurist proper does not ask whether a legal rule agrees with the
Law of Nature; he is content if he can establish its existence and show
how it is related to the ensemble of rules. Only in countries like ancient Greece "where the constitutions resembled natural arrangements
so little" would philosophers start their inquiries by asking who had
the right to make the law: "The problem of sovereignty which was to
claim so much attention, could originate only in a country in which
revolutions were permanent."[71] The philosopher, then, will always
reserve the right to question the validity of laws and to attempt modi-
fications; he will not recognize any authority superior to man's reason.
The Church attempted a synthesis between the peripatetic theory of
sovereignty and the Roman concept of State authority: "it imagined
that Divine grace enabled certain human beings to discern the truth."[72]
The Church can do no wrong. Today, Sorel believes, all intelligent
persons are agreed on the question of sovereignty: they have dismissed it from their minds. "The absolute is **banished** from politics,
and everybody holds that the **essence of democracy is liberty.**" Today,
"sovereignty is a purely ecclesiastic notion," and its sporadic re-
emergence in the world is due to the fact that "ideas of Catholic origin
still have a very strong appeal."[73]

   Hippolyte Taine explained the clash between the two societies,
spiritual and secular, as a conflict between faith and science rather
than that of socio-economic systems.[74] Sorel disagrees: "far from

---

[66]Sorel, op. cit., p. 150.   [67]Ibid., p. 151-152.
[68]Ibid., p. 153.   [69]Ibid., p. 154.
[70]Ibid. (September, 1901), pp. 326, 327.
[71]Ibid., p. 327.   [72]Ibid., p. 328.
[73]Ibid., p. 329. - Sorel's emphasis.
[74]Ibid., p. 330. - Taine, op. cit.(26. edition), p. 176.

growing in intensity, that conflict seems much less acute in our time than it has been in the past." Sorel suggests that even in the past the issue had not really been of a religious nature but a battle between two different types of science. Besides, the new, Galileian-Newtonian approach could have disturbed only the small world of the actual scientists; but "the great religious phenomenon of modern times is the mass deflection of the common people from the Church."[75] The Third Republic attacked the Church because the latter was too closely aligned with monarchic tendencies. The reasons for the break were historical, not ideological: "When the republican government decided to establish a system of lay education," it was because of the conviction of leading politicians "that the Republic could be made to last only if the new generations could be accustomed to identify Republic, Fatherland and France with each other."[76] To be sure, while the secularization of the schools was in process, a great deal of anti-religious propaganda was in evidence, but the purpose of that agitation was not to dechristianize the country. With the school reform completed, the excitement died down, so fast that some "rather naive" observers could not help wondering "how the country could suddenly have become so indifferent to philosophic and religious questions." But in truth "the country did not turn, it never had been anything but indifferent." It took the Dreyfus case to revive anticlerical polemics which had already passed into the limbo of the unintelligible and ridiculous.[77]

The political loss of the Church, Sorel believes, is its religious gain. The defenders of Catholicism try to tell us that the Church ought to enjoy, in a democratic country, a maximum of liberty because theology is really another type of that philosophic speculation so dear to the apostles of free thought.[78] But no, Sorel replies, the Church besides being a school, is also a body of priests dispensing sacraments under conditions established by them. The great defection of Catholics took place mainly among the rural population where the Christian faith had always been very superficial: The peasant looks upon Church rites as mere magic incantations for which he pays. If he leaves the Church nowadays, he does so, not because he has become converted by the free thinkers of the city, but because he is no longer as afraid of his curé as he has been before. The Church lost its purely magic power when it was shorn of its public right "to police the religious sentiment."[79] Where this police power is still recognized on a voluntary basis, the influence of the Church will remain strong. Nor can the Church surrender its claim to determine both faith and morals: the moment it abondons its exclusive existence and its intolerance, the Church is bound to dissolve into innumerable sects, and there is no reason to assume that the church will modify its strictly monarchic constitution in the future.[80]

---

[75]Sorel, op. cit., p. 331.   [76]Ibid., p. 332.
[77]Ibid., p. 333.   [78]Ibid., p. 334-335.
[79]Ibid., p. 335.   [80]Ibid., p. 336.

Some people cannot understand why the Vatican has in the past accepted the most vigorous measures against the French Church with comparative docility, but the explanation is simple: Rome does not worry too much about the fate of its French monks as long as the French Republic continues to remain the faithful "oldest daughter of the Church" outside of France, especially in the Near East, closing Catholic schools at home while subsidizing them abroad.[81] That would not make sense if the State were really to be understood as one person, facing another person called the Church. The difficulty disappears as soon as we analyze "the multiple components of the State," — a task which Sorel takes upon himself, with results highly suggestive of some recent theories about the ruling class in a democracy, theories not usually associated with the name of Georges Sorel:

The ancient philosophers "reduced the State to an infinitely simple being which, according to their definitions, should be the expression of the general will," their state was endowed with qualities borrowed from individual psychology. There was a core of truth in these speculations: "certain similarities do exist between the people of one and the same nation, so that the laws might be understood, to some extent, as the manifestations of a community of juridical thought." Actually, the law is not made by that community, nor even by the intellectual servants of the mass instinct who band together into groups in Parliament, — it is "a very small number of persons with a flair for politics" who make the real decisions: people "capable of drawing up the formulas to which the majority will give its consent, often without understanding the full meaning."[82]

It is this complicated process which the philosophers reduce to a simple manifestation of a social thought process, whereas Sorel believes that "it would be much more exact to say that national ideas are determined by laws imposed on the nation; the law being the core around which the popular instincts crystallize, instincts which without that support would remain in flux and indeterminate." Sorel does not deny that the laws, in the last instance, depend on the people, but that influence works only in a highly indirect fashion while the laws themselves "directly generate the popular ideas."[83]

The great complexity of the parliamentary system, expressly so divised as to erect obstacles to party whim, would not in itself sufficiently assure a certain continuity, were it not supplemented by other institutions, such as the judicial branch. In brief, the supposed unity of the state in domestic affairs is nothing but the illusion of

---

[81]Ibid., p. 339.

[82]Ibid. — Sorel is usually linked to the "Elitists" — Mosca, Pareto and Michels — because he shares with them the concepts of the myth and the elite; he might be given credit for the theories exclusively assigned to them, such as "the iron law of oligarchy" (Michels). Cf. Supplement 2.

[83]Ibid., p. 340.

people remote from government activities. On the other hand, in the field of external action the unity of the State is real because foreign policy making is of a different order. It is determined by the institutions of war: the traditions of the army and diplomacy. Domestic law evolves from popular instinct to become a juridic doctrine: what takes place is "a complete process of intellectualization."[84] The military order, however, represents instinct at its strongest. The administrative branch, Sorel remarks in an aside without elaborating, is placed halfway between the legislative and the military institutions; it operates "generally in opposition to the jurists."[85]

As the parliamentary regime becomes more and more complex, a rather rigid division develops between internal and external policy. The Church, in allying itself closely to the military and diplomatic castes, is not so much seeking protection from its domestic enemies than it is "trying to steer foreign policy in a direction useful to the Catholic interest." For thirty years, Sorel says, this alliance between the Military and the Church could operate in full liberty and generate a nationalistic fever-heat; "this propaganda remained completely unmolested; indeed, it profited from the patriotic indoctrination practiced by the public schools."[86]

Up to this point, the views developed by Sorel have been, with rare exceptions, those of the historian studying the Church in its relation to the State; he has, in the main, refrained from taking sides. He now becomes Sorel, the critic, the contemporary of a furious struggle. But deeply involved as he is emotionally, Sorel will not become a partisan of either side; he attacks both, fighting a two-front battle as a one-man troisième force: on the one hand, he censures the Church for having gone on record against the re-trial of Dreyfus, thus destroying with one stroke the diplomatic work of many years. By sacrificing its true interest to sentiments of "personal vendetta,"[87] the French clergy stirred up a hornet's nest: it brought upon itself the "revanche" of the radicals who, seeing the Republic threatened by a formidable coalition of the spiritual and military camps, rallied to the counter-attack.[88] The Church did not see it that way: it believed itself assaulted "by a sect which, from time to time, succeeds either by force or by a ruse, in taking possession of the state power."[89] Picturing the enemy after its own image, the Church "believes it has to fight a counter-church" with proper dogmas, a regular hierarchy and, perhaps, even a pope of its own.[90] Nor is the Church altogether wrong in

---

[84]Ibid., p. 341.
[85]Ibid. note. For Sorel's views on bureaucracy, see below, p. 89.
[86]Ibid., p. 342.
[87]Sorel, "De l'église et de l'état" (see note 45), p. 55.
[88]Ibid., p. 57-58.
[89]Ibid., p. 59. Sorel's emphasis.
[90]Ibid.

that assumption; there exists, in France, a "politico-scholastic party" of intellectuals, many of them university professors who, inspired by the "narrow ideas of the eighteenth century, attempt to dominate the minds." What is usually referred to as the struggle between Church and State, is in reality a conflict between church and counter-church.[91]

Sorel has no brief for either caste; the "professors and journalists" show exactly the same spirit as the Church while they combat; they have "all the ambitions of the old St. Simonists who tried to organize everything according to a hierarchic fashion."[92] Whichever faction wins, democracy will be the loser; in any case "the people would find pitiless masters."[93] Knowing what Sorel will later say about democracy, we are somewhat surprised to hear that it represents "liberty of thought," worth being protected from the masters; and our surprise becomes amazement as we read that this defense is the "highest mission of the State."[94] Has Georges Sorel completely forgotten his master, Karl Marx, and his dictum about the state as "the executive committee of the bourgeoisie?" Not quite. He even cites him, or, at any rate, the Marx who celebrated the Paris Commune of 1871 as the harbinger of genuine proletarian democracy. Just as Lenin will do, in his work on **The State and Revolution,**[95] Sorel sees the solution in a genuinely "federalist organization" of the state, which, by a system of "purely financial assistance" to education would break the intellectual influence of the old classes.[96]

The sincere socialist, then, will be a social-democrat, and as such he will, for the time being, take his place in the ranks of the active fighters against clericalism and militarism.[97] Especially the latter, with its strong appeal to the partiotic instinct of the people, is too formidable a foe for the Socialist parties to take on without strong allies: the best insurance against the stigma of antipatriotism is a Popular Front, or as Sorel calls it, "an amalgam of parties."[98] Unlike some intransigent dogmatics of the class struggle, Sorel is not at all concerned about the outcome: the rallying-cry of anticlericalism is good enough to unite the masses, regardless of class, in their "daily struggle against [the principle of] domination, for the priest is in daily contact with the citizen, whereas the military oligarchy exerts but an intermittent tyranny."[99]

Sorel is confident that, in the long run, his own cause stands to gain most from the coalition, in particular where that cause is still weak: "Nothing is as important for the propagation of Socialism in the countryside as the anticlerical action." The Proudhonian Sorel,

[91] Ibid., p. 62.   [92] Ibid., p. 64.
[93] Ibid., p. 64-65.   [94] Ibid., p. 65.
[95] On Lenin and Sorel, see chapter 10.
[96] Sorel, op. cit., p. 66.
[97] Ibid., p. 69-70.   [98] Ibid., p. 71.
[99] Ibid., p. 72.

unlike the town-bound Marxists, never turns his back upon the peasant. The power of reaction, he believes, must be struck in its rural strongholds held by the curé.[100]

Modernism and Antisemitism

Sorel was a hard man to please. He has called the anti-Dreyfus policy of the Church "its greatest blunder" since 1848,[101] but he censures, in a subsequent publication,[102] with equal acerbity all clerical attempts to appease the lay state. In still another study,[103] he restates once more his belief in the common front of anticlerical action, while at the same time frowning upon certain Socialist leaders like Emil Vandervelde who try to put water into their Marxist wine in order to please everybody. He mocks a "rich Israelite" who contributed heavily to the defense of Dreyfus; the cause of justice he sees turned into a Jewish plot. But hatred of the Jews, the bond that holds the Church party together in its struggle, he finds as distasteful as the "diamonds of M. Sachs."[104]

Writing on the occasion of the death of Pope Leo XIII, Sorel has lost much of his faith in the recuperative forces of Catholicism; what he had put in the affirmative two years earlier, he now puts in form of a question: "The great problem of the present is whether the Catholic world is able to engender mystical forces comparable to those it has produced in the past...."[105] It is because Sorel is no longer so sure of it that he turns against liberal Catholicism: the modernistic tendency within the Church is in his view a sign of its weakening. When the cause of the Franch monarchists became quite hopeless in the early years of the Third Republic, the Pope himself encouraged a rapprochement between Catholics and moderate Republicans.[106] But this attempt to match democracy (of anticlerical persuasion) by democracy (pro-catholic) only proves to Sorel once more the "disappearance of the old, heroic spirit (warlike or revolutionary)", that generally marks the new era after 1870. The Union Générale was, in reality, a device "to make the parasitism [of certain Jewish financiers] a monopoly of the great Catholic families."[107] Thus, on the upper level, racialism was the pretext for easy economic plunder; to encourage it was to promote the moral collapse of the bourgeoisie, to bring its corruption to a head. The average Socialist would deem such a result of ecclesiastic policy a most praiseworthy thing, as it would seem to hasten the transformation of the exploiting producers into mere proprietors, to be

---

100Ibid.   101Ibid., p. 55.
102Léon XIII. — See note 47.
103"A propos d'anticléricalisme" (see note 47), p. 242.
104Ibid., p. 151.   105"Léon XIII," p. 378.
106Ibid., p. 357-358.   107Ibid., p. 353.

expropriated without any adverse social consequences. Not so Sorel. Anticipating his peculiarly ambivalent notion of proletarian violence as a means to harden the resistance of the ruling class, he shows a strong concern for the integrity of both opponents: Church and Bourgeoisie. But this is only part of his indictment. The mortal sin of which he accuses the Vatican consists in that it catered to the worst of mob instincts.

In each great crisis of its history, the Church could rely on religious organizations which met the needs of the situation: Franciscans and Dominicans in the thirteenth century, the Jesuits in the sixteenth.[108] But today, "where would we find a genuine manifestation of the Catholic spirit?" Sorel asks. And he replies: "In antisemitism."[109] By giving antisemitism "its official protection," the Church indeed pursued "in a certain sense, a democratic policy." For antisemitism is, according to Sorel, a genuinely democratic phenomenon:"I believe political science made a very great step forward the day antisemitism was found to be one of the authentic forms of democracy." It is its ugly form: "a reactionary democracy fighting a socialist democracy."[110] This statement, made thirty years before Hitler demonstrated its truth, will even today sound odious to all those who failed to learn the lesson of the last two decades. Sorel, uniquely sensitive to social undercurrents, knew long before Fascism was born officially, that it is the perverted but direct descendent of contemporary, democratic mass society. He also knew that its most virulent manifestation "is no passing accident;" and, as a Socialist, he was convinced that it could be destroyed only "by economic reforms sufficiently attractive to the classes which furnish the main contingent of antisemitism."[111]

Citing Renan's "terrible invectives" against the modern Jew,[112] Sorel develops the distinction — which was to become a stock-in-trade of National Socialist propaganda — between industrialists (good people) and mere capitalists (drones). "There is nothing specifically Jewish" about Renen's rich hedonist, "that aristocrat who tries to reenact the follies of the great freedmen of imperial Rome."[113] Sorel does not frequent the cosmopolitan salons but his great stand-by, Paul de Rousiers[114] has described the type: "America continuously disgorges existences like that, people in search of a titled son-in-law" who will unlock the doors of the great houses for them. They are "the false Americans;" the true American is a builder and fighter. Parasitism, then, "has nothing to do with race," Sorel decides, "the problem is of

---

[108]Ibid., p. 378.   [109]Ibid., p. 379.

[110]Ibid., p. 363.

[111]"De l'église et de l'état," p. 54.

[112]"Nouveaux réquisitoires de M. Brunetière" (see note 47), p. 132. Sorel quotes from the 15. chapter of the 9. book of Renan's History of the People of Israel.

[113]Sorel, op. cit., p. 132.

[114]P. de Rousiers, La vie américaine, pp. 33 and 325.

an economic nature"[115] He holds the Jews, with many others, do not seem to feel at ease in the role of captains of industry, and "the weakness of Germany" may be due to the fact that "the great enterprises are, in that country, more completely in Jewish hands than elsewhere."[116] Again, this remark curiously anticipates the Nazi line. But with a difference: when Hitler ranted against Capitalists, he really voiced his hatred of the Jews; whereas Sorel's argument —which will become increasingly monotonous — is not with the Jews as such but with the middlemen and interlopers of a capitalist culture that has lost its stamina.

As for the Church, the Georges Sorel of 1903 doubts that a genuine revival is at all possible in his time, a period essentially "pacific and anti-revolutionary." This much he knows: If the Church is "to regain its lost heroism, it will not be through antisemitism."[117]

Once more Sorel returns to the general subject of Catholicism and Modernity. It seems that he is not yet satisfied with the preceding studies, although he does not say so openly. He now criticizes the view, held by two Catholic apologists, that "the old conflicts between science and faith have disappeared, or have become, at least, strongly attenuated," — a view which Sorel himself had expressed only a year ago.[118] He still accepts it as a more or less correst statement of fact, but rejects the conclusion: Far from having helped the Church, "the very process which produced that attenuation of conflicts, engendered the crisis" in which the Catholic Church finds itself.[119] Protestantism is in an even worse predicament, for it "cannot subsist once its only holy writ, the Bible, is treated as a profane text." The Catholic dogma is less endangered by liberal exegesis, protected as it is with the weapon of Papal infallibility.[120] Nor do the claims of modern science in themselves present a direct challenge to supermundane truth. "All modern mechanics is founded on the postulate that science need not know the nature of things."[121] Nor do the new scientific tendencies any longer lead to an absolute determinism, "one can understand how so many geometricians and physicists manage to reconcile their faith with their science...."[122] Sorel makes an observation, correct for his time but no longer true today: "The physical and natural sciences developed without concerning themselves with the problem of their own relation to philosophy. The difficulty had been great as long as one had tried to establish a contact between science and theology; the question of miracles posed itself, which could not be avoided."[123] But as

[115]Sorel, op. cit., p. 132-133.

[116]Ibid., p. 133.   [117]Léon XIII, p. 379.

[118]"La crise de la pensée catholique" (see note 47), p. 523. Cf. Sorel's own earlier statement cited on p. 80-81.

[119]Ibid.   [120]Ibid., p. 531-532.

[121]Ibid., p. 532.   [122]Ibid., p. 535.

[123]Ibid., p. 548.

the old rationalistic faith lost ground, as diffidence became the dominant scientific attitude, content with theoretical approximations and
important practical results, supernatural intervention could be regarded as a "particular relaxation of natural laws;" the "free" inter-
stices between territories conquered and explored seemed well fit to
accommodate a miracle, and to account for the factor X. Scientific
skepticism made for a religious neo-mysticism.[124]

However, "such a situation is altogether contrary to the Church
tradition;"[125] the belief in the absolute authenticity of revelation cannot be reconciled with scientific modernism. The quantitative indeterminacy of scientific doubt is unacceptable to the orthodox Catholic interpretation of a miracle as "qualitatively different from natural
events."[126] What causes "the grave crisis in Catholic conscience,"[127]
is thus not the over-assertive character of modern science, but, on the
contrary, the very lack of it. The great modification of scientific
claims should, on the surface of it, strengthen the position of religious orthodoxy; instead, the retreat posed a threat worse than the
great attack that had preceded it. The Church could suffer the naturalist to descry the scientific value of the sacred books and to replace
them by their own profane theology; even if that was rank heresy, it
still betrayed a faith in absolutes, expressed, as it were, in another
language which could be translated into, and assimilated to the ecclesiastic needs. At worst, that scientific certitude could be rejected, if
it could not be corrected. In other words, faith could live in the same
world with a counter-faith; it could survive the scientific doubt of God.
But it could not permit the scientific doubt of science. The new skepticism was intolerable because the sense of limitation from which it
sprang contained the germs of an irrationalism, utterly irreconcilable
with the rational Thomist tradition. The question in Sorel's mind was:
how would the Church fill the great void?

The Church did the obvious: "Ever since the middle of the 19th
century, the miracle has assumed an importance in Catholicism, such
as it rarely had enjoyed before." Sorel considers this development
both logical and promising: "From now on, Christian philosophy will
have to regard the mystical as the principal basis of its speculation."
In such a manner, Sorel holds, the present crisis could find its solution: "all doubt would disappear, and the religious life would serve to
explain the world; thus theology would reassert its role, which is, with
regard to science, the relation of a sovereign to his vassal."[128]

Will that come true? Sorel is vague about the prospect. He
throws out a few hints: "Ancient philosophy started from the most
general, from unity, from that which was as little human as possible;
the new philosophy would have to start from what is most deeply an-

---

[124]Ibid., p. 540.   [125]Ibid., p. 548.
[126]Ibid., p. 540.   [127]Ibid., p. 548.
[128]Ibid., p. 550.

chored in sentiment, from the individual, from those elements of man
that are not yet socialized."[129] A demand that, coming from Sorel,
will strike some readers as a great surprise. If we understood correctly, the new philosophy, to be created by the Church, would be a
Neo-Humanism, incorporating perhaps, we surmise, the most important elements of Bergson and Bergsonianism. Not without reason did
some critics find a strong affinity between that French philosopher and
the creed of the Church which he is said to have embraced before his
death in Nazi-occupied Paris.

Sorel has no doubts that it would be possible to proceed from this
new humanism to a study of animate nature; but he does not underrate
the difficulties of the next step: the reconstruction of the physical universe. Nor does he overrate the willingness of the Church to travel
the indicated road; he finds its lack of philosophic initiative "very curious," and his guess is that the impulse to a new Christian philosophy
is most likely to come from the outside, from the lay world.... [130]

Bureaucracy and Democracy

When Sorel sketched this Neo-Thomist program, Jacques Maritain
was still very much of a Leftist, and we may doubt he ever read the
essay or approved of the strange ally later on. But regardless of the
value of Sorel's suggestions, they are remarkable for the ambivalence
with which he, consciously or not, approaches the whole subject of the
Church-State relationship. He dislikes the Jews, but equally, or more
so, antisemitism; he attacks the Church, but only to defend it against
its attackers. Sorel, the Socialist, and Sorel, the historian of the
Church, seem strangely oblivious of one another. Likewise, Sorel,
the disciple of Proudhon, rejects the State and all it stands for; and
yet he musters enough objectivity, to give the State its due. Or rather,
Sorel studies the "two radically distinct aspects of the State...."[131]
They "mix so intimately that the theoreticians often do not even seem
to suspect that a distinction is in order...." But this distinction is of
paramount importance, since "those two forms are not two varieties...of one and the same quality; between them exists an absolute
contradiction."[132] There is, what Sorel calls "the Idealistic State"
which assumes the roles of "Will and Reason incarnate in some way or
another in the public services;" that State acts as "the master, educator and director of all the particular wills and intelligences...."[133]
It is to this type of activity that the philosophers refer in almost all
cases; their main spokesman is Hegel with his State as the realization

[129]Ibid.   [130]Ibid., p. 530-531.
[131]Sorel, Introduction à l'économie moderne, 2. edition (Paris, 1922), p.
225.
[132]Ibid., p. 229.   [133]Ibid.

of the moral idea. Sorel of course rejects that notion and agrees with
Engels, although not completely, for the Marxist class struggle theory
of the State "does not always apply exactly." But in the main Sorel
concurs: "the Idealistic State is a manifestation of quite other things
than **objective reason;** it stands for the domination of a group of men
who managed to seize organized and concentrated power."[134]

Secondly, Sorel identifies "the Administrative State" which has the
function of "providing mechanisms functioning with regularity." Frequently, that State will pattern itself after the economic institutions
which it finds in existence, and, indeed, "it ought to be the servant
rather than the master of society:" but in reality this is not so because
the Administrative State is continually deflected from its proper ends
by those in power. But the tendency, Sorel believes, is unmistakable:
Whereas the Idealistic State tends to play an exclusive role, rejecting
all really serious attempts of controlling it, the Administrative State
accepts the cooperation of the associations freely formed among the
people; indeed it will be difficult to offer a good reason why the State
alone should provide education or refuse charitable organizations the
right to mitigate the ill effects of a repressive justice.[135]

Surely, Sorel does not have in mind the State we know, with its
great proliferation of central agencies controlling, if not actually
managing the national economy. He could not describe what did not
exist in his own time, and particularly not in France. Thus he can say
that in the economic milieu proper the State suffers "a profound **capitis
diminutio.**" So much do the local economic units prevail, "that it is
legitimate to ask whether the field ought not to be abandoned to them
by the central power altogether." In the field of the productive forces,
the State fulfills its proper function only "on condition that it becomes
the opposite of the Idealistic State."[136] Again Sorel comes very close
to hitting on Gaetano Mosca's "balance of the social forces" when he
calls "that milieu best constituted where there is in existence such a
combination of diverse powers that no domination will ensue; in that
case the equilibrium is assured, the **neutralization** realized."[137] The
Proudhonian influence which pervades the entire work, is particularly
apparent here: a pluralistic society of the producers is envisioned,
controlled by a self-effacing central agency which will "not intervene
to pursue an ideal or to secure profits," but solely for the purpose of
"eliminating wills which constitute a hindrance to the [general] movement." This neutralization of the economic milieu is likened by Sorel
to "a suppression of friction in a machine."[138]

This is not necessarily a plea for free enterprise, although the
Introduction à l'économie moderne belongs in the main to Sorel's

[134]Ibid., p. 230.   [135]Ibid., p. 230-231.
[136]Ibid., p. 231. Sorel's emphasis.
[137]Ibid., p. 232. Sorel's emphasis.
[138]Ibid.

pre-syndicalist period. In stressing the local direction of economic activities, Sorel frequently mentions producers' and consumers' co-operatives as appropriate nuclei of economic enterprise. He notes the theoretic contribution which the Anarchists made in this field, without agreeing with their "often erroneous conclusions."[139] Their solution is too easy: even in a libertarian society there will be need for some sort of a "neutralizing" central agency, and "people are not very inter-ested — not systematically interested — in administrative matters that do not closely affect their passions."[140] Sorel reminds his reader of the short-lived civic reform movements in this country, which will, in a violent upsurge of popular indignation, oust their Tammany Halls, but never for very long.[141] The question of public control would be-devil even the Proudhonian "free" society. The division of powers is a remedy of sorts; at least, that principle holds out some hope that the separate branches of the government will check each other, especially if there is not one party strong enough to control them all.[142] But Sorel is not so sure about the degree of efficiency attainable under the principle of dispersed powers. Like Rousseau, he sees that the con-centration of powers had its advantages: it is "a good thing when it permits the management of affairs by a bureaucracy strong enough to enjoy a certain independence." The Frenchman and, we may suspect, the former civil servant speaks, and not the libertarian, when Sorel says that "the independence of the functionaries so far has been the best guarantee to assure their honesty."[143]

The great accomplishment of the old French monarchy was, in Sorel's view, the creation of a bureaucratic service which served as a model for all the countries of continental Europe.[144] In France, bu-reaucracy was "the **chef-d'oeuvre** of the legists," but juridical training does not necessarily engender civil service systems: Italy for in-stance held law studies in high honor, yet that country "did not pro-duce a bureaucratic administration."[145] This point is arguable; Arnold Toynbee for one holds that French and other royal administra-tions only carried out on a large scale what the Italian city states had perfected before them.[146] Sorel at any rate, believing as he does that the Italian administrators tried very hard "without achieving anything solid," derives from that, possibly faulty, observation "a fundamental law of history, according to which institutions do not arise when and because people feel a need for them; rather they are the result of **ex-ternal causes**, that is, of causes alien to the ends realized by those institutions when they have reached full maturity."[147]

---

[139]Ibid., p. 233.   [140]Ibid., p. 235.

[141]Ibid.   [142]Ibid., p. 243.

[143]Ibid., p. 244.   [144]Ibid., p. 244-245.

[145]Ibid., p. 245.

[146]A Study of History, Vol. III (London and New York, 1934), pp. 354-357; Vol. IV (London and New York, 1939), p. 198-199.

[147]Sorel, op. cit., p. 245.

For France, this argument seems to hold good; there, bureaucracy was originally nothing else but an instrument of royal aggrandisement: it developed "because, since the 12th century, the monarchy had been a conquering power, continually bent on the destruction of the local powers." In union with the standing army and the royal magistrates, the administration little by little conquered France for the King; thus, the strong unity which warfare was imposing on the State brought results not merely externally, but likewise at home: "The bureaucratic body was a sort of civil militia which never ceased to improve its performance. It represented the public interest to the extent to which that public interest was synonymous with the destruction of [feudal] particularism; but it also represented despotism."[148]

This administrative machine reached its perfection under Napoleon who managed to impart to it the same exacting discipline which he had imposed on his armies. Its decadence began as soon as it was placed under the command of the parliamentarians: "everything had to prostrate itself before the **majesty of national sovereignty.**"[149] If he has to choose between bureaucratic despotism and parliamentarian democracy, Sorel will take bureaucracy, because its personnel may be expected to observe a code of public obligation which is essentially non-capitalistic. So he exempts the civil servants even of the bourgeois State from the harsh accusations which he is in the habit of leveling against the other parasites of bourgeois rule: "That the routine and formalism [of the bureaucrats] are cumbersome and, sometimes, outright funny, no one will deny; yet that routine, that formalism was the price paid for the preservation of [our] independence."[150]

However, those times are irrevocably gone. "The process of decomposition goes on without interruption; democracy continues to demolish all that is left of tradition...." Thus far the voice is that of the disciple of Renan, and Taine, mourning the passing away of Le Play's "social authorities." But the next sentence sounds the clarion call of the good Socialist: "There will be no bureaucracy — in the historic meaning of the word — till Socialism triumphs."[151] The sentence, even with the saving grace of its parenthesis, may shock the reader who is liable to equate bureaucratic government with the loss of freedom. Sorel would answer him that freedom is more likely to exist under a civil service taken out of party politics, under functionaries freed from all considerations of **"raison d'Etat"** and merely "charged with a production job."[152] In other words, the bureaucrat would become a technician, and the question of how well he has accomplished his assignment would not differ from such argument as is likely to take place "between a merchant and his representative. We leave idealism behind to enter the realm of production."[153]

---

[148]Ibid.   [149]Ibid., p. 246. Sorel's emphasis.
[150]Ibid.   [151]Ibid., p. 247.
[152]Ibid., p. 251.   [153]Ibid.

4. THE GENESIS OF THE 'REFLECTIONS'

From Proudhon to Proudhon

To become aware of Sorel as a historian as well as a political thinker is an important step toward a better view of his full stature. But it is not enough. Looking for what joins the two Sorels together, we may well decide that "he was, and intended to be, a philosopher."[1] A mere catalogue of the philosophical subjects to which he devoted essays and entire books, would at least bear out the "intent". Starting out in his own field, engineering, Sorel takes up epistemological problems of physics and psycho-physics, of non-euclidian geometry, of atomism.[2] His **Socrates** is, as we saw, as much a treatise on metaphysics as it is a first sketch of Sorelian politics; his early book on Marx and Aristotle[3] contains the first reference to Sorel's favorite philosopher, Henri Bergson, who is treated more extensively in a long essay appearing in 1907,[4] and again in Sorel's very last book **On the Utility of Pragmatism.**[5] Earlier, the philosophical journals printed Sorel's views on such topics as **Science and Morals, The Metaphysical Preoccupations of Contemporary Physics,** and **On the Problems of Philosophy.**[6]

However, this list, impressive as it is, may give a wrong impression. Sorel's enquiry into metaphysical, logical, or ethical problems was not something separated from his interest in the politics of the day; rather it pervaded his entire work just sufficiently to baffle both the expert and the layman. The philosophically trained reader, irked

---

[1]See Part I, Introduction, p. 16 and note 5.

[2]"Sur les applications de la psychophysique" in Revue Philosophique, Tome XXII, 1886; "Le calcul des probabilités et l'expérience," ibid., Tome XXIII, 1887; "Contributions psycho-physiques à l'étude esthétique," ibid., Tome XXIX, 1890; "Sur la géometrie non-euclidienne," ibid., Tome XXX, 1891; "Fondement scientifique de l'atomisme" in Annales de Philosophie Chrétienne, 1892; "La physique de Descartes," ibid., 1892.

[3]See below, p.100, note 44.

[4]"L'évolution créatrice" in Le Mouvement Socialiste, October 15, December 15, 1907, January 15, March 15 and April 15, 1908.

[5]De l'utilité du pragmatisme (Paris, 1921), 471 p.

[6]"La science et la morale" in Questions de morale, Paris, 1900; "Les préoccupations métaphysiques des physiciens modernes" in Revue de Métaphysique et de Morale, November, 1905; "Vues sur les problèmes de la philosophie," ibid., January, 1911.

by the incessant interjection of non-philosophical matter, was likely to consider the author a dilettant (an accusation proudly borne by Sorel[7]), while the man in the street, if he read Sorel at all, could not but consider him obscure. Even Sorel's best-known work, the **Reflections on Violence,** may be said to contain philosophy to an extent that makes the relative popularity of that book something like a freak accident in the history of literary success.

Whether it was philosophical curiosity that started Sorel on his way toward political rebellion, or a primary practical interest, suggesting the use of philosophical lenses to bring political objectives into sharper focus, — the fact remains that the two authors who exerted the greatest influence on the political thinker, Sorel, were treated by him as metaphysicians first, and only subsequently as philosophers of social, revolutionary movements.

Sorel's whole work may be described in terms of a posthumous battle between Proudhon and Marx, as an attempt at reconciling two positions which were considered irreconcilable by the original protagonists. But it would be false to interpret Sorel's mature political thought as a mere combination of Proudhonian and Marxian ideas; it would be more correct to say that Sorel accomplished his synthesis by a double process of elimination and revaluation: he threw out such elements in both Proudhon and Marx which were not suitable to his own, Sorelian, purpose, while superimposing his own, very free interpretations on what was left. Of the two, it is no doubt Karl Marx who "suffers" more at the hands of his critic, — a fact which does not necessarily prove that Sorel was less impressed by Marx than by Proudhon, or that he was less critical of Proudhon than of Marx. Quite to the contrary, one has the impression that the impact of Marx on Sorel was greater, more of an excitement and incitement than the less cogently reasoned oeuvre of Proudhon. The latter's apparent eclipse, at least as far as Sorel's "early" writings are concerned, must, however, not mislead us: it was the novelty of Marx, the mystery about a work that had hardly begun to affect France, that attracted Sorel, whereas he knew his Proudhon well. As he became Marx-conscious, the Proudhonian heritage was more or less relegated to Sorel's subconscious, to reemerge in stages, as the Marxian image lost its initial charm for him. Or, to put it differently: Sorel can afford to submit to the influence of the German thinker precisely because the French tradition of Proudhonian libertarianism is a matter of course to him. He goes all out to Marx, but he comes to him from Proudhon. And he will return to him, in the end.[8]

---

[7]See his **Reflections on Violence** (Glencoe, Ill., 1950), p. 32 - 33.

[8]The second edition of Sorel's last political work, the **Matériaux d'une théorie du proletariat** (Paris, 1921), contains an appendix, "Exégèses proudhoniennes" (pp. 415-449), in which Proudhon's attitude toward nationalism is shown to be negative. Cf. chapter 8, note 40.

It is Proudhon who is the subject of Sorel's first long essay devoted to topics other than physical and mathematical.[9]   But all consideration of Proudhon's revolutionary, or religious ideas is explicitly excluded.[10]   What interests Sorel, is Proudhon's particular, semi-Hegelian use of the dialectic, his notions on freedom and determinism, his theory of value, his idea of education as a weapon to combat inequality. Sorel's careful survey of a life work "little read, and, above all, little studied,"[11] is free from all propagandist or critical connotations; yet the reader familiar with Sorel's later development will already discover all the elements which were to become part of his specific **Weltanschauung**: what Proudhon has to say about the moral and juridical aspirations of the proletariat, and about the "ethics of production," reads, in Sorel's sober exegesis, like something to be filed away for future reference. But no indication as yet of the tender, reverential tone in which Sorel was to speak of Proudhon ten years hence: it takes some time to cherish what is ours by birthright.

What Sorel says here of Proudhon may well be applied to his own work: "detaching the theories from an author's work...always a delicate transaction...is particularly difficult in the case of Proudhon: his thought evolved slowly; his very first **memoir** on property contains the germs of all his later doctrines; but he did not live long enough to give them their definitive form; hence frequent contradictions in his formulas, so that perhaps not a single of his books...is completely homogeneous."[12]   Thus, Proudhon's "best known work" on **Justice in the Revolution and in the Church** would be confusing[13] unless we take into account its supplement, published some years later.[14] Sorel believes that "this work, which we consider to be one of the most remarkable productions of the century," has not found sufficient attention. Not a few readers were shocked when they discovered in that book — Proudhon's **War and Peace** — "a justification of the right of force." But in developing that doctrine, Proudhon only follows in the footsteps of the classical Greek tradition without, however, being conscious of the "close relationship;" Sorel seems to describe his own attitude toward Proudhon when he characterizes Proudhon's indebtedness to Hellas with the words; "that parenthood is so powerful that,

---

[9] **"Essai sur la philosophie de Proudhon"** [in the following called **Proudhon**] in **Revue Philosophique**, June and July, 1892. - But Proudhon is already very evident in Sorel's **Socrates** (pp. 83, 85, 95, 97, 98, 158, 167, 180, 191, 204, 257, 267.)

[10] Sorel, **Proudhon** (June, 1892), p. 622.

[11] Ibid.

[12] Ibid.

[13] Ibid., p. 635.

[14] Ibid., (July, 1892), p. 44.

ordinarily, our author fails to realize...that he is reproducing theories borrowed from antiquity almost verbatim."[15]

What is that antique heritage which Sorel in turn has already taken over from Proudhon? In a footnote referring to his own Socrates, Sorel calls Proudhon the only modern genius who understood the old master.[16] The Proudhonian community is akin to the Greek polis which "had always been a congregation of soldiers; Aristotle's sole concern was how to form people into warriors full of energy and virtue; the Homeric culture could not have produced anything else." Proudhon saw war exactly as the great poets of antiquity saw it: it is war that "reveals our ideal to us, war that creates the great epics, war that reinvigorates nations gone soft." In war, Proudhon believed, "man discovers his own best qualities: courage, patience, disregard of death, devotion to glory and the good of his fellows, in one word: his virtue."[17] And Sorel, anticipating his concept of the proletarian class struggle in the Reflections, notes down: "the struggle must be chivalrous...'the true soldier neither hates nor despises his enemy'...."[18]

Within the polis, the notion of law, of justice is closely bound up with "the reciprocal respect of personal dignity among those soldiers all brought up in the cult of virtue, ready to die...for the defense of their country," so that Proudhon could exclaim: "What matters life, when justice is at stake? Is justice not man in his totality, is it not perhaps more than life, love, property and liberty?"[19] The sequence of the Great Words is remarkable, with liberty coming last. It is, in the formulation of a recent French writer, "a subjective right which belongs to those, and to those only, who are capable of defending it."[20] Democracy stems from defense. Sorel wonders whether the idea of justice is at all susceptible of peaceful evolution among certain nations: "the conception of the Greek polis being founded on war, its theses could not be understood by the admirers of Poor Richard or by the Asiatic races."[21] Even in our Western world, the great majority of people is all but untouched by the Greek tradition, Sorel contends,

---

[15]Ibid. "Georges Sorel and his disciples...do not think much of the rationalist Proudhon; they prefer the anti-contractarian and anti-democrat." Georges Guy-Grand in his introduction to De la justice dans la révolution et dans l'église in Oeuvres complètes de P.-J. Proudhon, Vol. VIII, Pt. 1 (Paris, 1930), p. 7. Cf. also Henry Moysset's introduction to La Guerre et la Paix in the same edition, Vol. VI (Paris, 1927), p. xciv, about the lasting impression which that work made on Sorel.

[16]Sorel, Proudhon (July, 1892), p. 44, note.

[17]Ibid., p. 44.

[18]Ibid., p. 45.

[19]Ibid.

[20]Bertrand de Jouvenel, Du Pouvoir, (Paris, 1945), American edition: On Power, preface by D. W. Brogan, transl. by J. F. Huntington (New York, 1949), p. 319. De Jouvenel is much indebted to Mosca.

[21]Sorel, op. cit., p. 45.

adding: It is true that the masses are ruled by minorities, but even these minorities seem not always able to grasp the significance of Proudhon's theory.[22] That is, perhaps, due to the fact that his explanation is incomplete: the Hellenic culture is not the sole basis of our modern notion of justice: "the question arises whether the just man does not owe something to Christianity." Proudhon himself pointed out the important contributions which Rome, Italy, France and Germany made toward the evolution of law. Sorel feels, therefore, justified in amending Proudhon's formula by saying: "The just man is the noble man as portrayed by our ideal interpretation of antiquity, transformed by our conscience refined under the influence of Christianity."[23]

As civilization develops, the notion of war undergoes a gradual transformation which tends to obscure the fact that peace, the peace of modern society, is still a state of war, only under different forms. From a divine ordeal, war had developed into the agency which brought forth such ideas as sovereignty, authority, government, and ruler, hierarchy and classes; from the right of force sprang the notion of law, and subsequently that of equality, first signifying the equal right of each one to go to war against each, later, as communities became pacified internally, the right of free contract, and, in our time, of free competition. But society always remains, by fact or by right, in a state of war.[24]

True, Proudhon knew that such a view of war would be one-sided and unrealistic. So he goes on to apply his own law of contradictions, and to reveal the "double face of war." It has both "the face of the archangel and the face of a demon."[25] What caused the degradation of the "ideal war?" Proudhon's distinction between poverty and pauperism helps him and Sorel to understand the modern type of rapacious warfare. While human desires are unlimited, production is always limited. Struggling against poverty man becomes free, master of himself, a moral being. But he always remains "poor." Poverty is decent; it is the greed of the mighty that led to ever increasing social disparity, to the disparagement of honest labor and to so much misery that wars of conquest seemed the only means left to restore the domestic disequilibrium.[26]

It is this kind of war which, as Proudhon declared, "humanity no longer wants."[27] As Sorel put it in an earlier work:[28] the polis of warriors had become a community of workers. The antagonism of the battlefield is now transformed into the social struggle bent on the

---

[22]Ibid., p. 45-46.   [23]Ibid., p. 46

[24]La guerre et la paix in Oeuvres complètes de P.-J. Proudhon (Paris, 1927), VI, 41.

[25]Ibid., p. 314.

[26]Ibid., pp. 338, 340 ff.

[27]Ibid., p. 510.

[28]La ruine du monde antique, see chapter 2, p. 62.

"production of an ever superior order" based on work.[29] And again
Sorel notes something for future reference: the examination of the
present condition of industrial society revealed to Proudhon a law of
singular importance; as progress grows, labor becomes not less, but
more exacting; if the physical demands on human energy have de-
creased with the increasing mechanization of production, the intellectual strain has become worse.[30] With Proudhon, Sorel will say
that the industrial revolution, far from realizing the hedonistic dreams
of a Fourier, generates a mentality contemptuous of the easy life.
The austere producer replaces the "decadent capitalist."

     Critical interpolations are not missing from the general assent.
Sorel remarks on the "hasty composition" of **Justice**;[31] the work lacks
clarity mainly because the important conception of "the right of force"
did not occur to Proudhon until much later.[32] Also, in 1846, when he
wrote his **System of Economic Contradictions,** Proudhon still held that
all antagonisms, natural or mental, are resolved eventually. Only
twelve years later "he recognized his error" and wrote: "the antinomy will never be resolved; what looks to us like a synthesis is merely
balance between the antagonistic forces ...." But, Sorel adds, Proudhon never quite rid himself of the Hegelian notion of the synthesis.[33]
He died "before the new industry came to maturity," Sorel writes
eight years later, "and he always remained somewhat under the influence of ideas dating back to the time prior to 1848;" that explains
why his reasoning is sometimes awkward, but it is also a reason for
taking him as a guide if one wants to understand social conceptions
current in his time.[34] In particular, Proudhon's federalist doctrine
may become a useful weapon against such Marxist state socialists as
Jaurès, who was just discovering Proudhon, as the French nationalists
will do a decade later.[35] Sorel notes that the influence of Proudhon
has so far been confined to the bourgeoisie, but now "the time has
come when the ideas of Proudhon ... will be important for the future
of socialism."[36] Yet one year later Sorel still has reservations:
"notwithstanding all the precautions which Proudhon took in order to
discard the socialist illusion:" the practical solutions which he

---

[29]Proudhon, op. cit., Vol. II, p. 374.

[30]Sorel, **Proudhon** (June, 1892), p. 633.

[31]Ibid., p. 635.

[32]Ibid., (July, 1892), p. 47.

[33]Ibid., p. 53.

[34]"Les aspects juridiques du socialisme" in Revue Socialiste, October,
1900, p. 579.

[35]"Quelques mots sur Proudhon" in Cahiers de la Quinzaine (13. cahier de
la 2. série June 22, 1901, pp. 21-24.

[36]Ibid., p. 25. About the "nationalist Proudhon," see chapter 8.

offered for the cure of economic ills were "influenced by **considerations of natural law.**"[37]

Sorel himself will soon be instrumental in restoring Proudhon's reputation among socialists, but not before he had submitted to the influence of Proudhon's erstwhile friend, rival and conqueror.

Enter Karl Marx

Sorel's first reference to the author of **Das Kapital** is a curious document.[38] Published as a letter to the editor of the revue that had printed his essay on Proudhon a year earlier, Sorel's statement reads like the eager exercise of a young acolyte accepting the new dispensation unreservedly, not capable of understanding how anyone could doubt its truth, and full of scorn for all those who dare to belittle it. Sorel was forty-five years old when he wrote this letter. Like almost all his writings, this one too was provoked by what he had read about Marx rather than by the original; in this case it is Gabriel Tarde, the great French sociologist, who arouses Sorel's wrath with a comparison of Marx and Hegel, both of whom he found tortuous, enigmatic, obscure.[39] Sorel answers with a blanket denunciation of contemporary philosophy which continues to "battle chimeras and to navigate through the empyrean;" its "captious and subtle objections" to the Marxian system miss the point completely; in the end, "the truly new metaphysics of Marx will triumph" over all that.[40] Sorel, once he caught fire, could be quite a pamphleteer; the three pages of **Science and Socialism** show him in white heat.

No wonder, he writes, many people consider socialism as just another form of Jacobinism: there is no denying that socialism is being exploited by the Jacobin demagogues of today, and that is a great pity; but how could it be otherwise, since the Jacobins alone are doing something for the masses. It is the fault of the enlightened classes themselves if the gap between them and the proletariat becomes wider and wider, with the educated people resigning themselves to a skeptical attitude which refuses to believe in anything. "Is it not an admirable spectacle," Sorel exclaims, "to behold the plebs remaining loyal to the old principles, still retaining faith in such absolutes as Right

---

[37]"Idées socialistes et Faits économiques au XIX siècle" in Revue Socialiste, May, 1902, p. 542. - Sorel's emphasis. - On Proudhon, see also chapter 6, p. 151.

[38]"Science et socialisme" in Revue Philosophique, May, 1893, pp. 509-511. It is Sorel's first **French** publication about Marx; he had already treated that subject in two Italian periodicals, in 1889 and 1890.

[39]Sorel, op. cit., p. 509. Tarde had criticized, in the **Revue,** a book by Jean Bourdeau, Sorel's admirer (see chapter 7, p.175), on German Socialism.

[40]Sorel, op. cit., p. 509.

and Truth?" For what does socialism mean? "That the public power
act in accordance with the rules of a rational state."[41] The socialist
demand for a rational organization of society stands and falls with the
claim that socialism can be a science, and that the system of Karl
Marx satisfies that claim. Anyone can invent "subjective formulas"
concerning the evolution of society (a thrust at Auguste Comte and his
ideal state of "bankers and priests"), but the central question is
"whether the exchange [of commodities] contains an element susceptible of becoming the object of a rational science, as K. Marx maintains,
or whether it is nothing but a phenomenon defying all possible scientific categories, as Aristotle seems to believe." And Sorel continues:
"If the Stagyrite is right, then all socialistic theses collapse; Marx
knew that well and he took great pains to justify his point of view."
But is his particular solution convincing? Sorel's answer is couched
in negative terms: the refutations proffered by the non-Marxian econ-
omists failed to convince him; "that boring tribe of scribblers has not
even grasped what their adversary was about." They are excluded
from the discussion for "the problem is of a philosophic nature; only
philosophers familiar with the study of principles could seriously approach it."[42]

The neophyte has to confess that he has been "trying for a long
time unsuccessfully to find the solution of that important question;"
nor has anybody else as yet responded to his quest.[43] Boehm-
Bawerck's massive attack on Marx's theory of surplus value was not
to appear for another six years; so the field seemed free for Georges
Sorel to attack the "philosophic problem" in his next major work. **The
Old and The New Metaphysics** or, as Sorel's disciple, Edouard Berth,
called the essay when he published it in book form forty-one years
after its first appearance in print, **From Aristotle to Marx,** [44] reas-
serts in principle Sorel's confidence in the scientific correctness of
the Marxian economics. The doubts will assert themselves soon
enough, and together with the German, Eduard Bernstein, and the
Italian, Benedetto Croce, Sorel will reject precisely the Marxian system and retain, for his own use, the *mystique* of the class struggle as
the essential, living part of Karl Marx's work. In doing so, Sorel will
reverse his position: the question of exchange value will concern him
less and less, as the "evolution of society" assumes main importance.
He will retain, however, notions already clearly developed in **Science
and Socialism,** notions which to the reader endowed with the wisdom
of hindsight, may appear as slightly less than orthodox Marxism: his
belief that the masses will defend the traditional concepts of morality
and law against the relativism of the bourgeoisie (a belief hardly to

---

41 Ibid., p. 510.

42 Ibid., p. 511.

43 Ibid.

44 "L'ancienne et la nouvelle métaphysique" in I.'Ere Nouvelle, March-
June, 1894; **D'Aristote à Marx,** preface by Edouard Berth (Paris, 1935), 275 p.

be reconciled with the Marxist principle of reducing all absolutes to historical, transitory reflexes of the superstructure); Sorel's proletarians, however revolutionary he may want them to be, will also be conservative.

The Primacy of Mechanics

The Old and the New Metaphysics was published thirteen years after Sorel's death, and the editor of the volume was convinced that the author, in his life time, would have refused permission to republish the work of his "first Marxist fervor," full of the very "scientism" which Sorel toward the end of his career had attacked and condemned so severely.[45] The essay, a close contemporary of the historical study later published as **La ruine du monde antique**, is in the main concerned with the problems of knowledge since Aristotle who established the position beyond which "no progress was made ... until our century:" not until "K. Marx [took up] certain questions where the Stagirite had left them."[46] Everything in between the two is rejected by Sorel, and his argument is not so much in favor of Marx versus Aristotle as an attack on Descartes (echoing Vico) and Kant (the British empiricists are not mentioned at all),[47] an attack in which Aristotle and Marx are viewed almost as allies: For the ancient philosopher had already posited, as the starting point, man as a social animal: all ethics is communal property. The medieval, Christian doctrines, on the other hand assumed "each individual as an isolated unit confronting a sovereign judge;" true, St. Thomas introduced the peripatetic principles of politics into his system, but "these rational theses ... constituted an anachronism, since they did not correspond to the prejudices of time and milieu." None of the catholic doctors could possible place themselves in the position of a philosopher living in a free Greek polis.[48]

Modern spiritualism merely adapted the theologian individualistic viewpoint to a secularized form: in Descartes' seventeenth century the regime of absolute monarchy "of necessity produced the same effects as those engendered by the ecclesiastic milieu of the middle ages." Idealist morality, according to Sorel, was based on the paramount fact of political life: the relations of the subject to the sovereign.[49] Not until the revolution of 1848 did the "chimera of sovereignty" begin to lose its hold on the imagination;[50] at present we live

---

[45]D'Aristote à Marx, p. 1.

[46]Ibid., p. 95.

[47]"For the last two centuries, knowledge has been explained as a process starting within us to proceed to the external world; materialism (in the Marxist sense of the term) takes a diametrically opposite view of things ... " Ibid., p. 190.

[48]Ibid., p. 256-257.   [49]Ibid., p. 257.

[50]Ibid., p. 258.

in the time of "the great disorder:" traditional morality, patterned
after the theologian model, no longer holds good, while "the social
conception of [human] acts has not yet been popularized." In order
to retrace "the good road," we must rediscover Aristotle's "social
animal," but we must go beyond him: Aristotle had denied, very
forcefully, that the moral domain contained anything rational and absolute.[51] Even less could he evolve any modern notions of political
economy; in a society based on slavery, that is, on the inequality of
men, economic values could not be treated in a scientific way:[52] "the
Stagirite treated of exchange in his Ethics, in connection with justice;" according to him, exchange belonged to the empirical phenomena, "he could not have thought otherwise, following as he did the dialectic method which begins with morals and politics to end with
economics."[53] Today, "we start with the genesis of economic phenomena and we get rid of the moral coating which lends a subjective
color to everything it covers. We are, at last, enabled to study the
things as they are, in their proper order —we are ready, in one word,
to see them in a truly scientific way...."[54]

This is a long way from "Aristotle's [ethical] probabilism,"[55]
frequently hampered by a confusion between private and public ethics,
a confusion easily understandable since the boundary between the two
is fluid. With us, the distinction has become unnecessary: all ethics
is social. And the social animal has become the "social worker."[56]

Antique philosophy, struck by the continuous changes in nature,
was searching for "the immovable science:" for an "intelligible answer."[57] The "barbaric state of Greek mechanics"[58] precluded truly
scientific methods; add to this the Greek tendency to confuse "what
we distinguish so carefully: mechanisms and organisms."[59] Hence
their need for what Sorel calls "the expressive support," a construction "explaining something else than the relations which need explaining." Here he finds the source of "the illusions on which ancient metaphysics thrived."[60] The moral need for certainty forces upon the pre-
scientific mind of man auxiliary explanations like "final cause,"
"prime mover" and other propositions about the unknown, which then
attain central significance; their sustaining role is forgotten, as is the
injunction that "questions concerning matters which are beyond scientific knowledge are not given in nature but result from the paraphysi-
cal interpretation of constructions made to explain the things."[61] The
supporting fictions are taken to be true and real.

Only if we place ourselves firmly, with Sorel, on the basis of

[51] Ibid., p. 260.
[53] Ibid., p. 260.
[55] Ibid., p. 261.
[57] Ibid., p. 161.
[59] Ibid., p. 129.
[61] Ibid., p. 155.

[52] Ibid., p. 238.
[54] Ibid., p. 260-261.
[56] Ibid., p. 253.
[58] Ibid., p. 160.
[60] Ibid., p. 131.

historic materialism, do we find that "the system of sentimental illusions is always the reflex of an economic system; the emotional action intervened to prevent us from seeing the reality of things and to hide from us the incoherence of constructions: but it creates absolutely nothing."[62] What is the object of true science? "To determine the hidden metaphysical entity which translates internal impulsions into abstract terms, and finally to signal the illusion, if the illusion exists."[63] It is "the analysis of machinism and its effects" which permits us to turn from subjective notions, from a fortuitous philosophy "to the objective, social, abstract data of science."[64] For the machine is the social creation **par excellence**; "it is even more social than language itself."[65] It operates in an order of things impervious to our moral prejudices.[66] Ancient materialism resigned itself to a determinism close to fatalism;[67] modern materialism grants us our freedom within "the artificial milieu"[68] which "is fabricated, worked and continually refined by [man], and all science of man which neglects that milieu is an anthropological phantasy."[69] The ancient metaphysicians, faced with the problem of free will, tried to answer it in mechanistic terms involving them in unintelligible difficulties due to their attempt to deduce human from cosmic laws: Truth is that "we can know nothing outside the artificial milieu."[70] But "we are free in the sense that we are able to build machines which are not patterned after cosmic models; we change no laws of nature, but we are powerful enough to create sequences endowed with an orderliness which is all our own."[71]

In his enthusiasm for this discovery which he assigns to Marx,[72] Sorel proclaims the new "ideal" in almost lyrical terms. "Go on then, and extend human activity; invent new machines and you will gain something on the domain of the unknown by enlarging the field of human cooperation with the energies of nature in the artificial milieu."[73] In his scorn for the "illusions of the bold metaphysicians," Sorel dismisses lightly the psychological impact of "moral illusions" which, "like all the emanations of our spirit, have their proper history, such as myths and legends." The theorist of the myth as the great moral motor of historic movements is not yet born; in 1894 those "sentimental" notions are nothing but "great errors which, at a given moment, dominate an entire people." He sees clearly the power and

---

[62]Ibid., p. 263.   [63]Ibid., p. 262.
[64]Ibid., p. 261.   [65]Ibid., p. 201.
[66]Ibid., p. 264.   [67]Ibid., p. 263.
[68]Ibid., p. 264. - About that concept see also Sorel's study on Vico in chapter 3, p. 67f.
[69]Ibid., p. 193.   [70]Ibid., p. 267.
[71]Ibid., p. 264.
[72]Sorel had at that time not yet discovered Vico.
[73]Sorel, **op. cit.**, p. 267.

persistence of those psychological forces which explain "that the illusions persist so long and exercise their influence," but Sorel still
thinks of that influence as merely "morbid."[74]

Only one modern philosopher besides Marx escapes Sorel's censure. Some writers are impressed with the fact that **The Ancient and
the New Metaphysics** signals the first appearance of Henri Bergson
on the mental horizon of Georges Sorel who greeted the author of **Les
données immédiates de la conscience** with the poetic words: "That
book is...like a vigorous tree rising in the midst of the desolate
steppes of contemporary philosophy."[75] The names of Bergson and
Sorel are forever linked: not even the most casual account of Sorelian thought will fail to mention the "decisive" influence the philosopher of the **élan vital** has had on the philosopher of the myth. No
amount of rectification will destroy this textbook tradition which might
be called another example of a myth triumphing over the brute evidence of facts.[76] In vain did Henri Bergson himself politely beg to
differ from the disciple;[77] and it will be probably no less in vain to
point out that Sorel, while acknowledging his great debt, from the very
beginning maintained a very critical attitude toward the philosopher
whose classes he used to attend, no doubt feeling quite out of place
among the fashionable crowd that was lionizing the brilliant lecturer.
The least that must be said is that Sorel's Bergsonianism did not become wholehearted until he had completely freed himself from the
scientism of his Marxist period, that is, not until the beginning of this
century.[78] In the essay under discussion he is as little disposed to
accept Bergson unqualifiedly as he is willing to make "the Stagirite

---

[74] Ibid., p. 262.

[75] Ibid., p. 167-168.

[76] "Sorel and Bergson met like Kant and Rousseau." A. Lanzillo, **Giorgio
Sorel** (Rome, 1910), p. 93. "Let us not exaggerate. Sorel was not suddenly
touched by the Bergsonian grace. Bergsonianism corresponded to some pro-
found leanings of his mind. Sorel, anti-intellectualist and mystic, was a
Bergsonian before Bergson." P. Perrin, **Les idées sociales de Georges Sorel**
(Algiers, 1925), p. 24.

[77] "It seems to me," he wrote to Sorel's biographer, Agostino Lanzillo,
"that you were successful in making us see the diverse aspects of that complex and original physiognomy, in relating them to one another and in explaining them by one another. In particular, you point out well how his philosophical
conceptions could meet with mine from a certain angle, even though I did not
treat of social questions and did not incline toward syndicalism....I would
have to make some reservations about several of your judgments, in particular about your views on democracy. It seems to me that we must aim to revive its enthusiasm, and there is no reason to assume that such task would be
impossible. But these are matters far too serious as to be treated in passing..." Lanzillo, **op. cit.**, p. 93.

[78] There was an interval of 18 years between Bergson's **Données immédiates** (1889) and his **Evolution créatrice** (1907). See above, notes 4 and 5.

responsible for all the nonsense attributed to him."[79] It remains strange how some students of Sorel could have overlooked the fact that, in **The Old and New Metaphysics,** he uses only one half of the vitalist philosophy.[80] By concentrating almost exclusively on Bergson's theory of the intellectual ego rather than of the intuitive self, Sorel tries to "rope in" Bergson for his own concept of a scientific, social knowledge operating in an "artificial milieu," while flatly rejecting Bergson's notion of free will.[81] Sorel could not well have judged differently at the time: in his Marxist world, there was no room whatever for such "spiritualistic tendencies" as indeterminacy.[82]

In conclusion, there remain to be signaled some Sorelian observations, almost casually interspersed, and almost forlorn in the midst of the epistemological argument, — shrewd apercus on social leadership which read like a sketch of what Sorel's friend, Vilfredo Pareto, was to develop later into an elaborate theory: the famous law of the "circulation of the elites" seems anticipated when Sorel describes the methods by which the bourgeoisie uses the panacaea of "universal education" to deprive the proletariat of potential leaders.[83] "It is wiser to subsidize the barbarians than to combat them."[84] We may wonder whether Pareto was inspired by that sentence when he treated of the "lions" and the "foxes." In turn, he was pleased to discover, in Sorel's **Reflections,** "the confirmation of several theories" developed in an earlier work of his own.[85]

L'Affaire Labriola

Sorel, always on the lookout for editors who would publish at least part of his notes-grown-into-essays, had by 1895 once more become an editor in his own right.[86] For a few years he could indulge

---

[79]Sorel, **op. cit.,** p. 130.

[80]A fact recognized by Pierre Angel in his **Essais sur Georges Sorel** (Paris, 1936), p. 89: "Sorel is eager to infer [from Bergson] that 'science is, in the last analysis a social adaptation of the individual to physical nature,' overlooking all the objections which Bergsonianism understood in its authentic synthesis, would raise against such tendencies."

[81]Sorel, **op. cit.,** p. 167.   [82]Ibid., p. 174.
[83]Ibid., p. 109.   [84]Ibid., p. 110.

[85]V. Pareto, **Manuel d'économie politique,** 2. edition (Paris, 1927), p. 480. Pareto refers to his **Systêmes socialistes** (Paris, 1902). Cf. also, Supplement 2.

[86]Of **Le Devenir Social,** together with Paul Lafargue and two other socialists (1895-1897). Earlier, he had been for a short time one of the editors of **L'Ere Nouvelle,** founded by a Roumanian, Diamandy. In 1899, he joins Hubert Lagardelle's new review, **Le Mouvement Socialiste,** for two years, rejoining it in 1906.

in the author's dream: to print what he pleased. The book section of the review he wrote practically single-handed, signing his **compte-rendus** with almost as many fictitious initials as the alphabet would yield; the authorship of some of those contributions is still being disputed. The list of collaborators all united in their endeavor to proceed along the trail blazed by Karl Marx, was as international as it was illustrious: the roster of writers who contributed, first to the shortlived **Devenir** and subsequently to **Le Mouvement Socialiste,** contained such names as Benedetto Croce, Friedrich Engels, August Bebel, Eduard Bernstein, Karl Kautsky, Jean Jaurès, Antonio Labriola, Rosa Luxemburg, Emile Vandervelde. Among these grandees of socialism, Georges Sorel played assuredly a minor but nevertheless an important role: as his correspondence with Benedetto Croce shows, he was a driving force in making Marx and Marxist literature better known in France which was, in that respect, trailing behind such countries as Italy, and even Russia. Forever trying to be helpful to others, Sorel was an indefatigable middleman between his friends and Paris publishing houses. Many a Paris editor was to rue the day on which he had promised Georges Sorel to publish the French version of some abstruse foreign treatise; the peaceful looking old burgher in the cape and bowler hat could be quite insistent. With the years he had become, few knew exactly why, quite a power in the small Parisian coteries that made the intellectual weather of tomorrow. People who knew him better would say that Georges Sorel's prestige was founded on his great discursive power which he used to exercise no matter where: pausing in the street to buttonhole a hapless young acquaintance, or in the **couloirs** of the National Library, but preferably in the backroom of his favorite **bouquinistes,** Péguy or Delesalle, where he would hold forth for hours, terrorizing his audience with his erudition, laughing heartily at his own jests, a Paris Dr. Johnson, a Nestor, a Guru.[87]

But nothing demonstrates more convincingly the status which Sorel had won for himself in the little world of Marxist **literati** than the prefaces he was asked to write, beginning with 1896, for other authors, some of them much better known than he was. In some cases, the authors were not altogether happy about the results, for Sorel was occasionally less than interested in saying the appropriate things about his protégés. A preface by Sorel was mostly about Georges Sorel. In at least one case, Sorel's insouciance wrecked a friendship. It was his very first attempt in the new field, a preface for the French edition of a work by Antonio Labriola,[88] and nobody was more surprised by the result than Georges Sorel. The memory of the **imbroglio**

---

[87]See also Part II, Introduction.

[88]Antonio Labriola, **Essais sur la conception matérialiste de l'histoire** (Paris, 1897), translation of **La concezione materialistica della storia** (Bari, 1895) .

rankled long in Sorel's memory: in 1898, two years later, he writes: "That preface was not reproduced in the following edition, Antonio Labriola having decided that I was not safe enough to be a companion for an orthodoxe."[89] And as late as 1909, introducing another Labriola, Sorel is still in a vindictive mood: "Ten years ago, my lack of admiration for the [Marxian] dialectic drew down upon my head the wrath of Antonio Labriola, who...not only severed all relations with me but also excommunicated me in solemn fashion, lest the inquisitors of the social democratic faith accuse him of having friends among the godless."[90]

Although this is clearly the language of hurt innocence, Sorel conceded Antonio Labriola's point. The Italian pundit who, together with Croce, may be said to have initiated Sorel into the complexities of Marxist lore, had a real grievance, for critical as one might be of certain moot points in the Marxian work, throwing out the dialectic altogether was really going too far. And no protestations of admiration for Labriola[91] could disguise the fact that the author of that preface was indeed a heretic. Sorel had crossed the critical line separating the orthodox from the revisionists of the Bernsteinite persuation, although he may not have been conscious of it at the time. Or was he? There is a section in the preface dealing with "what constitutes, in my eyes, the vulnerable part of the [Marxian] doctrine...." What is, Sorel asks, its "metaphysical basis?" If we are told, that there is no need for that inquiry because the proper method is provided by psychology, then we may still ask: "what psychologist is truly indifferent to the metaphysical problem?"[92] Marx put to work a great deal of psychological principles, but he did not, as a rule, state them in a scientific form. It will be "the duty of the disciples of Marx to complete the work of their master:" they will "recognize that they must give up that provisional state; that they must rise above particular analyses and have at their disposal a solid scaffold as a prop for the historical relations." Doing all this, would, in Sorel's view, not constitute a crime against the spirit of Karl Marx "who seems to have feared nothing more than to leave behind an altogether rigid and closed system; he knew that a doctrine is moribund when it is completed...."[93]

There is more in the same vein: "the prudence of Marx was extreme; he did not attempt to bring any theory to its conclusion; the

[89]Sorel, L'Avenir socialiste des syndicats in Matériaux d'une théorie du prolétariat, 2. edition (Paris, 1921), p. 82, note 1.

[90]Arturo Labriola, Karl Marx, L'économiste, Le socialiste (Paris, 1910), p. xxxiii, note 1. - Cf. also Sorel, letters to Croce, in chapter 1, p. 30.

[91]"The publication of this book marks a date in the history of socialism ....The work of M. Labriola belongs together...with the classics of Marx and Engels." Sorel in Antonio Labriola, op. cit., p. 19.

[92]Ibid., p. 12-13.   [93]Ibid., p. 14. Sorel's emphasis

recent discussion has shown that he had not said his last word about value and surplus value. What blindness to charge the disciples of Marx with the attempt to confine human thought within limits prescribed by the master!"[94]

Labriola could agree with the general tenor of these demands, since he considered his own work as an extension rather than as a mere exegesis of the Marxian oeuvre; but he read, between the lines, the intimation that in Sorel's opinion even he, Labriola, had fallen short of filling the "large lacunae"[95] in the master's work. Or what else did the Frenchman mean when he wrote: "There is no point in trying to set down the metaphysics and to define the psychology [of Marxism] when only a few studies concerning the basis of historical materialism are available?"[96] Again, the Italian could only applaud Sorel's mockery of those who would accuse Marx of scorning all morality just because he has scoffed at their own subjectivistic bourgeois morals.[97] But Labriola must have read with deep suspicion the following: "Inspired by Marx's principles, we may say that the social question no longer exists; we may even say that socialism (in the ordinary and historic sense of the word) is a thing of the past: indeed, the question no longer is what **society should be like,** — but what the **proletariat can accomplish** in the actual class struggle."[98] There is in this passage, nothing that could not be retraced to some Marxian utterance, and yet, the emphasis is different, perturbing....Did Labriola sense that here was, still in the embryonic stage, a new philosophy which, once matured, would elevate the working class, from a mere agent in the dialectical process to the main actor and exclusive hero?

Syndicalism

It should be clear by now that Sorel's capital work, the **Reflections on Violence,** did not suddenly spring from his mind like Pallas Athene from the head of Zeus. Rather, Sorel approached his subject in a hesitating, plodding way, taking his time: ten full years of his life already far advanced in years. To use the language of the engineer, Sorel: while patiently mining an ever lengthening lode of facts,

---

94Ibid., p. 14-15.   95Ibid., p. 14.
96Ibid., p. 15.   97Ibid., p. 16-17.
98Ibid., p. 3-4. - Sorel's emphasis. - "In the meantime, Sorel has delivered himself body and soul to the **Crisis of Marxism**...I was writing to the [old] Sorel, not to this new one...the **herald** of a war of secession." Antonio Labriola, **Socialism and Philosophy,** Preface of 1901 (Chicago, 1907), pp. 179-180.

he was at the same time constructing the "mechanics" to assemble his materials; it was a job of both recombination and conversion: not so much a matter of 'new lamps for old,' as the attempt to apprehend what was old in the new, and what new in the old. In a period of transition, the engineer, Sorel, was so busy retooling that he could never give too much attention to the product; nor could he ever be sure of the point reached in his work: hence the almost feverish pace and the fragmentary character of his output.

Convinced that Marx had failed to pay sufficient attention to the forms and ways in which the proletariat was expressing its own aims, Sorel now turns his attention from political socialism — led by bourgeois intellectuals — to the problem of labor unions and related organizations of authentic proletarian origin. He devotes a series of articles to **The Socialist Future of the Syndicates.**[99] This study, generally considered to be the nucleus of the **Reflections,** ends with the words: "To sum up my thought in one formula, I should say that the entire future of socialism is bound up with the autonomous development of the labor syndicates."[100] Sorel, the socialist, then may be said to have turned "syndicalist" as early as 1898, ten years before the final text of his philosophy appeared between the covers of a book.

However, the syndicalist of 1898, though already placing the accent on "autonomy," does not yet speak of revolutionary violence. Neither do we find expounded in the **Avenir** the "myth of the general strike." Sorel being the man he was, could not have done otherwise, for when he wrote the essay, French syndicalism was still in its non-militant phase; the Anarchists, whose influence was to alter the character of the syndicalist movement so radically, were only then beginning to join it in larger numbers.[101] But the fact that Sorel did not **speak** of the general strike does not preclude that he already may have **thought** of it. Sorel at any rate, does claim that he was ready to discuss the issue, but that he preferred to be discreet about it, so as not to embarrass his friends in the movement: "During that period," Sorel was to write seven years later, "the idea of the general strike was odious to most leading French Socialists; I thought it wise to suppress a chapter in which I intended to point out the importance

---

[99] **L'Avenir socialiste des syndicats** appeared originally in L'Humanité Nouvelle, March-May, 1898; it was republished as a brochure, with several additions, and a preface, in 1901; in 1905 Sorel published another preface, for a contemplated second book edition, in **Le Mouvement Socialiste,** under the title **"Le syndicalisme révolutionnaire"** (November 1. and 15) as well as two new chapters, **"L'esprit petit bourgeois"** and **"La Mutualité"** (ibid., September 1 and 15).

[100] **L'avenir** in **Matériaux,** 2. edition, p. 133.

[101] "We...have invented nothing at all, and even assert that nothing can be invented." Sorel, **Reflections on Violence** (Glencoe, Ill., 1950), p. 61. For the evolution of the Syndicalist movement, see chapter 12, p. 278.

of that conception. Since that time, great changes have taken place: in 1900, when I prepared a new edition of my article, the general strike no longer was regarded as mere anarchist insanity...."[102]

Sorel is still unwilling to **blame** Marx for his lack of attention to the problem of proletarian organization: he prefers to censure the disciples for forgetting the master's injunction: that the proletariat must acquire juridical and political capacity as the necessary prerequisite for victory.[103] Otherwise, without "sufficient preparation" the result will be either the "destruction of civilization"[104] or else the vaunted dictatorship of the proletariat will turn out to be "the restoration of social iniquities."[105]

Sorel is happy to report that the recognition of the danger has already dawned on the leaders of French syndicalism. These men, he says, are certainly not very great philosophers, but their instinctive distrust against all political organization demonstrates that "the **pure syndicals** have more to teach us than to learn from us!"[106] They are no longer taken in by the legend of the indispensable, superior intellectual: "experience shows that the qualities of leadership are nothing exceptional, and that they are quite commonly found among manual workers, perhaps more so than among intellectuals....It was with the greatest ease that the British labor unions found, among their own people, the men able to lead them."[107]

Even Karl Kautsky, Marx's German heir apparent, who pointed out that, after all, all the great leaders of incipient socialism, like Marx himself as well as Engels and Lassalle, had come from the ranks of the bourgeoisie, — even Kautsky "recognized that in one decisive point...the interests of the proletariat are diametrically opposed to those of the **intelligenz.**" [Sic][108] The intellectuals do not constitute

---

[102]Preface of 1905 in **Matériaux,** p. 58. Cf. note 99.

[103]L'Avenir in **Matériaux,** p. 81.

[104]Ibid., p. 82.

[105]Ibid., p. 87. In a later footnote, Sorel refers to **Reflections,** pp. 190-193. (1950 ed.).

[106]Ibid., p. 87. Sorel's emphasis. - Sorel paid tribute to two syndicalist leaders by writing prefaces to Fernand Pelloutier's **Histoire des bourses de Travail** (Paris, 1902) and to V. Griffuelhes and L. Niel, **Les objectifs de nos luttes de classe**(Paris, 1909).

[107]Ibid., p. 92. - Sorel's authority for this statement is Paul de Rousiers, **Le trade-unionisme en Angleterre,** p. 42.

[108]Ibid., 95. Sorel cites from the French translation of Kautsky's **Socialism and the Liberal Professions,** which had appeared in his own **Devenir Social,** May, 1905, p. 115, - his source is the same as that used by Lenin in **What is To Be Done?** (1902) where he quotes Kautsky's sentence that "Socialism and the class struggle arise side by side and not one out of the other," in order to prove his thesis that only political and not trade union work will condition the proletariat for revolutionary action. Cf. chapter 10, p. 236. Lenin, **Collected Works,** Vol. IV, Bk. II (New York, 1929), p. 122.

a class in the true sense; they are members of the so-called professional classes which would not fare well in a truly proletarian revolution.   The malcontent, or underpayed among them gravitate toward
the proletariat, but their influence is bad: "the true vocation of the
intellectual [turned socialist] is politics; the politician's role is very
similar to that of the courtier, requiring no industrial aptitude."[109]
It is against these self-styled rulers that the syndicals are in revolt,
and in the view of Georges Sorel, they are quite right, for they sense
accurately: "once the worker has accepted as his leader people alien
to the corporation of producers, he will never learn the art of governing himself, he will remain subjected to external discipline.   One
might use a different word, but it would still be the same thing: the
exploitation of the worker would continue."[110]

    This was written in the year that saw the founding of the Russian
Social Democratic Labor Party in Minsk, the party that split five
years later into Mensheviks and Bolsheviks.   But Gregori Plekhanov
had voiced the same ominous premonition as early as 1883,[111] and he
knew it had come true when Lenin came to power, while Sorel refused
to recognize the new Red discipline for what it was: the confirmation
of his own old fears.[112]

    The anti-intellectualism of Sorel, developed philosophically in
his **Socrates**, is now operative on the social ground; his distaste for
the revolutionary intelligentsia is no reactionary fad, nor does it link
him to the irrationalist movement that was beginning to show strength
in that very period.   Sorel declares himself against the intellectuals
because he sees in them a danger for the self-realization of the proletarian class.   They falsify its ends, by stressing the ends rather
than the means of liberation.   "I do not think," Sorel writes, "that the
social revolution will have much resemblance to a scene from the
Apocalypse."[113]   The aversion of so many Marxists to the humdrum
activities of union cooperatives puzzles Sorel.   As if the interest in
grocery details could spoil the worker's mind for socialism and the

---

[109]Sorel, op. cit., p. 98.

[110]Ibid., p. 98-99.

[111]"After having seized power, the Revolutionary Socialist Government ...
[will either have] to take its inspiration from modern Socialism - in which
case its lack of practical spirit as well as the insufficient advancement and
the habits of the workers will make it impossible to follow this course - or to
seek an issue in the ideals of patriarchal and authoritative Communism, by
modernizing it only to the extent that the socialized production will be controlled by a Socialist caste instead of by the 'Sons of the Sun,' and their functionaries, as in ancient Peru." Plekhanov, Introduction to **Socialism and the
Political Struggle in Collected Works** (Geneva, 1905), p. 141-142. Cited without page reference in N. de Basily, **Russia Under Soviet Rule** (London, 1938),
p. 96.

[112]See chapter 10.

[113]Sorel, op. cit., p. 112.

meaning of the class struggle.[114] Sorel believes in the worth of pragmatic self-education: What will become of the victorious revolution, he asks, if the industry will have to be directed by people who are today incapable of running a cooperative? To expect a miracle to happen, what else is that than "to call for the good despot of whom so many philosophers have been dreaming?" Not in utopia will the new productive forces unfold, but "in the very bosom of capitalist society," and together with those productive forces "the relations proper to a new social order: what might be called the moral forces of the future."[115] The important thing is the development, within the working class, of "new juridical notions." The old, individualistic relationships of seller-buyer, money lender-borrower "must make room for the notions of mutual help and solidarity."[116]

We are, Sorel believes, in the presence of a truly novel principle: Government by the totality of citizens never was more than "a fiction." Rousseau was well aware that his paradoxical General Will could operate only in the absence of all coteries and factions, but that was to make an assumption in the face of all the facts: for what is history if not "the history of political factions taking possession of the State to ply therein their petty predatory game."[117] The alignments of the past, since they were mostly formed for the sake of conquering power, attracted people of the adventurous type of mind, without much aptitude for work. In contradistinction, "the new groupings are professional; they are based on the production of material goods and they have the industrial interests at heart."[118] There is no reason why the social services provided by the bourgeois governments should not devolve upon the new producer groups themselves, no reason why such matters as labor exchanges, insurance, sickness benefits, or factory laws should not be administered by workers' associations: they would handle social welfare problems more efficiently than government officials.[119]

This, then, is the task of the trade unions as Sorel sees it: to wrest those rights, one after the other, from the public domain. This they must do by always pointing to the public interest, untiringly exposing inefficiency and graft. In the end, they will have taken over from the old forms all that which is worth preserving, leaving to the democratic state only its repressive function. For the proletarian struggle is not conquest and plunder: rather, its aim is "to empty the political organism of the bourgeoisie of all life and to pass on what usefulness it has to a proletarian type of political organism which will come into being as the proletariat develops."[120]

---

[114]Ibid., p. 111.   [115]Ibid., p. 112.
[116]Ibid., p. 114.   [117]Ibid., p. 118-119.
[118]Ibid., p. 119.   [119]Ibid., p. 122.
[120]Ibid., p. 123.

Coming to the close of his investigation, Sorel offers one more argument in favor of the proletarian form of social groupings. He borrows it from Emile Durkheim's famous study of suicide. By breaking up the old professional associations which held the individual wills together, the French sociologist believed, "we have destroyed with our own hands **the chosen instrument of our moral reorganization.**"[121] There is no other force that could replace the influence of group cohesion; education, religion, they all lose their hold on a society that has become atomized, Durkheim holds.[122] But Sorel does not share his conclusion. True, the question: will there be a new morality? is one that can be answered only by the future. But that question is misplaced: "our business is not to know which morality is better, but to determine whether there exists **a mechanism capable of guaranteeing the development of morals.**"[123]

And Sorel does not doubt where he must look for those mechanisms. They are the proletarian organs, using democratic methods for ulterior ends. "Vis-a-vis the state, the action of the proletariat is of a double nature: it must fight its way into the existing political arrangements in order to obtain a **social legislation** favorable to its own development," but the aim transcends, or, rather, bypasses political democracy. "The proletariat must endeavor to emancipate itself, today, from all direction that does not come from within....Its first rule of conduct is: to stay exclusively labor, that is, to exclude the intellectuals...."[124] Their function can be no more than auxiliary.[125] The proletariat must learn how to stand on its own feet. It must find itself before it can create the new society, or, rather: re-create society inside the proletarian self. The conservative, defensive essence of Sorel's syndicalism is unmistakable. For all the elements he added later on, that essence will remain unchanged.[126]

Merlino

Another Italian Marxicologist to whom Sorel owed a great deal, was Saverio Merlino, whose **Pro and Contra Socialism** had been critically reviewed by the book editor of the **Devenir**.[127] In July 1898,

---

[121]Ibid., p. 127. Sorel's emphasis. He cites **Le suicide**, p. 439. (the 1. ed. was published in Paris, 1897).

[122]Sorel, **op. cit.**, p. 126. - Durkheim, **op. cit.**, pp. 431-428.

[123]Sorel, **op. cit.**, p. 127. - Sorel's emphasis.

[124]Ibid., p. 132.   [125]Ibid., p. 133.

[126]Sorel's most recent French commentator agrees: see Fernand Rossignol, **op. cit.**, p. 226.

[127]Saverio Merlino, **Pro e contro il Socialismo** (Milan, 1897), reviewed by Sorel under that title in **Le Devenir Social**, October, 1897.

Sorel wrote a preface for the French edition of that work,[128] an essay of 45 pages, in which he continues his own multi-front battle pro and contra Marxism.[129] He is still breaking lances for the master: "Back to Marx, is, in my view, the order of the day;"[130] he is still ridiculing sundry vulgar-critics of Karl Marx as well as the vulgar-marxists who try to put their author into the straight-jacket of a rigid dogmatism. He now takes his stand openly by the side of the revisionists led by Bernstein, endorsing their belief that the working class should come to its salvation through reforms achieved within the framework of the democratic process. But the Protean nature of Sorel again asserts itself: while granting the "universally recognized need for a rigorous revision of the doctrine left behind by Marx and Engels,"[131] including the belief in the impending economic catastrophe of capitalism,[132] Sorel at the same time insists on a proletarian militancy deriving its strength from the belief in the "moral catastrophe" to be inflicted upon "an adversary treated as irreconcilable." Here is, we may safely say, the new Sorel who declares, with Merlino, that "socialism is a moral question."[133]

Antonio Labriola is not the only person to become incensed by this changed attitude: Sorel notes calmly that Charles Andler, the great French expert on socialism, had accused him of "having abolished Marxism" by rejecting historic determinism.[134] Sorel replies: not so. If anyone has "falsified" Marx, it is Engels, "by introducing a philosophy of history which he called dialectic, a philosophy which he has never justified, and which is very difficult to comprehend."[135] In contradistinction, the true Marx, Marx minus Engels, opened up "truly scientific ground"[136] with his conception of a "social mechanism formed by the classes."[137] Yet there is "a great

---

[128]Formes et essence du socialisme (Paris, 1898), being an abridgment of the book listed in the preceding note as well as of a brochure of the same author which, under the title, L'Utopia collettivista, had appeared in Milan, 1898.

[129]To mention some of Sorel's contributions to the Marx debate of that time: "La crise du socialisme" in La Revue Politique et Parlementaire, December, 1898; "Y-a-t-il de l'utopie dans le Marxisme?" in La Revue de Métaphysique et de Morale, March, 1899; "Morale et Socialisme" in Le Mouvement Socialiste, March, 1899; "L'éthique du socialisme" in La Revue de Métaphysique et de Morale, May, 1899. See also chapter 1, notes 21 and 42.

[130]Sorel, preface to Merlino, op. cit. in note 128, p. xxxix. - Sorel's emphasis.

[131]Ibid., p. iii.   [132]Ibid., p. v.

[133]Ibid., p. xlii. - Sorel's emphasis.

[134]Ibid., p. x. - Andler's attack on Sorel: in Revue de Métaphysique et de Morale, September, 1897, p. 657.

[135]Sorel, in op. cit., p. ix - x.

[136]Ibid., p. vii.

[137]Ibid., p. v. - Sorel's emphasis.

indeterminacy in the historic system of Marx:"[138] according to him, the social movement depends on the social cultures, but historical materialism does not help us to determine the exact nature of that dependence; we are given no explanation of how the political conditions and popular sentiments combine to engender the juridical consciousness of a class. All we can do, therefore, is "to borrow indications from the sociological study, indications permitting the man of action to construct the springs to regulate his conduct, and to construct them freely."[139]

If certain Marxists had their way, the proletariat would be concerned exclusively with its own material interests. Fortunately, the most important socialist organization, the social-democratic party of Germany, chose another way: it "makes the effort to appeal to the sentiments of the entire society;" superficially seen, this seems to violate the principle of the class struggle, but the German socialists are nevertheless on the right track, Sorel believes. By stressing the general principles of Truth, Justice and Morality, as postulated by the statute of the "International,"[140] the German party does not merely manage to attract to itself disgruntled, exploited members of the bourgeoisie,[141] but it has hit on "the only means to safeguard the sentiment of justice among the laboring masses." For, "in emancipating itself, the proletariat must emancipate all those who suffer."[142] Thus, while the mechanism of social change, as defined by Marx, is geared to the "material transformation of the conditions of life," the social-democrats, "employing more subtle tactics ... rely on a moral transformation in the manner of making [moral] judgments." Society in its totality is to become a unified moral whole, under the direction of a proletariat that has become ready for the task.[143]

But whereas Marx had assumed that the new justice would be established after the victory of the proletariat, with the advent of a classless society, Sorel, in what is perhaps his most radical departure from the Marxian scheme, takes the view that the new legal concepts must be worked out prior to the victory of socialism: "Experience teaches us that a new culture cannot become efficacious without very long preparation: therefore, the means to realize that new juridical constitution must be developed now, in capitalist society."[144] The implications of this notion are momentous: the "moral transformation" becomes "a juridical question"[145] to be answered by the proletariat, that is, by the class which, in the Marxian system, performs the function of antithesis and could not, therefore, under

---

138 Ibid., p. xi.

139 Ibid., p. xi - xii. - Sorel's emphasis.

140 Ibid., p. xiii - xiv. - Sorel's emphasis.

141 Ibid., p. xvii.   142 Ibid., p. xvi.

143 Ibid., p. xviii - xix. - Sorel uses the term, capable, following Proudhon (De la capacité de la classe ouvrière, 1865). - Sorel's emphasis.

144 Ibid., p. xv.   145 Ibid., p. xix.

capitalist rule, achieve the new synthesis of classless justice. For Sorel, on the contrary, that synthesis is a slow growth anticipating socialist society and the condition for its realization; a synthesis to be worked out, in the daily struggle with the bourgeoisie, by a working class that finds the answers in its proletarian consciousness. But that again implies that proletarian morality is not something to be overcome, to be abolished in the classless stage, but to become the basis of the new society of the producers: the working class is the hero, not merely the victim, of the great drama called the industrial revolution, or, in Marxist terms: the proletariat is — **horribile dictu!** — the "demiurg," not the mere "agent" of the historic process. With Merlino, Sorel comes to reject the notion of "many socialists who, mislead by some utterances torn out of context from the work of Marx, have believed that the political organization is a secondary product of the economic basis."[146] Sorel does not quite dare to turn a famous Marxian dictum upside-down and to say that "It is not the social being of men that determines their consciousness, but, on the contrary, the consciousness of men that determines their being,"[147] but Sorel's assumption that socialist ethics can and must precede socialist economics if there is to be a socialist society at all, can hardly be reconciled with the Marxian view.

It is in connection with the new morality, that piecemeal political reform becomes so important for Sorel. Merlino, he believes, "is right when he maintains that political and economic reforms are indissolubly connected."[148] The growth of the state power in modern society is, in the Marxist view, nothing but the superstructural reaction to the growing intensity of the class struggle, which, in turn, is the result of the growing concentration of capital, as predicted by Marx. But if the Socialists permit this process to develop "automatically," that is, without attempting to control it by political reforms, then the future proletarian state will be just another kind of Leviathan who simply refuses to 'wither away.'[149] This is a remarkable anticipation of certain recent theories distinguishing between democratic socialism on the one hand and "bureaucratic collectivism" or "managerialism" on the other.[150] The economic concentration of power

---

[146]Ibid., p. xxi - xxii.

[147]Karl Marx, **Selected Works** (New York, 1942), Vol. I, p. 356.

[148]Sorel in op. cit., p. xxii.

[149]Ibid.

[150]Both the "Managerialists" (James Burnham) and the "Bureaucratic Collectivists" (Anton Ciliga, **The Russian Enigma,** London, 1940, Dwight Macdonald, **"The End of Capitalism in Germany,"** in Partisan Review, May-June, 1941, and, **"The Root is Man"** in Politics, April, 1946,) - both schools agree that Soviet Russia is not socialist but a "bureaucratic totalitarianism." They find theoretical ammunition in a statement made by Rudolf Hilferding in 1940: "The controversy as to whether the economic system of the Sovial Union is 'capitalist' or 'socialist' seems to me rather pointless. It is neither. It

will not of its own make room for the 'free associations of producers'
living in a 'realm of freedom.' Again and again Sorel will refuse to
believe that a truly socialist legality could be conjured by the proletarian genius out of nothing 'after the event,' that is, following the
overthrow of capitalism. A truly democratic control over the proletarian state, as postulated by Marx in his description of the Paris
Commune, must be preceded by a capitalist state already limited in
power by a series of political and economic reforms.[151] These limitations will be the result, not of some abstract notions about "natural
right," but of the historical "struggle for rights" in which the dominated assert their demands for justice and express them in new institutional forms.[152] As these juridical creations achieve legal status,
they, in turn, enable the class of the ruled to broaden and to deepen
their juridical convictions.

Where are the institutions to be found through which the proletariat can express itself? Sorel commends the Belgian socialists for
their struggle "against the extension of the governmental power" and
for their attempts to steer "the political evolution along libertarian
lines."[153] But, though still professing faith in political action, Sorel
believes that something else holds out a greater promise: "Marx
considers the trade unions to be the first layer of the proletarian
pyramid; those organisms are not meant to last forever; but in their
time they will have served to develop the sentiments of solidarity...
among the workers."[154] Since Sorel had dealt with the trade unions
in his **Avenir** only a few weeks earlier, he only touches on the subject
here, to turn to a discussion of Bernstein's that "the movement is
everything, the goal nothing." Sorel, unlike the Kautskys, is not
shocked. On the contrary: "the great socialist writer has been misunderstood." Since capitalism still has a long way to go, it would be

---

represents a totalitarian state economy to which the economics of Germany and
Italy are driving closer. A state economy...eliminates...the autonomy of
economic laws. It represents not a market but a consumers' economy....
Prices have become symbols of distribution and no longer comprise a regula-
tory factor in the economy....The Marxian sectarian cannot grasp the idea
that the present-day state power, having achieved independence, is...sub-
jecting social forces and compelling them to serve its ends." Rudolf Hilferding,
"State Capitalism or Totalitarian Economy" in **Modern Review**, June, 1947,
pp. 271, 266, 267, 270.

[151]Sorel, **op. cit.**, p. xxii.

[152]"When we are thinking about the future...we actually reason about how
to change the present." **Ibid.**, p. xxiv. About Sorel's notion of "the struggle
for rights," which he had taken over from Rudolf von Ihering's celebrated
work of the same name, cf. Sorel, preface to N. Colajanni, **Le socialisme** in
Matériaux, p. 188; also Michael Freund, **Georges Sorel** (Frankfurt a. Main,
1932),p. 98.

[153]Sorel, **op. cit.**, p. xxii.

[154]**Ibid.**, p. xxv.

idle to evolve a program for the society of the future, — that would be
utopianism. But since "it is imperative to know in which direction we
ought to move," we must inspect "the psychological content of those
institutions which are on the way to their realization; it is necessary
to know the movement in the midst of which we are living .... " Thus
understood, it is possible to say that "movement and final result become identical in our mind."[155] From here it is only one more step
to the notion that the efficacy of a social "myth" does not depend on
its realization.

     Marxism, Sorel believes, stands at the cross-roads: one way
points in the direction of utopia which attracts many a socialist despondent over a dogma which has become "fossilized" under the hands
of the commentators. The other way is that of the "true movement,"
requiring "active participation in practical life, the pursuit of reforms, be they ever so small."[156] Reformism, Sorel insists, does
not preclude revolutionary ardor: in its daily struggle against capitalism, the proletariat "acquires catastrophic notions [about] property ... it can, therefore, accomplish a great historic mission, in that
it confronts society, incessantly, with a new juridical system."[157] As
he will do later in the **Reflections,** Sorel compares the modern proletariat with the Christians of the second century A. D. who "felt called
upon to destroy all the institutions characteristic of pagan society."
Although living in the midst of that society and able to work out their
own way of life in autonomy, those early Christians had still preserved
"the sentiment of their revolutionary role."[158] In the same manner
Sorel's proletariat finds itself in an irrepressible conflict with the
old society "at the same time that it is able to introduce ameliora-
tions into the existing system."[159] Sorel even sees fit to make use of
"a celebrated expression of Nietzche" [sic][160] for his conclusion:
"**The great originality of contemporary socialism consists in** [the]
revaluation of all values by the militant proletariat."[161]

     Sorel too is still at the crossroads: his proletariat is both mili-
tant and democratic, revolutionary and reformist; it is in the old society but not of it; on the other hand, the workers are not yet requested
by Sorel to secede from society, to insulate themselves against the
bourgeois virus by **scission:** violent severance. But the Sorelian
strictures against Marx are approaching an intensity which makes his
cry, "Back to Karl Marx" sound rather forced; it is a strangely
changed Marx to whom Georges Sorel proposes to return. Through
the Marxist varnish of the picture we can see emerging the old features of the moralist Proudhon.

----

[155]Ibid., p. xxvii. - Sorel's emphasis.
[156]Ibid., p. xxxix.   [157]Ibid., p. xliv.
[158]Ibid., p. xliii.   [159]Ibid., p. xliv.
[160]Ibid., p. xlii.
[161]Ibid., p. xlv. - Sorel's emphasis.

The Missing Links

For three years Sorel hammers away at his new thesis; in article after article he insists that Marx was a moralist **par excellence**, that socialism was the movement of the proletariat, not a theory about it, revolution and reform were one and the same. A few examples may illustrate Sorel's indefatigable syncretism:

"M. Merlino's book does not propose a new social doctrine ... the work done by Marx will not be in vain, quite on the contrary.... A few comrades and I try to unearth the treasures ... buried in his books.... Socialism is not a doctrine, a sect, a political system; it is the emancipation of the working classes organizing themselves, educating themselves and creating new institutions."[162]

"Marx ... never failed to bring out the juridical side of the social wars. In his view, the modern class struggle aims at a transformation of the **principles** of legislation." It is a case of "right rising against right; not merely a conflict of interests." We must separate what Marx said about the struggle of the proletariat against capitalism, from the theory of the "**mission of the proletariat,** which plays a decisive role in his doctrine, a mission with an essentially moral aim."[163]

It becomes evident to all the world, Sorel believes, that "each historic period reveals, not a uniformity, but a diversity of co-existing economic forms.... If this view is accepted, all that is utopian in the Marxist theses disappears [and] it is no longer necessary to look for problematic laws regulating history...." The question arises: what is socialism, if not the search for the society, described by Engels in such "sybillinic" terms? "The answer seems simple to me: socialism is the labor movement, it is the revolt of the proletariat against the institutions of the masters, it is the organization, at the same time economic and ethical, which we see emerging under our own eyes, to struggle against the traditions of the bourgeoisie."[164]

The Sorelian doctrine of the social myth, already adumbrated in his **Socrates,**[165] makes its second, still tentative appearance in an essay on socialist ethics of the same year: "Little does it matter ... whether communism is realized sooner or later," or that we do not know how many stages must precede it: "the essential thing is our

[162]Sorel, **"La crise du socialisme"** in **Revue Politique et Parlementaire,** December, 1898, p. 612.

[163]Sorel, **"Morale et socialisme"** in **Le Mouvement socialiste,** March 1899, p. 209.

[164]Sorel, **"Y-a-t-il de l'utopie dans le marxisme?"** in **Revue de Métaphysique et de Morale,** March, 1899, p. 175.

[165]See chapter 2, p. 50f.

ability to render account of our own conduct. What is called the final goal exists only for our internal life." Once more Sorel gives credit to Merlino for the view that "socialism realizes itself every day;" it comes into its own "as we discover what socialist conduct is and as we learn how to master the institutions." We will have socialism "to the extent that a socialist ethics takes shape in our consciousness and in our actions."[166]

In a postscript written in 1914 Sorel explains that the theses developed by him in the preface to Merlino's book "arose in a very evident way, from the conditions created by the Dreyfus case in the middle of the year 1898." Disregarding the advice of some of their leaders who believed the scandal was a strictly bourgeois family affair and of no interest to the proletarian cause, the socialist and anarchist workers of Paris joined the "Dreyfusards" with so much vigor that Sorel could, for a moment, see the proletariat as the spearhead of the democratic drive. "I was grievously mistaken," Sorel confesses.[167] The popular coalition against the reactionary forces of army and church turned out to be "the anti-church." Directed by "Jacobine" politicians, the "radical" regime seduced many an ambitious socialist; it threateded to annex and tame the proletarian ally. The time had come to draw the line.

In 1899, however, Sorel was still a democrat and the piece introduced by the remark just quoted is one of several that "echo my illusion."[168] One of them contains, however, what Sorel thinks is the first indication of his doctrine of the myth,[169] although he does not yet employ that term. Briefly, Sorel's "discovery" amounts to this; The concept of the class struggle, according to Sorel the key to Marx's system, — that concept **simplifies** "the excessive complexity of the social structure." Yet, without the division into two camps, proletarian and bourgeois, socialist propaganda would be clearly impossible. Therefore, the Marxists "cannot permit themselves to subordinate their class conceptions to the facts.... Without [assuming] the dichotomy it would be impossible for them to make the **revolutionary idea** understood, just as without the description of an ideal future they could not fill the mass mind with the notion of the **moral catastrophe.** It is one thing to study social science, another **to form the consciousness of people."**[170]

Marx was a passionate man who could never separate in his own mind the scientific from the educational approach. Often he managed to express his abstractions figuratively, in form of a historic account

---

[166]Sorel, **"L'éthique de socialisme"** in Revue de Métaphysique et de **Morale,** May, 1899, p. 298.

[167]Sorel, **Matériaux,** p. 173.

[168]**Ibid.**

[169]Sorel, preface to N. Colajanni, **Le socialisme** (Paris, 1900) in **Matériaux,** p. 189, note 2 (added in 1914).

[170]**Ibid.,** p. 188. – Sorel's emphasis.

which, at best, is not more than an artistic device to help us assimilate his idea. A striking example of that method, in the opinion of Sorel, is the famous prophecy of the last-but-one chapter of Das Kapital. "Taken literally, that apocalyptic text, is only of mediocre interest; interpreted as a product of inspiration, as an image designed to form the [proletarian] consciousness, it...illustrates well the principles which Marx thought necessary" to derive the rules of socialist action.[171]

Sorel compares the "generally happy use which Marx made of that social poetry" with the deplorable dogmatism of the epigones for whom the class struggle assumed "the nature of a veritable magic force operating as cunningly as Eduard von Hartmann's Unconscious...."[172]

This then is how Sorel extracts the "essence of socialism" from the Marxian mixture of science and vision: or, to use one of Marx's famous similes: under Sorel's and "his comrades'" prodding, the living substance of the Marxian work will burst, so it was hoped, through its integument of dead dogmatic matter. What is taking place, around 1900, is the process which Sorel will later call The Decomposition of Marxism.[173] That is a title open to misunderstandings: we are tempted to think of a corpse decomposing, and many observers were then indeed convinced that Marxian socialism was dead. But Georges Sorel did not agree; he hoped, at any rate, that it could and would find another lease on life in proletarian, syndicalist organs. To them, he held out his new Marx, — a Marx who had not really intended his elaborated theories to be taken at their face value; a Marx who had not employed images to make his dogma comprehensible, — it was to be the other way around: his doctrines had been only images appealing to the feelings rather than to the ratiocination of his followers....

Three years later, Sorel once more takes up the theme of the myth in his major work on economic questions,[174] a study inspired by Le Play's theory of the social authorities and Proudhon's distinction between the "economic milieu" and production proper. In a later edition of the book, Sorel explicitly links his remarks about the myth both to the past[175] and to the future.[176] "I wonder," Sorel wrote in 1903, "whether it is possible to furnish an intelligible exposition of

---

[171]Ibid., p. 189. - Sorel's emphasis.

[172]Ibid., p.189-190. - Sorel's emphasis. - About Hartmann, cf. Introd. i, p. 17.

[173]Sorel, La décomposition du marxisme (Paris, 1908), 64 p.

[174]Sorel, Introduction à l'économie moderne (Paris, 1903).

[175]He cites what he had written on the Marxist myth in his preface to Colajanni. (Introduction, 2. edition, Paris, 1922, p. 396.)

[176]"In the Reflections on Violence the theory of the myth received a more concise form." Ibid., p. 394, note 1.

the process by which principles are transformed into action, without
resorting to myths." He appeals to the historians of philosophy to
take up the neglected study of the "considerable role which the myths
have played in human thought;" he refers to Plato's use of the myth, a
subject not yet sufficiently elucidated.[177] Having made this suggestion, which, if not original,[178] was still remarkable for its time,
Sorel turns to his special field of interest: the proletarian myth: "I
wonder if we should not treat, as myths, those theories which are no
longer acceptable to the **learned men** of socialism, while held as
'axioms not to be questioned' by the militants." Sorel again advances
his belief that Marx intended his catastrophic theory of history to be
taken "as a myth, illustrating, very clearly, the class struggle and the
social revolution." If this view is accepted, it will, Sorel is convinced,
go a long way toward overcoming the seemingly hopeless predicament
of Marxist socialism: once we can show that "the myths are necessary [for] a social philosophy which refuses to fool itself and to accept as science what is not science — then we can also and unques-
tionably, demonstrate that the **contested theories** are required by
modern revolutionary action;" and at the same time it will probably
be evident that the "learned constructions" of the semi-socialist sociologists are nothing but a bogus science.[179]

Sorel concludes: "The moment may not be far off when it will be
recognized that the old revolutionary socialism is infinitely more
imbued with the spirit of philosophy and closer to science than is the
hyperjuridical socialism of our reformist academicians."[180]

The last illusions of the Dreyfus days are gone: Sorel has lost
all faith in the peaceful reform of capitalism. More and more the notion of proletarian **violence** creeps into his writings. The most powerful weapon of organized labor: the strike, and in particular, the general strike is seen in a new light. In an essay first published in
1900,[181] Sorel already speaks of the strike as "some sort of experimental preview" of the final catastrophe which socialism wants to
bring about.[182] But the experience of class solidarity brought about
by a strike is not limited to labor: the employers too might profit
from it. In the revolutionary tendencies of the proletariat, Sorel sees
a potential "moral force capable of arousing the bourgeoisie from the
slumbers into which prosperity makes people lapse so easily."[183]

---

[177]Ibid., p. 394.

[178]We already noted that Sorel was influenced by Le Bon (Introd. i, note
10), Renan (Chapter 2, p. 48), Alfred Fouillée (Introd. i, note 11 and Chapter 2, p. 51).

[179]Sorel, **Introduction**, p. 396.

[180]Ibid., p. 397.

[181]Sorel, **"Les grèves,"** originally published in **La Science Sociale**, October
and November, 1900, reprinted in **Matériaux**, pp. 395 - 413 as **"Grèves et
droit au travail."** Citations from that reprint.

[182]Ibid., p. 411.   [183]Ibid., p. 412.

The reader of the **Reflections** at once recognizes another feature of that work, a feature more than any other responsible for the impression that Sorel was offering advice indiscriminately to either side. But that impression is erroneous. If Sorel wishes for a vigorous bourgeoisie, it is because he believes that without it, the class struggle would slacken and end in a democratic compromise in which the proletariat was bound to loose all its stamina. And the only class of which Sorel believed most of his life could redeem Western society happened to be the proletariat.

The anti-reformist, anti-political note is even more accentuated in the preface which Sorel wrote for the book edition of the **Avenir**.[184] There we read: "For the workers, the revolution is something quite different than the victory of a party; it is the emancipation of the producers freed from all political tutelage; it is the decomposition of power; the organization of social relations outside of a government of non-workers."[185] We no longer hear of cooperation, of socialism as a "labor movement in a democracy:" the scission is complete. Its symbol has become the total social action: "The general strike then would [no longer] be the tool of a political party, but the conscious revolt of workers fully organized and able to dispense with the counsels of any and each political party."[186]

This is no wishful thinking: when Sorel wrote these lines, revolutionary syndicalism in France as well as in Italy provided him with the facts for his theoretical analysis. The movement was at its peak strength when Sorel published the article which more than anything shows the complete continuity existing between his first, tentative and his final treatment of syndicalism. Written as a supplementary preface to the earlier work[187] in the very year which saw in print the first Italian sketch of the **Reflections,**[188] the article entitled **Revolutionary Syndicalism** states flatly that "the times for revolutions made by politicians are over."[189] The proletariat refuses to submit to a new hierarchy. Reform has lost its spell: not only does it fail to appease the masses, on the contrary: "each time the democrats tried appeasement, the syndicalists intensified their attack, and the most certain result of that experience seems to be, in my opinion, that **the belligerency** [of the proletariat] **increased in the same proportion as the bourgeoisie made peace offerings.**"[190] Besides, the workers only do what the middle class had done when it was in its prime: the industrial revolution achieved by the bourgeoisie was a revolutionary accomplishment untrammeled by any preconceived plans. It was, to use

---

[184]See note 99.

[185]Sorel, **L'avenir** (Paris, 1901), p. vi.

[186]**Ibid.**, p. vii.

[187]See note 99.

[188]See chapter 1, note 91.

[189]1905 Preface to **L'Avenir** in **Matériaux,** p. 59.

[190]**Ibid.**, p. 74. - Sorel's emphasis.

W. Y. Elliot's phrase a "pragmatic revolt."[191] "Why," Sorel asks, "could not the proletariat follow the same road and march forward without imposing on itself any ideal plan?"[192] It is a question put to the Marxist orthodoxy. Theory, all "theories are the offspring of bourgeois reflection."[193] (Sorel hastens to add, in a footnote: "I except here what is essential in Marxism," that is: what Sorel has declared essential.) Sorel does not claim that syndicalist thought, rejecting what is bourgeois theory in Marxism, ought to rely on sheer, instinctive spontaneity. True, Syndicalism is at present vindicating Vico's law of the ricorsi: it is passing through its primitive, barbaric phase, "in which everything is instinct, creative and poetic...." Socialism could not possibly renew the world unless it forms itself in the same fashion.[194] With the passing to time, it will undergo "the evolution prescribed by the laws of Vico: it must rise above instinct, and perhaps that process has already begun;" Sorel mentions the "rejuvenated" Marxism, in other places also referred to as the "new school, represented in France by Lagardelle and Berth," modestly omitting his own name. Syndicalism in its second phase would thus be characterized by conscious action, but it would not try to foretell history, but rather be content to master the facts intellectually as they occur.[195]

Sorel's return to the Viconian theory of catastrophic breakdowns is at the same time a partial rapprochement to the position held by the most orthodox of Marxists, Kautsky, who had maintained all the time that due to its "internal contradictions," capitalism could not be reformed. Sorel now shares that view, but claims that he has given content to an abstract formula: "The general strike expresses Kautsky's thesis in a concrete manner."[196] The elevation — or shall we say, reduction? — of that concept to a myth in the Reflections is already indicated; the final showdown in the social war becomes remote, and at the same time something that is experienced daily, in foro interno: "Each strike, be it ever so limited in scope, is a skirmish in the great battle called general strike. So simple are the associations of ideas in that case that to indicate them to the strikers is enough to turn them into socialists. Today, the need to uphold the idea of war is more imperative than ever...."[197]

All the links are now assembled to complete the chain of the Reflections. In writing the synopsis of ten years of work, Sorel will say with more assurance and in concentrated fashion what he had been accumulating for so long, but he will still be mindful of his own injunction against dogmatic thinking: since scientific principles are altogether absent in his field, it is impossible to arrive at any precision

---

[191]W. Y. Elliott, The Pragmatic Revolt in Politics (New York, 1928).
[192]Sorel, op. cit., p. 65.
[193]Ibid., p. 67.   [194]Ibid., p. 66. Cf. chapter 3, p. 74.
[195]Ibid., p. 67-68.   [196]Ibid., p. 60.
[197]Ibid., p. 61.

and clarity. He goes so far as to counsel against "using language with too much exactness, for it would then be at odds with the fluent character of reality, and therefore misleading."[198] The words are almost identical with those used in the letter thanking Daniel Halévy for the editorial help which transformed still another series of Sorelian essays published in a little-read revue into a well known, famous and infamous book.[199]

---

[198]Ibid., p. 58.
[199]Cf. **Reflections on Violence** (1950 ed.), p. 33.

5. THE MEANING OF VIOLENCE

"We have limited ourselves to defining the historic bearing of the notion of a general strike. We have tried to show that a new culture might spring from the struggle of the revolutionary trade unions against the employers and the State." In these modest words Sorel describes the task which he had set himself in his **Reflections.** They were to remind the modern reader that violence was no residium of the barbaric past, bound to disappear from a peaceful society, but a persistent and decisive fact of social life. Beyond that, Sorel does not claim to have discovered anything new: "our greatest claim to originality consists in our having maintained that the proletariat can emancipate itself without being compelled to seek the guidance of that section of the middle classes which concerns itself professionally with matters of the intellect."[1] Such is Sorel's involved way of saying that the working class ought to work out its own salvation without any help from the intelligentsia.

The "Letter to Daniel Halévy" from which the preceding quotations are taken, was written in 1907.[2] Looking back on his syndicalist phase three years later, Sorel sums up the reasons which led him to pay attention to the fact of proletarian violence. He takes us all the way back to the Dreyfus days again, when "the men of violence played a decisive role ... in forcing through the revision of the trial...."[3] It was the "direct action" of the Anarchist and Allemanist[4] workers which accomplished two things: one the one hand, to intimidate the forces of reaction, on the other, to expose the weakness of the parliamentary socialists. If the conservatives refrained from using the whole power of the state against the Dreyfus coalition, it was because they were afraid of taking on the Men of Violence, who, in the last analysis, made the liberal regime of Waldeck-Rousseau possible.[5]

---

[1] Reflections on Violence (1950), p. 61.

[2] Published in Le Mouvement Socialiste, August 15 and September 15, 1907.

[3] Sorel, "Mes raisons du syndicalisme" in Matériaux d'une théorie du prolétariat (2. ed.), p. 282-283. The piece originally appeared under the title "Confessioni" in Divenire Sociale, Rome, March 1 - May 16, 1910, and as a brochure, with the subtitle, "Comme divenni sindicalista" in July of the same year. The printed French version is a free reconstruction of the original, as Sorel remarks in a note (Matériaux, p. 239-240).

[4] The followers of Jean Allemane, French labor leader who, in 1890, excluded from the Federation of Socialist Workers, founded a new group, named "Socialist Revolutionary Labor Party," but usually called after its leader. They were hostile to parliamentary socialism.

[5] Sorel, "Mes raisons" in Matériaux, p. 282.

But Sorel made it clear both in the book and in the later commentary, that he was not so much interested in the practical achievements which may or may not result from "direct action" as in its effect upon the proletarian mind: in the Reflections he declares that "to examine the effects of violence it is necessary to start from its distant consequences and not from its immediate results.... We should inquire what will result from the introduction of violence into the relations of the proletariat with society."[6] In 1910, he declared himself disinterested in the question "whether direction action should remain the general rule of future coalitions in France." What matters to him is not the material impact of the Dreyfus affair, but how it influenced "the genesis of ideas." An accumulation of historical incidents during that time made it possible to understand the true nature of proletarian violence, previously regarded as an accidental by-product which, at rare intervals, disturbed the normal evolution of the labor movement.[7]

What Sorel did, then, was to look at the phenomenon of social violence and to explain it as well as he could. He was quite conscious of his limitations: "I do not claim that I have, in this book, said everything there is to say about violence, and still less to have produced a systematic theory of violence," he confessed in the introduction to the first edition of the Reflections.[8]

He declared himself satisfied with the role of the observer who refrains from taking sides: "It is not the business of the historian to award prizes for virtue ... or to establish any catechism whatever ... and so I am not at all concerned to justify the perpetrators of violence, but to inquire into [its] function...."[9] But the fervid tenor of his language tells against him: the Reflections are the work of a determined partisan. He knew it too, and said so, on other occasions. Georges Sorel considered himself "a Socialist writer" and openly boasted that he was helping "to ruin the prestige of middle-class culture."[10]

This partisanship does not necessarily impair the value of Sorel's discoveries, but it goes far to explain why he never managed to evolve "a systematic theory of violence." To do that, it was not enough to look at "violence," to analyze its nature, and to point out its importance. We want to know why violence should be discovered as, and elevated to, a prime mover in a society as civilized as France and by a writer as pacific and as middle class as Georges Sorel. In other words: the theory of violence, in order to be comprehensive, must be supplemented by a theory of the theorist of violence, transcending his own, self-imposed limitations. Sorel felt that need dimly; but all he did was to inform us how, under what circumstances he became aware of Violence; he never said why he decided to identify himself with those who practiced it.

[6]Reflections, p. 71.

[7]"Mes raisons" in op. cit., p. 284. — Sorel's emphasis. [8]Reflections, p. 73. [9]Ibid., p. 69-70. [10]Ibid., p. 62.

The problem is not merely one of Sorel's personal psychology: it poses difficulties which will have to be met without the assistance of Sorel, although, if possible, on his own ground. The theory of violence, if it is to be taken seriously, must be more than the private speculation of an isolated thinker: it will have to be corroborated by additional proof, preferably non-political in character. Such evidence would go a long way to convince us that Sorelian doctrines are not merely interesting in themselves, but are expressive of a general, contemporary thought process. The first step would be to establish such a trend. The second, and much more difficult, an inquiry into its significance.

The cognate field of study promising to throw some light upon our subject, is, we suggest, music, in particular the modern opera. Once before a musical analogy served to explain a puzzling cultural phenomenon, when Friedrich Nietzsche drew a parallel between Greek tragedy and Richard Wagner's operatic work.[11] It was a tour de force which should have called forth some appreciative response from the philosopher of the Myth. But Sorel, though much interested in aesthetic problems,[12] did not see fit to mirror his own work in music. Yet, it is surely more than mere coincidence that the Sorelian theory of violence was born precisely when a new, veristic style of violence conquered the world of operatic make-believe, at first in Italy (Leoncavallo and Mascagni), with Germany and France following suit. The Karl Marx of the musical Sorels was, of course, Wagner: in both instances the rebels tried to reassert their independence from "the master," while assimilating from his work what suited them. They got rid of the system, while retaining the idea of the class struggle and the mobility of the Wagnerian orchestra, respectively. But the analogy shall not be pressed. Not the similitude of style concerns us here, although the evolution of the contemporary music toward a dissonant and polytonic "pluralism" is once more suggestive of Sorel. The point at issue is, however, not the violent expression of post-Marxian,

---

[11]In The Birth of Tragedy from the Spirit of Music (1871), already cited in chapter 2 in connection with Sorel's Socrates.

[12]See Sorel, "Esthétique et psychophysique" in Revue Philosophique, Tome XXIX, 1890; "L'évolution moderne de l'architecture" in La Revue Scientifique, 4. Serie, Tome III, 1895; "La valeur sociale de l'art" in Revue de Metaphysique et de Morale, May 1901; "Le mystère de la Charité de Jeanne d'Arc de Charles Péguy" in L'Action Française, April 14, 1910; "L'Otâge de Paul Claudel" in L'Independance, July 15, 1911; "Charles Péguy" in La Ronda I, April 1, 1919; see also Sorel's colloquies on "Art and Artists" in Jean Variot, Les propos de Georges Sorel (Paris, 1935), pp. 171-249, dealing with novels, plays and operas. His musical taste was conservative and exacting: he detested Massenet and Meyerbeer, he admired, with reservations, Wagner, he loved "the great Verdi," especially the last Verdi of Otello and Falstaff; of the moderns of his time, he mentions kindly Debussy. Beyond that point in musical development Sorel did apparently not go.

post-Wagnerian feeling, but the spirit that informs it. Since music proper lends itself to almost any kind of misinterpretation, we do better to consult the texts which the composers chose for their librettos. We shall single out two works of the late Richard Strauss, whose veristic period closely coincided with the genesis of Sorel's theory of violence. The selection is not arbitrary, since, whatever one may think of **Salome** (1905) and **Elektra** (1909), both operas, or, rather, dramas set to music, are, by general consensus typical of the whole period.

The Quick and the Dead

Oscar Wilde's dramatization of the death of John the Baptist[13] was denounced as an offense to public morality, because it glorified perversion (necrophilia); its performance met with many obstacles. The Straussian score made matters even worse: to the first audiences, it seemed to amplify the morbid, decadent, sensationalist elements of the original beyond endurance; the one act opera accordingly was banished from such distinguished stages as the Metropolitan Opera in New York. Today, the whimsical young princess can embrace the severed head of her unwilling prophet lovingly without our being shocked; we even may discern a moral thread in the apparently amoral if not openly immoral story of her amorous girations around the cistern-dungeon of the raucous saint.

Vindications of Strauss' heroine have been attempted before, without much success: her final savage monologue conveyed to some an erring soul touched, and redeemed by genuine love: the murdered moralist has won his battle after all. But this solution is too simple, and it is not borne out by the music which proclaims the triumph of the murderess; if there are in her funeral song any trembling undertones, they only serve to humanize, but not to moralize the struggle between lust and ascetism. If the story contains any moral at all, we must look for it elsewhere; from the two protagonists we must turn to the chorus of the tragedy.

In appraising and commenting upon the dramatic action and its agents, the chorus represents the common sense of public, average morality. Now in Wilde's play the chorus role of passing moral judgment is given to a figure, which, unlike most choruses, steps forward in the end to execute it. By abruptly calling in his soldiers to put Salome to death, her stepfather Herod, after long brooding over the crime which he helped to perpetrate, cuts short the agonizing trance of Salome, restoring, by his intervention, a sense of public decency and justice. If his decision strikes us more by his brutality than by its rather tardy justice, it is because the judge from which it comes, is very strange indeed: conventional morality is here asserted by a tyrant prince who has himself committed fratricide and incest, and who had been coveting

---

13Matthew 14, 1-11.

his wife's own daughter. Yet, it is he who finally redraws the line almost obliterated in the course of the dramatic action, between good and
evil, licit and illicit, violence and order. To be sure: he acts for his
own safety, superstituously afraid as he is of the hoary man of God.
He did not hesitate to jail the irksome preacher, but he is not bold enough
to silence him for good, and when the Princess Salome reveals that she
has no such inhibition, his rage against her is the typical dislike we
feel against those who do have the courage of our own concealed intentions. But his slowly mounting indignation has a genuine ring all
the same: in some submerged depths of his corrupted, neurasthenic
nature, the old sinner really respects the prophet. Hence his frantic efforts to persuade the Princess not to take him, Herod, at his royal
word. When he implores her "to be reasonable," his own incoherence
becomes almost moving. At the end of his wits, he concedes defeat,
but it is this defeat that generates in him the will to murderous destruction. It is the last resort of an exasperated reason which has given up
all hope in the efficacy of rational intercourse: It is indeed the ultima
ratio which is said to be the king's, when all the means of peaceful
litigation are exhausted. Violence, although approved in its communal
form of war by the collective moral conscience, meets with severe
moral censure when it takes the form of individual action as with Herod;
and yet his command to do away with Salome, though technically a judicial murder, Herod's regal status notwithstanding, may be looked upon as a vicarious private act committed in the public interest. There
is no doubt about it: when the curtain falls, we feel that, in some way,
the world has been set right again. If this feeling does not quite alle-
viate the deep uneasiness of the experience, the reason is that though
the forces of good seem to triumph in the end, its agents in the drama
do not live to see it. Indeed, both representatives of decency, the hapless young lieutenant, Narraboth, who tries to warn the Princess, and
the prophet himself, are annihilated in the struggle; retribution seems
to be a family affair: justice can claim as little credit for the punish-
ment of evil as the police for any gang murder that took place in the
underworld. Violence has failed to prove its moral alibi convincingly.

That is no longer so in Richard Strauss' next drama of nocturnal
bloodshed. His Elektra shifts the scene from hellenistic Judaea to pre-
classical, archaic Greece; but the change is not so much apparent in
the musical style (which attempts to be more monumental than the
sinuous, vibrating Salome); it is the ethical direction that has become
more assured, and at the same time easier to grasp: the Mykenian
night is darker than the moonlit hour in Herod's palace, but the dawn
is also brighter; two lives have to be taken, and though the deed be
good, it still is done with much low cunning, stealthily. But for the first
time, the avengers have clean hands. Their father had been slain by
their own mother and her lover. The line seems clearly drawn between
those who are evil, and those who are good. But again, matters are

not quite as simple. For whereas in Salome all figures in the drama
were eccentrics, extreme cases, in Elektra the arch-villain, Aegisthes,
who has murdered Agamemnon, is a coarse, but plain good fellow, almost likeable in his besotted folksiness. And this characterization,
made even more explicit by the guileless Bavarian yodeling in the
score, is deliberate and has a definite meaning. No longer are the
worlds of common sense and common place synonymous: Herod,
although himself not completely normal, could still represent the side
of normalcy and shocked propriety. Now, on the contrary, the moral
law is being broken by a philistine and upheld by two outcasts: the ill-
used Elektra, and Orestes, her young brother, who returns from lowly
exile. Even more significant is the case of Elektra's sister, young
Chrysothemis who is not only innocent of any crime but shockingly
conventional: when she refuses to join the conspiracy against the guilty
couple, expressing instead the wish to get married and have children,
the older sister knows no bounds in her contempt; in her own, somber
dream, there is no place for humdrum satisfactions. The ethical responsibility lies with the hero and the heroine, determined on an act
of violent grandeur against a petty murderer, an act in which they can
expect no help from average society. The tables are reversed: one
more comment will help to make fully clear how far the revolution of
the musical New School against the founding father has progressed.
In Wagner's Ring, the demi-god and superman, Siegfried, is singled
out by Wotan to transcend his own morality, an undertaking of which
the divinity itself despairs. Siegfried is slain, but joining him in proud
self-immolation, Brunhild, the heroine, precipitates the Twilight of the
Gods: the transformation of all values is at hand. We may presume,
that Siegfried became the main godhead of the new Walhalla; his amoralism no longer the fulcrum of a revolutionary protest, is now a routine
respectability, eagerly taken up by all the mortal Siegfrieds of the new,
triumphant middle class. Aegisthes, who inherited the bed and board of
the war-weary chieftain Agamemnon, is that heir: the perfect bourgeois,
formerly perhaps the major domus who enjoys the full regalia of a
power which he had long coveted, enjoying it, however, with the uneasy
conscience of the upstart who made good. The comparison between
him and a Siegfried worn by time and habit, is not as farfetched as it
will seem at first glance: musicians who know both their Wagner and
their Strauss will at once recognize the strikingly Siegfriedian characterization of the happy slave driver, Aegisthes: a borrowing of which
Strauss almost certainly was unaware, but which was none the less a
feat of psychological transvaluation worthy of a genius: the war profit-
eer become respectable, the dashing fellow who still swaggers as of
old and hums the forceful scales of Siegfried forging his good sword.
And around him, hovers a new generation, unintelligible to him, therefore adjudged treacherous, immoral, criminal. They murder him! His
final outcry is that of a worthy man surprised by so much black

ingratitude. Had there been violence in his own past? But that was
long ago, and what would happen to authority if every disgruntled youth
took it upon himself to change the law?

To this, the man of violence, Orestes — for in the act he has become a man — could answer that he and Elektra acted under duress.
For had his sister not attempted to come to an understanding with her
mother, the diseased and conscience-stricken Klytemnaestra? Indeed,
the children did not move until all arts of peaceful litigation had been
tried, all means of rational exchange had been thoroughly exhausted.
The dialogue between the mother and the daughter is perhaps the best
scene Strauss has ever written, which is saying much; it is known that
he composed it not less than three times before he was contented.
Compared with this stupendous music which penetrates through layer
after layer of the human soul to probe the blackest depths of human
suffering, deceit, abominations and endearments, compared with this,
all that precedes it is a feeble prelude, and the stormy sweep of the
finale merely grand opera. It is, literally, the last word that is here
spoken between enemies so close to one another that they both divine
what each one leaves unsaid. And then again, the simplest words go
wrong, they no longer convey a truth, because with language become
such a subtle instrument, truth too becomes bewilderingly subtle. There
is no longer one, but many truths, or is there none at all? Only a nought
that kept you wide awake, night after night? You could not see or grasp
it, and yet, something was there, gnawing at your heart and sucking it
dry, mercilessly. Are there no means, to put a stop to this? cries
Klytemnaestra. There must be means. And, jubilant, Elektra: Yes,
mother: strong means. An offering, to satisfy the greedy gods. And
out she blurts: yourself, it is yourself that you must sacrifice. De-
spairing of all words, afraid of murdering the mother, she attempts to
hypnotize her into suicide. But Klytemnaestra, although a mere shadow
of her former self, is still a formidable foe: she will not surrender to
semantic violence, the intellectual poison that serves him who can no
longer use the dagger.[14] Thus the conversation ends, the last attempt
to settle matters by debate has failed.

But without the attempt the following explosion would remain completely meaningless. For what takes place is not a blind act of destruction, an assault on some unknown, uncomprehended kind of reason,
but an act of liberation, the revolt of reason against values shared and
understood only too well. It is indeed a family affair, whether enacted
under the walls of Mycenae or between two classes or whole nations

---

[14] "It is customary to say of ... periods of corruption that they are milder....
But ... I only grant so much — namely, that cruelty now becomes more refined.... The men of the period of corruption are witty and calumnious; they
know that there are other ways of murdering than by the dagger and the am-
bush...." Nietzsche, The Joyful Wisdom, transl. by Thomas Common (New
York, 1924), No. 23, p. 64.

arraigned one against the other — the parties to the struggle nearly always belong to the same world, sharing the same values, even if they disagree about their meaning.[15] And even when the argument breaks up in fisticuffs, it still remains a dispute about something; it is hardly ever mere pugnaciousness. That this is so, may be seen by the very effort necessary to break up the great community of values; before we can think of destroying what refuses to agree with us, we must first commit acts of intellectual mayhem: classes, nations have to become diabolical to one another, and the storm trooper can be inhuman only after being taught to look upon his victims as subhumans. Elektra and Orestes too could not have touched their mother unless convinced that she had sunken to the level of the beasts. Or, rather, by her association with Aegisthes, she had lowered herself to the social level of those who can be slain with impunity. If not for the queen's loss of caste, she might have been forgiven her great crime by the avenging children.

Violence thus understood is not essentially in opposition to benevolence, but its extremity: unwillingness to accept mere pretense for the genuine article. Violence is not essentially opposed to reason, but the last means of achieving a new, "better" kind of reason. What Strauss and Sorel, the composer and the writer, had in common was that they were products but not representatives of decadence: while working in the medium and within the limitations of their time, both the musician and the social thinker were too healthy specimens as to succumb to the debilitating influence that prompted them. They had a right to say what Nietzsche had said of himself: "Agreed that I am a decadent, I am also the very reverse.... I placed myself in my own hands, I restored myself to health.... A typically morbid nature cannot become healthy at all, much less by his own efforts. On the other hand, to an intrinsically sound nature, illness may even act as a powerful stimulus to life, to an abundance of life."[16]

Our musical examples could be amplified from many other sectors of artistic creation; Sorel's Reflections were paralleled by similar convulsions in contemporary literature, poetry and painting: futurism (which Sorel despised)[17] and expressionism are only two names for the great anxiety that heralded the crisis. An entire civilization stirred uneasily, not yet quite ready, but preparing to come to blows with itself. Fast approaching the point where debate ceased to be meaningful, the Western world began to shed its former values — not because people wanted to live without any values, for that is impossible, but because the new social facts defied traditional interpretation. There

15For instance, the religious wars of the 16th and 17th centuries brought so much misery to Europe, not because the foes spoke different languages, but precisely because they argued about a common intellectual heritage.

16Nietzsche, Ecce Homo transl. by Clifton P. Fadiman, p. 6-7 in The Philosophy of Nietzsche, The Modern Library (New York, 1937).

17See Sorel's remarks against Marinetti and cubism in chapter 7, pp. 189 and 190.

seemed to be a pressing need to remove forcefully what would not yield
to reason. If there was to be debate at all, it seemed to be in need of
a new platform first. Destruction of the tumbled-down old scaffold
would not be the vandalism of "external proletariats,"[18] but an act of
conservation; not an invasion, but a break-out from the catacombs.
There will be no final cataclysm, but there will be partial breakdowns
which demand alertness and firm intervention, lest the true barbarians
come and scatter the new building stones among the wreckage of the old.

Limitations

If we should grant Sorel that he ennobled the term, Violence, so
that we no longer regard it as a synonym for Evil, we would have gone
just as far as the philosopher of the Reflections went himself. To do
for him what his good sense or intuition vetoed, that is, to make Violence a synonym for Virtue, would lead to results not only alien, but
completely unacceptable to the Sorelian. He will grant us that men
may resort to violence in order to restore imperiled absolutes, but he
will deny in the same breath, that such action makes an absolute of
violence. He will remind us that Sorel himself confined himself to
treat of violence as a phenomenon pertaining to a distinct social class,
the proletariat; as a philosophical pluralist he could not well claim for
that one class a monopoly of goodness; all he could assert without vio-
lation of his code, was that each class must choose its proper absolutes,
and that his own allegiance to the proletariat was his personal decision.
We also know that he did not at all reject the possibility that proletarian
violence might well result in a strengthening of the bourgeois will to
resist — a prospect not at all displeasing to Sorel.[19]

This position, merely sketched in Sorel's work, is most elab-
orately stated by Pareto. Violence is something approved or disap-
proved of, according to the varying and fluctuating interests involved.
As seen from the ruling class, "insurrection was legitimate against
kings and oligarchies; it is never [held to be] legitimate against 'the
people'."[20] Since indeed there is a widespread sentiment "that social
stability is a good thing," and since "organized society would fall to
pieces...if, the moment a large or small group ceased to be satisfied
with certain norms...it flew to arms to abolish them," the ruling class

---

[18]In the Toynbeeian sense.

[19]"Everything may be saved, if the proletariat, by their use of violence,
manage to re-establish the division into classes, and so restore to the middle
class something of its former energy; that is the great aim towards which the
whole thought of men...must be directed." Reflections (1950), p. 113.

[20]Vilfredo Pareto, Mind and Society [Trattato] di Sociologia generale,
Firenze, 1916; French ed., 1917-19 , transl. by Andrew Bongiorno and Arthur
L. Livingston, edited by Arthur L. Livingston, (New York, 1935), vol. IV. p.
1526, § 2182.

may claim to defend more than just itself when it enlists against potential rebels all kinds of "living faiths" (Sorel's myths). They "may be
useful within certain limits, and have in fact proved to be so, as absurd
as they may be from the scientific standpoint."[21]

Insofar as Sorel's theory of proletarian violence not only presupposes but thrives upon forceful retaliation by the ruling class, Pareto
would deny that it reflects the actual situation, for he writes of "theories
designed to justify the use of force by the governed" that they "are almost always combined with theories condemning the use of force by
the public authority."[22] In turn, proletarian violence is termed illegal
by the governments. "The strikers might answer, and in fact sometimes do, that they are using illegal violence because they are cut off
from using the legal variety. If the law were to constrain people [the
employers] by use of legal violence to give them [the workers] what
they demand, they would not need to resort to illegal violence." Pareto
seems to relish using the terms, legal and illegal violence, in close
conjunction and without expressing any moral preference, because a
few lines later he repeats: "People who use illegal violence would
ask for nothing better than to be able to transmute it into legal violence."[23] The "salient point" is neither the legality nor the morality
of violence, but its utility. In the Paretian scheme of things the dispute
concerns "the relative merits of shrewdness and force, and to decide
it in the sense that never, never, not even in the exceptional case, is
it useful to meet wits with violence, it would be necessary first to show
that the use of cunning is always, without exception, more advisable
than the use of force."[24] But that depends entirely on the relative
proportion of mobile and stabilizing elements in the decisive classes,[25]
and, therefore, "one cannot assert in general that stability is always
beneficial or that change is always beneficial." Violence is neither an
absolute summum bonum nor a summum malum: "Every case has to
be examined on its particular merits, and the utility and the detriment
appraised to see whether the first overbalances the second, or vice
versa."[26] The quest after a principle of "right" is hopeless: "The
classes that have the greater strength, intelligence, ability, shrewdness, take the lion's share." The rest is illusory, mere subjectivism:
"Every individual certainly has his own principle for a division [of the
social spoils] that would seem ideal for him. But such a principle is
nothing more than an expression of his individual sentiments and interests...."[27]

Sorel could have no quarrel with Pareto's exposition; indeed, his
own philosophy imposed on him indentical beliefs as to the relativity of

21Ibid., p. 1527, § 2184. 22Ibid., p. 1527, § 2185. 23Ibid., p. 1530, § 2189.
24Ibid., p. 1530-1531, § 2190. 25Ibid., pp. 1531-1536, §§ 2190-2194.
26Ibid., p. 1536, § 2195. — Pareto here approaches closely Bentham whom
he loves to ridicule.
27Ibid., Vol. III, p. 962-963, § 1509.

all historic "right." But he was also the great moralist, and it is here
that he diverges from Pareto — and from his own precepts. Like Karl
Marx, whom he praised for it, Sorel did not always obey his own injunctions; he did not always avoid the impression that violence should
indeed be considered as a summum bonum for the proletariat. He may
be questioned on that point, on his own premises. Violence, for Sorel,
is not an end in itself; he never advocated violence for the mere sake
of violence. It is a means, to keep the body politic intact. But if this
doctrine is accepted, for the sake of argument, it follows that it does
not necessarily apply at all times. There may be situations in which
violence would appear not only superfluous but positively detrimental
to the proletarian interest; for instance, in case the condition of the
working class has radically changed. Sorel quite obviously assumes
the permanence of the specific kind of class relations he found in his
time; by absolutizing the class struggle and its epiphenomenon, proletarian violence, he treated as a continuum and absolutum what is,
on the strength of his own tenets, only a passing phase. In this point,
Pareto, who is frequently accused of the same sin, is the much more
consistent, if less enthusiastic and attractive thinker.[28]

6. OLD ACCOUNTS SETTLED

With the **Reflections on Violence** Sorel's life work was done. At least, that seems to be the agreed judgment of posterity. But Sorel continued to produce reviews, articles, and books, for fifteen more years, from 1906, through war and revolutions, until 1921, one year before his death. During that period, his mind was not stagnant; on the contrary, twice he radically changed his political allegiance: away from syndicalism to a premature national socialism, and back again to the belief in proletarian internationalism.

His publicly stated views on the two revolutionary movements of our time will concern us later, together with the question of Sorel's influence. The study of his work, limited to the **genesis** of the Sorelian mind, would be at an end, if not for the fact that some of his later works were actually conceived and even published, in a rudimentary form, prior to 1906. They are, therefore, to be considered as belated, yet legitimate, expressions of Sorel's formative period. As such, two books and three essays will be treated here, all of them products of Sorel's most fruitful years, from 1906 to 1909.

Stylizations and Images

Through all of Sorel's writings we may see the engineer at work checking his tools: the story of his quest for a consistent methodology runs through his entire oeuvre like one of those desert rivers which appears and disappears and reappears again.

The **Introduction to Modern Economics** has already been touched upon on two occasions;[1] the third arises now, since that work is the link in the methodological chain connecting Sorel's **Vico** with Sorel's **Renan**.

"Three rules" we read, "seem to me to be fundamental for the scientific study of social phenomena...." The first: "All classifications, all the relations which we establish between phenomena as well as the significant aspects under which the facts present themselves, depend on the practical end which we pursue...."[2] What sociology needs is "to adopt, on the outset, an openly subjective attitude;" it must know what it wants to do; it must subordinate all its research to the kind of solution it desires to recommend. After having thus declared himself for a pragmatic sort of coherence theory, Sorel goes on to say that "socialism offers the great advantage that it approaches all questions in a well determined spirit, it knows where it wants to go;...at

---

[1]In chapter 3, p. 89, and chapter 4, p. 121.

[2]"Observations genérales" in Introduction a l'économie moderne, (1. edition, Paris, 1903), cited from the revised 2. edition (Paris, 1922), p. 384.

any rate," Sorel adds, "as long as the labor movement brings sufficient pressure to bear" [on its leaders]. If socialism seems of late to be going astray, the reason is, that it has begun, like sociology, to think of itself as above the economic conditions: it has become idealistic.[3]

The second rule commands us to treat social facts not as the solid and unchangeable objects of Greek epistomology, but rather as "nebulae, changing their position, their aspects and dimensions every instant." It is the nebulosity of social facts that leads us to believe of them "whatever we wish"; objects will be represented by way of "projections which recall, by their clumsy, arbitrary design, medieval maps."[4] There are, of course, methods of separating the essential from the accidental, but the fact remains that there is not a formula without an equally convincing contradiction.

There is only one way out: "to abandon the old Greek method, patterned after the requirements of geometry, and to try to attain reality, mobility and continuity." We must, in other words, abandon Hegel for Bergson. Sorel finds Bergson's strictures against traditional philosophy "particularly applicable to sociology."[5] The human mind can overcome the obstacle by a device which is as safe as it is simple: Our study of social phenomena must be an art. It sees the facts "against a background of what may be called stylized projections, so arranged as to give the impression of being auxiliary realities, each one possessing its proper principle of life, order, development." The social facts thus will be wrapped up in "systems of images," none of which, to be sure, has any absolute value, because certain "stylized projections" may be very helpful in one case, and absolutely useless in another.[6] One might despair of the efficacy of the method, were it not for the evidence of its successful operation in the arts: good painters and sculptors "know how to discover aspects which will lend themselves to stylization" with the net result that "the tension of immobility evokes the clear impression of mobility." This artifice is so old as to make us wonder why the sociologists did not make use of it.[7] "The method of imagining motion in motionless tension is all the more successful when the changes are more regular" or more likely to suggest the existence of a law; "or when they are, as it is sometimes said, more rhythmical." Why make risky guesses about the future, when all we have to do is to examine the facts at hand? When Bernstein coined his phrase about the movement being everything, he was more of a philosopher than he knew.[8]

Third rule: We cannot help resorting to ideological constructions,[9] but we must beware of idealism which is nothing but "lies and deception."[10] To be rejected: all conclusions that have not as their object

---

[3]Ibid., p. 386. [4]Ibid., p. 387.
[5]Ibid. [6]Ibid., p. 388. — Sorel's emphasis.
[7]Ibid., p. 389. [8]Ibid., p. 390.
[9]Ibid. [10]Ibid., p. 392.

"institutions, usages, empiric rules well grounded in, and formed by clearcut practice." Vico showed the way which we must follow.[11]

Return to Renan

If some philology-minded student of Sorel should feel called upon to investigate the question: what writer did exert the greatest and most lasting influence on our protean author, he should have no trouble in finding the right answer. Ernest Renan did more for Georges Sorel than the one book in which his name is in the title would suggest; citations from Renan's writings overcrowd the pages of each and any of Sorel's works, crowding out even Proudhon, who, when all is said, must still be called his supreme master. Why this preponderance of Renan, even at times when other figures, such as Marx, seem to attract Sorel's main interest? It has been said that "Sorel looked upon Renan as the personification of that republican France which stood between French Caesarism and the slowly rising France of mass democracy...."[12] The traditionalist, Sorel, could indeed find an affinity with Renan, "the greatest representative of the old conservative-liberal elite"[13] which entered the "graveyard of aristocracies"[14] in the wake of the Dreyfus revolution.

But if Sorel was strongly influenced by the political and social attitudes of Renan, it was even more the historian of the **Life of Jesus** and **The Origins of Christianity**, who both attracted and repelled Sorel, the passionate student of historic origins and ends in general, and of religious movements in particular. It was this aspect of Renan's work that early stirred Sorel's curiosity about Judaea, Greece and Rome. This great debt, frequently acknowledged by Sorel, cannot be cancelled by Sorel's equally frequent rejection of Renan's own conclusions.

The question of originality need not hold us up. Was it Renan who directed Sorel to his studies of the Bible and Socrates, or did Sorel turn to the writings of Renan because they happened to deal with the problems relevant to Georges Sorel? That question may remain unanswered. What matters is the role which Renan occupied in Sorel's intellectual development. It may be suggested that Renan served him as a foil; but the same could be argued for Karl Marx, and to a lesser

---

[11]Ibid., p. 390.

[12]Michael Freund, **Georges Sorel** (Frankfurt a. Main, 1932), p. 20.

[13]Ibid. See Sorel, "Les 'Cahiers de Jeunesse de Renan'" in Le Mouvement Socialiste, May, 1907: "Renan defines well the aim of that grave conservative oligarchy" (p. 475); "I believe that La monarchie constitutionnelle en France and La Réforme intellectuelle et morale are [Renan's] most remarkable writings" (Ibid., p. 476). The last-named work is discussed below, on p. 134 of this chapter, and in chapter 8, note 8.

[14]The term is Vilfredo Pareto's, see **Mind and Society** (New York, 1935), Vol. III, § 2053, p. 1430.

extent, for Proudhon: their ideas were the matrix out of which Sorel lifted what he needed for his own purpose. But whereas he continued to be fond of Proudhon (although taking him to task for his rationalistic residues[15]), while he retained a basic respect for Marx even after he had made him over radically in his own Sorelian image, — his attitude toward Renan became increasingly embittered, until, after many asides, he finally devoted to him a whole book marked by an iconoclastic harshness.[16] Nothing is easier than to say that Sorel turned against the older man precisely because he was so indebted to him: that the act of liberation had to be so violent because what bound him to Renan was so much stronger than all other ties. But Sorel did not really expel Renan from his own system; he merely transformed him from a foil into a counterfoil. He did not actually attempt to exorcise Renan — he needed him as a perpetual reminder of everything he, Sorel, no longer wished to be. Sorel seems to exclaim, pointing at the author of the sentimental romance[17] about Jesus: there, but for the grace of Marx, goes Georges Sorel. Hence his reluctant recognition, his outbursts alternating between praise and condemnation. Renan's role in the life of Sorel was to play Dr. Jekyl to a redeemed Mr Hyde afraid of a relapse. And it may well be that his fear was justified after all, and that, while turning Renan "upside down," while viewing historic phenomena as collective rather than individual acts, Sorel had become the author of a twentieth century romance in which the hero was played by an entire group, the proletarian generators of a new religion called, by Sorel, "the morality of the producers." That proletariat was presented with a myth by Georges Sorel, — but what if the proletariat should itself turn out to be a myth? By 1950, the capacity of "the producers" for free self-expression is no longer an article of the intellectual credo; the Sorelian faith in the creative genius of the proletariat has not been borne out by the events. Political and administrative manipulation, not the "institutions of the working class," determine the fate of the new society. Perhaps Sorel had the right notion about the true character of his producers after all and merely failed to draw the last conclusion. He wanted the syndicalist movement to be "anti-political," meaning that it should shun "politics," not that it was to forego political action of its own. But it is just possible that the laboring man if left to his own devices —

---

[15]See chapter 4, p. 94 f.

[16]Sorel "is terribly harsh with Renan. The basic insincerity of that Breton with the Gascon atavism, his perpetually equivocal insinuations, his malicious double-entendres, his beautiful phrases flavored with a vague, honeyed and sugared religiosity, his idealistic galimatias — that historian of Christianity, who definitely understood nothing of Christianity, has been spared nothing...." Edouard Berth, reviewing Sorel's Système historique de Renan in Le Mouvement Socialiste, August 15 and September 15, 1907, p. 187.

[17]Sorel, Le Système historique de Renan (Paris, 1906), pp. 34 and 61. Subsequently called Renan.

which he never is — becomes "anti-political" in the full sense of the word, that is: indifferent to all collective action. It has been said, in connection with a great English writer of proletarian background, "that the aesthetic genius of the working class, when it is occasionally released, may be anti-political, religious, ardently concerned with an inner life and even esoteric."[18] Omit the word "aesthetic" from the statement, and it would be Sorel with a vengeance. It would also be a vindication of the individualist Renan.

Psychological and Scientific History

The Historic System of Renan "incorporates what good there was in an old book of mine about the Bible," Sorel informs friend Croce.[19] Again, Sorel sets the heavy machinery of exegetics in motion. This time he follows Renan in reassigning the Fourth Gospel to a later phase of Christian history: he believes it to be contemporary with, if not a product of, the Montanist movement (second century, A. D.).[20] However, Sorel is unwilling to give up without a fight his theory which makes the gospel according to St. John not only the most authentic, but also the earliest record of Christ. And so he insists that "the Montanists obviously did not introduce the Fourth Gospel into the Church," but rather that "they prodiguously enhanced the importance of a little book hardly studied prior to their time."[21] According to Sorel, this "little book" was "probably an ancient Hebrew document, written a few years after the Passion of the Lord and translated into Greek at a much later date by someone who no longer understood the text too well."[22] Throwing all caution to the winds, Sorel winds up by saying: "It is extremely likely that the Fourth Gospel is anterior to the Judean catastrophe."[23]

But it is the first part of the work, an introduction of almost ninety pages, which concerns us here. In it, Sorel develops his new methodology, contrasting his view to that of Renan. He distinguishes two systems:

"The first assumes that history is made by determined individuals. The second views these individuals as symbol-carriers rather than originators. The first is full of biological analogies; the second reminds one rather of geology. The first pretends to penetrating, by way of psychology, down to the roots of real life and to explain it to the full; the second makes no claim but to explain the past and is content with throwing light on certain aspects of things." Sorel calls the first method

---

[18]V. S. Pritchett, reviewing Richard Aldington's Portrait of a Genius But.... (D. H. Lawrence) in The New Statesman and Nation, April 29, 1950, p. 488.

[19]Letter to Croce (La Critica, 1928, p. 439), November 20, 1912. — Cf. chapter 2, note 43.

[20]Renan, p. 262.   [21]Ibid., p. 264.

[22]Ibid., p. 435.   [23]Ibid., p. 452.

"psychological," the second, "scientific."[24] The first is that of Renan, while the second is Sorel's. In terms of Renan's subject, the conflict may be expressed in the question: Is Christ the founder of Christianity, or did Christianity create the Christ we know? But the formulation of the question's second part is misleading: if taken literally, it makes the rejoinder easy enough. As a Catholic author asked the partisans of David Friedrich Strauss: If Christ is a creation of the early Christian church, who then created the church? But, says Sorel, if one considers Christ as a creation of the Church...the purpose is to understand "how the portrait of the gospels is related to all kinds of preoccupations which assaulted the first Christian communities." These groups formed under the impact of a series of fortuitous events which were nothing short of miraculous, and so "in their enthusiasm over the resurrection of Jesus, they projected everything that could be interpreted as supernatural, upon their hero." And that is how it should be, for "the great fact of nascent Christianity is the belief in the Resurrection: how such a belief came into being is a very useless question."

Repeating himself,[26] Sorel places the supreme event of church history on a plane with a much later and decidedly less central datum of the Christian tradition, by saying that "the miracle of the resurrection occupies here the same place as the stigmatization of St. Francis does in the history of the Franciscan order."[27] "Science," that is: scientific history, has nothing to say about the origins of religious "images"; its task is to establish "the relations existing between such images and the conditions under which the primitive communities existed."[28]

What follows are the passages which evoked the severe criticism of Sorel's most eminent reader, Benedetto Croce,[29] a criticism which gave Sorel pause, without however swaying him from his position:

"This kind of historiography, exclusively devoted to the scientific study of the mores, institutions and ideas, may well live together with theology, each discipline having control over a greatly restricted area without ever coming into conflict with each other unless the historian oversteps the proper limitations of his science...."[30] Sorel's belief in a "concordate between science and theology"[31] is based on his rejection of the psychological method of history. The theologian is interested in explaining origins, though he does it in a different way than the psychologist: "he wants to demonstrate that the various dogmatic decisions are well justified...as being steadily improved interpretations of the revelation." The enemy of the church, on the other hand, maintains that those decisions can be understood only with the help of a character study of their authors, of their philosophical and political

24Ibid., p. 5-6. 25Ibid., p. 20-21.
26See chapter 2, p.59. 27Renan, p. 21.
28Ibid., 29See chapter 1, p. 41, and Supplement 1.
30Renan, p. 21. 31Ibid., p. 457.

prejudices.[32] As to the revelation, the psychologist will treat it as a miracle, that is, as something not worth the attention of the serious scientist.

Sorel believes that this is the position of Renan, who, "without any doubt...had the ruin of Christianity in mind;"[33] at one point Sorel even claims that "Renan understood nothing of Christianity."[34] For he, Renan, believed "that history is able to bear witness against the Christian theories;"[35] whereas, according to Sorel, "the theologian is free to explain events his way, by a supernatural act," and that right cannot be denied to him by the historian to whom events are, or ought to be, strictly indeterminate[36] — "and there is nothing less determinate than Christianity."[37] One might, of course, "imagine causes of some sort...but if one does, one has stepped outside science."[38] Naturally, as long as the historian insists on discovering the origins of the Church, he cannot help enquiring after the true nature of "the fact that gave birth to the illusion of the miracle of the resurrection; but once the question of the origins has been abandonned, all difficulties disappear."[39] The historian and sociologist should follow the example of the modern physicist who does not reason about the beginning or the end of the world.[40]

"Thus, in the case of the stigmatization of St. Francis, we do not have to know the nature of the sores; we must find out what [the people of] the Middle Ages thought of it." Their faith is the fact that affected history and "does not depend on the problem of physiology."[41] And again: "Those causes [of a new religion] are so disproportionate to the facts that it becomes a matter of indifference for historiography whether or not the fact has ever happened."[42] The sole task of the historian is "to bring into a system the conditions under which the events occur, without ever attempting to determine the origins.... The theologians are not satisfied with what they call the appearances or outward side of things; [if] they wish to separate that which is human and that which is divine in the world," then they, in turn, must leave the realm of history and concentrate exclusively "on the divine aspect" of things.[43] The historian Sorel is satisfied that "the belief in the resurrection of Jesus [is] the principle which tells us a great deal about the Christian origins." But that this belief itself "is not susceptible of explanation; there is a mystery which science must not try to hide, and which the theologians may regard as their exclusive property."[44]

    [32]Ibid., p. 21-22. [33]Ibid., p. 68. "I may be one of those who make a revolution." Renan, as cited by Sorel in his review of the **Cahiers de la jeunesse** (see note 13) p. 461.
    [34]Renan, p. 66. [35]Ibid.
    [36]Ibid., p. 74. [37]Ibid., p. 469.
    [38]Ibid., p. 74. [39]Ibid., p. 37.
    [40]Ibid., p. 23. [41]Ibid., p. 37.
    [42]Ibid., p. 280. [43]Ibid., p. 458. [44]Ibid., p. 458-459.

It is easy to see where this kind of reasoning may lead: Sorel may be suspected of "working both sides of the street;" his "scientific" disinterest in causes, in the origins of great historic movements, leaves the road open to arbitrary constructions, as long as they do not make any claim of being based on demonstrable fact. Translated into secular terms, the freedom of the theologian may become the revolutionary, mystical authority of the "inspired" manipulator of our readiness to believe, to believe something, almost anything. This is, of course, not what Sorel intended, but that is what happened. As Ernst Cassirer said, "henceforth, myths can be manufactured in the same sense and according to the same methods as other modern weapons — like machine guns or airplanes."[45] Sorel did not, be it repeated, foresee that development, but his thought is indicative of the mental condition in which such a development becomes intelligible and — in wide parts of the world — acceptable.

The Illusions of Progress

The book of that title[46] is an offshot of the meditations from which issued the **Reflections**: it may be called a subsidiary of that work, developing in greater detail Sorel's theories about the character and function of the bourgeoisie and its specific dogmas of democracy and progress. In a larger context, the book continues the historical analysis, colored by Karl Marx's materialism, of the great Western tradition, — the study which Sorel had started in his **Socrates** and in the **Ruin of the Ancient World**.[47]

As in most of his works, Sorel begins with and against Proudhon: as before, his perennial conversation which his spiritual ancestor is one of **Sic et Non**. Proudhon's **Philosophy of Progress**[48] which probably gave Sorel the idea for his title, is a tantalizing mixture of idealist and positivist elements. In assuming absolute laws of development which assure us that society always advances, the progressivism of Proudhon retains Hegelian features; when he defines progress as the negation of the Absolute and predicts that the cult of the supposedly absolute Being

[45]Ernst Cassirer, **The Myth of the State** (Stamford, Conn., 1946), p. 282. A. D. Lindsay's "operative ideal" (**The Modern Democratic State**, Oxford, 1947, p. 37 ff.) becomes a propaganda device.

[46]Les Illusions du progrès, (1. edition, Paris, 1908). Its chapters had been serialized in **Le Mouvement Socialiste**, August-December, 1906. — The citations are from the 4. edition (Paris, 1927). The work shows the influence of Taine in many, lengthy references.

[47]Sorel explicitly returns to the great subject of the last-named work in a series of articles devoted to G. Ferrero's **Grandeur et décadence de Rome** in **Le Mouvement Socialiste**, July 15, 1906, February 1907, and July 15, 1908.

[48]Théorie du progrès (1. edition., Brussels, 1853).

will be replaced by the culture of humanity,[49] then Proudhon rather
sounds like St. Simon and Auguste Comte. But he also says that "civilization is proceeding unbeknown to the legislators and statesmen, under
the cloak of opposition, revolution, and war."[50] Every moment we expect "the Marxist doctrine of the class struggle to make its appearance,"
but Proudhon, being "in the first place a great moralist," is convinced
that morality is independent from the class structure. And from this
he concludes that "all ideologies are configurations of the spirit on
which the life of the classes has only a secondary influence."[51]

It is in the 18th century that Sorel finds the conditions which gave
rise to the great dogma of permanent progress. A new class comes
into being which will soon enough be "the conquering bourgeoisie." If
we want to understand the ideology of the rising thiers etat, we must
realize that it grew strong as "the auxiliary of the crown," as "a class
of clerks."[52] Their position of relative power was not so much the result of their own strength as the effect of royal policy: the bourgeois
were the beneficiaries of the struggle between the monarchy and the
feudal fronde. Bourgeois mentality thus was not unlike that of the freedmen of imperial Rome. Such a class "cannot construct its ideology
along the same lines as a class of masters; for it reasons not so much
upon its own affairs as upon those of others."[53] It attacks given tasks:
the administrative and jurisdictional objectives of absolutism. It cannot
fail to be impressed by both the methods and the spirit of the institution
it serves. It is no accident that modern French democracy took over
the devices of Royal bureaucratic centralism; Sorel cites an enthusiastic modern testimonial to the greatness of Richelieu who is characterized as the "great leveller, forerunner of the democratic work."[54]
The bourgeoisie, "inheriting the admiration which the Ancien Regime
had for the state," developed its unitary concept even further. For,
whereas in a perfectly regulated monarchy nobody was supposed to
raise his voice against the prince, in a democracy each citizen is pre-
sumed to have willed (at least by indirection) what he is commanded
to do.[55]

What impressed the contemporaries of Louis XIV more than anything else, according to Sorel, was the way in which "the royal power
managed to establish itself above misadventure, to an extent that seemed
definitive;" they were thus sufficiently disposed toward ascribing every
social activity to an impulse derived from the royal authority; the result was that "they looked upon the royal institutions as a constant

---

[49]Op. cit. in Oeuvres complètes de P. J. Proudhon, Vol. XII (Paris, 1946),
p. 73-74.

[50]Sorel, Illusions, p. 8, quoting Proudhon, see op. cit., p. 124.

[51]Sorel, op. cit., p. 6-7, note 1. [52]Ibid., p. 80.

[53]Ibid. [54]Ibid., p. 67. The quotation is from Gabriel Hanotaux, Histoire
du cardinal de Richelieu, (Paris, 1893-1947) tome II, p. 483.

[55]Illusions, p. 9.

force which, each day, added some new improvement to the improvements already made." From there, the idea of "acceleration" followed as "a rather evident and necessary" truth. The notion of stability and the impression of an ever-quickening improvement of conditions both combine to form the first crude basis for a theory of progress. Sorel is so impressed by his discovery that with him even the emerging modern science was conditioned by the fact of absolutist rule: he finds it quite possible that Galileo's law of the increasing speed rate of falling bodies was suggested to him by political analogies; for in his time the power of the monarchs was already absolute enough to indicate a type of steady force. But, feeling that he might have gone too far, he qualifies: "It could be that the idea of acceleration, after having descended from the political sphere to physics, consecutively travelled the way in reverse; accordingly, the theory of the accelerating speed rate of falling bodies would have contributed to give a greater precision to the idea of progress. The evolutionist theories furnish us with an analogy: though reared in the philosophy of history, they had to take a detour through biology before they could decisively win over the historians."[56]

Relying heavily on the work of a man whom he had much abused before,[57] Sorel finds that the theory of progress owes much to Descartes, particularly to his theses relative to science: that science is not separate from practice and that it keeps growing all the time. But once again we are asked to insert before the word, practice, the adjective, "political": since Descartes' time, Sorel insists, it was quite evident to the observer "that the new model governments with their concentrated power and their regular administration, were well fitted to execute their plans with a reasonable amount of exactness, thus being able to achieve the unity of theory and practice. . . . The royal power appeared to be infinite . . . nothing seemed to be impossible to royalty; science could not fail to keep abreast of those who needed it in order to rule."[58]

But the most important aspect of the new scientific movement is the manner in which it adapted itself to the interests of a society of noble dilettants and became a vulgar science. Again, it was Cartesianism that contributed most to the spread of scientific interests; but it could do so only by adapting itself to the lighter moods and limited horizons of polite drawing room conversation.[59] Descartes himself cannot, strictly speaking, be made responsible for this development,[60] and yet, in a way, he was. Sorel "pauses for a moment" to explain what happened, and his explanation reads to us as if he might have had himself in mind:

---

[56]Ibid., p. 34, and pp. 34-35, note 2.

[57]Ferdinand Brunetière, Etudes critiques. Brunetière had been Sorel's bête noire in the Dreyfus years. See chapter 3, p. 86.

[58]Illusions, p. 35-36. [59]Ibid., p. 36-37.

[60]The rule of Descartes began rather late, Sorel says, following Brunetière; the influence of Cartesianism in the 17. century is a myth. (Ibid., pp. 37, 38.)

"The creator of a system operates like an artist, interpreting with utmost liberty what he observes around himself; if that system has sufficient contact with the current ideas, it will last and become the favorite doctrine of another generation, a generation which may understand it in an entirely different sense than the contemporaries did." What had been of secondary importance only may now become all significant; the judgment of posterity may even reverse the original scale of values entirely, yet "the final judgment of history will be based on the adopted version."[61]

For this work of adaptation Descartes' philosophy, as Sorel says, was admirably suited: whenever it was necessary to explain any known or novel fact, "any intelligent person familiar with the Cartesian way of reasoning could find an answer to everything." Indeed, when Descartes formulated his famous principle of methodic doubt, he was doing nothing else but "introducing the habits of the aristocratic spirit into philosophy."[62] The affinity between Cartesiansim and upper-class skepticism was by no means the weakest reason for the success of the new philosophy. The noble amateur scientist demanded, and was easily satisfied with, explanations which appealed, without imposing too heavy a strain on his attention, to his "common sense," and Sorel cites Taine citing the words of Descartes' successor, Malebranche, as an illustration: "To attain truth, it is sufficient to pay attention to the clear ideas which everybody finds in himself."[63] Simplification and summarization, these were the tasks the 18th century philosopher was asked to fulfill by a society eager to transform everything "into pleasant subjects of conversation." In Condorcet's words: "there came into being in Europe, a class of people less concerned with discovering the truth... than with spreading it."[64] The great accomplishment of the philosophes was to bring about the diffusion of a broad body of knowledge which gave social status to the knower.[65] It was the admission ticket of the bourgeois anxious to belong, or, at least, to be tolerated by polite society.

At first, the clerks had to be careful in their speculations lest they infringe on subjects which the masters reserved for themselves. Hence the tendency of middle class philosophers to take up topics removed from reality, the more abstract, the better. The church had always shown a great amount of toleration for bold thought as long as it did not impinge on the questions that really mattered, such as theories about natural right and its ramifications. The monarchy followed the church in that it showed little concern over eloquent manifestoes in praise of republican institutions. An attack on the salt tax, that would

---

[61]Ibid., p. 37. [62]Ibid., p. 45.

[63]Ibid., p. 46. Sorel adds that the church soon discovered the potential danger of the new philosophy; evidence: Bossuet's attack on Malebranche (Ibid., p. 47).

[64]Ibid., p. 53.

[65]See Daniel Mornet, Les origines intellectuelles de la révolution française (4. edition, Paris, 1947).

have been something else again. It was the very obscurity of the new
theories that made them seem so innocuous. And so, in order to appear innocuous, the philosophes deliberately cultivated an ambiguous
style. Since there was safety in obscurity, obscurity became the hall-
mark of a literature in which a class of clerks, excluded from concrete responsibilities, expressed abstract ambitions which grew with
their mounting wealth and self-assurance.[66]

But the masters made one miscalculation, if they can be said to
have been at all conscious of their danger: the middle class took deadly
serious what was being written by the people with the good, aristocratic
connections; the more reckless the thought, the more the bourgeoisie
admired it. The rationalistic propaganda of the enlightenment did not
promote the spirit of acute criticism: its sweeping generalities engendered a naive conviction that the boldest schemes could be immediately
translated into facts.[67]

It is, of course, impossible even to touch on the wealth of material
with which Sorel attempts to document his thesis, but it should be clear
by now what his conclusions are: the theory of progress is the creation
of a class, the bourgeoisie, and as that class, time-bound. Moreover,
progress, like its concomitant, democracy, are rationalist, unitary,
and utopian concepts, begotten in an atmosphere of unreality, but later
on used to gloss over the harsh facts of hierarchy and class rule on the
one hand, and to maintain the phantom character of social solidarity
and democratic justice on the other. But with a difference: the bourgeoisie, after its triumph over the old masters no longer makes an effort "to justify its claim to power by resorting to the philosophy of
history. The notion of progress has lost much of its importance in the
eyes of the people who play a role in bourgeois science."[68] But the
slightest criticism of the dogma still draws fire from the apologists of
middle class rule: anyone who ventures a protest against the illusion
of rationalism, is immediately branded as an enemy of democracy."
A man like Bergson, Sorel has been told on several occasions, is the
greatest threat that ever faced the modern spirit.[69]

This modern spirit reminds Sorel of the declining days of the
Ancien Régime: it has inherited its cynicism and superficiality: "actually, there is not much difference between our great journalists and
the encyclopedists."[70]

Sorel sums up: "At the beginning of our search we met with a
small charge philosophy of fashionable people who wished to enjoy their
riches unrestrained by the commands of prudence under which their
fathers had been living for so long."[71] It was a time of optimism, of
greatest expectations; a world of laughter and gossip; one would not
expect any social consciousness from a class that had no proper function

---

[66]Illusions, p. 82-83. [67]Ibid., p. 133-134.
[68]Ibid., p. 265. [69]Ibid., p. 50-51.
[70]Ibid., pp. 59, 285. [71]Ibid., p. 275.

in society. The parallel Sorel wishes to draw is obvious: he believes that history repeats itself in once more pitting a new class which is productive, against one that has become oblivious of its social function and rules merely by force and deceit: "Today we have descended to election ballyhoo which permits the demagogues to marshall their armies in dictatorial fashion and to assure themselves of a good life."[72] The bourgeoisie, in short, has abdicated in favor of a parasitical elite. It had not always been that way: there was a time of bourgeois greatness when the middle class did know its proper role. In the parliamentary regime of early nineteenth century liberalism that middle class found its ideal institutional expression, and it also found its great historians who were celebrating the new system as the crowning end of a development willed by necessity.[73] The ideology of progress which inspired that drive, had then some meaning, for, as Sorel says, "there is in the capitalist world, a **real progress**" which is equally welcomed by the prospering ruling class and by the socialists who see in it the promise of a revolutionary overturn. "This real progress... takes place in the technique of production"[74] and replaces the old sentiments of property by "the affections which every truly qualified worker feels toward the productive forces entrusted to his care."[75] It is not actually a "new" affection: the same relationship of man to his work can be observed in rural life; Sorel likens the way the factory worker feels about his machine to the love with which the farmer tends his field, his vineyard and his cattle. "All the virtues attributed to property would be unintelligible without the virtues engendered by a certain manner of work." What makes work vital to us, Sorel wants to say, is the creative effort that goes into the production process: "The purpose of property is to transform the farmer into an artist," and the same is true for the industrial craftsman (Sorel's whole doctrine of production is colored by the fact that in his time French industry was still primarily of the small atelier type of production). But his further statement that "the modern shop is a testing ground... for the inventive spirit of the worker"[76] is no less true of mass production industry, as the experience of the second world war showed conclusively.

It is Sorel's familiar view of the relationship between man and machine (he explicitly refers to the end of his **Reflections**[77]) which explains his diatribes against democracy: because that new, creative attitude toward work must be protected and developed by all means, he is suspicious of all methods designed to perpetuate the old, tired ideology of a class no longer production-minded. It is precisely because the old creed of progress is no longer in itself convincing that the bourgeoisie, in order to preserve the benefits derived from it, has to use methods of persuasion which are alien to the spirit of the new

---

[72]Ibid., p. 276. [73]Ibid., p. 275.
[74]Ibid., p. 276-277. — Sorel's emphasis. [75]Ibid., p. 281.
[76]Ibid., p. 281-282. [77]Ibid., p. 283.

producers, which is also a new moral and juridical view of society. True to the spirit of their own beginnings, the old rulers use the highly improved mass media of information to assure conformity: "The experience of our days shows that the vulgarization of knowledge does not make the people able to choose and control their elected representatives."[78] If Sorel would write today, he very likely would have a great deal to say about the standardized, canned brand of education which more than anything else is responsible for homo semiliteratus Hitleriensis. Sorel foresees the danger of a uniformity which could result from an exaggerated and perverted emphasis on democratic unity;[79] in 1909, he adds another chapter to the Illusions, in which he analyzes the affinities between democracy and mediocrity.[80] It is what he once called "the great preoccupation of my life,"[81] his concern for the preservation of our Western culture, that makes him write: "Since education has no other purpose than to impart to the people mental habits which the bourgeoisie in turn had borrowed from the old nobility, it is of no use to the proletariat."[82]

The reader whom these definitions of democracy strike as unduly narrow and beside the point, should recognize that Sorel's overstatements are deliberate: for all the concrete data which he offers to give body to his mythical producers, there is something airy, indeterminate about the notion which calls for a strong, auxiliary idea — a counterfiction to set off the myth in stark relief. The angelic tidings of the great rebirth make the demonization of "democracy" almost imperative.

The Two Democracies

Sorel knows very well how to distinguish between the type of democracy which is good although hardly ever practiced, and the other kind, confectioned by and for the demagogues and orators for purposes of power politics. It is for the second type, which dominated the French scene so ostentatiously, that Sorel reserves the contaminated term, Democracy. The good kind he identifies by various names, but never once does he use the word, democratic, to describe his own ideal state. He prefers to speak of a republic, following Proudhon; he wonders if

---

[78]Ibid., p. 59.

[79]Cf. appendix i of the Reflections, entitled "Unity and Multiplicity." See chapter 11, p. 264 and chapter 12, p. 274-275.

[80]Added as appendix i to the 2. edition of the Illusions (Paris, 1910). The essay, originally published as "Evoluzione e decadenza" in Divenire Sociale, December 1909 - March, 1910, must not be confused with Sorel's critique of Ferrero's history of imperial Rome (cf. note 47). See also chapter 11, p. 258.

[81]See chapter 1, p. 41.

[82]Illusions, p. 60.

the true self-government of Le Play's "social authorities"[83] could be revived in the form of the industrial syndicate. Because there are inherent in the democratic order self-defeating tendencies, too often frustrating the very freedom and equality which they proclaim, Sorel rejects the democratic form, retaining faithfully its essence. Nowhere did he make clearer what may be called his theory of associational democracy than in an essay published simultaneously with the Illusions and entitled The Organization of Democracy.[84]

The theory is Proudhon's, whose influence completely dominates the study. It reflects, negatively, his revulsion against Caesarism, or, as Sorel calls it, the "bonapartist spirit"[85] evinced by modern society no matter whether it is ruled by rhetors or an emperor. It is the rule of or for the "omnipotent multitude,"[86] a regime that will deny all values of the past simply because they are of the past. Sorel has very harsh words fo the German social democrats who "managed more successfully than any other popular party, to win over multitudes of devout voters by their intransigent denial of traditional values." It is interesting to note that, already in 1906, Sorel censures "the levity, incoherence and cynicism" of an "unrelenting agitation," thanks to which the German proletariat sighs for the day on which the old authorities would disappear. The list of the authorities with which Sorel, by implication, sympathizes, includes "the Prussian army, the pedantic civil services and courts...the church."[87]

As a result, our modern democracies are made up exclusively of the type of individual who "feels no obligation toward the past, no deep affection for his home and is only mildly concerned for the well-being of the future generations;" he is obsessed by the mirage of riches gained by force of sheer wits rather than by serious work. His place is "the big city where human beings pass like shadows;" where "political committees take the place of the old social authorities ruined by the revolutions."[88]

---

[83]Le Play's term for the rule of the associated family-heads of the substantial families in rural society, frequently referred to in Sorel's Introduction a l'économie moderne (see chapter 3, p. 92); see also below, p. 159, and chapter 8, note 8.

[84]"L'organisation de la démocratie," an article (written à propos a book by the Belgian, Adolphe Prins, De L'esprit du gouvernement démocratique), first published as "L'Organizzazione della democrazia" in Divenire Sociale, November 16, 1906, and as "De L'esprit du gouvernement démocratique" in Le Mouvement Socialiste, November, 1906, and included in Matériaux d'une théorie du prolétariat (2. ed., 1921), pp. 365-394.

[85]Op. cit. in Matériaux p. 367, note 1.   [86]Ibid., p. 379.

[87]Ibid., p. 384. Sorel is very partial to the merit system of public administration as opposed to the spoil system. Cf. chapter 3, p. 91.

[88]Matériaux, p. 386-387. Le Play's term italicized by Sorel. — Note the Spenglerian tone of the sentence which shows the author in a rare poetical mood.

This "negative nature of democracy"[89] is contrasted with the neighborhood type of home rule as described by Proudhon. His meditations led him to pay more and more attention to the rural origins of lay.[90] The primitive democracies, of which we find survivals in 19th century Switzerland and among the North African Cabyles, were cantonal associations of large families united by ancestor worship. Religion imposed stern moral rules on the clan ruled by the most distinguished family heads (Le Play's "social authorities").[91] Aristotle had an inkling of this type of government after which he tried to pattern his own policy; unfortunately Greece no longer offered him a living model; his theory of social authorities therefore had to confine itself to a few abstract hints from which we can learn little.[92]

Proudhon's ideal republic comes much closer to expressing the primitive, rural democracy. Libertarian, anti-militarist, federalist,[93] it achieves freedom through the greatest possible dispersal of power. Of the five prerequisites which Proudhon lists as essential for the realization of his polis, the most important are: Administrative decentralization and restoration of "provincial and communal life." "Given these conditions, authority will disappear in the end, and the state, the public thing, res publica will be erected on the unshakable basis of law and local liberties, corporative as well as individual; it is the interplay that constitutes the freedom of the nation."[94]

This passage strongly suggests Gaetano Mosca's pluralistic doctrine of "juridical defense" based on a balance of the social forces; his "ruling class" comprises Le Play's and Proudhon's "social authorities." We are now in a position to settle the question as to whom belongs the priority of the ideas common both to Mosca and Sorel.[95] The answer is that both go back to older sources: Mosca does not seem to be indebted to Proudhon, but rather, like Proudhon himself, to the tradition made into a system by Polybius and transmitted to modernity by Machiavelli.[96] As to Sorel, the evidence is clear: it is Proudhon, not Mosca, who inspired the theorist of the Reflections as well as the author of Das Kapital when he predicted, in a sentence also quoted by Sorel, that the state would eventually wither away: in Proudhon's society of freemen "government, in a strict sense, no longer exists." What

89Ibid., p. 384.

90Ibid., p. 390. Cf. Sorel, Introduction a l'économie moderne, Part I ("De l'économie rurale au droit"), which is inspired by Proudhonian principles.

91Matériaux, p. 385-386. — For once, Sorel fails to refer to Vico.

92Ibid., pp. 388-389. 93Ibid., p. 380.

94Ibid., p. 377. Sorel cites De la justice dans la Révolution et dans l'Eglise, tome V, p. 179; see Oeuvres complètes de P.-J. Proudhon Vol. VIII, Pt. 2 (Paris, 1931), p. 309.

95See also Supplement 2.

96Cf. James Burnham, The Machiavellians, Defenders of Freedom (New York, 1943).

characterizes a republican government of law and liberty best is ... "its impersonality."[97] And whereas Marx spoke of the time when "labor has become not only a means of life but also the primary necessity of life,"[98] Proudhon, the son of artisans and peasants, foresaw a community of artists. Following the counsel of Genesis and Voltaire's Candide, a free humanity would cultivate its garden: "When the exploitation of the soil, once left to the slave, has become the first of arts, as it is the first of the industries, man's life will be spent with senses tranquil and the mind serene."[99]

That Proudhon was not himself too hopeful about seeing his dream ever come true, is borne out by the extremity of his advice: "I see only one way ... to divide France into twelve independent states and to suppress Paris."[100] But cantonalization would not in itself remove the difficulty raised by Sorel. Proudhon himself did not exclude the possibility that his republic might evolve from a constitutional monarchy;[101] he was less certain of that outcome where the system in existence was already "democratic." Proudhon was very much aware of "the extreme facility with which democracy passes into despotism and vice versa."[102] Why, Sorel asks, should the exploiters of democracy reform themselves? The optimism to which Proudhon clung against his better insight, Sorel will have none of. To him the real trouble is that both types of democracy, the unitarian and the pluralistic kind, are in reality so closely intertwined that they are likely to confuse even the theorist.[103] If there are ever to be genuine popular self-government and jurisdiction, there is little chance, Sorel believes, that they will issue from our present democratic institutions. And he asks: "Will not the workers' syndicates be able to perform the role played by the old social authorities?"[104]

Sorel's Rousseau

The fondness which Sorel has for Proudhon is unmistakable even when he disagrees with him. It is not often that the comment will be as harsh as the following: "Proudhon has become almost unintelligible because he too emulated the pulpit-style to a great degree." The statement links Proudhon with one he hated and despised: Jean Jacques Rousseau.[105] What did Sorel himself think of the man? A first guess

---

[97]Matériaux, p. 377.

[98]Karl Marx, "The Criticism of the Gotha Program" in Capital, The Communist Manifesto and Other Writings (New York, 1932), p. 7.

[99]Matériaux, p. 390. Sorel cites De la justice, tome III, p. 370; see Oeuvres complètes, Vol. VIII, Pt. 3 (Paris, 1932), p. 412.

[100]Materiaux, p. 381. [101]Ibid., p. 378.

[102]Ibid., p. 379. [103]Ibid., p. 385.

[104]Ibid., p. 393.

[105]Sorel, "Jean Jacques Rousseau" in Le Mouvement Socialiste, June, 1907, p. 532, note 1.

would be that he shared Proudhon's revulsion; indeed, there are in the
Illusions references to Rousseau as one of the apostles of modern,
idealistic "obscurity."[106] One would not even have to know what Pierre
Josephe thought of Jean Jacques, to expect Sorel's reaction to be one of
radical antagonism to the abstract speculations of the Social Contract.
It is indeed difficult to imagine two men farther apart than Sorel and
Rousseau in mind and temper. It seems wrong even to compare them.
Perhaps it is their very distance that made Sorel's judgment of Rousseau
surprisingly non-belligerent, and, at times, almost sympathetic. Or
it could be that he was simply following his instinct for fair play when
he defended the Genevan against a crowd of posthumous dragon slayers.[107] But even this does not fully explain his cautious, all but reverential attitude toward Rousseau. He had made fun of the "General
Will" in the Avenir, but a later footnote [108] explains that "in 1898, I
had not yet been sufficiently aware of the... so-called democratic
institutions existing in the old Swiss cantons," the models to which
Rousseau returned, "in some instinctive way." It is a full apology,
with "social authorities" and Cabyles thrown in for full measure.

While the Illusions are exclusively concerned with Rousseau's role
as a main representative of contractarian theory, the special essay
emphasizes the psychologist and educator, defending him against various accusations such as that he was a traitor to the causes of the encyclopedists, a reactionary madman, an inhuman monster. Sorel suggests that Rousseau was all these things, and, in addition, a religious
genius who could speak with many tongues without ever being untrue to
himself; one who could give new luster to old meanings: he alone in
that great age spoke with authority. It is in this connection that Sorel
writes the beautiful lines, ostentatiously referring to Rousseau's Thérèse Levasseur, but thinking of his own deceased companion, "Happy the
man who has found the devoted consort, strong and proud of her love,
the wife who will always keep his youth alive in him, who will never
let him become self-satisfied, forever recalling his duty to him; the
wife who, at times, can even reveal to him his genius,"[109] — words
of Proudhonian ardor and noblesse, of which Sorel himself was so fond
that he repeated them twice: once in a letter to his Italian translator
and biographer, Agostino Lanzillo;[110] and as a post-script to the fourth
edition of the Reflections, the last published in his life time.[111] The

---

[106]See above, p. 148.

[107]Sorel's essay is directed against the tendency — which became fashionable once more with anti-fascist writers of the recent past — to portray Rousseau as a schizophrenic, responsible for the authoritarian outrages of the
French revolution.

[108]Matériaux, p. 118, note 1. Added in 1914.

[109]Sorel, "Jean Jacques Rousseau" in loc. cit., p. 513.

[110]February 20, 1910. See also Part II, Introduction, p. 162.

[111]1919. — The citation occurs in a note on the last page of Sorel's plea
"In Defense of Lenin," of all places: (Reflections, 1950 ed., p. 311).

irony of Sorel's ecomium is that it does not apply to Thèrése; she was not what that strange man needed. As Sorel, reverting to prose, puts the case: "It did not work out for Rousseau."[112]

Acting as a second for Rousseau against that beau sabreur, Jules Lemaître,[113] Sorel cannot admit of the contention that the terror of the revolution was the logical result of the Contrat social. The policy of the Jacobins violated Rousseau's most important rule: they were that "partial association" of which he had said: "When one of these groups becomes so large as to swamp all the others...the general will does not then come into play at all...."[114] Only by way of gross distortion could the Social Contract be made to serve as a program for the revolution. "In our day, the work of Marx gave birth to similarly inept commentaries...."[115] Rousseau's work was misunderstood by the men of the revolution because it was so much steeped in the tradition of pulpit eloquence, a genre which lends itself naturally to exaggeration. We are so used to it in its practitioners, that we never expect society to conform to their orations. Like they, Rousseau wanted to stir up in his contemporaries "an emotion engendering useful but indeterminate reflections upon their manner of life;" in order to achieve his purpose. "He presented them with highly colored images which have to be accepted as an indivisible whole," instead of being merely sample propositions to be sifted out by the empiricist. More than once, Rousseau cautioned his readers against confusing the fictitious world of his Emile and the Contrat social with the realities of the century: such a mixture could not but produce absurd results in his opinion. But that was precisely what the politicians of the revolution did with the work of the man whom they had made their god. Their error was that of the many medieval sects which tried to practice what the church fathers had written about poverty.[116]

On the negative side, there is to be listed the tremendous influence which Rousseau exerted on the "sensibility" of his epoch. The cultivation of the tender feelings became a mere fad, an affectation which failed to make better people of the revolutionaries. One may even wonder if it did not kill their sense of pity; moved to tears by soulful perorations, the Robespierres got their Rousseau mixed up with

---

[112]"Jean Jacques Rousseau," p. 527.

[113]Who had just published a book, Jean-Jacques Rousseau (Paris, 1907). Together with Anatole France, Lemaître is the frequent butt of Sorel's literary criticism: "Lemaître is the Anatole France of the Right, and France the Jules Lemaître of the Left." (Jean Variot, Propos de Georges Sorel, Paris, 1935, p. 176; also 140-143, 242).

[114]"Jean Jacques Rousseau," p. 529. The citation is from Contrat Social, Book II, chapter iii (translation by Gerard Hopkins, in Social Contract (New York, 1948), p. 194.

[115]"Jean Jacques Rousseau," p. 528-529.

[116]Ibid., p. 530-531.

the proscriptions of the wicked. A generation of bourgeois misread what had been "written for a very refined aristocracy which could admire the beauty of Rousseau's ideas, much as they were outside of the main current." The great public too wished to admire, but it was unable to understand, the reason being that "Rousseau was lyrical in a time when nobody else was." The misunderstanding resulted in a caricature of Rousseau's thoughts; but "Jean Jacques was no more responsible for inept imitations than Raphael was for the academic style."[117]

What is responsible for the unusual mildness of Sorel's critique? The reason given: that it is a counter-critique, does not quite explain the unmistakable inflection of sheer sympathy in Sorel's voice. Behind the arguments, we may detect a feeling not simply reducible to the already mentioned sense of fair play. It may not be reducible to anything in Sorel's conscious mind. Could it be that there is some real kinship between the two: the great erratic of the 18th century and the 20th century dissenter?

Sorel has been likened to Socrates; René Johannet felt reminded of Dr. Johnson,[118] the Tharauds of Stendhal;[119] to other the profusion of Sorel's work may recall Jeremy Bentham about whom he wrote in his last publication.[120] It was Guy-Grand who compared Sorel to Rousseau: he called him "a Rousseau assuredly less gifted as an artist, as much lacking the gift of the writer as the other one possessed it;" on the other hand, Sorel is "a purer Rousseau..." besides, he is much better versed in many sciences of which Rousseau had hardly a presentiment. But like Rousseau, Sorel is "a man of sentiment rather than of dialectics; a man as opposed to the positivism and intellectualism of today as Rousseau was opposed to the rationalism and optimism of the Encyclopedists." And again, like Jean Jacques, Sorel is "in love with solitude." Both were dreaming of a new man who would recreate civilization on a higher, nobler level: Rousseau's "natural man" becomes Sorel's heroic proletarian....[121]

The parallel may easily be overdrawn; in fact, the comparison breaks down at an important point.[122] Still, it has merit, though the merit may be rather one of negatives: what makes Sorel and Rousseau look alike, is less their share of common qualities, than the great distance separating them from a rejected and rejecting world. Not that Sorel ever thought of himself as an outcast, — on the contrary, it was

---

[117]Ibid., p. 532.

[118]René Johannet, "L'évolution de Georges Sorel" in Itinéraires d'Intellectuels (Paris, 1921), p. 178.

[119]See Introductory ii, p. 165.

[120]Sorel and L. Auriant, "Jeremy Bentham et l'indépendance de l'Egypte " in Revue Le Mercure de France, April 15, 1922.

[121]Georges Guy-Grand, "Georges Sorel et les problemes contemporains" in La Grande Revue, Paris, December, 1922, p. 300.

[122]See chapter 11, p. 262.

he who was doing all the casting out. But Sorel knew that this was not enough; repulsion creates nothing unless it is coupled with attraction. Sorel did not completely lack attractive power; but because it was not strong enough, — not nearly as strong as Rousseau's, — Sorel could never afford the same independence; he needed points of support: he had to be a member of some coterie, even though he was more often than not its preceptor. But, unlike Rousseau, Sorel wanted to belong. Hence his frequent shifts from one group to another; hence those many changes, so-called, in his intellectual outlook. Rousseau too was a seismograph of influences playing on his morbid but acute sense for the slightest changes in the intellectual climate. But his genius was to form the current as much as he was himself formed by it. That much cannot be said of Georges Sorel. He lacked the other's confused single-mindedness. And yet, his work was to have the same destiny, if not the influence: its ambiguities led to the same grotesque misunderstandings; like Rousseau, Sorel was claimed by, and for, several contending schools of thought. In recognizing Rousseau as a lyricist who was writing for an aristocratic public, Sorel might well have wondered about his own audience. It turned out to be, not as he would have himself believe, the proletariat, but the very class of people against whom he wrote: the intellectuals and politicians. His work was fated to attract a small bourgeois elite taking the place of Rousseau's aristocracy, and to provide some cues for the eternal demagogue. Whether he knew it or not, in pleading for Rousseau, Sorel was, in fact, merely stating his own case.

Crisis

In 1907, the impetus of revolutionary syndicalism had already passed its peak, without fulfilling Sorel's expectations. The **Reflections** had not yet been published in their final form, when Sorel already felt that something was amiss. Like Marx in his later years, he began to doubt that the great revolution was as close at hand as he had been led to believe only a few years earlier. "The bourgeoisie," Sorel writes in an essay published in June, 1907, "may find resources to defend itself for a long time to come."[123] Looking back on his syndicalist period three years later he will say diplomatically: "A new series of chance developments have not been very favorable to the progress of ideas."[124] But that was an official statement; in his correspondence Sorel is less reticent: the truth is that he has become quite disillusioned about his syndicalist friends.[125]

---

[123]"La crise morale et réligieuse" in Le Mouvement Socialiste, July 15, 1907, p. 36. — (The same issue contains contributions by Robert Michels, Edouard Berth, Arturo Labriola and Hubert Lagardelle).

[124]"Mes raisons de syndicalisme" in Matériaux, p. 286.

[125]Cf. chapter 7, p. 185.

But the capitalist class will have to pay a price for its survival;
"I am convinced," Sorel writes, "that from now on the bourgeoisie is
destined to live without morals."[126] He compares our society with
Aristotle's polis and the Rome of Cicero. In the latter case particularly,
the decomposition of the old society was all but complete; yet it took
another three centuries for Christianity to bring its new ideals to fruition, and even then only in a very imperfect manner.[127]

What impresses Sorel is the fact that economic structures seem
to have a staying power of their own, regardless of the decay of the
moral forces, and inversely: the morality of a civilization seems to
be "much more independent of the economic basis than are the juridical,
political, and even the religious ideologies." That would be a shocking
discovery for a good Marxist to make, but the Sorel of 1907 does not
even bat an eye as he, in half a dozen lines, submits that there may be
a "complete disagreement" between moral superstructure and the
rest.[128] Not that the statement constitutes a new departure in his
work, but never before has the autonomy of ethical values been proclaimed by him in such a matter-of-fact way.

Yet the radicalism of the severance is deceptive: Sorel, no longer
a Marxist, is still a socialist. The principle discovered is immediately
put to proletarian advantage. If bourgeois economics can persist without the corresponding bourgeois morals, then the proletariat will be
able to develop its own ethics independently of the prevailing bourgeois
economics. If Sorel is right, "a class could create for itself moral
conceptions which may be in complete disagreement with the total social
structure." Hence the importance of the efforts to protect the proletariat against the moral sophistries invented by bourgeois philosophers
in lieu of defunct middle class morality.[129] In saying this, Sorel merely
restates the views already expressed in his prefaces to Colajanni and
Merlino ten years earlier.

He is now ready to sum up. In two brief works he looks back on
the battles which he had fought in the Dreyfus period. **The Decomposition of Marxism** as well as **The Dreyfus Revolution** bring the insights
of Sorel's apprentice years to readers not familiar with the most important phase of his development. They need no special treatment in
this study. In particular, the work first mentioned[130] goes back to an
old essay dealing with a book by Anton Menger,[131] the Austrian

---

[126]"La crise morale et réligieuse," loc. cit., p. 35.   [127]Ibid., p. 36.   [128]Ibid.
[129]Ibid., p. 36-37.   [130]La décomposition du Marxisme (Paris, 1908), pp. 64.
[131]"Les aspects juridiques du socialisme" in La Revue Socialiste, October
and November, 1900, based on Anton Menger's Das Recht auf den vollen Arbeits-
ertrag (1886), translated into French as Le Droit an produit intégral du travail
(Paris, 1900). An English translation had been published earlier (The Right to
the Whole Produce of Labour, (London, New York, 1899).

economist; it is a survey of "Sorel, so far," throwing no new light on his intellectual genesis. **The Dreyfus Revolution,**[132] occasioned by Daniel Halévy's apology for his own Dreyfusard youth,[133] is the critical appraisal of a movement which, starting as a crusade for justice had ended by destroying the institutions so dear to Le Play and Renan. Both "desired the administrative mechanism inherited from the Ancien Régime and the revolution, to be replaced by a more humane order, founded upon the respect for the social authorities."[134] But time was running out for the old notables of a liberal past inspired by German conservativism: "The course of contemporary history threatens to destroy all that is still left of a civilization which Renan admired."[135] For the name, Renan, we may substitute that of Sorel; in his own "historic system," Renan, the sentimentalizer of the Gospel, ultimately becomes the defender of an aristocracy which stood for "individual privilege and the limitation of power, and which strove to save the modern worlds from the exaggerated notion of the State, the ruin of the ancient world."[136] The independence of Renan's Germanic feudatories becomes Georges Sorel's new feudalism of the free producers.

---

[132]*La révolution dreyfusienne* (Paris, 1909), pp. 64.

[133]"Apologie de notre passée " in *Cahiers de la Quinzaine* (10. cahier de la 11. série), April, 1910.

[134]Sorel, "**Germanesimo e storicismo di Ernesto Renan**" in La Critica (1931), p. 363. — See also Francis Graham Wilson, The Case for Conservatism (Seattle, 1951), p. 45, about De Tocqueville and the "Social Authorities."

[135]Ibid., p. 444.   [136]Ibid., p. 441-442.

PART TWO

THE INFLUENCE

Introductory ii:

FRIEND, TEACHER, PROPHET

The most remarkable thing about the career of Georges Sorel is, without any doubt, its late start: he did not write for publication until his fortieth year. Such tardiness is almost unique in history. There come to mind the camel driver and merchant Mohammed who became the inspired founder of a world religion at the age of forty; there was the bashful church organist and school teacher, Anton Bruckner, who did not dare to think of himself as a composer until he had reached the age of forty (1864). But in neither case the new career was such a radical break with the past as that which separates the free lance writer and social philosopher from the engineer and government official, Georges Sorel. Did an internal crisis precipitate the change, did financial considerations postpone for years what he had already decided for himself? We do not know: Sorel is silent about the most important event in his intellectual life; he is not very communicative about himself: "My biography can be summed up in a few lines."[1]

We learn that he was born in Cherbourg in 1847. Thus he was a fellow countryman of that other famous son of Normandy, Gustave Flaubert who showed an equal reluctance to inject his personality into his work. According to one source young Georges was born into "an excellent family of very good French bourgeois stock,"[2] while another biographer assigns him to the lower middle class.[3] He received a solid education culminating in three years of Paris engineering school (1865-1867). About his twenty-five years of service with the National Department of Bridges and Highways, Sorel says not a word; we know, however, that he had to move around a great deal: his duties called him to Algeria, and even to Spanish Catalonia.[4] We are safe in assuming that he used the many hours of provincial boredom to the limit by assimilating anything the poorly equipped local libraries would yield.[5] When he emerged as a new author in 1886, Sorel could fall

---

[1]Letter to Agostino Lanzillo, February 20, 1910, cited by René Johannet, "L'évolution de Georges Sorel" in **Itinéraires d'Intellectuels**, (Paris, 1921), p. 227.

[2]Georges Valois (Alfred Georges Gressent), **D'un siècle a l'autre** (Paris, 1921, cited from the 4. edition, 1924), p. 132.

[3]Pierre Andreu, "Du nouveau sur Georges Sorel" in **Le Figaro Littéraire**, July 10, 1948, p. 6. — The author, who has done some special research into Sorel's family background, hinted to the present writer at some grave financial difficulties which had brought Sorel's father down in the social scale.

[4]Johannet, op. cit., p. 227, note 1.

[5]Cf. Sorel's complaint to Croce concerning the lack of good source materials see chapter 2, notes 20 and 43.

back on more than a quarter of a century of truly encyclopedic if
scattered readings. In 1892 at last, Sorel crossed his Rubicon: in
order to write as he pleased, he retired without claiming the pension
to which his service entitled him, with a small family inheritance
providing the existential minimum[6] for him and his wife.

His wife — he calls her so, although they were not legally married. Sorel never mentions that fact which was only recently un-
earthed by one of his biographers.[7] It appears that his parents
frowned upon the marriage. Marie-Euphrasie David came from a
family of poor peasants; she was thirty years old — two years older
than Sorel — a servant girl in a Lyon hotel where he had fallen ill,
when they first met. It seems that she looked after him, and that the
patient fell in love with his nurse; when he recovered, he took Marie
with him as his wife. As she was almost illiterate, he provided for
her education by hiring a private teacher for her. She learned fast —
up to a certain point: she was and remained a devout Catholic who
never took to her husband's agnostic ways. One would assume that he
tried to "reform" her, but, surprisingly, he never interfered with her
religious worship and parish activities; on the contrary, he encouraged her charitable work among the victims of a cholera epidemic
while on duty as an engineer at Perpignan. After her death, he always
carried with him a religious medallion which had belonged to her, and
one day when he thought he had lost the souvenir, the widower was
frantic until he recovered it.

According to bourgeois tenets, the union was clearly a **mesal-
liance,** but Georges Sorel was happy in it. Marie, if not his intellectual equal, was to him a source of intellectual inspiration; or rather,
in her simple ways, she made alive for him what otherwise might
have remained dead, bookish information: Georges Sorel, the student
of the proletariat, got to know it intimately in her person. Marie
David probably never knew, or, if she knew, could not appreciate what
her husband wrote, and still, Sorel was justified in saying, after her
death, that she "had been part of his existence as a socialist writer."[8]

Yet the women whom the neighbors knew as "Madame Sorel"
never became his lawful wife, not even after his parents had both
died. This failure to legalize his "menage" could not have been due
to any disdain of conventional morality on his part, for Georges Sorel
was, like Karl Marx, most meticulously middle class in all his

---

[6]"I do not expect to go to Lausanne for **M.** Pareto's jubilee: at seventy one
does not move without good reason, and, honestly, a small income like mine
demands the strictest economy." **Lettere di Georges Sorel a Roberto
Michels"** in **Nuovi Studi di diritto, economia e politica** (Rome, 1919, p. 291),
June 28, 1917.

[7]Andreu, **loc. cit.**

[8]Letter to Lanzillo, **loc. cit.**, p. 228.

private dealings. Nor is there any reason to suspect, as some did,[9] that he could not marry his Marie because she was already married to somebody else. The explanation offered by Andreu, seems to be most consistent with Georges Sorel's character: "Bound, perhaps, by some vow, or simply out of filial loyalty, Sorel continued to respect the wish of his departed parents."[10]

Be that as it may, there is no question that Sorel's devotion to his Thérèse Levasseur[11] was the axis around which his life revolved until her death in 1897. The writer whom the Paris literati were to know for twenty-five more years, was the disconsolate widower who wrote: "I can say that I worked ever since to erect a philosophic monument which would be worthy of her memory," and who transferred his conjugal affection to the family of his departed wife, living with one of her married nephews in a small suburban home surrounded by a tiny garden, where "in hours of discouragement," he is "sustained by the memory of her" to whom "I dedicated two of my works."[12] He is "a robust old man, with the clean complexion of a child, a short, white beard and superb eyes of the color of Parma violets," reminding one of his admirers of an old Viking.[13] Another witness compares him to a vintner, "the eyes full of goodhearted malice."[14] Sorel seems to have suffered from a slight physical deformity: "a small hump which hovered behind him like the owl on the shoulder of the drinker in the painting of Franz Hals."[15] With his friends he was relaxed, a teaser, giggling with a high-pitched voice, fond of a good drop or two. Strangers were impressed with his old-fashioned politeness and simplicity.[16] With them, he was "very much the gentleman, a bit old school, very bourgeois, in his deportment much more the man of letters ... than the revolutionary." Like Stendhal, Georges Sorel never failed to wear his decoration, the ribbon of the **Légion d'honneur,** which was given to all state employees of a certain rank (Sorel had ended his career as a chief engineer). Robert Michels who reports this touch of vanity, and who is very anxious to assert his independence

---

[9]Andreu names Edouard Dolléans and Jean Variot.

[10]Andreu, **op. cit.**   [11]See chapter 6, p. 154.

[12]The **Reflections** and **Saggi di critica del Marxismo** (To Lanzillo, **loc. cit.,** p. 228).

[13]Jérôme et Jean Tharaud, **Notre cher Péguy** (Paris, 1926), I. 255.

[14]Valois, **op. cit.,** p. 133. — "I imagined Georges Sorel tall, meager and sallow like his brother, the colonel, to whom life in the colonies had given a slightly Chinese look. I found him small of stature, plump, grey-bearded, with a round and jovial face. The only thing the brothers had in common was their blue eyes." Letter written by Madame Henry Coullet, reproduced in Edouard Dolléans, **"Le Visage de Georges Sorel"** in **Revue d'Histoire Economique et Sociale,** Vol. XXVI, No. 2 (1940-1947), p. 112, Post-Scriptum.

[15]Tharaud, **op. cit.,** p. 257.

[16]Johannet, **op. cit.,** p. 179.

from the older man, adds that the ribbon "did not exactly add-to Sorel's subversive appearance."[17]

The author of **Political Parties** had good reason to fight off the spell of the "strong thinker," for there is overwhelming testimony about the forcefulness of Sorel's personality. "When he enters a bookstore to inquire for the most recent publication, the clerk immediately thinks: 'there is an extraordinary man.'" Or, if you should happen to sit next to him in the **Collège de France**, "seeing him bite his lips and push up his moustache is enough to convince you: 'my neighbor is an extraordinary man.'"[18] The electrifying impact of Sorel's **debut** is well attested: when he entered, Georges Valois reports, "those present began to shiver mentally; all conversation ceased."[19] Even the most casual conversation partner felt with him like a wild beast under the omnipresent eye of its trainer, who descends upon it "quiet, subtle, powerful, sure of himself...immune against attack."[20]

But if he was the dominating figure in whatever gathering he chose to enter, Sorel was not domineering: "actually, there was no more modest, self-effacing man than he." The author of the frightening **Reflections on Violence** was really a most pacific man who shunned noise, politics, publicity, and, if he could, all personal activity.[21] Yet, there he was, among the revolutionary fire-eaters, and no one ever looked upon him as an intruder, engaged, like so many other intellectuals, on a proletarian slumming tour: "What inspired us with the greatest confidence was the fact that Sorel had nothing of the bourgeois about him who goes to the people. He came quite simply as a scholar on the search for a congenial audience."[22] However, the word, scholar, does not seem to be quite fitting either: "Since there was not the faintest streak of pedantry in him, since he was, on the contrary, quite affable and playful, always ready with an anecdote to liven up his dissertation, listening to him was unbounded delight.... He could talk for hours without anyone wanting to interrupt him."[23] The ideas which had been accumulating in him throughout sixty years came pouring from his lips as effortlessly as water spouting from a spring: "He knows everything...he has read everything, from Gilgamesh to the latest news tidbit...."[24] One has to see Sorel at a debate, "his body thrust forward, hands in his pockets...to get an idea

---

[17]Michels, loc. cit., p. 289, note 4.

[18]Johannet, op. cit., p. 178.

[19]Valois, op. cit., p. 133.

[20]Johannet, op. cit., p. 179.

[21]Valois, op. cit., p. 133.

[22]Valois, op. cit., p. 134.

[23]Ibid. Valois relates that Sorel was not averse to savoring his discourse with plain gossip.

[24]Johannet, op. cit., p. 180.

of the ardent youthfulness of this old man,"[25] who combines Stendhal's passion for truth[26] with the wisdom of an ancient sage. Sorel must be imagined leaning against a Greek background, and he is unthinkable without a circle of disciples, Johannet feels,[27] and Michels makes the comment: "Strange, Sorel, essentially a solitary, cannot endure solitude. Like all theoreticians, he stands in need of acolytes . . . ."[28] He is not of this age: "His place is Ionia, and I can well see him there, withdrawn into a temple like Heraclitus, only much more benign than the Dark One, welcoming anyone who cares to enter . . . ."[29]

Obviously, this is a very youthful chorus of admirers, and the only voice that sounds slightly off pitch, is always that of Robert Michels: "He impresses greatly by his age, being at least twenty years our senior, and even more by his drive. He is utterly intransigent, intolerant, peremptory (too much so for my taste)."[30] Georges Valois disagrees with this diagnosis: "We respected him not for his fifty years but for what he had to say."[31] Still, the relationship between Sorel and his audience was of necessity one-sided: his crushing superiority simply did not admit of any true debate; their rejoinders, if any, fell as flat as those with which the Socrates of Plato's dialogues had to contend. Like Socrates, Sorel completely disregarded, or slyly chose to overlook the inferiority of his interlocutors: "He honored me by assuming that I too knew everything, had read everything. He would say: 'you know, what Renan says on page 47 of his **Antichrist**,' or 'You will remember the passage in Karl Marx . . . .'" Tharaud "received the blow without flinching, it made things easier for him," and gave the victim a chance to admire "that brain which never ceased to throw out new ideas, quickly discarding . . . the crust of banality which always clings to them, to penetrate to the live tissue of thought."[32]

Such was Sorel's hold on young minds which "at last received intellectual guidance from a man who, manifestly did not covet any office, influence, or honors."[33] They called him their "dear master" or "Papa Sorel:" it was indeed a father and son relationship which rallied the new generation to the garrulous preceptor. Some left, unable to endure his all-encompassing mental paternalism; a few turned into prodigal sons, resolved to explore to the bitter end the avenues of thought which he had only gazed upon with half-closed eyes. This

[25]Ibid.
[26]Tharaud, op. cit., pp. 259 and 262.
[27]Johannet, op. cit., p. 181.
[28]Michels, loc. cit., p. 290, note 5.
[29]Johannet, op. cit., p. 180.
[30]Michels, loc. cit.
[31]Valois, op. cit., p. 133.
[32]Tharaud, op. cit., p. 259.
[33]Valois, op. cit., p. 133.

Socrates too had his Alcibiades who went out to take arms against the
mother city, turning anti-socialist: Georges Valois and Benito Mussolini vie for that doubtful honor. But most of the disciples went
through their apprenticeship not only unharmed but enriched for life:
in finding their preceptor, they had found themselves.[34]

Wanted: A Boswell

Valois, Variot, Johannet, Michels, the Tharauds, — all keenly feel
both the magnificence and the futility of Sorel's writings; all are
agreed that he was, above all, a master of the spoken word: "It is by
his discourse that M. Sorel exercised his greatest influence "[35] His
oral oeuvre was "a thousand times vaster than his written work, which
was considerable enough."[36] Even such an independent thinker as
Péguy depended for his intellectual information on the weekly ramblings of "that old vagabond in the world of ideas."[37] Sorel was not at
all particular about his audience: "As soon as somebody appeared in
the door frame, he would grab him, like some providential godsend,
and at once made him partake of his thoughts of the moment," or else
he would abruptly change the subject and turn, with astonishing ease,
from, say, a description of cavalry uniforms to a discussion of Ploti-
nus or St. Thérèse.[38] But the old vagabond preferred to be surrounded by a steady clientele; he was forever on the lookout for some fixed
locale where he would show up with pedantic regularity to take the
chair reserved for him. The places changed as often as the "little
mags," but the type of lecture hall always remained about the same:
the backroom of an editorial office or a bookstore. The American
reader familiar with the ways of Europe, will remember that a Paris
bookstore besides being a place where books are stored, has in addition, the important function of serving as a kind of cultural exchange
club whose informal members will frown upon the uninitiated intruder
from the street bent on an errand as pedestrian as spending money on
a book. The chair on which Sorel presided over one of his favorite
"academies" — the bookstore of his publisher Marcel Rivière in the
rue Jacob — still stands in the corner from where the old man used to
scrutinize with his light Norman eyes each newcomer, smothering
him by a pointed silence; if the stranger seemed to be a likely prospect, Sorel's big rosy face would express faint pleasure, with a by-
mixture of puzzlement, as if he were wondering: 'And who are you to
interrupt me?'[39]

---

[34]Georges Valois felt that way; see chapter 11, p. 254.
[35]Johannet, op. cit., p. 179.
[36]Variot, Propos de Georges Sorel (Paris, 1935), p. 1.
[37]Tharaud, op. cit., p. 261-262.
[38]Ibid., p. 256-257.
[39]Variot, op. cit., p. 16.

For many years Sorel met regularly once a month with the group around Hubert Lagardelle, the editorial director of Le Mouvement socialiste. From one of the habitues, Robert Michels, we have an account of these meetings which suggests a literary salon in the grand Parisian tradition, with Lagardelle's Russian-born aristocratic wife, Sinaja, making the honneurs, assisted by other femmes précieuses, like Madame Berth and Madame Delesalle, surrounded by an international elite of intellectuals, such as Edward Benes, Arturo Labriola and the Bulgarian nobleman and later Bolshevik diplomat, Christian Rakovski.[40] After he had parted ways with Lagardelle, Sorel found a similarly congenial, although less fashionable audience in the editorial offices of Péguy's revue, the Cahiers de la quinzaine, which he visited faithfully every Thursday afternoon. The break with that friend deprived him of a platform which he never could replace. Before the first war, Sorel was often to be found at the small bookstore of his syndicalist friend Delesalle, but there he no longer had the numerous and brilliant public to which he had become accustomed at Péguy's. Most of the time, the store was empty, and Sorel was confined to one patient listener, Delesalle's wife, Leona, a "very sweet and knowledgeable lady,"[41] but, according to another source, also quite deaf.[42]

This anti-climax seems to be almost symbolical: the audience shrinking to the point where Georges Sorel is talking to himself. But has his talk not always been a monologue? True, but in order to be good, the monologist needed listeners. His spoken word depended utterly on some receptive ear, it was the audience which elicited from him more than he ever managed to express in print. What a pity that this wealth should be lost for all those who had never had a chance to hear Sorel! Would there ever be a Boswell, one of the disciples wondered, to record the talk of the latter-day Dr. Johnson? The difficulties which that Boswell would have to overcome would be enormous: he would have to recreate an entire "theo-socio-politicogony, of novel, disconcerting dimensions," an esoteric world, completely independent and remote from ours, surrounded by an atmosphere which would be "incommunicable."[43]

But Georges Sorel did find his Boswell, or almost so. To what extent the notes which Jean Variot took of Sorel's talks throughout many years, are trustworthy, it is difficult to say. Sorel saw all but one (the very last, dealing with Lenin), and though he slashed them mercilessly, what was left sounds authentic enough. But there remain a few disturbing aspects which call for caution. How could anyone so close to Georges Sorel as Variot err about the date of his master's death, and not only once, but twice? (he gives it as 1924, instead of

---

[40]Michels, loc. cit., p. 288, note 1.
[41]Ibid.
[42]Tharaud, op. cit., II 142.
[43]Johannet, op. cit., p. 179.

1922)[44] Also, we will have to remember that the chronicler was a
Conservative, whose royalist sympathies were likely to color the
record.   Yet, he does report without any apparent restraint the rant-
ings of the old man against such dignitaries of Nationalism as Maurras or Barrès.   We may suspect Variot of over-emphasizing what
sympathies the ultimate Sorel expressed with regard to Benito Mussolini, but these statements are corroborated from other sources.
Likewise, the version of Sorel's simultaneous love affair with Lenin
has a true, unexpurgated ring: it is transcribed without any apologetics
or censure.   But it is possible that retrospective editing has endowed
certain Sorelian prophecies with a significance not warranted by the
original dicta.   It is with these qualifications that the reminiscences
of Variot must be judged.

Variot's particular relationship to Sorel is worth contemplating.
Like Boswell, he does not mind being occasionally humbled, and even
insulted by greatness; he seems to take a singular, impish pleasure
in acting the young scamp who will not and must not be taken seriously.   There are vast advantages to be gained by that method, for a man
who suffers himself to be treated as a fool, thereby acquires the priv-
ileges of a fool: to tell the truth and to make fun of his employer with
impunity, — rights of which Jean Variot availed himself with prudent
moderation, but somehow implying, in a stealthy way, that Georges
Sorel found in him quite an equal in conversation.   There is the self-
effacing type of whom it may be said that "he is not important enough
to be as humble as all that!"[45]   Now Variot's modesty is limited, yet
by successfully putting Sorel at ease, by goading him into reckless,
off-the-record statements, he went far in pulling Sorel down to his
own level of humdrum humanity.   No doubt, he did it with the best of
intentions; and, indeed, the portrait of a brawling, cackling Sorel who
occasionally seems to be deep in his cups, does not detract one inch
from the man's stature; the immense gusto of his quixotic tilts with
long forgotten nine-day-wonders of French politics and letters is as
irresistible as it is lovable.   For Sorel was an angry man not because
he bore life a grudge, but because he was fond of it.   His towering
prophetic rage was generated not by weakness, but by strength.   We
owe to Nietzsche the insight into the ambiguous character of our af-
fects: two people may be possessed by what seems one and the same
passion, of identical strength and effect, and yet, in one case, the affect will be a symptom of abundance, of life affirmation; in the other,
of privation, of resentment.[46]   It may be profitable to investigate the
nature of Sorel's affective reactions in that light, to the extent that
they reveal themselves in, and are relevant to, his political and social

[44]Variot, op. cit., pp. 8, 14.

[45]An utterance attributed to Thomas Mann. The "Victim" was a very
famous German writer who shall remain unnamed.

[46]See Beyond Good and Evil in The Complete Works of Friedrich Nietzsche,
Vol. V (Edinburgh and London, 1909), p. 122-123.

doctrines. Sorel seems to have used Variot almost exclusively as a receptacle for uninhibited confessions.[47] A choleric vindictiveness is such a marked characteristic of these conversations, that it is difficult not to suspect frustration as the real and sole reason of so much aggressiveness.

But such a judgment would be rash, for while Sorel was beyond any doubt a very wrathful man, his wrath has a remarkably infectuous and exhilarating quality. These furies are not those of a frustrated man. Behind the thunder and the lightning one perceives a serene sky, the inward equanimity of one sure of himself. His indignation is that of an intellectual millionaire, not of a beggar. If he seems ill disposed toward an argument, it is not that he is averse to arguing as such, but because he is unwilling to argue on a level which he deems unworthy. His rage is, as his doctrine of the general strike, essentially defensive: it is intellectual violence intended to protect rational standards. The Sorelian kind of irritation runs no interference with thought, — it is a derivation from it: another mode of reasoning. In short, the volcanic force at work in that man is not anger reasoning, but angered reason.

This interpretation will not be acceptable to those who view Sorel as an irrationalist, as the apostle of intuitive, instinctive drives. But close inspection will reveal, if it has not already done so, that Sorel, who recognized the major role of mythical concepts in the life of man, was not himself a man of myth.[48] He was concerned with the subconscious, dark part of the soul, his understanding went out toward it, not from it. He knew that one can be too clever to grasp the complexity of things, but that is not the same as underrating the role of intelligence. He never did commit the "treason of the clerks."[49] In pointing out the limitations of the intellect, Sorel was no more an irrationalist than David Hume.

Democratic Illusions and Realities

Being a Rightwinger, Jean Variot was naturally predisposed to play up Sorel's anti-democratic bias; and since that bias became more acute when Syndicalism seemed to have succumbed to the lure of democracy, the notes which Variot took during the time of Sorel's disillusion (between 1908 and 1912) are particularly careful and revealing.

---

[47]"One could observe a curious contrast between the good natured expression of his round and rosy old face and the trenchant pronouncements which he sometimes made upon his contemporaries." Variot, **op. cit.**, p. 128.

[48]See chapter 11, p. 262.

[49]The reference is to Julien Benda's book, **La trahison des clercs** (Paris, 1927), translated by Richard Aldington as **The Great Betrayal** (London, 1928) and **The Treason of the Intellectuals** (New York, 1928).

Any partisan will rejoice when he finds the enemy deficient in organic strength or moral energy; not so Sorel. Any weakness or neglect of duty is to him something to be rejected even in a foe. This objectivity, which perhaps deserves the name, scholarly, was notable in his critique of the Church;[50] it shows itself again, when he combats the French bourgeois republic. He criticizes it, not for being too powerful, too efficient in keeping the people in place, but for not being powerful enough. Sorel appoints himself champion of the great political realities which he calls la grande politique — against the great illusions of the democratic myth. The state, whether it is democratic or monarchic, has to make war incessantly: at home, on "the utopian spirit, which also may be called the spirit of disorder; abroad, on the diplomatic combinations...of the enemy."[51] There is no royal or republican grande politique, but always the same need for a "political logic" as "the only shield which will protect the vulnerable points of any agglomeration of people."[52] It is the sum total of all acts required to satisfy "the superior needs of the collectivity."[53] Without it, no national progress toward the good life.[54] But in terms of la grande politique, "the equivalent of what, in military language, is called the direction of the large units,"[55] the collectivity is nothing but a fiction, "because of its inability to understand its proper interests."[56] The parliamentary regime merely obscures and complicates matters: the masses, Sorel says, with Michels, with Pareto and with Mosca, are today not less led than before;[57] "they thought they voted, but all they did was to give themselves masters."[58] Sorel does not say that the state is man's supreme creation; on the contrary, he assumes that our "atavistic instincts" were those of the solitary anarchist: who knows, he exclaims, perhaps Cain, the asocial, antisocial murderer is the prototype of "normal" man![59] But once organization is conceded and the usefulness of the state is accepted, "the obligation of the state to make decisions, and the obligation of the mass of people to obey will have to be admitted."[60]

If this is so, and if the primacy of la grande politique is a condition which cannot be violated with impunity, then it is hard to understand, how democratic governments can be so easygoing. Not to enforce in their administration the strict order which they expect of their armies, simply does not make sense to Sorel.[61] In his opinion, no community can make the slightest progress unless its management is under severe discipline and thoroughly accountable for all its acts.[62]

---

[50]See chapter 3, p. 75. ff.

[51]Variot, op. cit., p. 101.   [52]Ibid., p. 97.

[53]Ibid., p. 108.   [54]Ibid., p. 101.

[55]Ibid.   [56]Ibid., p. 108.

[57]Ibid., p. 100.   [58]Ibid., p. 99.

[59]Ibid., p. 110-112.   [60]Ibid., p. 99.

[61]Ibid., pp. 104, 107-108.   [62]Ibid., p. 107.

Thus, travelling a not at all devious way, that great enemy of the state, Georges Sorel, ends up in the vicinity of the authoritarian school. There is even an intimation that non-democratic systems bestow greater social benefits on their own citizens than does the Third Republic: "The German worker is much happier than the French. He enjoys the same pleasures as the bourgeois, he finds his entertainment in the same beerhalls...."[63] There is even a touch of demophobia in the notion that the people never act unless they have been stirred up by intellectuals and bourgeois orators.[64] Still, there is no inconsistency in all this; Sorel had never favored the Revolt of the Masses; his revolution was to be one of minorities. Nor does it preclude order and authority: "Syndicalism...confides its interests to specialists whom it obeys. Therein lies its strength. It has much more of the sense of la grande politique then our [French] statesmen have who are men of laissez-aller. But laissez-aller has never been a social method."[65]

This utterance was made in 1909, at a time when Sorel no longer considered himself to be a syndicalist. But the old sympathy still lingers on, although Sorel has lost all hope in any revolutionary change in his own country: "It is possible the public will have had enough of all these [parliamentary] shenanigans one day. But do not therefore believe that things will greatly change....You don't know our good Frenchmen, if you think they will renounce their habits."[66] If there is to be any cataclysm, it will be brought about, not by a revolution, but by war.

"We shall see great things." These are the first words Jean Variot hears Sorel say in 1908 [67] Today, in 1951, we are not overly surprised by the announcement that "the war will come from Russia," nor was it so surprising even then, in the year of the Bosnian crisis. But when Sorel proceeded to say that war was "the normal European condition," he was far ahead of most of his contemporaries.[68] "Before ten years are over," he predicted, "Europe will founder in war and anarchy, as she is used to doing twice or thrice a century."[69] The rotten Tsarist despotism will unleash the war, and "naturally Pan-Germanism will also have its say,"[70] but the real culprits, in Sorel's opinion, will be the democracies, and above all (here Georges Sorel is very French) Great Britain, with her policy of non-commitment. A clearcut military pact with France would clarify the air, but that vague system called Entente cordiale is neither here nor there.[71]

"They talk of federating Europe," after the pattern of the United States of America. Those people forget that the U. S. A. are held

[63]Ibid., p. 100.   [64]Ibid., p. 115.
[65]Ibid., p. 108.   [66]Ibid., p. 98.
[67]Ibid., p. 15.   [68]Ibid., p. 17.
[69]Ibid., p. 18-19.   [70]Ibid., p. 17.
[71]Ibid., p. 35.

together by a homogeneous culture, by a common language, whereas Europe .... [72] Nor does Sorel accept the evidence of the Swiss federation: the old cantons which threw off the Imperial yoke were held together by nationalist interests, and they, in turn, attracted, by sheer force the French and Italian territories which now make up Switzerland together with the German-speaking sector.[73] Far from having spent its force, nationalism is still making headway: it captures even countries where it was supposed to have fulfilled its mission long ago. No wonder: "all European nations live under permanent menace. Hence the exasperation of nationalisms."[74]

Yet the philosopher of violence cannot be called an advocate of war. He calls it "that ignoble stupidity which changes nothing." But the inevitability of war is a fact which must be met squarely. "The issue cannot be met with Socialist twaddle; only with Nationalistic principles. I really am curious how the European Socialists will act, when the nations will be ready to hurl themselves against each other." Does that mean that Sorel is a friend of nationalism? He scoffs: Because I study it? **"Sapristi!** Facts are facts, and once more facts!"[75] War, he agrees with Durkheim and Le Bon, is a form of collective insanity, collective suicide. Supposing, six million draftees in France and Germany would refuse to answer the call. The governments would send the police after them. Then, what would happen? The police could not arrest six million people. But each one among the six million will believe that he will be among the few arrested. Sorel describes astutely the psychology of terror used by the totalitarians afterwards: "Threatened by implacable laws, we flee forward to escape them, in a kind of death acceptance which amounts to a vast suicide ...." In 1870, the Parisians shouted **A Berlin!** and the Berliners **Nach Paris!** "And they were singing songs. But that was nothing else but resignation," although the young soldiers of course did not know it. "Europe is a graveyard, populated by nations which will sing before they kill each other. The Germans and the French, they will soon sing again. Ah! Holbein was quite right to depict in his **Dance of Death,** Death as a fiddler striking up a little tune to lead men to their destiny."[76]

And afterwards? "Let us assume, the war will not end well for Germany. Then the old German disorder is bound to return. Who will be the man, the German, capable of reassembling the dismembered limbs of the Germanic body? If ever Germany should fall apart, because she is no longer held together by authoritarian force, ...a genius ten times bigger than any other country would need to restore her." To which Variot adds in a note: "Seven times Sorel talked to me between 1910 and 1912 about the type of man who could

---

[72]Ibid., p. 17.   [73]Ibid., p. 22.
[74]Ibid., p. 25.   [75]Ibid., p. 27-28.
[76]Ibid., p. 29-30.

refashion Germany in case of a downfall of the Hohenzollerns. This anticipation of Hitler is rather curious. On the other hand, did Hitler in his prison perhaps read the **Reflections on Violence?** What else is his authoritarian socialism but a German version of Sorel?"[77] Published in 1935, when Hitler, like Mussolini, was held in respect by many respectable people, that comment was meant to enhance Sorel's prestige; today, the author doubtlessly would wish it had remained unwritten. It might be asked why Sorel's name should not be linked to that of Hitler. It has been linked, and justly so, with Mussolini. But aside from the point that Sorel liked only **certain aspects** of Italian fascism,[78] he never identified himself with the principle of authoritarian government. It was for him simply another fact of history, which must be recognized: the remedy of national self-preservation in a time of trouble. This Sorelian conviction is borne out by an utterance he made in 1910: "Whatever the future may hold in store for us, we can affirm one thing: if Marxism should ever come to power somewhere in the world, it will be by the use of authoritarian violence."[79] It is not likely that Sorel was thinking of Russia at that time (1910); rather it was Germany he had in mind, with her seemingly so powerful social democratic party. Still, it is a surprise that Variot did not deem the statement "curious" enough to give Sorel credit for having foreseen the Soviet regime seven years ahead of time. Variot may have refrained from doing so also because Sorel, whenever he refers to red Russia before 1917, spoke of her in a very disparaging way: "Russia? Don't talk to me of Russia. The Russians will always be Russians.... Let us not talk of their public spirit, nor of those frightful Romanoffs who all together did as many criminal and stupid things as Peter the Great and Catherine did to help those impossible Russians...." (The great historian seems to have forgotten that Peter and Catherine too were Romanoffs.) Only at the tag end of his diatribe, Sorel permits himself to express some hope for the Russians but again, as in the case of Germany, he makes it conditional upon a miracle: "Only a genius could restore their national and social dignity."[80] But this is enough for Variot to vindicate his prophet once more: in a footnote he refers to the things Georges Sorel will have to say about the red Tsar of the Russians twelve years later.[81]

During the war, our author and his Boswell did not meet, but we can fill the gap in the account of Sorelian predictions from other sources. One of these concerns the Reich again: "If Germany should be defeated," he writes Croce, "the Social Democrats will by no means pursue the customary democratic policy; instead of working for the downfall of the country, they will help to bolster German discipline."

---

[77] Ibid., p. 31.
[79] Variot, op. cit., p. 116.
[81] Ibid., pp. 66 ff ; see chapter 10.

[78] See chapter 9.
[80] Ibid., p. 32-33.

And Croce adds, in a note: "That is exactly what happened."[82] And
in another letter to Croce, Sorel confesses his innate dislike and distrust of all things Russian: "It is not the Slavic domination which
could give birth to a new Middle Ages...." " (in the preceding sentence he had discounted the possibility of a Viconian rebirth) "The
Slavs are strangers to the main ideas of our civilization...." " But
the danger is not merely one of Slavic conquest; it threatens from
within as well, and the term, Slavic, thus assumes an ominously double
meaning: "As we fall into decadence, we become Slaves ourselves;
we are ripe for the Russian domination."[83]   When Croce read this,
thirty-five years ago, he must have thought Sorel wildly extravagant;
today, the great philosopher could probably add to the text another,
gloomy note of approbation.

The day before the peace treaty was signed in nearby Versailles,
the two men ran into each other on the **Pont de la Concorde.**   Sorel at
once resumes the conversation interrupted for four years: "Listen,
Variot. You went to war, you saw things happen...." " And Variot,
remembering the words which Sorel spoke when they first met, repeats: "Yes, the great things...." " But Sorel will have none of it: "No,
great stupidities.... And the end is not yet. Believe me, you're still
young. Nothing will change. Class wars, national wars, always the
same pretexts for buffoons." Is there anything left? Yes, the ideas:
"they are the granite which will outlast the place-hunting, the prejudices, the cheap politics."[84]

The old purveyor of ideas, notwithstanding his brave words,
sounds downcast, almost tearful; his belligerency seems all gone. To
the astonishment of Variot, he has nothing but praise for Romain Rolland, whom he had execrated as a phrase-maker and feeble novelist.
Now he admires him for the steadfastness and courage of his wartime
pacifism. But the peaceful mood does not last long. His expectation
that the peace would be as sordid as the war had been had already
come true; the decomposition of Marxism, of which he had written
long ago, had ended with the dismal collapse of the vaunted International; French nationalism had teamed up with the forces of "bank-
ocracy" — all that could hardly be surprising to Sorel. Yet his **post-
mortem** still sounds like that of a very angry man. However, a new
note has crept into the strident denunciation: he had known the feeling of defeat before; he had resigned himself to intellectual loneliness.
But never before had he sounded so apologetic; never before had he
been so humble and at the same time so dreamily detached from his
own work: "I'm a self-taught man. I compile my materials in the hope
that someone will make use of them. If no one does, that is too bad.
Or is it? Who knows?"[85]

[82]La Critica (1929, p. 116), January 4, 1915.
[83]Ibid. (p. 295), December 12, 1915.
[84]Variot, op. cit., p. 46.   [85]Ibid., p. 48.

7. A LIFE IN LETTERS ii

(1908 - 1921)

"I retire into my hole."[1] The reasons which Sorel has offered in justification of his withdrawal from syndicalism, such as intrigues within the movement, infiltration of careerists, waning of the revolutionary spirit — these reasons sound impressive enough, but somehow they seem to explain too much. The startling coincidence of Sorel's saying good-bye at the very moment that his main syndicalist publication reached the public, suggests another, simpler explanation, — one to be found in Sorel's character: once he had answered an intellectual question for himself, he was likely to get restless, fed up. Having said, for the time being, what he had to say, he liked to drop the issue, not without providing himself with a good excuse, and turn to something else.

For the moment, at a loss what to do next, Sorel is in a dejected mood: "I will try to do some small books," he writes Croce, "but I do not have much courage, and it takes much courage to write something that is useful."[2]

He has been attacked as a Romanticist because of his **Illusions of Progress**. But "I am nothing of the sort." And he instructs the critic, Jean Bourdeau of **Les Débats,** to take due notice of that **démenti**. The work is to appear in an Italian version, but "I do not know whether this translation will have any success because the book is very French in its subject matter."[3]

Sorel does not remain long in his "hole." A letter dated September 18, 1908, reveals, though in a rather devious and apologetic fashion, the new interest, the new attraction: "I am sending you a revue with the French text of my article on modernism ... the Italian translation was too free and full of nonsense. I could not remake the article because that would have brought me too many attacks for giving something to the revue of young royalists; but I could let them have

---

[1]See chapter 1, p. 45.

[2]Letters to Croce (**La Critica,** 1928, p. 108), June 24, 1908. One of the "small books" will be **La décomposition du Marxisme** (pp. 68), another, **La révolution dreyfusienne** (pp. 64). See chapter 6, p. 158 - 159.

[3]To Croce (**loc. cit.,** p. 108), September 12, 1908. Sorel stated that prior to the **Reflections** he enjoyed no publicity "except the one which Bourdeau devoted to [his writings] in **Les Débats** and **La Revue Politique et Parlamentaire.**" (To Robert Michels, November 13, 1905, cited in "Lettere di Georges Sorel a Roberto Michels," **Nuovi Studi di diritto, economia e politica,** Rome, September - October, 1929, p. 289).

the [original] French text. These youngsters are very intelligent.
Since they cite my books all the time, I could not well refuse them a
collaboration of this sort. I communicated to them your judgment on
modernism which is so correct."[4]

It is not easy to follow Sorel in his argument: the fine distinction
which he draws between contributing a new article to the organ of the
"enemies" of yesterday (a reprehensible act) and letting them use the
original of a translation, is too clearly self-defeating as to require
any further comment. He is obviously embarrassed; the way Sorel
tries to draw Croce into the affair shows an uneasy conscience. But
the young people flatter him, and he is lonely. Or is Sorel for once
less than candid? Are the flattery and the embarrassment only pretexts behind which he conceals the fact that those Royalists are something more than just "very intelligent:" was it that Sorel, a general
who had just lost an army, saw in them new allies in his fight against
the Third Republic and its bourgeoisie?

It is no accident that Sorel's bias against Jews, which had been a
mere undercurrent in his thought, now begins to be an obsession with
him. It is an element too conspicuous in his work to be passed over
in silence here. Quoting Arturo Labriola, Sorel notes that "in Milan
a part of high finance is Jewish and socialist."[5] As he grows older
and more bitter, the erstwhile Dreyfusard will forever be on the trail
of Jewish influence in commerce, literature, politics. There is, in
that pursuit, nothing inconsistent with his general aversion against
bourgeois traders (in ideal and material goods) as parasites exploiting what the actual producers are creating.[6] The anti-semitism of
Sorel is a conservative's concern about the Jewish "element of decomposition."[7] Nietzsche too had written in that vein, but the comparison would be unfair to him, because his attitude toward the Jews
combined contempt of the middleman with admiration of the Hebrew
genius, denunciation of their "slave morality" with subtle sympathy
and understanding. Whereas Sorel betrays nothing if not the dour
suspicions of the peasant in conjunction with the sullen phobia of the
petty bourgeoisie, anticipating, it must be admitted with regret, in an
uncanny way the vulgar notions of a Streicher, Himmler, Hitler.[8]

---

[4]To Croce (loc. cit., p. 108). The article mentioned was «Le modernisme
dans la Religion et dans le modernisme; the royalist revue in which it appeared, was the Revue Critique des Livres et des Idées (1908). The Italian
version had been printed by the Divenire Sociale of November 16, 1907, under
the title, "Modernismo nelle religione e nel socialismo."

[5]To Croce (loc. cit., p. 190), October 24, 1908.

[6]Cf. chapter 3, p. 85f.

[7]Theodor Mommsen, Auch ein Wort über unser Judentum in Reden und
Aufsaetze (Berlin, 1905), p. 416-417.

[8]He will make an exception of Henri Bergson, but even in his case Sorel's
bias asserts itself, as will be seen.

Fortunately, Daniel Halévy is officially not of the Hebrew dispensation, or else Sorel would not dispatch and recommend to Croce his
biography of Nietzsche.[9] "I believe," Sorel says, "this book merits ...
serious examination," although, he adds, it would have gained had the
author been more alert to the fact that "there were, around Nietzsche,
people who contributed a great deal to his misery, and who prevented
him from producing what could have been expected of him; all those
messieurs were quite injurious to Nietzsche."[10] A very typical remark: even where Sorel is appreciative of the great Dionysian, which
is not too often, he distinguished between the Nietzsche who could
have been and the actual man who became a Nietzschean.[11]

Between proof-reading the Italian **Reflections** Sorel still finds
time to act in his favorite role, as a literary matchmaker, by seeing
to it that Edouard Berth reviews Croce's **Philosophy of the Practical**,[12] and by urging the author to send another copy to Bergson "who
told me that your **Aesthetics** interested him greatly." Follows one of
Sorel's rare personal remarks: "I am all smashed and I don't know
when I will be in shape again for doing some reading, let alone serious
work." As if he had said too much already, Sorel turns, in the next
sentence, to Giuseppe Prezzolini who "seems to have recovered a bit
from his pragmatism."[13] That Italian writer, he notes gleefully in his
next letter, had informed him that [Giovanni] Papini too has ceased to
be a Pragmatist: "He should have started that way; what seduced
those two to adopt pragmatism, was its novelty and a certain touch of
Machiavellian dilettantism." Prezzolini had sent him an article in
which the philosophy of Creative Evolution was traced back to Hegel,
a construction which would "surprise Bergson a great deal" because
the latter "sees no relation between his own and Hegel's ideas."[14]

The matchmaker continues his efforts: "The other day, I met **M.**
Bergson who is very anxious to meet you. He will probably go to
Northern Italy on his vacation, and when I told him that you pass your
summers very often in Perugia, he answered that it would probably
not be too difficult to arrange a meeting. I believe you would please
him by suggesting a rendez-vous ...."[15]

Earlier in the year (1909), Sorel is worried because he has not
heard from the friend "for ages," but he can guess the reason: "that
terrible catastrophe, in which you must have lost more than one

---

[9]**La vie de Frédéric Nietzsche** (Paris, 1908).

[10]To Croce (**loc. cit.**, p. 191-192), November 23, 1908

[11]He comes closest to endorsing some of Nietzsche's views in the **Reflections**, (1950 Am. ed.), pp. 256-264.

[12]**Filosofia della pratica** (Bari, 1908); Engl. transl., London, 1913.

[13]To Croce (**loc. cit.**, p. 192). December 9, 1908. — On Prezzolini, cf.
chapter 9, p. 217.

[14]To Croce (**loc. cit.**, p. 192), December 23, 1908.

[15]**Ibid.** (p. 197), August 6, 1909.

friend."[16] Sorel worries about still another friend: "I received Pareto's **Manuel d'économie politique.** Apparently, he took some of your comments on the Italian edition quite seriously, although your remarks really were gentle enough."[17] He acknowledges receipt of the Italian **Reflections,** which were published by Croce's house, Laterza: "the edition is much more beautiful than the French one....I thank you for all the trouble you took in that matter."[18] But his real interest is elsewhere:

"My brochure on the Dreyfus affair begins to cause me much annoyance. Because I did not care to argue about Dreyfus's innocence or guilt, I find many people inclined to boycott me...but I am used to that kind of treatment, and I shall continue on my way." We learn on this occasion that the booklet about the Dreyfus Revolution as we possess it, is the condensed version of a "fairly thick volume" which Sorel had then decided not to publish because it seemed "unnecessary." He almost regrets his decision now, for many of the troublesome remarks, so he believes, would have passed unnoticed in the larger context.[19]

The people who are boycotting him, are of course the socialist and syndicalist friends of yesterday. But they have enough worries of their own: "the socialist revues are passing...through a terrible crisis," Sorel notes, not too unhappily. "They have nothing more to say." And he lists the whole lot of them: **Die Neue Zeit,** Karl Kautsky's organ "has been reduced to babbling nonsense;" the **Revue Socialiste** which printed so much of Sorel, shows a "distressing insignificance;" Lagardelle's **Le Mouvement Socialiste** has enjoyed "a few years of prosperity (strictly in the intellectual sense, I am told); but [the editors] saw to it that Berth and I had to withdraw." And ever since, "the revue has sunken to the level of mere platitudes." How much more stimulating, in comparison, is the production of the anti-socialists and anti-democratic Right: "You may have received the volume of G. Valois, which I announced to you...." He is noncommittal, at first: "that movement certainly will not bring the political results expected by its promoters; but it will have some influence on the intelligent because Maurras and some of his friends are very well educated, and people begin to be disgusted with the definitely mediocre crowd which, with great insolence, monopolizes the best [academic]

---

[16]**Ibid.** (p. 193), February 3, 1909. — Croce's footnote: "the earthquake of Messina."

[17]**Ibid.** (p. 194), February 12, 1909. Croce criticised Pareto in an essay reprinted in his **Materialismo storico ed economia marxista** (Bari, 1900), French transl., Paris, 1901; **Historical Materialism and the Economics of Karl Marx** (London, New York, 1914).

[18]To Croce (**loc. cit.,** p. 194), March 23, 1909.

[19]**Ibid.** (p. 195), May 10, 1909.

positions."[20] Valois is much on his mind; once more he presses upon
Croce the "curious volume written by a young royalist; G. Valois is a
commercial employee whose literary gifts are considerable."[21] However, Sorel is not ready yet, as he will be a few years later, to take
Valois's scheme of a social kingdom seriously: "He certainly is under a delusion if he thinks that the relationship between some revolutionary syndicalists and the monarchists of L'Action Française will
be of any consequence; still, his book contains quite a few observations
which attest well to the author's high intelligence and perspicacity."
And coming to his point: "I would be obliged if you could read his
book and say something about it." He is already engaged, but not yet
committed.

The New Patriotism

Commenting on a literary feud between Croce and Luzzatti, the
historian Sorel makes this curiously matter-of-fact remark: "Who in
France today regrets the horrible persecutions of the Albigensians?
What would France be if she had lost her Southern province?"[22] Sorel is of course thinking of the potential cultural loss; still, his conclusion seems to be that Right is what is good for the national interest, a sentence which has been made famous by somebody else. As
for Sorel, the parallel to the great cause celèbre of his country is
quite obvious. Indeed, Luzzatti is called a Dreyfusard in the next letter, half of which is a lengthy quotation from Joseph Reinach's volu-
minous History of the Dreyfus Affair, one of the works that provoked
Sorel into writing his own account of the event. With something like a
pleasant shudder, Sorel relates what even such a Dreyfusard as
Reinach has to say about the Jews: that they had always been revolutionaries; first with their prophets; then, in the Middle Ages, as the
artisans of Averroism and pantheism; their exegetics is to be found
in the cradle of the Reformation, their Cabbala in the cradle of Free-
masonry; and finally, since 1789, they were among the principal archi-
tects of the modern world, while their socialists, Lassalle and Marx,
conspired for its downfall. To Sorel this passage constitutes "a monument of insanity" and, though "the author is remarkably well informed,
his work is marred by countless half-truths," — product of the kind of

---

[20]Ibid. (p. 195-196), June 27, 1909. — The book by George Valois was La
monarchie et la classe ouvrière (Paris, n. d.).

[21]To Croce (loc. cit., p. 334), August 11, 1909. — About Valois, see also Introduction to Part II, p.164f, and chapter 11, p. 254 - 255.

[22]To Croce (loc. cit., p. 335), November 18, 1909. — The subject of Croce's
criticism was David Luzzatti's book, La libertà di coscienza e di scienza.
Cf. Croce, Pagine sparse I (Naples, 1919), pp. 287-290.

nationalism, in this case Jewish nationalism, "with which you simply cannot argue."[23]

Turning to philosophy in the next paragraph of the same letter, Sorel notes that William James's **Pluralism** is to be translated into French. He adds: "In the mind of W. James, pluralism seems to have the function of explaining the existence of evil in the world; the fact of evil poses some difficulties for philosophers with optimistic leanings (as are the English and Americans); they account for it in a crude way by assuming that there are several worlds and several gods. (**Varieties of Religious Experience** has an intimation of that thesis.) In a general way, the problem of evil is the stumbling stone of modern thought, unwilling as it is to hear of anything derogatory to its optimism." But then again, we see Sorel engaged in propagating James in France: he wants his publisher, Rivière, to follow up the **Pluralism** by the translation of **The Meaning of Truth**,[24] and, in connection with a Crocean article on Marx and Hegel, he indicates the **raison d'être** of pragmatism: "I wonder whether it is a mere accident that Hegel never had a real successor; perhaps his system was the last one that could be constructed. Nothing like this probably occurred before; each system was in turn supplanted by another; but Hegel's never was. Is it at all possible to replace it? Perhaps Marx was right in not creating a new system, and pragmatism is the obvious indication that something has happened in the history of thought."[25]

Marx, Hegel — these old themes are being crowded out by the new interests. Two books arouse Sorel's curiosity. One is written by Lucas de Pesloüan, the other by Péguy. The first-named is "a former army officer who had been with the engineers and left the service because he is rich, but who continues to be interested in mathematical questions."[26] But it is not mathematics that Sorel is so much interested in at this particular moment, as the close relationship existing between Lucas de Pesloüan and Charles Péguy. The two men are comrades-in-arms in the new movement on the Right: the mathematician has just published an analysis of Péguy's work, and Sorel finds the article "important, since the author is a friend and relative of

---

[23]To Croce (**loc. cit.**, p. 336), November 27, 1909. Sorel's citation is from Joseph Reinach, **Histoire de l'affaire Dreyfus** (Paris, 1901-1911), tome IV, p. 444.

[24]To Croce (**loc. cit.**, p. 338), April 1, 1910.

[25]**Ibid.**, April 10, 1910.

[26]**Ibid.** (p. 337), February 11, 1910. — The parallel with Sorel's own career is striking. Daniel Halévy who considers **M.** de Pesloüan to be a thinker as great as he is unknown, spoke to the present writer of the sympathy which the two retired engineers felt for one another. Unlike Sorel, de Pesloüan wrote very sparingly. The book mentioned in the letter, **Les systèmes logiques et la logistique** (Paris, 1909) has remained the cardinal work of Sorel's friend.

Barrès."[27]   Of **The Mystery of St. Joan's Charity,** the work in which
the erstwhile Dreyfusard Péguy proclaims his return to fatherland
and church, Sorel says that "its literary value has been generally
recognized; the genre is new, at least, in France; the writer, Charles
Péguy, wishes very much to be discussed; he would be grateful to you
for a full appraisal in **La Critica.**"[28]   Sorel ventures a prediction:
"Perhaps Peguy will become **the great writer of the renewed patriotism;** there seems to be something after all to that rejuvenation of the
patriotic sentiment the Dreyfus crowd is making so much fun of
lately."[29]

Once Sorel is on the trail of a good subject, he pursues it with
unbending loyalty. Barrès, although a relative of Péguy's friend, had
been less than appreciative of the **St. Joan,** the reason being, in Sorel's
view, that Barrès "is too much the **psychological romancier,** unable to
appreciate a **"mystery of lamentation, supplication and lyrical glorification."**   The old agnostic in Sorel is only slightly embarrassed by
Péguy's ardent Catholicism: after all, the Christian element in the
work merely lends color to what is essentially "a national subject."[30]

A very international subject interjects itself into the correspondence: Theodore Roosevelt had visited Paris; his reception at the
Sorbonne elicits the following undiplomatic comment from Sorel:
"That yankee [sic] is quite a nuisance and the European enthusiasm
for him is difficult to understand; I can see why the diplomats should
play up to him if he is really, as I read ... singled out for a Caesarian
destiny; but that should be an additional reason for the rest of us to
show reserve!"[31]   From this excursion into the realm of world politics, Sorel returns to William James and pragmatism. The coldness
with which he looks back on the philosophy of action proclaimed only
two years earlier in the **Reflections,** may be gathered from a reference to the French edition of Croce's **Philosophy of the Practical,**
which was about to appear. The work might impress Paris, Sorel believes, since "everybody talks in a helter-skelter fashion, of the philosophy of action, of practice and experience...."[32]

On June 28, 1910, Sorel writes Croce one of his longest letters,
full of interesting revelations.[33] He begins by recommending to his
correspondent a young compatriot who is to become Sorel's Italian
translator and biographer, recipient of some of the rare communica-
tions in which the old author tells something about himself.[34]   The

[27]**Ibid.**
[28]**Ibid.** (p. 336-337), January 24, 1910.
[29]**Ibid.** (p. 337), February 11, 1910. — Sorel's emphasis
[30]**Ibid.** (p. 337-338), February 28, 1910. — Sorel's emphasis.
[31]**Ibid.** (p. 339), May 10, 1910.
[32]**Ibid.** (p. 339), May 21, 1910. — See note 12.
[33]**Ibid.** (pp. 340-342).
[34]See also above, p. 177 and below, **pp.** 189, 195, 201.

new confidant is Agostino Lanzillo who will end up as a Fascist. In
1910 he is a collaborator of Il Devenire sociale, Sorel's old mouthpiece. That review is about to fold up like so many other little organs
of the Left; so young Lanzillo needs another job. Could Croce help?
As for Sorel himself, the fate of the periodical that published the first,
rudimentary Reflections leaves him cold, and all the more so as
"some young people who seem to have sufficient means, plan to found
a revue here, of which I would be the director. This presents me with
a very tough question, on account of my health." But his sense of duty
toward a good friend wins out: "I have accepted, on condition that
Berth is made co-director; thus, if the enterprise should prove to be
successful, I could quit and leave Berth in an established position."
Any doubts about the political character of the new enterprise are
quickly dispelled: "so far, [Berth] has not had much luck with socialist literature; he must leave that dead alley in order to make his
talent known...." In his eagerness to allay Croce's suspicion, Sorel
drags in Bergson. The philosopher had used his influence to force an
article by Berth about Péguy's St. Joan upon a hesitating editor. Such
pressure would not have been necessary, "if Berth had already been
co-editor of a revue (insignificant as that revue might be)." Quod erat
demonstrandum: Sorel must oblige certain well-to-do young people,
who would not be found in a socialist dead alley, in order to make
Edouard Berth sufficiently acceptable to all and everybody.

As if he were ashamed, Sorel turns — still in the same letter — to
a subject dear to Croce. It occurs in a new essay of Sorel's[35] in
which he "reached the same conclusions as you did: Hegel's historic
significance lies in the fact that he made an end of the ancient dogmas
and initiated a new era. What you want retained of Hegel's work is an
ensemble of attitudes which [the philosopher] must assume in the
presence of reality if he intends to master it." In his anxiety to please
the Neo-Hegelian Croce, Sorel places himself on what may charitably
be called a high plateau of safety: his definition of the correct philosophic attitude describes to him "the essential function of all philosophy; as soon as it begins to be dogmatic, scientific fallacies creep
in."

Whenever he is in an intellectual or moral quandry. Sorel announces that he is a sick, old man. He wants to write more philosophic articles; but will he have the necessary strength? At present,
he is hardly able to do any writing at all; the best he can do is brief
meditations, a few pages each: "that is perhaps what I shall do in the
projected revue...confining myself to a chronicle of ideas." In a
circuitous way, he has returned to the awkward subject in which his
own role is apparently to be entirely non-political. Is Georges Sorel
afraid of Croce's answer?

------

[35]"Vues sur les problèmes de la philosophie" in Revue de Métaphysique
et de Morale, September, 1910, and January, 1911.

But the next letter[36] solemnly announces the prospectus of "a revue scheduled to appear on the first of November."[37] Only a few friends like Pareto will receive the declaration of intention, because the editors do not wish "to be attacked before the first issue is out." Croce's collaboration is solicited with the imploring and assuring words: "I accepted a very heavy burden; I shall retire as soon as the revue is on its feet...." And he accepted only under severe pressure: "the founders declared my participation indispensable for the success of the project." Once more, he applies the Hegel treatment, this time in conjunction with a Bergson testimonial: "I saw Bergson yesterday, and he told me that your book on Hegel convinced him of the usefulness, for his own purpose, of re-reading Hegel more attentively than he had done before." A Croce essay on **The Masonic Mentality** arouses Sorel's "enormous interest" because of its insistence on the autonomy of philosophic thought from the demands of cultural mediocrity; Sorel wants the friend to expand the article into a booklet: "the response would be tremendous." But the most important item of this letter, at least to Sorel, is relegated to the very last sentence; a piece of sad news in two lines: "The revue of which I sent you the program, will not appear; there are too many complications."

A week or so before, Sorel seems to have hoped that there would only be a short delay in publishing the new revue: "We have been forced," he writes Lanzillo,[38] "to postpone publication...to December 1...." And he unburdens himself to his new disciple: "Some people say that I am making a great mistake in linking myself with Monarchists, as if a revue had always to be the creature of a party...." But the philosopher's mission is **"to understand those movements which he deems important;"** in order to accomplish that, "he does not have to side with those who are in the movement." The philosopher Sorel "wrote about religious questions too without belonging to the church;" is it necessary to be Catholic to understand the Catholic religion? But if detachment is a philosophic duty, it is not to be confused with distance: "we must place ourselves inside the movement and acquire an intellectual love for it; without that sympathy we cannot ever hope to get to the root of things." For once, Sorel has a kind word to say for academic education: "Our university culture enables us to make that effort, in the same way as...an architect identifies himself with the mentality of Renaissance man, or the Gothic or Egyptian period...."

Croce too, no doubt, expected to be told about the reasons which lead to the fiasco of the **Cité Française;** but he had to wait almost two

[36]To Croce (**loc. cit.,** p. 342), September 5, 1910.

[37]**La Cité Française. —** Cf. chapter 8, p. 204.

[38]The letter appeared in the **Giornale d'Italia** of November 20, 1910. Cited from Réne Johannet, **L'évolution de Georges Sorel** in **Itinéraires d'Intellectuels** (Paris, 1921), p. 216-217. — Sorel's emphasis.

months for the next letter.[39] It provides another illustration of the
oblique way in which Sorel likes to communicate his major interests:
"Please have a look at the chapter which I added to the **Illusions of
Progress.** I believe I have opened a promising road for the philosophical investigation of history by showing that the movements toward greatness are always **forced,** whereas the movement toward
decadence is always **natural;** our nature is irresistibly carried in the
direction considered bad by the philosopher of history, whether that
be barbarism or decadence."[40]

After this preamble, Sorel condescends at last to tell the story of
the still-born literary magazine: "The revue **La Cité Française** will
not appear; the two founders, members of **L'Action Française,** wanted
to dominate the scene; I would have been without any real influence
while bearing full moral responsibility. The first issue went to press
but was not put on sale." The membership of the two founders in
L'Action Française mentioned for the first time in this correspondence, must have been known to Sorel for quite a while; that he kept it
a secret for so long, is another proof of his bad conscience.

But he is not at all downcast, and for good reason, because another project has already taken shape. **La Cité Française est morte —
vive L'indépendance!** For that will be the title of the new revue of
which Sorel sends Croce still another prospectus.[41] As the founder,
he names "one of my old associates, Jean Variot. He met at once with
ardent support which permits hope of success." This time, the subjects are to be neither philosophy nor politics, but art and literature.
What of it! Sorel is in a jaunty mood: "Hopes are that the artistic
crowd will come across with not a few subscriptions." Again, Croce's
collaboration is requested. Could he write something about Carducci?

But then Sorel proceeds, in perhaps his longest letter, to reveal
more fully the skeleton in the closet of the editorial office that never
opened. His ex-friend, Lagardelle, we hear, was "greatly afraid" that
Sorel's association with two actual members of **L'Action Française**
might hurt his own good standing in the syndicalist movement, especially since he was running for parliament. "The poor boy ... actually
tries to convince himself that he and I had been associated in order to
surpass democracy, not to **destroy** it; evidently he is not familiar with
the Hegelian meaning of the word, 'surpass'. . . ." Lagardelle speaks
the Hegelian language of Russian girl students gathered for a

---

[39]To Croce (**loc. cit.,** p. 343-345), January 25, 1911.

[40]The new chapter added to the **Illusions** was called **Grandeur et décadence**
(appearing as Appendix i): "The present hour is unfavorable to the idea of
greatness, but times will change; history teaches that greatness will not fail
indefinitely that part of humanity to which belong the incomparable treasures
of classical culture and Christian tradition." (**Illusions,** 4. edition, Paris,
1927, p. 335.) — On decadence, see chapter 11, p. 258.

[41]See chapter 8, p. 204f.

revolutionary tea party. What the authentic Hegelians meant to convey was that "history never makes **tabula rasa**; revolutions preserve some things while destroying others." Marx certainly believed that social-ism would take over what was sound in the capitalist economy; "but to preserve its democratic organization is to perpetuate the omnipo-tent politician, and that is definitely not what Marxists understand by revolution." With that, we may add, Lenin would for once spontane-ously agree.[42] "However," Sorel goes on, "such considerations will not stop a man [Lagardelle] who so many times derided 'parliamen-tary cretinism' and who now wants to become a deputy!"

That paragraph, so typical of the Sorelian mind, in which the bat-tles of the century are likely to be crowded out by more ephemeral skirmishes, is followed by a summary **post mortem** of his recent past: "I believe, with you, that socialism has collapsed; Lagardelle's example is sufficient proof of the fact that the socialist mind has be-come devoid of all ideas; I am thoroughly convinced that, in dealing with these questions, one must start with the assumption which I made in...The Confessions, — fully developed, it would state that social movements cannot last unless they are sustained by a strong ideolo-by....Socialism, in becoming political, loses the strength to form such an ideology." For a moment it had looked as if syndicalism did possess that strength, but it soon fell into the hands of **"hyperdema-gogues"** who do not comprehend the "power of ideas."[43] These are the reasons which determined him "to write no longer about syndical-ism. There are more interesting questions to examine."

After this great **apologia** he has still some irritations left: "Therefore, I shall leave it to Lagardelle and his emulators to **sur-pass** democracy[44]....I understand Lagardelle plans to bring his gospel of hyperdemocracy to the Italians. **Bon voyage.**"

His mind now finally at rest, he ends the letter with the usual re-mark on Bergson: "This year, he gives his course on personality; I am not going; I know that he has an enormous crowd...." Poor Bergson, the **femmes précieuses** have taken him over; they will end by making a caricature of Bergsonism which may wreck his reform work.

Who is to Blame?

With so much of his energies absorbed by the new venture, Sorel continues to display an intellectual curiosity of truly appalling

---

[42]For the disagreements between Lenin and Sorel, see chapter 10.

[43]Sorel's emphasis. — The passage from the **Confessions** is to be found in **Matériaux d'une théorie du prolétariat** (2. edition, Paris, 1921), p. 249-250.

[44]Sorel's emphasis.

dimensions. A catalogue culled from a single letter[45] will bear out
this point: He thanks Croce for promising a contribution which will
deal with the last fifty years of Italian literature; he mentions André
Gide as the "grand chief" of the group around the **Nouvelle Revue
Française** and speaks approvingly (because Daniel Halévy vouched for
it) of a drama by the French consul in Prague, Claudel; he apologizes
for remarks he made on Hegel,[46] which "must appear extremely insufficient" to Croce; in connection with Hegel he refers to Renouvier,
once well known, today totally forgotten, as the only French philosopher who was not a Hegelian. Follows a complaint, **à propos** a book
on the Sorbonne, about the low level of instruction at that institution,[47]
in turn followed by another comment on Marxism; an article about a
"very curious" book by Arthur Drews[48] elicits the remark, echoing
ideas of his **Socrates** and the **Renan**: "Why don't the German philosophers apply their theses to St. Francis of Assisi, whose history is so
much more accessible to critical examination than the life of Jesus."

In this crazy quilt, the Marxian patch is easily the most revealing: "I am very much afraid," writes Sorel, "that what you said about
the death of socialism, is only too true."[49] In the capitalism which
Marx knew and described, the entrepreneurs were complete masters
of their house, unhampered by collective wage contracts or by government regulations. But that kind of capitalism no longer exists. "The
leaders of organized labor find advantages in entering relations either
with the owners or the government: moral advantages because those
relations raise their own status with the rank and file, and material
advantages [elision in the text] on which it is not necessary to enlarge."[50] Thus socialism becomes sheer demagoguery, "both in the
trade unions and in the political struggle ...." That is why, Sorel
reiterates, "I decided never again to write about that subject. Berth
too has arrived at the same conclusion...." Who then remains in
the socialist movement? The bright "young men who found agitating
[for socialism] an easier road to success than membership in any of
the older parties."

Do these remarks add a new note to Sorel's disenchantment?
They do. His disappointment with a proletariat prone to using

---

[45]To Croce (**loc. cit.**, p. 346-348), February 19, 1911.

[46]See above, p. 182.

[47]Sorel attacked the university in an essay, **"Lyripipi sorbonici moralisationes;"** see chapter 8, p. 204.

[48]**Die Christusmythe** (Jena, 1909); Am. transl., **The Christ Myth** (Chicago,
1911).

[49]Interview, published in **La Voce**, February 9, 1911, later published in
Croce, **Cultura e vita morale** (Bari, 1914), pp. 150-159. Also referred to by
Sorel in **Matériaux d'une théorie du prolétariat**, (2. ed. Paris, 1921). p. 3-4.

[50]Did Croce expunge a Sorelian allusion to corruptible and grafting labor
leaders?

democratic bargaining techniques, is still bitter, his vituperation of
the pseudo-proletarian leadership as grim as ever; yet there is a
touch of resignation in his voice: what happened to the movement has
an element of inevitability; as human nature goes, the proletariat
could not have developed otherwise under the changed conditions of
which Marx knew nothing. But if so, who then, is to blame if Sorel's
expectations come to nought? Has he lost faith in the validity of his
own, radical demands on the Heroic Proletarian? He certainly would
have denied any such thing, and several years later, he did deny that
he had ever entertained a doubt. But if, for the time being Georges
Sorel did not concede the point, he, at any rate, turned his back upon
the question.

For a while the correspondence centers again around Vico, because Croce had just published his important work on the Neapolitan.[51] Sorel at once puts pressure on his Paris publisher to have the
work translated into French. In the discussion of the Crocean work,
Sorel displays a rabid partisanship. One critic, Giovanni Amendola,
"has not much to say about a question which, in my opinion, has been
settled satisfactorily by you; Vico was not in the least concerned with
the religious problems of his time."[52] And when Papini, who had
labelled Vico an eclectic, receives a critical thrashing at the hands of
Croce, Sorel is delighted: "The Italians must have become iconoclastic maniacs to question the originality of Vico," he says and gives
his pragmatic definition of originality: "Vico's principle was original
since it was fruitful."[53]

Even more disturbing is the success of the poet who calls himself
the Angel Gabriel of the Annunciation, whose fame had attained international proportions. In one and the same breath, Sorel disposes of
Romain Rolland to whom the Italians attribute a position "which does
not belong to him in our literary history."[54] He still thinks highly of
Claudel and is convinced of his "complete sincerity;" there is no doubt
in Sorel's mind that only the protection of the Berthelot clan saved
the poet-diplomat from being recalled from his post because of his
too "vehement Catholicism."[55] Croce remarks at this point: "Sorel
later changed his opinion about Claudel whom I, until that time, had
not managed to relish." Indeed, fifteen months later, Sorel will write,
on the occasion of Claudel's **Partage du midi:** "I am unable to understand the enthusiasm of the Italian critic... it seems to me that this
is one of Claudel's most deplorable productions."[56]

---

[51] **La Filosofia di Giambattista Vico** (Bari, 1911), translated by R. G. Collingwood as **The Philosophy of Giovanni Battista Vico** (New York, 1913).

[52] To Croce (**loc. cit.**, p. 432), May 24, 1911.

[53] **Ibid.** (pp. 435, 436), January 27 and April 5, 1912.

[54] **Ibid.** (p. 432), July 8, 1911.

[55] **Ibid.** (p. 433), July 27, 1911. — The Berthelot family practically ruled
the **Quai d'Orsay** for many decades.

[56] **Ibid.** (p. 438), October 15, 1912.

Is D'Annunzio slipping too? One of his plays, **The Martyrdom of St. Sebastian,** is a flop, and Sorel wonders whether the author will ever recover from the setback. He does not like the man; he does not like the Jews, but that still gives the Jews no right to claim D'Annunzio as one of their own:[57] "The Jews love to annex illustrious men to their own nation, even if the evidence is pretty flimsy. I would like to know what there is to that claim, because Elémir Bourges told me the other day that D'Annunzio impressed him as a typical Jewish **littérateur."**[58] Sorel's obsession becomes most obtrusive during the time of his association with **L'Indépendance,** in which he publishes an article entitled **On Some Jewish Pretensions.** His admiration for Bergson remains intact although that great philosopher too is of Jewish origin. When Julien Benda (another Jew) writes something critical of Bergson, he becomes a publicity monger who "wants to get talked about by attacking Bergson, because he had been unsuccessful as an author of **pornographic stories."** But when a certain Jean Florence in turn comes to Bergson's defense and counter-attacks Benda, that can serve no good purpose either, because Florence is actually "a Jew called Blum, a great bluffer, who dared to join the **Action Française."**[59]

(It seems that Sorel's anti-Semitism stops at the Atlantic shore, for he does not mind writing a preface for **The Economic Interpretation of History** by Edwin R. A. Seligman, whom he calls simply, and correctly, an "American.")[60]

So incensed is Sorel by what he suspects to be a Hebrew plot against the Hebrew, Bergson, that he writes an article (not published) unmasking the "powerful forces which are today at work to block the propagation of Bergson's ideas." Why would the Jews be against

---

[57]Rumor had it that he was born with the not so poetic name of Rappaport.

[58]To Croce (**loc. cit.,** p. 437), August 11, 1912. — Elémir Bourges: another of Sorel's intellectual friends. About him, see Variot, **Propos de Georges Sorel** (Paris, 1935), pp. 234-242, a conversation about Barrès, Aeschylus, Don Quixote, Massenet, Georges Ohnet and Jules Lemaître, with Variot acting the part of Boswell, while Sorel and Bourges alternate in the role of a very hilarious Dr. Johnson.

[59]To Croce (**loc. cit.,** p. 437, September 3, 1912. — Sorel's emphasis. — Julien Benda, co-author of Sorel's essay, "The Metaphysical Preoccupations of Modern Physics" (see chapter 4, note 6), later consistently hostile to Sorel. Best known by his **Treason of the Intellectuals** (see introductory ii, note 49). His candidacy to the **Académie Française** led to the intrigue that ended with the break between Sorel and Charles Péguy. (See chapter 8. p. 209) — Florence-Blum: not, of course, to be confused with the late Socialist statesman, Léon Blum.

[60]To Croce (**loc. cit.,** p. 437), September 21, 1912. — First published in New York, in 1902; in French as **L'interprétation économique de l'histoire** (Paris, 1911). As usually, Sorel's preface has hardly a word to say about the author and the work he is supposed to introduce.

Bergson? They "cannot forgive him that he put the modern world on the road toward realism." Their natural allies are the university professors: when Bergson talks about God and the soul, he speaks of subjects which do really excite him; "but when Boutroux and the Sorbonne idealists talk about God and the soul, it means nothing." Bergson begins to see that the academicians will always be against him; "his trip to the United States will only reinforce his realistic tendencies, and so the ditch which separates him from the merchants of logic, will only become deeper."[61]

The Catholics are against Bergson too, thus joining the camp of their own worst enemies, a fact which makes Sorel exclaim: "What blindness!"[62] His irritability in these months is extreme. Does all go well with his **Indépendance**? Never before has he been so sweeping in his judgments, so contemptuous of the Great and semi-Great. For instance, he had always slighted Friedrich Engels, blaming him for everything that was wrong with Marx; but he never would have said before what he says now, discussing a work about the minor of the **Dioscuri**: "So many pages to explain the thoughts of one who did as little thinking as Engels did."[63]

Indeed, not all is well with **L'Indépendance,** and the surest indication of another crisis in the making is Sorel's avowal that he is rather ill. The revue is less than a year old, when he writes: "I am having another attack of the stone, more violent than ever; I wonder when I will be able to do any useful work again, for I feel very low. I would like very much to take advantage of my misfortune and withdraw from **L'Indépendance.** I find the mentality of most of the younger editors too compromising for an old man of my type. I don't care so much for their (very Parisian) habit of deciding questions which they hardly understand."[63]

In the next letter nothing more about the matter; instead, a fit of rage caused by a new artistic craze: **"Cubism** is exploited here by painters taking advantage of some silly and rich foreigners, particularly Russians." He is surprised that the Italians too should have their cubists. Sorel speaks with Cassandra's voice: does Italy want to commit suicide?[64]

The letters of the last two years before the first world war are, as compared with the rest, disappointing both in volume and in content. If Sorel was despondent over the eternal failure of his literary schemes, he did not say so.[65] Nor does he mention to his friend

---

[61]To Croce (**loc. cit.,** p. 439-440), November 24, 1912.

[62]**Ibid.** (p. 442), June 22, 1913. The work in question was **Il Materialismo storico in Federigo Engels** by Rodolfo Mondolfo.

[63]To Croce (**loc. cit.,** p. 439), December 20, 1913.

[64]**Ibid.** (p. 439-440), November 24, 1912.

[65]Sorel mentioned the subject only once: "What do you think of **L'Indépendance**? I believe it is on the wrong track." (November 24, 1912.)

another association which had started in 1912: his — unofficial — contact with **L'Action Française** by way of a society which was to bring French monarchists and revolutionary syndicalists into a joint anti-democratic front.[66] He must have known: the liberal, Croce, would not have approved of the new **"Circle Proudhon."** But the — temporary — slump in the long correspondence between Croce and Sorel is no reflection on their feelings toward each other. The simple truth seems to be that Sorel had reached the nadir of his intellectual life. His hopes in a Viconian generation of the West had all been disappointed — first by the Left, then by the Right. It seemed to him that he had really reached the dead end. He still wrote a great deal, but what he wrote, was mainly a rehashing of the old ideas; more and more he indulges in a retrospective mood, looking upon himself as a strange, obsolete survivor from a revolutionary past forever gone. He begins to collect his early, unknown prefaces and essays for a rambling volume which, significantly will have the diffident title: **Materials for a Theory of the Proletariat.** Meanwhile, in his letters, he keeps up the usual chatter about books and authors, Marinetti's futurism (nonsense!), Bergson (who bergsonizes now) becomes a member of the Academy (Barrès tried to block him, but the Archbishop of Paris called the hunt off); yet his heart does not seem to be in it. The shots of Sarajevo have been fired, but they find no echo in these letters: on July 21, 1914, Sorel still speaks about Dumas and Scribe, about Flaubert, Maurras, and Daniel Halévy, as before, apparently forgetting his own premonition.[67] The war of which he spoke in 1908, will finally destroy the world which Georges Sorel had known and throw him into new depths of despair, but also open up for him a world of new emotions, new hopes, new illusions.

<u>The Longest Years</u>

It is not easy for Americans to understand what the first world war did to Europe: they know that the old nations came out of the struggle decimated, impoverished materially, no longer the unquestioned rulers of the globe. But what the war meant for the **mind** of Europe, very few non-Europeans can fully realize. One has to consult such diverse works of the European élite as André Gide's war diaries, the final volumes of Proust's epic, the Cornwall episode in D. H. Lawrence's Australian novel, **Kangaroo,** or Thomas Mann's **Magic Mountain,** if one wants to grasp the full impact of the war upon the soul of Europe. Those writers knew the truth: a great civilization which had lasted many centuries, was dead, it had committed suicide. Life, to be sure, went on, but they knew in their hearts that it was

---

[66]See chapter 8, p. 206f.
[67]See Introductory ii, p. 171 f.

mere pretense. The pitted fields would heal, the shattered houses rise again; young authors would receive the **Priz Goncourt,** unheard-of musical styles would be tried out on alert, delighted audiences. Ghosts, dancing upon their own graves! In the agony of the four war years, those Unhappy Few already consummated the experience which it took the rest of mankind three more decades and another war to comprehend. The deadly truth they knew **was final;** hence the oppressive sadness, the prophetic savagery, the icy self-contempt of those sepulchral documents. Gide, Lawrence, Proust — all three endured the supreme penalty: the degradation of man's faith, the ultimate destruction of his soul. So, in his way, did Georges Sorel, though with a difference: he sensed that the great war was both an end and the beginning of a new historic phase

September 22, 1914: Sorel sought refuge from the war in the small town in which his wife is buried: "I left my Paris home like many others on the advice of the authorities; I regret I did, because the trip killed me, and to go back means new fatigues! The events overwhelm me; I feel...all Europe is busy rejecting what was still left of the institutions dear to Renan; there will be nothing left to hold up to shame the Jacobin politicians, financiers and big town slickers." This sentence sets the tone of Sorel's war letters: the patriotic note will be conspicuously absent throughout. He is a European and a historian: "The Prussia of old, which felt itself getting absorbed by the new, industrial Germany, seems to be dying in a flood of blood...." Sorel, apparently, has no great doubt about the outcome: the defeat of Germany; "we shall see something analogous to the Judaean war: who will be the poet, the historian or the philosopher of that dreadful catastrophe?" It will not be Sorel, for "I am a man of the past; I have nothing more to say...."[68]

But though his world was dying, Sorel understood the social, revolutionary meaning of the war, even at this early stage: "We are entering a period more startlingly new than the revolution had been...." But if the war is **La Terreur** of Jacobin France, only on a world scale, then Sorel can see no sense in it and no hope for the future. He is reminded of Proudhon, "who in the last years of his life must have had similar impressions...."[69] As so often before, he turns to Croce, urging him to carry on: "You are the younger man; you could give us the philosophy of the new revolution."

---

[68] To Croce (**La Critica,** 1929, p. 51). — The Judaean war: Vespasian's campaign of extermination against the Jews, ending with the destruction of Jerusalem by Titus, 70 A. D.

[69] In **"La marche au socialisme,"** a chapter written in September, 1920 and added to the 3. edition of the **Illusions** (Paris, 1922), Sorel used passages from Proudhon's letters to express his own despair. See chapter 10, note 56. — Another Frenchman felt the same way about the war, cf. Marcel Le Goff, **Anatole France à la Béchellerie,** 2. ed. (Paris, 1947).

At the very same time, as a man in Switzerland, who called himself N. Lenin, was beginning to see the great revolutionary potentialities of the "imperialist war,"[70] Sorel writes to Croce: "It seems to me that one result of the present war will be the liquidation of socialism...."[71]

From Paris he writes Delesalle: "I came back a month ago; my trip was not happy, because it brought me a bronchitis which, according to the doctor, will only go away with warmer weather." He worries about his young relatives at the front. Fortunately, all his "many nephews" are at present safe behind the lines: "two have been wounded but are well again."[72] Sorel reacts like any family man,[73] but as the casualty lists grow, he will bemoan all losses, regardless of blood ties and nationality. It is the intellectual bloodletting which appalls him most. The war is only four months old when he already writes: "I am shocked by the complete nullity of the literature produced by this war; I wonder whether philosophy is not in need of a popular, artistic and religious basis which we lack completely."[74] Unlike Bergson, Sorel cannot make himself believe in a "regeneration of the French genius."[75] The souls of Péguy and Claudel, two men who had shown so much talent, are now "absolutely empty."[76] As to the politicians, their threats to root out all the despotisms of Europe recall the worst excesses of the **Directoire**.[77] All opposition has been silenced: "Here, we live in Plato's cave; the censorship lets nothing through.... What has become of that vaunted **public opinion**, which was supposed to rule the world?" There is now less of it than under Louis XV. "The future is immensely gloomy." Like other Frenchmen, Sorel is suspicious of the English ally: the papers cannot praise the great effectiveness of his artillery enough, but "one of my nephews writes me that the English gunners are far from brilliant."[78] This war, he knows, will last a long time; and the British do not mind. They "evidently hope to exhaust Europe for the greater glory of their country...." Like the Russian exile in Switzerland, Sorel sees nothing but imperialistic tendencies at work, but he does not share Lenin's hopes: "Here, the little people talk incessantly of revolution; nothing

---

[70]See his **Imperialism, The Highest Stage of Capitalism.**

[71]To Croce (**loc. cit.**, p. 51), October 26, 1914.

[72]Sorel, **Lettres à Paul Delesalle** (Paris, 1947, p. 111-112), November 22, 1914.

[73]He was very fond of his wife's family which he had adopted long ago as his own, although his fondness was not always reciprocated. Cf. Part II, Introduction, p. 162 - 163.

[74]To Croce (**loc. cit.**, p. 114), November 14, 1914.

[75]**Ibid.** (p. 120), April 8, 1915.

[76]**Ibid.**, April 25, 1915.

[77]**Ibid.** (p. 117), January 19, 1915.

[78]**Ibid.**, January 30, 1915. — Sorel's emphasis.

could be more dangerous than such confused rumors."[79] There is a
revolution going on, but in another sense. Using Nietzsche's term,
Sorel declares: "This is the hour of the universal slave revolt." He
is referring to the nationalist independence movements within the
Habsburgian Monarchy, the ambitions of the Roumanians in Trans-
sylvania who a century ago had been mere slaves of the Hungarians.
Another illustration of this trend is to be found in Croce's own Italy.
That country, still at peace, is in the throes of the great argument
between the advocates of intervention and the party favoring neutrality, an argument which will soon be decided in favor of war. Sorel is
horrified by the war whoops of the clique behind D'Annunzio: "the
follies of the avanguardist youth which is at present dishonoring the
name of Italy, are completely worthy of the asiatic slaves which made
up the bulk of the Roman population since the time of the Gracchi."[80]
These people "represent a curious survival of the **graeculus exuriens**,
a type which, to the major detriment of Italy, had reappeared during
the Renaissance, to ruin a country which seemed predestined to such
a great future...." It would not be surprising if the present Italian
commotion, which finds its artistic outlet in such absurd forms as futurism, were "the harbinger of a grave national affliction which may
destroy all the results of the **Risorgimento.**" All symptoms indicate
that "Europe is going to sleep intellectually." Once more, Sorel compares his Frenchmen to their ancestors under the **Directoire:** they
obey orders with the same docility; the patriotic literature is as it
was until the Restoration introduced some new ideas. Those who do
all the agitating nowadays, like the Italian hotheads, will only prolong
the slumber.[81]

Italy has entered the war; the fighting on the Western front has
become a stalemate. Sorel incurs censor trouble for the first time:
an article of his has been mutilated, and he takes pains to supply
Croce with the sentences and words missing in print. But who cares
about mutilated words, while hecatombs of human beings are being
sacrificed on the Aisne and on the Carso? "It seems the world has
not yet seen enough slaughter. Never have the governments shown so
much thirst for blood, nor the nations such servility... "[82] D'Annunzio delivers a patriotic sermon at a church service held at the
front, which strikes Sorel as "utterly grotesque" and reveals to him
the real function of this war, which is to free all the base instincts
which have been accumulating in mankind for a whole century."[83]
He must be thinking of his own high expectations when he writes

---

[79]Ibid. (p. 119), March 14, 1915.
[80]Ibid. (p. 123), July 18, 1915.
[81]Ibid. (p. 122-123), June 28, 1915.
[82]Ibid. (p. 292-293), September 26, 1915.
[83]Ibid. (p. 294), November 24, 1915. — (For further Italian developments,
see chapter 9).

dejectedly: "The nations show more resignation in this war than heroism .... The socialism of which I had been dreaming, was based on the
existence of epical sentiments .... Those who believe in Vico will look
in vain for any signs of a rejuvenation." He is told that "the socialists
hope to profit greatly from this war. That is quite likely." But it
would not necessarily mean a triumph for Sorel's ideas: nationalization of industries made necessary by the needs of war production, will
leave a deep impression on the popular mind everywhere, but it will
favor in the main "a certain type of socialism" which Sorel rejects:
State socialism. This development may be accompanied by outbursts
of the kind of popular violence particularly hateful to Sorel: "What
prolongs the war, is the fear the ruling class has for its life; there is
talk that the homecoming soldiers will kill the chiefs of the government and not a few of their own officers. The office holders wish to
delay the day of reckoning as much as possible."[84]

Like the German, Thomas Mann, Sorel, the Frenchman from Germanic Normandy, fights against the type Settembrini who wants to
make the world safe for his supposedly superior Latin civilization.[85]
"It is evident," Sorel writes,[86] "that all the changes which the influence of Taine and Renan seemed to have made so secure, are definitely lost; we went back to the intellectualism of the 18th century ....
It would be interesting to compare the declamations of the **Dreyfusards** of fifteen years ago with those addressed today to Germany, in
the name of Truth and Justice!" Some people have high hopes of a
religious revival which would come after the war; but Sorel wonders
"whether the supposed Catholic renaissance will not be submerged by
the masonic triumph."[87] "It has come to the point where clerical reaction [in France] and Germany are identified, so that the anticipated
victory of the Entente is taken to be synonymous with the triumph of
free thought .... Our return to the insanities of the Voltairian bourgeoisie may last a century and perhaps even longer."[88] The decline
of 19th century liberalism is developing apace. But if some observers

---

[84]**Ibid.** (p. 295-297), December 5, 1915.

[85]The ridiculed spokesman of Western rationalism in the **Magic Mountain,** the work in which Thomas Mann expressed in novellistic form the ideas
of his untranslated book of essays, **Betrachtungen eines Unpolitischen,** written
at the same time.

[86]To Croce (**loc. cit.,** p. 356-357), April 5, 1916.

[87]**Ibid.** (p. 358), May 30, 1916. — Until recently, Latin free-masonry, unlike its Anglo-saxon counterpart, had retained its distinctly political role as
a rallying point for secularist, liberal, and, particularly, anticlerical sentiments. Hence the fierce persecution it suffered in countries conquered by
Fascism. Hence the recent Vatican pronouncement on participation of Catholic priests and laymen in such civil service clubs as Rotary because of
their possible affiliation with Masons.

[88]To Croce (**loc. cit.,** p. 359), July 8, 1916.

think that this means we are returning to the Hegelian state, they are mistaken: instead, we are marching toward "the Jacobin, the Jesuit, the plutocratic State," for the idea of organization is an historical conception, whereas "at present all historical relations are dissolving, not to be reborn, unless an unpredictable **ricorso** takes place. Liberalism presupposed a regime respecting the laws which safeguard individual existence;" but today, "the idea of law is dying all over the world under the blows of triumphant democracy."[89]   Does Croce really believe an intellectual and moral reform is still possible?   If it is, then only on condition that the people chose the path of penitence, as Renan had wanted them to do in 1871.   They did not listen to him then, and today they are less likely to repent than ever.[90]

His health has improved somewhat, but he is still confined to his home: until recently, he informs Delesalle, his stomach refused anything but iced juices.[91]   To the same friend Sorel confesses: "I believe this crisis marks the end of my intellectual production; a few years ago, I still imagined I had a few things to say, but now I see I will have to resign myself to old age, idleness."[92]   But worse is to come: before the year is over, he comes down with a severe case of emphysema, which frightens him greatly.   The doctor told him that he might have suffered a heart stroke on his daily promenades between Boulogne sur Seine and Auteuil.   Again, he must submit to a very strict regime; he must not even climb the stairs leading to his study.[93] Deprived of all and any work, his mind returns to the past: "A few months ago, I sent you a picture of myself, aged twenty; here now is a photograph of my wife, taken when she was approximately thirty years old." It seems that Delesalle had never been told to whom the **Reflections** had been dedicated, for Sorel tells him: the "compagnon of my youth" was she, his wife. "I wrote the book almost ten years after she died," but he knows that "she would have approved its ideas."[94]

There follows a peculiar episode which throws light on his family relations.   Sorel wants to send a money order to a cousin of his wife's, but since the nephew with whom he stays, does not like her, he asks Delesalle to do the errand to the post office. "I shall repay you when you come to see me."[95]   What a pathetic confession, and what a conspiracy to dispatch fifty francs! It must have been hard on the upright, proud old man to go such devious ways; he must have pondered the affair at great length and with great misgivings, motivated by fear of the relative on whose good graces he had to depend, and yet resolved to help the niece who could well use the little he could spare.

[89]Ibid. (p. 441), January 10, 1917.
[90]Ibid. (p. 441-442), January 20, 1917.
[91]To Delesalle (**op. cit.**, p. 114), August 6, 1917.
[92]Ibid. (p. 116), August 12, 1917.
[93]Ibid. (p. 119), December 6, 1917.
[94]Ibid. (p. 122-123), December 28, 1917.
[95]Ibid. (p. 123), December 31, 1917.

Exciting news from Russia begins to intrude into the correspondence,[96] but neither war nor revolutions can distract Sorel for any
length of time from his passionate interests in strictly intellectual
problems: "I met Bergson yesterday," he informs Croce. The two
men discuss the relationship between philosophy and art. "In our time
the complete separation of art and philosophy will be bad for philosophy," said Bergson. It was quite different with the Greeks. If the
medieval schoolmen misunderstood Aristotle so frequently, the reason
was, Sorel believes, that they were altogether lacking in artistic
sense. Descartes too was completely unartistic. It might be worthwhile to pursue this idea, Sorel concludes.[97] The mind of the old in-
valid is as vigorous as ever. So is his temper. Despising Paul
Claudel has by now become an old habit with Sorel: new victims seem
to be highly desirable. One presents itself readily in the person of a
Harward [sic] professor named Santayana who has written a book on
the errors of German philosophy: "This work seems to indicate an
irresistible trend pulling philosophy toward a journalism comprehensible to shopkeepers...Ferrero is far surpassed in that genre by the
professor from Harward [sic again] and by Boutroux." Sorel uses the
opportunity to give his general view of American civilization, which
was, and still is, commonplace among the European intelligentsia:
"Could it be," he asks dramatically, "that Europe is ready for the
great American ideas: **mediums** and **Christian Science?** It is to be
feared that our fall into the petty bourgeois lower depths is final."[98]
The topic recurs several times: Proudhon was right when he wanted
Napoleon III to put a check on the American conquests by consolidat-
ing the regime of Juarez (!) in Mexico and by assisting the Confedera-
cy. "Today the danger menacing civilization is much greater than it
was at that time."[99] Those Americans, with their dollars and their
arrogance, how Proudhon despised them! Today, "all Europe puts
herself on their niveau." Why, a young officer of the general staff
even told him that very few Americans knew William James, "the sole
philosopher whose fame has crossed the ocean."[100]

When Sorel wrote this letter, the armistice was already six weeks
old. What has Sorel to say about the great event? We read about his
second flight from bombarded Paris (yielding to "the imprecations of

---

[96]For Sorel's views on the Russian revolution, see chapter 10.

[97]To Croce (**La Critica,** 1930, p. 42), September 7, 1917.

[98]**Ibid.** (p. 43), October 25, 1917. — The italics and the English terms,
mediums and Christian Science, in the original. — Santayana's work was **Egotism in German Philosophy** (London, New York [1916]), which appeared in
French as **L'erreur de la philosophie allemande,** with an introduction by
Emile Boutroux.

[99]To Croce (**loc. cit.,** p. 46), July 29, 1918.

[100]**Ibid.** (p. 47), December 6, 1918.

my niece"[101]); he announces his return trip to the capital,[102] but when the end has come at last, it is not even mentioned. Not one word of rejoicing, of relief. The flow of Sorel's letters continues without a ripple. This attitude of "business as usual," — was it due to some intuition that the revolutionary war had really not ended, that it was fated to go on for two full decades in the disguise of a spurious peace which, for all purposes, was a mere armistice?

The business at hand is the, belated, publication of his **Materials for a Theory of the Proletariat,** which he dedicates to Delesalle and his wife, cautioning them against accepting the dubious honor: since much in the collection could be considered as reformist socialism, the revolutionary syndicalist Delesalle might feel embarrassed.... [103] But Delesalle was used to his friend's frequent moods of self-abasement. He did not take too seriously such letters as the one Sorel wrote him from Malix par Tenay, his refuge from the German Gothas and Long Berthas:

"I have been asking myself for a long time how useful all the work was which I did for Socialism in these past thirty years." Today, he even wonders if his theories, "granting they had some effect" were not perhaps more wrong than right. He carefully considers the alternatives: "If the workers had remained what they had been in 1848: the foremost fighters for democracy, the bourgeoisie would not today be prostrate at the feet of Barrès." On the other hand, the workers would, in that case, not have listened with such complete confidence to those who orated about the class struggle; "the syndicalists were sold by their chiefs like sheep in the market; the theory of the class struggle therefore turned out to be bad for the workers."[104]

Few thinkers will be found, courageous enough to commit to writing, even in a letter to a trusted friend, such complete recantation of a creed held for so long. However, if Paul Delesalle was worried, it was not to be for long, for only shortly afterwards, the class struggle will again look good to Sorel, namely the way it is conducted by the former Russian refugee to Switzerland.

Europe in Transition

The chaotic state of the defeated Reich makes Sorel wonder, as we are wondering today, about the future role of Europe's heartland: "The great question is: what does the present Germany stand for in Europe? I believe it was a major error to assume that the German

---

[101]To Delesalle (**op. cit.,** p. 134), April 23, 1918.

[102]Ibid. (p. 170), September 22, 1918.

[103]Ibid. (p. 174), December 2, 1918.

[104]Ibid. (p. 152), June 23, 1918. — He adds: "My opinion of my work is modest," but even that question "no longer interests me..."

Empire represented the military oligarchy; in my opinion, Emperor William was the chief of the capitalists; actually, the defeat did not affect the Germans as much as one was led to believe, because it is the capitalist bourgeoisie which was beaten; the Junkers are still full of hope." But their time seems to be over: "the capitalist bourgeoisie is triumphing everywhere;" and at that time Sorel believed this to be true, even for Russia where the Bolsheviks were fighting what looked to him like a losing battle. And he asks: Will Germany be the exception?[105] Hating the bourgeoisie as he does, Sorel would rather have the Junkers reassert themselves in Germany, because they represent the military class, for which Sorel, an anti-militarist of long standing, had developed a new sympathy. "The great question of the 19th century," he writes to Daniel Halévy,[106] "was how to check the power of the merchants...." The socialists tried to resolve the problem by mobilizing the working class. "But in truth the only institution capable of mitigating the tyranny of gold is one built on a strictly military tradition." Some ancient philosophers had an inkling of that truth. Sorel must be thinking of Plato, although he does not mention the philosopher he dislikes almost as much as Descartes. Nor does he, in the following, name Nietzsche, although Nietzsche did write very much in the same vein: "Napoleon brought some very archaic elements back to the surface....most likely, Prussian militarism will perish as Napoleon did," but it may "leave behind an anticapitalistic furor of which we cannot yet have an exact idea. I cannot resign myself to the thought that the world must remain under the rule of the financial speculators." Who, then, is to avenge Napoleon and Wilhelm? "Who knows, perhaps the German socialists, made wise by the war, may yet become more formidable enemies for the Wilsonians than Prussian militarism had ever been." As if intimidated by that vision, Sorel breaks off; it is too early for such "bold hypotheses."[107]

That was in 1917; in 1919 Sorel feels bold enough to praise the right-wing Socialist regime in Germany: "The German experience is

[105]To Croce (loc. cit., p. 48), December 20, 1918.

[106]October 16, 1917, cited in Fédération (Paris, November, 1947), p. 4.

[107]The Wilsonians: Sorel shares the belief of "many people that the League of Nations is destined to impose the hegemony of Anglo-saxon capitalism on the smaller countries rich in mineral resources." (To Croce, loc. cit., p. 50, February 1, 1919.) In a letter of February 9, 1919, written to G. Castellano, the editor of Croce's Pagine sparse, Sorel judges the League of Nations more favorably. He believes in its potential usefulness provided it does not attempt to become a super-state, limiting itself instead to strengthening international law in such matters as freedom of the seas, the respect of neutrality (Belgium, Switzerland); his ideal is the regime such as it existed, until the second world war, in the international settlement of Shanghai. (Croce, Pagine Sparse II, Napoli, 1919, p. 300-302.)

immensely interesting: for the first time, a great country is governed by workers; so far, they acted more intelligently than our bourgeois did in 1848; all the intellectuals are scandalized, while the Independent Socialists represent the old Jacobin spirit...."[108]

It would be easy to point out that Sorel's mind was, at that time, torn between two irreconcilable assumptions: on the one hand, he endorsed the revolutionary radicalism of a Lenin; on the other hand, he holds up the arch enemies of Bolshevism, the German right-wing socialists, as paragons of proletarian rule. He misunderstood both: Lenin was not a Russian syndicalist, nor were the Scheidemanns and Eberts anything but good bourgeois, but these were merely false judgments, whereas Sorel's simultaneous acceptance of both revolutionary and revisionist Marxism seems to make no sense at all. And yet, the difficulty will disappear, once we remember that the great preoccupation of Sorel's life always was the defense of variegated cultural vitality against the deadening and levelling force which he identified sometimes with intellectualism, sometimes with utopianism, always with democracy. As Sorel had exclaimed early in the war, "the bourgeois spirit is invincible" — meaning that eternal, classless human penchant for the satisfaction of the "basest instincts."[109] It was the hatred of the moralist against prudential commonplace expediency, a fighting man's contempt of unheroic compromise. What he said of Napoleon, Sorel could well have applied to himself, for he too was a revenant from the archaic past, a citizen of Athens prosecuting the first rationalist, Socrates; a latter day Tertullian talking with the voice of Pierre Josephe Proudhon.[110] It is Sorel's great fear of decadence that makes him easily accept such contradictory allies as Lenin, Ebert, Mussolini.

But to accept leftist, moderate, and "rightist" versions of the class struggle with almost equal appreciation is one thing, another to

---

[108]To Croce (loc. cit., p. 51), February 21, 1919. — in 1918, the radical wing of the German Social-Democratic Party broke with the conservative leadership of Ebert, Scheidemann and Noske, to form the U.S.P.D. (Independent Socialist Party of Germany), taking a position to the right of the Spartacus League, led by Karl Liebknecht and Rosa Luxemburg. The right wing of the new group rejoined the mother party soon afterwards, while the left wing merged with the new Communist Party of Germany, heir of the Spartacus League. Sorel's approval of Socialist reformism (cf. also Introd. ii, p. 173) finds another expression in a post-script to his **Matériaux** (2. edition, Avant-propos, p. 53, note 1): "Does the defeat of Germany mean the end of the feudal, Prussian aristocracy or that of the liberal bourgeoisie? I am inclining toward the second hypothesis.. "

[109]To Croce (**La Critica**, 1929, p. 289), September 1, 1915.

[110]In his book, **Guerre des Etats ou Guerre des Classes**, (Paris, 1924), Edouard Berth called Sorel, "Le Tertullien du Socialisme." (Appendix, pp. 424-437.)

confuse them with each other. Sorel is too much the historian to overlook the national component; he is prevented by his pluralistic world
view from reducing the Italian, German, Russian systems to a common
denominator. This lack of unitary outlook in Sorel yields rich results.
It makes it possible for him to differentiate between Lenin, the dictator of the proletariat, and Lenin, the red Tsar of Russia, and even to
praise Lenin as the leader of a Russian, national revival, but at the
same time to denounce Slavic expansionism. It is in this connection
that Sorel endorses the Italian aspirations in Dalmatia: the lines of
the West must be restored.[111]   In his concern for Latin culture Sorel
does not mind encouraging Italian nationalism, while frowning on Barrès and other advocates of the same sentiment in his own France.[112]

"I no longer take any medicines; but I am still rather feeble. The
doctor advised me not to take the **métro** on account of its stairs and
crowds."[113]   That means he is cut off from Paris, from visiting his
friends and his beloved **Bibliothèque Nationale** in the **Rue Richelieu.**
But he continues to perform his Lynkeus role: "Here, a new league is
formed each day which wants to regenerate France; I don't have much
confidence [in them]."[114]   The way most people think and act, it
seems as if "the war years were for them merely an intermission
between boxing and soccer matches."[115]   Bergson has been attacked
"by Maritain (grandson of Jules Favre, former anarchist, converted
by Leon Bloy)" and by Gentile; Sorel uses the opportunity to remark
that Bergson never said anything that could not be accepted by contemporary thought.   And in that he was right, in the sense that the
philosopher should always be in accord with the established science
of his time.   "Aristotle understood philosophy in that manner."   The
question is, however, whether Bergson did not sometimes take for
science what was only a metaphysical interpretation of it.   Sorel believes that Bergson was much influenced by Schopenhauer: it is very
likely that the **Creative Evolution** in its first shape was much more
pantheistic than the final draft. "Even now many theologians still discover in the work a great amount of **pantheistic poison,** and we must
not underrate the judgment of the theologians; they always proved to
be the subtlest critics of **dangerous books.** When it comes to orthodox
literature, they are much less perspicacious."[116]   He reads with

---

[111]Sorel, **"La Dalmazia è terra d'Italia"** in **Il Tempo,** February 15, 1919.
[112]Sorel attacked Barrès' book, **Le Génie du Rhin** in an article published
by **La Revue Communiste,** April 14, 1921. — See also his **"Exégèses proudhoniennes"** in **Matériaux** (cf. chapter 8, p. 211, and note 41).
[113]To Delesalle (**op. cit.,** p. 181), March 23, 1919.
[114]To Croce (**La Critica,** 1930, p. 119), August 16, 1919.
[115]Ibid. (p. 121), February 17, 1920.
[116]Ibid. (p. 190-191), April 11, 1920. — Italics in the original. — Sorel
wrote at that time his last book (on William James and Bergson), **De L'utilité
du pragmatisme** (Paris, 1921).

great interest Croce's critique of "Ostwald [sic] Spengler," who
"could very well have derived his idea of historic predestination from
Gervinus's Introduction to the History of the XIX Century.... This
method belongs, in his opinion, "to the current of **scientism**" which
overflooded the philosophic consciousness of the course of that century. That current was by no means a typically German phenomenon:
"That such conceptions could meet with success in Germany, shows
that today many Germans have permitted themselves to be taken in
tow by Anglo-French **scientism.**" Besides, Spengler is not more absurd than Haeckel with his History of natural creation, who dressed
up as a scientific work what actually was a philosophic fiction à la
Timaeus. [117]

"A young man who, I believe, is one of your friends," he writes
Croce, "delivered a public lecture about Georges Sorel:" "The author
was so kind toward me, that I fear he will be accused of exaggeration."
But Georges Sorel is pleased: "the acclamations of the very young
are the true consolation of old age."[118] He needs it badly, for the
Plea for Lenin which he added to the fourth edition of his **Reflections**
alienated many of his friends. "I am about to become an outcast," he
writes because his book on pragmatism is being given the silent
treatment in **Les Débats.**[119] His correspondence ends on that note of
despondency, occasionally brightened by a pleasant piece of news such
as an amiable letter from Bergson, which he copies for his publisher
"in order to console him for the poor sale of my [latest] book I did
not hope to find many readers, but Bergson alone is worth...a multitude...." And in all modesty, Sorel might have been thinking of himself when he went on to say: "Some years ago, Bourget said of the
Jeanne d'Arc of Péguy: 'A man who writes such beautiful books,
should know that they won't sell.'"[120]

Perhaps the dying Georges Sorel was not despondent after all.
We do not know for sure, for during the last year of his life he no
longer wrote Delesalle or Croce. In one of his last letters, he sighed:
"I often wish I could escape my hermitage; but the doctor will not let
me go to Paris; that makes me fear that something is the matter with
my heart which he does not dare to tell me."[121] That he did not obey

[117]To Croce (**loc. cit.** p. 192), August 13, 1920. — Sorel's emphasis.

[118]Ibid. (p. 193), 1920 (No further date given). — The young author: Max
Ascoli, author of **The Power of Freedom** (New York, 1949), at present publisher
and editor of the political revue, **The Reporter.** — The French text of his
Georges Sorel, with a preface by Berth, was published by Delesalle (Paris,
1921).

[119]To Delesalle (**op. cit.,** p. 233), July 7, 1921.

[120]Ibid. (p. 236), July 13, 1921. — Paul Bourget, wrote the drama, **La Barricade,** in which he put Sorel's doctrine of violence to a pro-bourgeois use.
Cf. Pareto's comment on Sorel's lack of material success cited in the Supplement of this study, p. 297.

[121]To Delesalle (**op. cit.,** p. 233), July 7, 1921.

doctor's orders we know from Robert Michels who entered into his diary, under the dateline, Paris, March 22, 1922, (that is, five months before Sorel's death): "Saw Sorel today in the back room of the book-store of his faithful friend, the bookdealer Paul Delesalle, in the rue Monsieur le Prince, quite close to my hotel near the Odéon. Although suffering from a bad heart ailment, Sorel comes once a week from his suburban Boulogne sur Seine to Paris, where he receives his friends, for just one hour, **chez M. Delesalle** .... "[122]

But whether holding court at Delesalle's or staying home, Sorel continued to be active to his last breath: scanning the papers for a bit of encouraging news, or lying in wait for visitors who would submit to his harangues, his scoldings and enthusiasms, his reminiscences and prophecies, until the final visitor arrived to silence him, who was the Don Quixote of twentieth century political philosophy.

---

[122] **"Lettere di Georges Sorel a Roberto Michels,"** loc. cit., p. 293, note 4.

8. THE SOCIAL MONARCHY

We are used to thinking of fascism, amalgam of nationalism and (pseudo) socialism, as a thing of Italian origin, and of Mussolini as its founder. But without exaggerating very much, one might call France its breeding ground, and say that the great counter-revolution[1] against the ideas of 1789 was conceived in the same metropolis from which most modern revolutions sprang. Eight years before the Duce constituted his first combat squad in Milan, five years before he hit on his **idée maitresse**, the doctrine, or at any rate, a program that came very close to it, was formulated by a circle of young intellectuals in Paris. The year of this first dress rehearsal: 1912.

In the center of the play, taking the role of the embarrassed and embarrassing protagonist, though personally keeping off stage, was Georges Sorel, who at that time enjoyed the status of a minor patriarch among the **literati** of the Left Bank. As the theorist of revolutionary syndicalism, he was admired by those who did not know that he no longer counted himself among its admirers; and he was wooed, with cautious eagerness, by others who did know that Georges Sorel was ready to try something new, whatever it might be. As early as 1908, in the very year in which his **Reflections** appeared in book form, he had confided to Jean Variot his strong interest in the "only serious nationalist movement existing in France: the group following Maurras, the monarchists of the **Action Française**."[2] Two years later, he placed his disappointment in syndicalism on record, writing that he felt "too old to wait for distant hopes to come true; so I decided to use the few years I have left to look more closely into other questions — questions in which the French youth takes a lively interest."[3] Realizing that his new turn called for some explaining, Sorel added that his socialist studies never constituted the most important part of his work.[4] He spoke the truth: the bulk of his writings deals with religion, ethics, and history. Yet the note of asperity in these explanations is unmistakable: from the very first, Sorel felt ill at ease in his new role as the darling of the **Camelots du Roi** with whom he was to work together for the next two years.

---

[1]"Counter-revolution understood, not as a movement of "reactionary" tendencies, but as **another** revolution.

[2]Jean Variot, **Propos de Georges Sorel** (Paris, 1935), p. 27. (Statement made on November 14, 1908.)

[3]From the introduction to **Le Confessioni: Come divenni sindicalista** (Divenire sociale, March 1-May 16, 1910) omitted from the French version (**Mes raisons de syndicalisme** in **Matériaux d'une theorie du prolétariat**) because Sorel had, in the meantime, renewed his allegiance to the cause of labor.

[4]Letter to Agostino Lanzillo, published by the **Giornale d'Italia**, November 20, 1910.

It was young Jean Variot who brought Sorel in touch with the founders of a new periodical, called L'Indépendance, after another project named La Cité Française, with Georges Sorel as the spiritus rector, had foundered before the start.[5] He joined the "Independence" group, if for no other reason than that he needed a literary outlet for his always feverish production. The journal could boast of a very distinguished board of directors, which included, among others, Vincent d'Indy, the famous composer, the dramatist Paul Bourget who had popularized Sorel's ideas in his play, La Barricade; the poet Francis Jammes, and the nationalist leader, Maurice Barrès.[6] As the editor in chief (together with Variot), Sorel contributed, besides many book reviews, no less than fifteen articles to the shortlived (1911-1913) organ, articles which show us more of the polemic than of the creative writer, Georges Sorel. His crime, if any, was one of omission rather than commission: although he went far in accommodating the peculiar prejudices of his new associates, he cannot be called a turncoat; after all, he never had been partial to semitic bankers either; nor had he ever been a real Marxist. Yet, there is no denying that a negative streak runs through all these essays in which he is still belaboring democracy, while no longer informed by any positive objectives: the enthusiastic inspiration of his syndicalist writings will not be discovered in his contributions to L'Indépendance.

Once more, then, he attacks the educational monopoly of the French intellectuals.[7] In particular, Sorel accuses the French educators of being foreign agents, cultural fifth-columnists, as we would say today, because, believing that it had been the Prussian schoolmaster who had won the war of 1870, they had copied slavishly the methods of Germanic scholarship, and worse: they had adopted its principle of aristocratic exclusiveness, thus transforming the centers of higher learning into so many strongholds of a scientific oligarchy, parasitical in character, subservient to the no less parasitical interests of the big bourgeoisie, while claiming for themselves "a sort of divine right of intelligence vis-à-vis the productive classes."[8]

---

[5]The little-known prospectus of that still-born publication, full of anti-democratic sentiment, is reproduced in René Johannet's Itinéraires d'Intellectuels (Paris, 1921), p. 206-208. — Cf. chapter 7, p. 183.

[6]See Gaétan Pirou, Georges Sorel (Paris, 1927), p. 43, and note.

[7]Lyripipi sorbonici moralisationes in L'Indépendance, April 1, 1911.

[8]Le monument de Jules Ferry, Ibid., March 1, 1911, p. 3. It is interesting to compare these two essays with one Sorel wrote four years later on Renan's Reforme Intellectuelle et Morale (published posthumously by Croce under the title, Germanesimo e storicismo di Ernesto Renan in La Critica, 1931, pp. 110-114, 199-207, 358-367, 430-444). There, Sorel reverses his previous stand, praising Renan for taking the unpopular view that German influence had made possible the intellectual recovery of France after the revolution, and that the only salvation for the young Third Republic, weakened by defeat, was in preserving the Germanic heritage of strong "social authorities" against the Gallic, democratic onslaught. Cf. also chapter 6, p. 159.

The question of war guilt is the subject of another article dealing
with the same national defeat: according to Sorel it is French liberalism, typified and lead by Emile Olivier, Napoleon the Third's last foreign minister, that must be blamed for the imperial policy of revanche
pour Sadowa. Parliamentarian pressure and a series of misjudgments
as to the true power of the enemy (Germany, the country of the poets
and philosophers) had brought about the great débâcle of the first Sedan.[9]

After the war, it was German influence that tipped the scales of
French domestic policy against the conservatives led by MacMahon;
Sorel suspects the republican chieftain Gambetta of secret dealings
with a German agent sent by Bismarck; a three-week trip to Germany
which the erstwhile firebrand of national defense made in 1876, so impressed him with the power of the new Reich that he not only gave up
all hope of revanche but even contemplated the idea of a German-French
alliance. Sorel could not well deny the fact that the Conservatives had
carried the elections for the constituent assembly of the new Republic
because they stood for peace with Germany; but he insists that the
pacific sentiment of the French masses, shrewdly exploited by Léon
Gambetta, ultimately sealed the defeat of the French Right, on contributing to both the failure of General Boulanger and to the victory of the
Dreyfusards.[10]

In connection with that famous case, the anti-semitism of Sorel once
more asserts itself.[11] Again the Jews are denounced as the grave-
diggers of all traditions; their guilt is shared by the French radical
intelligentsia. In particular, it is the anti-clericalism of the Republican Left which Sorel singles out for heavy criticism: the dogmas of
the church, no matter whether we believe in them or not, "at any rate
constitute pragmatic verities which always must be scrutinized by our
intelligence, but which cannot be dismissed simply because they are
not susceptible of scientific demonstration."[12] In fact, Catholicism has
considerably gained in strength during the 19th century by following a
course quite contrary to the advice of the enlightened people: "the
Church has bolstered its theology, it has increased the number of its
monastic institutions; it has treated miracles with an attention which
had not been paid to them since Medieval times."[13]

No wonder, some critics speak of this Sorelian phase as a "Return
to Traditionalism."[14] So furious is Sorel about that term that he

---

[9]Responsabilités de 1870 in L'Indépendance, May 1, 1911.

[10]L'Abandon de la revanche, Ibid., April 1, 1911.

[11]In Urbain Gohier, Ibid., January 1, 1912, and Quelques prétensions juives,
Ibid., May 1 and 15, June 1, 1912.

[12]Si les dogmes évoluent, Ibid., September 15, 1911, p. 33. — Sorel's emphasis.

[13]Quelques prétensions juives, loc. cit., p. 292-293. — Cf. chapter 3, p. 88.

[14]See Frederic D. Cheydleur, Essai sur l'évolution des doctrines de M.
Georges Sorel (Grenoble, 1914), chapter VII: Le retour au traditionalisme.

underlines it four times in a letter explaining his position to Edouard
Dolléans. The latter had been told "that Berth and I have abandoned
our old ideas and are leaning toward traditionalism. This discovery
makes my head swim." For the term, traditionalism, which was used
to designate a particular philosophical system eighty years ago, has
lost all distinct meaning today. But he is nevertheless willing to be
"called a traditionalist, as I was called a pragmatist, because in epistemological criticism I do attach a major importance to the evidence of
the historical development. When I took the part of Vico against Descartes sixteen years ago, I was, in a certain sense, a traditionalist;
all students of architecture are traditionalists...." But why is Sorel
so incensed? Because, "for the last few years, the tendency has been
to call traditionalists the partisans of monarchic and catholic institutions; it has even come to pass that this label is being applied to the
friends of Maurras...."

The implications seems to be, that Maurras and his friends of the
Action Francaise are not traditionalists in the Sorelian sense, but that
is not his point at all: "Therefore, if your [informant] wanted to insin-
uate that I am marching behind Maurras, he has committed a grievous
error.... You would oblige me very much by asking him to point out a
single publication where I act the part of a traditionalist, in the sense
in which the word is understood by the politicians."[15]

It is experiences of this kind which at last determine Sorel to withdraw: "Sit down and listen," he tells Jean Variot. "L'Indépendance
has been labelled reactionary and nationalist, rightly or wrongly, I
wouldn't know, but there it is, and I don't like it. I am going to use
my stone as a pretext to quit."[16] And laughingly Sorel confesses that
he knows the truth quite well: "You can't deny, m'lord, your little
gang talks with a nationalistic twang."[17]

The New Proudhon

He left L'Indépendance, but nationalism continued to intrigue him,
and so, when his best friend, Edouard Berth, was approached by some
extreme Monarchists with the proposal of joining them in a new "study
group," the Master gave his blessing. To be sure, this time, he with-
held his personal collaboration, but he did not protest when Berth and
other ex-Syndicalists teamed up with George Valois, the noted Monarchist,[18] to form the Cercle Proudhon. This was a new association,

---

[15]Letter of October 13, 1912. See Dolléans, Le Visage de Georges Sorel
in Revue d'histoire économique et sociale, Vol. XXVI, No. 2 (Paris, 1947),
p. 106-107.

[16]Variot, op. cit., p. 41. The date of the conversation is Easter, 1913.

[17]Ibid., — Variot intimates that Sorel, when well-lit, was fond of address-
ing him with fancy titles.

[18]Author of L'homme qui vient (Paris, 1906), La monarchie et la classe
ouvrière (Paris, 1909), d'un siècle a l'autre (Paris, 1921). See also chapter 11.

part club, part seminary, which was to create quite a stir on the Left
Bank from 1912 until the war broke out in 1914 and put the new French
nationalism to the test — not without radically changing its character,
submerging, for the "duration" at any rate, all monarchistic and authoritarian tendencies in the flood of a general, republican patriotism.

It was the appeal of the great name, Pierre Josephe Proudhon, that
lured Sorel into the new, strange company, — an appeal that was skill-
fully exploited by the Monarchist founders of the circle. Proudhon, the
non-Marxian socialist, Proudhon, the sturdy Frenchman, had he not
always been the strongest source of inspiration to Sorel? [19] One could
quote the author of Le guerre et la paix and De la justice page after
page, as Sorel was wont to do, and vice versa so similar were the two
writers' problems and reactions: their moral austerity, their dislike
of socialist utopias, of the bourgeoisie, their insistence on production,
on a stateless society of free producers....

Proudhon was the patron-saint today as he had been yesterday, and
still, Sorel's old friends were outraged by what they regarded as a piece
of reactionary forgery: under the conjuring hands of Georges Valois
and his companions, Proudhon seemed to turn into a Nationalist, a Conservative, almost a Royalist! The Royalists replied, contemptuously,
that it was high time Proudhon be rescued from his democratic worshippers. [20] Had not a notorious flunkey of the stock exchange, the
President of the Republic, Monsieur Fallières, recently outraged all
decent feelings when he dared to dedicate, at Besançon, the latest
monument erected to the genius of Proudhon? [21] Surely, capitalistic
democracy had no claim on the great Burgundian, — and Georges Sorel
said so too. The prospectus of the newly-founded organ of the group,
the Cahiers du Cercle Proudhon, stated it clearly enough: whatever
the differences separating founders and associates, "integral" nationalists and syndicalists, in matters of theory and practice, they were all
agreed, with Proudhon, on one thing: "Democracy is the greatest error
of the last century." [22] Democracy is the deadly sickness of all modern
nations. The new Proudhonians will yield to none, not even to Karl
Marx, in their praise of capitalism as the great constructive force that
made the world over; it is against the destructive aspects of capitalism
that they proclaim themselves, again with Marx, anti-capitalists, pro-
posing to abolish what they call "political capitalism": the corrosive
influence of plutocracy, as the main obstacle to true creative liberty.
The later, Fascist, distinction between the "mechanical" egalitarian

---

[19]See chapter 4, pp. 93-99.

[20]See Georges Valois, Pourquoi nous rattachons nos travaux à l'esprit
proudhonien in Cahiers du Cercle Proudhon, No. 1, January-February, 1912,
p. 34-41 (reprint of an address made at the first conference of the Cercle
Proudhon, on December 16, 1911).

[21]See Charles Maurras, A Besançon, Ibid., p. 3-8.

[22]Cahiers, No. 1, p. 1-2.

liberty of the democratic system and the "concrete" liberty made possible, and safeguarded by the State, is already anticipated in this pronunciamento made in the name of Proudhon and spelled out, in the same first issue of the Cahiers by a certain "Jean Darville" who was no other than Sorel's authentic mouthpiece, Edouard Berth.[23]

But the royalist partners of the circle went even further. Having "roped in" Sorel and his minute group by using the Proudhonian lasso, they proceeded to build up Sorel as the living Proudhon. The second issue of the revue contains a long, glowing account of Sorel's work;[24] it is followed, in the two next numbers, by a grand symposium in "Homage to Georges Sorel."[25] Interestingly, although perhaps not surprisingly, the fame of the "master and great philosopher," in the view of his new admirers, rests on his criticisms of the liberal past and present, while his syndicalist futurism remains unmentioned in the roster of his merits: it is the Georges Sorel who wrote about the Illusions of Progress and an Introduction to Modern Economy, two little known books, and not the author of the famous Reflections who becomes the second patron-saint of the Neo-Proudhonians, — with an emphasis that indicates a tendency toward the arty, an esoteric point of view contemptuous of established reputations.

Apparently, some of the more narrow-minded charter members of the circle looked upon the newcomer from the revolutionary left with strong misgivings, for Georges Valois, their intellectual chief, took great pains to explain[26] that the merger of extremes did not require the surrender of cherished convictions by anyone: the royalists would continue to be faithful to their King in exile, and the leftists would remain republicans; the nationalists would go on demanding a strong state, a France freed from the rule of the coteries; the syndicalist militants would retain their old opposition to the state, any state.

That seemed to be a sensible enough arrangement to safeguard a lively exchange of opinions. But would the compromise hold good beyond the talking stage? Did the activities of the Action Française seriously contemplate building their French Kingdom together with and for the working class? Or was that friendship a mere armistice, to be terminated the day after the overthrow of the despised Republic?

Although that day did not seem to be close, the question was too serious to be shelved. Of the solutions offered one was judged acceptable, a constitutional scheme as ingenious as it was tenuous:[27]

---

[23]Ibid., p. 9-28. (Second conference of the Cercle, January 10, 1912).

[24]Gilbert Maire, La philosophie de Georges Sorel, Ibid., No. 2, March-April, 1912, p. 57-81.

[25]Contributors: Georges Valois, Sorel et l'architecture sociale; René de Marans, Grandes rectifications soréliennes; Henri Lagrange, L'oeuvre de Sorel et le Cercle Proudhon: all in Cahiers, Nos. 3 and 4, May-August, 1912, p. 11-133.

[26]Ibid., p. 150-160.   [27]Ibid., p. 161-163.

In it, the Republic, One and Indivisible, would be replaced by a system of divided powers, with a king who was to assure national sovereignty against the outside world, and, at home, against the encroachments of big business. Beyond that point, the royal competence was not supposed to extend, except in a case of great social emergency. The nation was to retain its autonomy under the king, articulating itself into regional republics, corporations, workers' syndicates, each one administering its own affairs, and all sufficiently "well armed" to safeguard their own liberties, — if necessary, even against their royal protector. From this peaceful tug of war, there would result, so the planners of the Cercle Proudhon hoped, a balanced and yet vigorous new French society. The eternal penchant of the government to overstep its boundaries would be checked by the equally strong tendency of the "republics" to narrow down and circumscribe the power of Leviathan. The function of the syndicates would be "essentially to limit and confine the State; the syndicalist opposition to democracy stems precisely from the fact that democracy is, above all and inevitably, the State which penetrates everything and becomes the modern substitute of ancient Providence." The passage taken from a work by Edouard Berth,[28] states very aptly the position assigned to syndicalism in the blueprint of the Royalists.

We are faced with the spectacle of the disciple dragging the teacher behind him, down a path on which few of the old crowd followed. The only friend, besides Berth, who appeared still to see eye to eye with him, was Charles Péguy. But now even that good compagnon of his Dreyfus days left Georges Sorel. There came the day when Péguy, terrified by the relentless flow of Sorelian oratory, whispered to one of the Tharaud brothers: "I can't stand it any longer, let's get out!" His flight was followed by a letter in which he "excommunicated" Sorel in two terse sentences: "I recognize your hand in everything done against the Cahiers [de la Quinzaine]. I beg you not to come to our Thursday meetings in the future."[29] Péguy's son, Marcel, told his side of the story afterwards. It appears that Péguy had suspected his old friend of an intrigue against Julien Benda, who had broken with Sorel and who was Péguy's candidate for the Académie Française.[30] In contradiction of that view, Variot holds that Sorel's intrigue took place entirely in the imagination of the poet, Charles Péguy. But Jean Variot agrees with the Tharauds that Sorel resented Péguy's return to the

---

[28]Les méfaits des intellectuels (Paris, 1914), dedicated to Sorel and with a preface by Sorel in which Proudhon is called "the greatest French philosopher of the XIX century." This quotation is from the 2. edition (Paris, 1929), p. v, the quotation in the text: Ibid., p. 9-10.

[29]For details, see Jérôme et Jean Tharaud, Notre cher Péguy (Paris, 1926), II, 137-143.

[30]Marcel Péguy, La rupture de Charles Péguy et de Georges Sorel (Paris, 1930).

Church. He simply could not believe that the erstwhile socialist and Dreyfusard was very serious about his much publicized conversion. He never saw Péguy again, but whenever he met a common friend, Sorel never failed to inquire after him and to sigh: "Poor Péguy!"[31]

Sorel did not recover from that loss, for pleased as he was with youthful companionship, what really mattered to him was to match his wits against someone intellectually his equal, a Benedetto Croce, a Pareto, even a Jaurès. Now, as he was looking over his new friends, the younger generation looked promising enough; he had himself "contributed" to their number such faithfuls as Variot and Berth; and the rest, Valois, Lagrange, Maire, de Marans, seemed quite acceptable, and perhaps malleable. But what about their chiefs who, if not of Sorel's own generation, at any rate were mature men, — what about Maurras, Léon Daudet, and above all, Maurice Barrès? Georges Sorel's critical conscience, never to be lulled into sleep for very long, began to stir uneasily.

Between Sorel and Barrès there was much mutual curiosity and even more misunderstanding which a meeting, arranged by Variot, did not remove. Sorel, who considered Barrès above all a great master of French prose, talked literature throughout the interview, while Barrès, being under the impression that the interests of his guest were confined to politics, politely steered the conversation away from literary topics to the affairs of the day.[32] Under these conditions, the meeting of the minds which might have influenced the history of modern France, could not materialize. Sorel commented on the meeting afterwards: "Your Barrès is a very charming man. He has a superior education, and he is courtesy itself, but he is not very communicative. Did you notice how he would not tell me whether he wrote easily or not? For years I have been burning with curiosity to find out!" Whereas Barrès confided to the same Variot: "Your Sorel! What a devil of a fellow! I wanted to find out so many things from him...and he, what does he do? He makes me talk literature and how difficult it is to write.... And, say, he does not mince his words, does he. A curmudgeon, that's what he is."[33]

As to Maurras, Sorel continued for some years to hold the regard he had expressed for him in 1908, as a man who "knew about the proletariat."[34] Maurras alone among the right-wing radicals had understood that the strong state which he envisioned, needed a strong social basis; it is this insight which made his teachings attractive to quite a few French workers. In 1910, Sorel called Maurras "the most eminent theoretician monarchy has ever had.... Maurras is doing for the monarchy what Marx has done for socialism. He is a power."[35] But the Third Republic will not be destroyed by brilliant pamphlets. Revolutionary,

---

[31]Variot, op. cit., pp. 250-268. [32]Ibid., p. 153-159.
[33]Ibid., p. 160. [34]Ibid., p. 27 (Cf. p. 203 and note 2).
[35]Ibid., p. 123.

"direct action (violence) alone is efficacious."[36] The question is: will Maurras act? Sorel does not think so. French monarchism had become infected by the spirit of bourgeois reaction: "The real enemies of the Action Française stand on the right."[37] And after the inevitable war? Two forces, nationalism and Marxism, would confront each other. "After the foreign war, civil war. It is always like that."[38] Which one of the two extremes is likely to prevail? In France, most probably, neither one. The parliamentary system, Sorel thought, had so corrupted both the nationalists and socialists that it might well be able to prevail, even without a civil war. In that case, "the Action Française would have been preaching in the desert, before a few convinced Marxists, and, like they, in complete isolation."[39]

Much as Sorel may have tried to forget these doubts, he had them on his mind throughout his honeymoon with Royalism, until he could bear the strain no longer and, once more, pleaded poor health to withdraw completely from all contacts with the New Proudhonians. And did not the events of the next years bear out his doubts of 1910? For the last period of his life, before and after the peace of Versailles, Sorel would taunt the King's Men who had joined the patriotic wolf's pack in the democratic crusade against the Central Powers. Once more, war, national war, became anathema in Sorel's work, as the philosophy of the class struggle reassumed for him its old importance. Not only did Sorel speak of himself as "an old man who wants to remain, as did Proudhon, a disinterested servant of the proletariat;"[40] he also tried to prove from Proudhon's correspondence that the great French libertarian had never been a nationalist, the implication being that the Rightists had no claim on him at all.[41] Maurras and his ilk stood exposed as journalists who had declaimed against the Third Republic merely because their revues and papers did not sell.[42] Their abhorrence of plutocracy would cease the day they were to become eligible for high office. Actually, Maurras was a democrat: "L'Action Française tries to persuade the educated youth that the democratic idea is on the wane...." If that were to come true, then Maurras would be rightly

---

[36]Ibid., p. 124. [37]Ibid., p. 126.

[38]Ibid. [39]Ibid., p. 127.

[40]Matériaux (1. edition, Paris, 1919), Dedication. The book was ready for publication in 1914.

[41]Exégèse proudhoniennes, Appendix to the 2. edition of the Matériaux (Paris, 1921), pp. 415-449. Written in June, 1920. — Henri de Lubac, in his Proudhon et le christianisme (Paris, 1945) disagrees with Sorel's interpretation. He calls Proudhon a genuine patriot and "the numerous passages quoted by Sorel... merely show that he was not a lover of the blind chauvinism or jingoism of the mob." Cited from the American edition of De Lubac's work, entitled The Unmarxian Socialist, transl. by R. E. Scantlebury (New York, 1948), p. 56.

[42]Letter to Croce of January 19, 1915 in La Critia (1929), p. 117, cited in chapter 9, p. 224.

called one of the "masters of the hour." But, "is not he himself imbued
with the democratic spirit? The modern authors whom he admires so
much (Stendhal, Balzac, Sainte-Beuve) completely lack that aristocratic
distinction, which represented the hall-mark of good literature to our
ancestors." This was the ex-collaborator's judgment of French monarchism in June, 1914.[43] "What Sorel wants to say, is that the positivist
and intellectual, Maurras, repudiated only the political side of democracy and not its philosophical foundations."[44]

The Amalgam

The harshness of his afterthought bespeaks the remorse of a man
who had strayed from the narrow path of proletarian virtue, to contemplate another revolutionary order. His denunciation of the company
he had kept with "reaction" was essentially, the renunciation of that
terrifying new idea. He had had a glimpse of the forbidden fruit, and
he had shied away, leaving it for younger men to reap. So terrified was
he, that, when the new idea at last came to life, warped, coarsened, but
still clearly recognizable, Sorel did not dare to claim any credit for
himself.[45] He was too old, and too much of a socialist "traditionalist"
to pursue the tempting thought to its inexorable end....

For this was to be the new order, as proclaimed by the Neo-Proud-
honists: the class struggle formalized into a dualism reconciling the
desiderata of both monarchists and syndicalists, state and masses.
Obviously, their over-artificial formula was never meant to be more
than a plank, laid down for hesitant leftists to cross the ditch into the
nationalists camp, a sop to assuage their doubts about the future status
of labor under a government no longer limited by the considerations of
political democracy.

And yet, the frail construction contains many, if not all the elements
of Mussolini's corporate state — a state which, to be sure, never left
the blueprint stage, since the "republics" of the labor syndicates which
he installed, were never granted genuine autonomy within the framework
of his highly centralized administration. But the fusion of the socialist
and nationalist extremes, envisioned by a score of Paris intellectuals
in 1912 did become a reality in Italy a decade later. The interesting
question is not so much why that new idea did not take roots in the
country of its origin — for Pétain's shortlived "French State," although
hewing rather closely to the corporate and nationalist, anti-democratic
line, cannot very well be called a free creation of the French mentality —
the question is rather how it was possible that the members of the Cercle
Proudhon could even for a moment seriously believe in a success of
their conspiracy against the Third Republic. On the surface of it, the
situation was not at all favorable to a revolution or a coup d'état. The

---

[43]Matériaux p. 17-18, note 1.   [44]Pirou, op. cit., p. 46.
[45]See chapter 9, p. 230.

regime of the French middle class was never more secure. Social discontent, of course, persisted, but it was precisely because the revolutionary ardor of the workers was abating, that Sorel had turned to new horizons. He was a general without an army now, and if the Monarchists who humored him were under the impression that they would acquire, through Georges Sorel, the mass basis which they were lacking, then they were, at best, very naive.

But it is possible, and perhaps necessary to discard that view. Instead of writing off the Paris episode as an experiment in fascism that had to fail because it was, for one thing, premature, we might decide that it was Mussolini's matured, full-fledged Fascism of 1922 that went wrong because it went off the tracks laid out in 1912, — tracks that may still be waiting for someone to use them. . . .

It is, of course, quite likely, — as Sorel himself thought — that the gentlemen and labor theorists who, in the midnoon of the Third Republic, were day-dreaming about the social monarchy, had been talking with their tongues in cheek. Still, there remains to be considered their official credo; taken at its face value, it may disclose some valuable if partial truth regardless of whatever nationalist partisan considerations tended to defeat it. The Camelots du Roi may have been foxes scoffing at the sour grapes of mass success, but their record definitely shows that they did not seek out the mob. On the contrary, the group did shun, if not publicity, then, at least, popularity. Their attitude was one of primness and austerity, sometimes carried to the point of snobbery and dandyism. The better word is: esoteric. Their professed aim was to assess, not the day, but the age. The time to act was not yet, although it was bound to come as surely as the people would come to appreciate, if instructed, the need for an act of social surgery that would be both incisive and conservative. That act would be the result of their own free will, not of coercion. The people will have to become persons first before they may become a nation. As long as society remained the melting pot of masses, masses that share only one thing: a profound loneliness, only one thing was left to those who craved salvation: withdrawal, radical secession, for the sake of new communion. Isolation, yes, but of small, tightly-knit bands, united in their determination not to be ground into the mass of solitaries. Non-cooperation with the democratic demos, cooperation with the group — that was to be the seed of a new world.

Such notions were not at all alien to Sorel's philosophy of the "producers." His proletarians too were to withhold cooperation and to form their own communities, as the early Christians had done: living in this world, but not of it. Between the masses and the decadent manipulators, the new aristocracy would grow up in proud independence: alert, hardworking and austere, the proletarian élite was to keep the tired old masters at arms length until the time when they could be replaced. And if that time should never come, the struggle for that end would

still have been worthwhile; fighting it, the genuine producers, heirs to
a civilization that must be preserved, would revive the old heroisms,
that had been the glory of the Western world.

To say that the pre-Fascist Paris failure was a case of too little
and too early, would be a mere side-stepping of the question that demands an answer. Most assuredly, in 1912 the situation was not "ripe"
for any concerted onslaught from the Right and Left on the foundations
of French middle-class democracy. But that fact by itself need not
have precluded the slow underground growth of a movement that might
very well have found its historic chance in the great social crisis which
exploded with a muffled report in the Paris street riots of 1934. The
point is that Monarcho-Syndicalism never "jelled" so as to issue in a
real movement be it ever so small; it remained the brain-child of a
coterie, still-born.

The gentlemen who tried to hitch their wagon to Proudhon, were
revolutionary officers in search of cadres. By flattering Sorel they
hoped to infuse their idea of a nationalist state with social content. No
psychological acumen is required to see at once that the French workers — suppose Sorel had been in a position to "deliver" any proletarian
following — could not have possibly developed any confidence in a scheme
presented to them by a cavalier intelligentsia whose syndicalist sympathies were, at best, rather sudden. It did not take more than plain horse-
sense to see that the cumulation of leftist and rightist grievances against
the Third Republic was not enough to inspire anyone with rebellious
enthusiasm: hatred against the same enemy is not enough to promote
community of love. And there was, in particular, one element of the
Neo-Nationalist program which the French workingman was constitu-
tionally unable to make his own: the symbol and design of monarchy.

Again, to state that it was sheer romantic foolishness to lecture
modern Frenchmen, more than half a century after the fall of Louis
Philippe, about the advantages of the monarchic system, would be to
say the obvious. Yet, the anachronistic symbol, ill-chosen as it was,
responded, in a certain way, to a need dimly felt and deprived of expression in the new, industrial society.

This was the need and longing for a new authority or new authorities, to replace the old and to make possible the ordering of life, the
balance, if not the suppression of those forces which were making for
social frustration and mass unrest. That balance, the new masses had
come to feel with increasing clarity, was not to be achieved, in twentieth-
century Europe at any rate, by the nineteenth-century mechanics of political democracy. More and more people failed to feel themselves and
their concerns expressed and represented by the legislative and executive agents who, supposedly, did their, the people's bidding. But as the
belief in the regal overlord was gone, and trust in the infallible truth
of democracy was on the wane, no new authority was in the offing that
could have filled the institutional void. Since politics will tolerate a

vacuum as little as does nature, a frantic search for new forms of authority began. Mankind often when halted on its path, turns around to find its bearings in the past. If post-democratic society was to achieve the social harmony democracy had not been able to produce, the new state had to stand above the classes; it had to be, at last, Plato's Republic: man writ large, the state in which each one could recognize himself. That power, both impersonal, "disinterested," and most personal — why could it not be a French king, removed by general consensus from the clash of petty interests, God's own vicar and at the same time Rousseau's most democratic sovereign, the General Will personified?

In making kingship the centerpiece of their new institutional arrangement, the New Proudhonians were both right and wrong. Right, insofar as the simmering revolt against democracy was indeed a protest among other things against the ever growing dehumanization of civil society, a refusal to go on travelling a road that must end in the total depersonalization of all social relationships. But the promoters of the social Monarchy were wrong when they believed that modern man was really tired of representative democracy. They failed to see what his dissatisfaction really meant: that he wanted more of it. He could not, try as he might, identify himself with any distant dynast evoking merely unpleasant memories of a despostic past. What twentieth-century man wanted, was a much more direct system of representation — some way that would enable him to feel that he was truly managing, if only in a limited sphere, his own personal affairs. Sorel had expressed the deepest urge of our period when he said that the future elite would be masterless.[46] By that he meant, of course, not a return to primitive anarchy but a technological condition of society which would enable the producers to be at once masters and subjects of the social process. They would, again, be real persons. Authority would no more be some enigmatic, hostile force, but within their own reach, no longer an abstraction but the living symbol of man's freedom.

But that time was not yet, and with human nature what it is, unwilling to grope patiently for the right way, contemporary man's urge for a more personal expression of his social, or potential social power, in brief: his wish "to belong," if only vicariously, contented itself with a shortcut, fashioning the new, intensely personal authority of the dictator.

---

[46]Reflections (1950 ed.), p. 264.

9. GIORGIO SOREL — A PROTO-FASCIST?

In 1920 Sorel wrote: "Our socialist party bureaucrats would rather sacrifice the emancipation of the proletariat than their habit of political control. But France has lost her intellectual leadership in Europe. Many reasons led me, long ago, to the conclusion that what an Hegelian would call the **Weltgeist** is today looking at Italy. Thanks to her, the light of a new age will not go out."[1]

That sounds suspiciously like an apostrophe of rising Fascism. However, in 1920, Sorel (as will be shown) could have only the haziest idea of Italian things to come. Also, his high opinion of that country's potentialities, and his faith in its cultural predominance, are nothing new: Sorel speaks the plain truth when he asserts that he had always thought that way about the Latin Sister. In this regard, an objectivity, rare in a Frenchman, is mixed up with highly personal considerations.

For whereas Georges Sorel was known in France as the old master of a Happy Few, Giorgio Sorel was a renowned Italian publicist and author. Rarely will be found such an example of bi-national repute. Nor was Sorel's Italian oeuvre, which in size is at least equal to his French production, a mere matter of translation: some of his books[2] and many of his essays appeared merely in Italian and were never published in the author's country. Another point that is remarkable: while we hear nothing but complaints from Sorel about the great trouble he has in placing articles with French periodicals, he seems to have met with no such adversity in Croce's country. But although it is true that he owed much of his Italian **rennomée** to that great man, it would be superficial to explain it merely by the fact of patronage. The reasons for Sorel's success in Italy lie deeper, and they are as complex as the political and social situation of that country.

As everywhere, the mass diffusion of the new ideas which took root in Italy in the first decade of this century, originated with some minute nuclei of **homines novarum rerum cupidi.** Even if a notion is already "in the air," it still has to be formulated on an intellectual

---

[1]This is the conclusion of a preface written by Sorel for a projected collection of articles which he had contributed to various Italian journals between 1910 and 1920. Published and introduced by Mario Missiroli under the title **l'Europa sotto la tormenta** (Milano, 1931 and 1941). The preface was published as **Ultime Meditazione** in **Nuova Antologia,** 7. series, (Rome, September-October, 1928), pp. 289-307.

[2]**Saggi di critica del Marxismo** (Palermo, 1903), pp. xlviii and 401; **Insegnamenti sociali della economia contemporanea** (Milan, 1906), pp. xxii and 398.

level, before it can become the rallying point of first, smaller groups, and then the masses. Thus, in our semiliterate age, even the most hackneyed social slogans may be traced back to some highbrow review of negligible circulation and a life expectancy of a few months. When they fold up, their editors will try again, or, more likely, they will go on to some newspaper to exploit what reputation they have managed to establish for themselves. By now, the new idea has acquired some scattered bridgeheads, from which it can percolate in vertical and horizontal directions, until the infantry of common people comes up to close the gaps between the isolated strongholds, then establishing a solid front line, ready to advance. To stay within the simile, the bridgehead which Sorel acquired in Italy seems easy to identify: it was **Il Divenire sociale,** the periodical that printed the first text of the **Reflections.** But ideas seldom are successfully disseminated in such open and straightforward fashion: rather they prefer to spread in roundabout and surreptitious ways. More influential than the **Divenire** for the propagation of Sorelian thoughts became another organ, for which Sorel never wrote a piece. "What is this **Leonardo?**", he asks in a letter,[3] referring to a Florentine revue that had expressed itself quite disrespectfully about Croce's **La Critica.** But **Leonardo** was to rise again, after its early demise, as **La Voce,** edited, as its predecessor, by the two G.s, Prezzolini and Papini, who, between them, did much to introduce new figures of artistic, literary or political importance in their country: "Besides familiarizing themselves with the literary work of Claudel, many Italians through the **Voce** first became acquainted with the work of Gide, Rimbaud, James, Weinninger [sic], Tyrrel, Sorel."[4] The last-named did not right away reciprocate the interest with sympathy: he was an avid reader, but an acid critic, partly perhaps influenced by Croce who had no use whatever for the esthetic theories which Prezzolini and Papini advanced in their journal.[5] Besides, in a book on syndicalism Prezzolini had attacked Sorel "with considerable fury." Like all authors, the writer of the **Reflections** is convinced that his critic either did not read his work or read it in a most cursory fashion. That Prezzolini ranked him on a par with Henri Bergson is small "comfort" to Sorel. His modesty (or pride) is touched to the quick: "I have no pretension whatsoever to be compared to Bergson."[6]

But in the same degree as Georges Sorel draws closer to the nationalists, he finds The Voice increasingly agreeable. The tune

---

[3]To Croce, (**La Critica,** 1928, p. 97), December 8, 1906.

[4]Peter M. Riccio, **On The Threshold of Fascism** (New York, 1929), p. 107.

[5]"I am surprised that **La Voce** is so partial to the Modernists whom you consider to be farcical." Sorel to Croce (**Op. cit.,** p. 197), July 17, 1909.

[6]To Croce (**Ibid.,** p. 194-195), April 5, 1909. — The first chapter of Prezzolini's book, **La teoria sindicalista** (Naples, 1909) was ironically entitled: **Notre maître Sorel.**

becomes familiar: "Besides advocating a nationalism that stressed
domestic improvement and internal achievements, the Voce also
helped to spread the new syndicalist theories of Georges Sorel."[7] Not
only had Prezzolini reversed himself, he even used his influence to
open the columns of the Resto del Carlino to Sorel;[8] that famous Bolognese daily was to become an important carrier of Sorelian ideas
from there on.

With his new insight in the dynamics of twentieth century nationalism, Sorel could view Italian expansionism with a detached and yet
sympathetic understanding. When, in 1911, La Voce, parting ways
from more extreme imperialists, protested violently against the Tri-
politanian venture, Sorel wondered whether the Italian people really
were as opposed to that colonial venture, as the passionate polemics
of the press would indicate. The Italians, he suggests, are not at all
adverse to making conquests — provided they are profitable, "for nowadays, all nations hanker after colonies in the moon."[9] Besides, the
anti-war stand of the socialists appears to be disturbingly inept.[10]

But with this one exception, the La Voce group may be said to
have nurtured the latent anti-democratic sentiment of the Italian middle class which Mussolini later was to turn to his advantage; sharply
critical of the ineptitudes and scandals of the liberal regime on the
one hand, and of the pseudo-revolutionary antics of official socialism
on the other, Prezzolini and Papini looked with favor on the rebels in
both classes: "To Prezzolini must go the credit for being among the
first to reveal the importance of the works of Gaetano Mosca and Vilfredo Pareto...."[11] Of equal, if not greater, consequence was the
entente cordiale established between the Voce group and the Italian
Nationalist Association (later National Party), founded by Enrico Corradini, whose theory is characterized, by Franz Neumann, as "a
hodgepodge of...French 'integral nationalism' and of revolutionary
syndicalism....He incorporated into his own work, the doctrines of
Georges Sorel and transformed them into means of ensnaring the
working classes."[12]

The extent of Sorel's influence on Corradini has been questioned
by Giovanni Prezzolini, who insisted that the nationalist leader derived
his ideas from Pareto and Mosca.[13] However, there exists a letter

---

[7]Riccio, op. cit., p. 162-163.

[8]Sorel to Croce (op. cit., p. 342), June 28, 1910.

[9]Ibid., (p. 434), September 23, 1911.

[10]Ibid., October 14, 1911.

[11]Riccio, op. cit., p. 163. — See Supplement 2.

[12]Franz L Neumann, Behemoth (New York, 1944), p. 193-194.

[13]L'Aristocrazia dei briganti in G. Prezzolini and G. Papini, Vecchio e
nuovo nazionalismo (Milan, 1914), p. 38, cited by Joseph Rossi in 20th Century Political Thought, ed. by Joseph S. Roucek (New York, 1946), p. 568-569.
Erwin von Beckerath seems to share the same view: see his Wesen und
Werden des Fascistischen Staates (Berlin, 1927), p. 28, note 2.

from Sorel to Croce who had sent him a piece written by Enrico Corradini, about which Sorel is enthusiastic: "...remarkably intelligent ....The author realizes very well the value of my ideas. If I had his address, I would write and thank him "[14] This would indicate that Sorel gave the nationalist leader his official blessing, although, as Erwin von Beckerath points out, Corradini gave the myth a very unSorelian content: "with the syndicalists it was the general strike; with the nationalists, the nation."[15]

Be this as it may, the fact remains that the **La Voce** circle served successfully the purpose which **Le Cercle Proudhon** had failed to achieve, that is: to provide a platform on which revolutionaries of the Left and Right could build in common.[16] Whether the formula reads: Corradini = Maurras + Sorel, or: Corradini = Maurras + Mosca + Pareto, — in view of the affinity of thought between Pareto, Mosca, and Sorel, the distinction is quite immaterial. But the dispute illustrates the fallacy of isolating one man's work, and of attributing to him what was a multiple and cumulative contribution. Even so, the fermentation process was not yet complete. The formula employed by Corradini had a sequel: as his own credo was a blend between Maurras and syndicalist ideas, so Mussolini's fascist solution in turn reconciled the statism of Corradini[17] with his own anarcho-syndicalist past.[18]

Enter: Il Duce

While Georges Sorel was still alive he endorsed Lenin who thought very little of him.[19] When Sorel was dead he was acclaimed by the Duce of fascist Italy as his foremost teacher,[20] although Sorel had never publicly endorsed Mussolini.

---

[14]To Croce (**Op. cit.**, p. 195), May 4, 1909.

[15]Beckerath, **op. cit.**, p. 31.

[16]"Prezzolini's **Voce** was the connecting cell in the texture of the new Italy that rose before the first world war," wrote Mussolini's biographer, Margherita Sarfatti. (Cited by Riccio, **op. cit.**, p. [61].)

[17]"The nation is a spiritual person," E. Corradini, **L'Unità e la potenza delle nazioni** (Firenze, 1922), p. 115. "The state is the organic and active nation." **Ibid.**, p. 122. "The state stands for the will of the united nation, which transcends the warring wills of its component parts." **Ibid.**, p. 125.

[18]An ardent Italian patriot linked **La Voce** with the early, irredentist labors of the later **Duce**: "Even you, Benito Mussolini...were discovered by Prezzolini when you were up there in the [Austrian] Trentino, to which you will return, followed by us, to terminate with other arms the battle which you were then unable to complete." A. Di Staso in **Il Popolo d'Italia** of November 28, 1914. (Cited by Riccio, **op. cit.**, p. [145].)

[19]See chapter 10, p.

[20]The French journalist, Emile Schreiber, asking the **Duce** whether it was true that he had been inspired by the author of the **Reflections on Violence,** was told: "That's quite correct. Georges Sorel has been my master." **L'Illustration** (Paris) of September 17, 1932.

While it is comparatively easy to extricate Sorel from his self-confessed position as a Communist — the task of dissociating him from a cause he never avowed presents much difficulty.

The puzzle will never be solved unless it is realized that there were many facets of Georges Sorel's personality — in the case at hand, two: the partisan of the proletariat who had no use for the state, any state; and the student of historic forces, capable of considerable enthusiasm for any sign of a moral revival in Europe even if it took the forms of nationalism and strong-man rule. It appears that Sorel considered both of his intellectual attitudes as compatible if the working class had made genuine advances during this process of moral revival. Then the autocrat could have been forgiven for using and even strengthening the old techniques of ruling, so that a plea for the dictator was in order, although he might be a patriot and statesman first, an internationalist and syndicalist second.

When Sorel died in 1922, Mussolini, though not invested with official power until two months later, in all but name, was already the conqueror of Italy. Sorel had been following the latter's career with close attention, and is said to have predicted Mussolini's spectacular future as early as 1912.[21] In turn, the other had been quoting Sorel year in and year out in his capacity as a socialist editor and party leader.[22] The development of both men shows a remarkable parallelism, with the old philosopher always a step ahead of the young politician. Both had been Marxists before they broke away from the official party that had become reformist, although it was still mouthing the old revolutionary phrases. Both had become exponents of syndicalist, direct and non-political action. To be sure, Mussolini did

---

[21]"Our Mussolini is not an ordinary Socialist. Believe me: one day you may see him at the head of a sacred battalion saluting the Italian flag with his sword. He is a fifteenth century Italian, a **condottiere!** It is not known yet, but he alone has enough energy and ability to restore power to the government." Jean Variot, **Le Père Sorel,** in L'Eclair, (Paris) of September 11, 1922, as quoted by Gaétan Pirou, **Georges Sorel** (Paris, 1927), p. 53.

This startling prediction, published on the eve of the March on Rome, is not included in Jean Variot's final collection of the master's pronouncements, **Propos de Georges Sorel** (Paris, 1935). There, he has Sorel merely state: "I have heard about him before the war." (p. 56).

Another disciple, René Johannet, reported in his **Eloge du Bourgeois Français** (Paris, 1924), p. 338, that Sorel told him after the Italian Socialist Congress of Ancona in 1914: "This young man will make himself a name in the world." But that was at the time when Mussolini was a left-winger with syndicalist leanings.

[22]An extensive account of Mussolini's Sorelian as well as anti-Sorelian editorials is to be found in Gaudens Megaro, **Mussolini in the Making** (Boston and New York, 1938), pp. 228-245.

not need Sorel in order to develop his own form of radicalism,[23] but he could use Sorel's terminology to good advantage. The theory of violence elevated the crude vernacular of syndicalist propaganda to the dignity of a literary idiom.

Later on the two men parted ways for a while when, around 1910, Sorel, disappointed in French syndicalism, looked for other allies in his perennial struggle against the republic of "merchants, intellectuals and politicians."[24] Unlike Mussolini, Sorel did not wait for World War I to rediscover that stubborn fact, the nation. With his hypersensitive flair for forecasting social trends, Sorel tried to harness the new current for his revolutionary purpose, only to be showered by that staunch left-winger, Mussolini, with a torrent of abuse.

Again, in 1914, while Italy was still a neutral in the war, Mussolini became the socialist patriot and interventionist, whereas Sorel was decrying the imperialistic carnage and restating most emphatically his old, proletarian allegiance.

By 1920, Mussolini and Sorel had, each one, reached the other's starting point. Sorel's development was more involved than that of the Italian former socialist: if we omit his pre-Marxist puppation stage, he had moved from the revolutionary Left to the extreme "Right" and was now back in the syndicalist fold. Mussolini's itinerary was, in a sense, more straightforward than the Frenchman's: it simply ran from the extreme left to the extreme "Right."

But as the situation looked to Georges Sorel in 1920 the Italian prospects for a vital change in the political and social system were incomparably better than in France. In Italy, the **rapprochement** between syndicalist and nationalist forces had gone much farther; the regime was infinitely more disorganized than its French counterpart. What Sorel saw South of the Alps, was an exasperated proletariat which seemed capable of anything, if only it found the right leadership. As to the nationalist protest, it was less — if at all — dependent on a royalist solution.[25]

The nationalist propaganda for a strong state was felt to be directed against the cynicism and graft of the liberal regime rather than against the existing institutions of the labor class. If in France

---

[23]"His temperament and home surroundings would seem sufficient to indicate why he had little or nothing to learn from 'literary' apologists of violence or force like Nietzsche and Sorel." Megaro, **ibid.**, p. 104. "Those who ramble about Mussolini's intellectual father ... would do well to pause and consider the influence of his real father." **Ibid.**, p. 318.

[24]A phrase coined by Edouard Berth and used as title of an essay expounding the syndicalist credo: **Marchands, Intellectuels et Politiciens,** serialized in **Le Mouvement Socialiste,** July 15, 1907 — March, 1908.

[25]Since monarchy, in Italy, was not a mere wish but a reality, and, at that time, the tool and ally of the ruling liberal parliamentarians.

Sorel and his friends had for a moment expected that the revolutionary initiative might come from the right, in Italy the future seemed to
favor left-wing revolution, with a specifically Italian twist.

The future brought precisely that result, but with the added feature, entirely unforeseen by Sorel or anyone else, that the proletarian
leader of the revolution turned against his own class, by sacrificing
syndicalist principles to the nationalist concept of the omnipotent
state.

The fact that Sorel was not prepared for a fascist Mussolini is no
discredit to Sorel's analytical ability, when it is remembered that as
late as April, 1920, the budding Duce still declared: "I start with the
individual and strike at the state ... [not at] this or that state, but
against the state in itself .... Down with the state in all its forms and
incarnations: the state of yesterday, of today, and of tomorrow; the
bourgeois state and the socialist state."[26]

If Sorel did not comment on this or any similar pronouncement
coming from the same source, it was because at that time hundreds of
Italian syndicalist orators were saying exactly the same thing. The
anarchist Mussolini could not impress Sorel as very original. Besides, the founder of fascism spoke for a group of urban syndicalists,[27] while Sorel's speculations about a possible Italian revolution
developed in a different direction. Sorel knew that the Italian economy
was preponderantly one of peasants, and of poor peasants at that, badly exploited by their landlords who were barons on a latifundian scale
in the backward South of the country. In contrast to the leaders of
Russian Marxism, Sorel seems to have entertained hopes that the
class struggle — in Italy, at any rate — might be decided in the rural
sector rather than by the industrial proletariat. More than twenty
years before the March on Rome, Sorel had written an introduction to
the French edition of an Italian Socialist's work[28] — an introduction
which Sorel later published independently under the title "National Socialisms."[29] Still later he included it in a collection of miscellaneous
older writings[30] which appeared after the war, when Mussolini's break
with the reformist Socialist party was already a fact of public knowledge.

-----

[26]Megaro, op. cit., p. 319.

[27]The first assembly of the new party took place in March, 1919, at Milan,
the capital of Italian industry, and was attended by 145 persons, in the main
Syndicalists; the meeting sent a message of sympathy to workers who had occupied a factory at Dalmine. The intellectual make-up of the initial fascist
group was sharply distinct from that of the middle-class elements who were
to join later on. (Beckerath, op. cit., pp. 19, 20, 24).

[28]G. Gatti, Le socialisme et l'agriculture (Paris, 1901)

[29]Socialismes nationaux in Cahiers de la Quinzaine (Paris, April, 1902),
pp. 33-63.

[30]Matériaux d'une théorie du prolétariat (2. ed., 1921), pp. 201-237.

"There are," Sorel wrote, "at least as many kinds of socialisms as there are great nations."[31] In Italy, he believed, socialism might evolve along the line of the rural cooperative which was becoming increasingly popular with the poor tenant farmers. Was this perhaps to be the proletarian institution with which they would fight and win the class struggle in Italy? Sorel tended to believe it:

"If the system of agricultural cooperatives is really the school that is preparing the Italian peasant for socialism, then it is clear that socialism is destined to be developed by our neighbors along lines highly significant for the future....More than once Italy has been the educator of Europe; she could well assume that role once more, because she seems to have reached a stage favorable to the development of doctrines which would bring about a revival of socialism...."[32]

This prognosis of an Italian peasant revolution does not occur anywhere else in Sorel's work; that he incorporated it into a book to which he attached particular significance, without any change or annotation, does not necessarily indicate that he still believed in 1919 what he had written in 1901. His general faith in a coming Italian revolution, however, remained unshaken. In 1912, at a time when his opinion of French syndicalism was very low indeed, he told Jean Variot: "I do not believe that Italy's future will be the result of a normal, evolutionary process. I believe the syndicalist Italian youth, the most serious-minded of Europe, will make Italy greater because it knows best that the socialist theories, infected by democratism, are no longer tabu."[33]

However, up to this period no reference can be found to Mussolini, at that time chief of the radical wing of Italian socialism which had driven the reformists into secession.[34] The name "Mussolini" occurs for the first time in Sorel's correspondence with Benedetto Croce, and the reference is not a favorable one. Late in 1914, when Italy, still a neutral in the war, although being prodded by D'Annunzio and Mussolini toward intervention, Sorel complained about Giovanni Papini's recent popularity: "That does not surprise me too much, but it saddens me. After having adhered to the Futuristic movement, now he goes and becomes one of the lieutenants in the new Socialist party

---

[31] Ibid., p. 202.

[32] Ibid., p. 235.

[33] Variot, op. cit., p. 32.

[34] After the Socialist party congress at Reggio Emilia in July, 1912, the defeated right-wingers set up their own Italian Reformist Socialist Party while Mussolini, who had been instrumental in their expulsion, was made a member of the executive committee of the official party and, in December of the same year, editor-in-chief of the party organ, Avanti.

founded by Mussolini. It is to be feared that fifteen years of serious work in Italy have been in vain...."[35]

If he had not fully appreciated the impact of the new nationalism before, now, during the war which he hated and despised, Sorel saw the warmongers of the right unmasked: "I am not extremely surprised by the turn the discussion among Italian nationalists is taking...they are behaving like street Arabs....Italian nationalism reveals, at this occasion, its democratic soul just as our **Action Française** has done ...the majority of our great idealists are at bottom demagogues complaining about democracy when the circulation of their newspapers is disappointing...."[36] Shortly after Italy's entry into the war on the side of the Entente, Sorel wrote: "So the die has been cast...let us hope Italy will not have to suffer too much in consequence of her folly...."[37]

Sorel is not to be found in the camp of Italian interventionism in which Benito Mussolini figures so conspicuously. Sorel was saddened by the southern ally's heavy losses in the field, but not without hope that something good might come out of the slaughter. On January 9, 1916 he confided to Croce: "I believe Italy is marching toward the republic...the Socialists act with a sagacity of which I would not have thought them capable, by keeping themselves in reserve for the hour of collapse. Most certainly many Catholics adopt the same viewpoint."[38]

Sorel drew great comfort from a statement made by one of the "street Arabs," Corradini, saying: "Will the syndicate kill off parliamentarism? That is indeed our opinion." Sorel copied these lines for his friend Delesalle and added triumphantly: "Truth is on the march!"[39] A few months later, however, he was no longer so sure the Italian Socialists would exploit their opportunity. "I am told," he wrote Croce on December 25, 1918, "that the Socialist party may win a majority in the coming elections. This eventuality will put them to a harsh test; they could not do otherwise than replace unitary monarchy by a federal republic."[40] Sorel, the pluralist, speaking as the

---

    [35]To Croce (**La Critica**, 1929, p. 115), November 28, 1914. — The vanguard of Italian painters and poets led by Marinetti first teamed up with the nationalists led by Corradini. In 1919, a delegation of Futurists attended the first meeting of the Fascist party. (Cf. Beckerath, **op. cit.**, p. 19).

    On October 20, 1914, the executive committee of the Socialist party rejected Mussolini's semi-interventionist formula of qualified neutrality; he thereupon left the party and founded for his followers a new, interventionist organ, Il Popolo d'Italia.

    [36]To Croce (op. cit., p. 117), January 19, 1915.

    [37]Ibid., (p. 121), May 26, 1915.

    [38]Ibid., p. 354.

    [39]Georges Sorel, **Lettres à Paul Delesalle** (Paris, 1947), p. 145. Henceforth cited as "To Delesalle."

    [40]To Croce (**La Critica**, 1930, p. 48).

enemy of the centralized state, must have been hoping for a syndicalist order of the associated producers.

Crassus, not Caesar

The end of Sorel's correspondence with friend Croce, coinciding
with the end of Italian liberalism as well as proletarian freedom, does
not tell the whole story. In announcing the publication, the recipient
reserved the right to omit passages from Sorel's letters, "especially
of those written during the last years."[41] Written in the fifth year of
the Fascist regime, this remark suggests two possibilities. One is
that Benedetto Croce, since he had to use discretion, suppressed references unfriendly to Mussolini and his party, dating from the critical
last phase of Sorel's life (1920-1922). The other is that Croce who
consistently refused to kowtow to Il Duce, chose to leave out Sorelian
comments favorable to the system. Asked for the explanation, the
philosopher confessed that he does not recall what he did more than
twenty years ago, but he is sure the passages in question "could not
have contained any allusions against Fascism, for in that case I would
have been obliged to publish them." No, "Sorel, being the impression-
able man he was, in principle was favorable to Mussolini He hated
the professional politicos, and saw mistakenly in Mussolini "a spontaneous and beneficial force."[42] There remains, then, the bare possibility that our second surmise is correct. But have we a right to
assume that Benedetto Croce would have let his anti-fascism prevail
over his duty to the deceased friend? Such speculation is undignified.

There is no doubt about Sorel's infatuation with the future Duce;
all the more surprising is the unmistakable gloom of his last letters:
"I am passionately interested in the affairs of Italy, which present
themselves under such a mysterious aspect." They reminded him of
"the last days of the Roman Republic. The unrest instigated by the
financial magnates recalls to us the times of Crassus." The Italian
intellectuals were bought and "the people who listen to them do not
know that the writers, lawyers and politicians are the agents of finance capital. It seems to me the Socialist party too is not altogether
blameless in this matter."[43]

If this statement does nothing else, it reveals a deeply disturbed
Sorel: he tried to be the "detached" observer, lumping together im-
partially the Socialists with all those who committed the ignominious
"treason of the intellectuals" in Italy's fateful hour; but his past
loyalties were stronger then his will to objectivity: like any other
orthodox Marxist, he dismissed Mussolini as the modern replica of
Clodius and Milo.

[41]Ibid. (1927, p. 38, note).
[42]Letter to this writer (May 14, 1950).
[43]To Croce (op. cit., 1930, p. 191-192), July 30, 1920.

As the struggle neared its end, Sorel felt sorry for the defeated Socialists. "The Italian situation," he wrote on March 25, 1921, "resembles very much that of Ireland; the Socialists are treated somewhat like the Sinn Feiners are treated by the Black and tass" [sic].[44]

In but one published letter, the last he wrote to Croce,[45] did Sorel give credit to Mussolini's movement, if only for forcing socialism into decisive action before it was too late: "The adventures of fascism are, perhaps, at present, the most original social phenomenon in Italy; they seem to me to surpass by far the combinations of the politicians." It appeared to Sorel that Mussolini had already accomplished one thing: to instill "in a growing number of rural Socialists" the desire to enter the government. But their leader, Turati, "is hesitating because he is afraid his socialist personnel might not be up to governmental standards; however, he will end by taking the big plunge because even a brief delay would turn his abstention into a **gran rifuto.**" When Turati finally made up his mind, in July, 1922, it was too late; by then the Socialist party had lost the last remnant of its bargaining power.

For a last time, Sorel reverted to those rural syndicalists on whom he had set such great hopes at the beginning of the century. But Italian socialism had already made its final Great Refusal when, in 1920, it had not dared to follow up the occupation of the factories by decisive political action.

The unexploited "constructive" strike[46] of the north Italian workers was the Gettysburg of the Socialist confederates; Sorel did not live to see Appomatox. "What a sad future we have before us," he wrote Croce, and he comforted himself with the thought that, being seventy-four years old, he would not see "the still worse days to come."

If the letters Benedetto Croce saw fit to print impress us as coming from a man extremely circumspect in his evaluation of Italian fascism, the correspondence with Paul Delesalle, published in liberated France, shows the intimate Sorel who speaks his mind without restraint. Here, if anywhere, it is possible to find out what Sorel really thought of Mussolini.

The first fact that impresses the reader of the **Letters to Delesalle** is the total lack of any reference to fascism before 1921. The

---

[44]Ibid., p. 194.

[45]Ibid., (p. 195), August 26, 1921. — Croce, disturbed by Sorel's silence following this letter, asked for news, "but his physical condition did not permit him to answer me, and a year later, having been suffering for a long time, he passed away." (**Ibid.**, note 2).

[46]Mussolini vaguely endorsed the action of Italian labor: "Whether the factories belong to the workers rather than to the industrialists does not interest me. What matters is that people should work" Quoted by Stephen Raushenbush, **The March of Fascism** (New Haven, 1939, p. 173. Cf. also Megaro, **op. cit.**, p. 324.

explanation is that Sorel's interest in the years immediately following the first World War, was concentrated on Lenin's Russia; and that the French recipient of Sorel's letters was not, as Croce was, preoccupied with Italian affairs. When the topic was first mentioned, in a letter dated February 2, 1921, it was done in a single sentence: "In Italy, fascism does not seem ready to calm down; only a few days ago, Ferri was chased from his class room by the students of Rome "[47] This passage sounds noncommittal to the point of callousness, considering the fact that Enrico Ferri, professor of law, and leading Socialist was an old acquaintance of Sorel's. However, it is apparent that Sorel did not mean it that way, for soon afterwards, on March 19, 1921, he wrote: "Everybody in Italy expects new elections soon; I am very much afraid that they will result in a Parliament inclining the fascist way...." After having thus stated unequivocally where his sympathies lay, Sorel made one of his inspired guesses, a speculation backed up by no evidence whatsoever but one that time eventually proved to be uncannily accurate: "I am convinced that the clandestine, but real chief of the Fascists is the King — the King, who, in 1915, forced Italy into the war in order to destroy socialism."[48] One may refuse to follow Sorel in making Victor Emmanuel III personally responsible in both instances, but it is a fact that before the war the royal government had been greatly disturbed by the upsurge of proletarian unrest. The settimana rossa of 1914 was a clear warning signal of worse to come, and the Socialist party of Italy had fought intervention to the last moment, only to be stabbed in the back by their own left-winger, Benito Mussolini. It is known now that the only two forces on which the King could rely after the war, the Italian civil service and the army, did give Mussolini at least passive assistance and often active encouragement. The fascist terror squads somehow had access to army arsenals and public transportation. Sorel noted in the same letter: "As long as fascism continues to dominate the street, socialism will be weak, because the triumphant violence of the syndicates had been the essential element of its strength."

Sorel, unlike most Italian Socialists, knew the score: the Italian working class had lost the initiative in the class war, it was put on the defensive. Hence the theorist of violence as a means of keeping the two main classes of modern industrial society distinct and "in form" could have no quarrel with that fact, provided Mussolini's terror was indeed nothing else but the bourgeois answer to the proletarian provocation. As his reference to the King as the secret head of fascism reveals, Sorel at that point still unreservedly identified fascism with reaction. It is convenient to refer in this connection to a letter dated April 9, 1921, in which Sorel, speaking of the Italian peasants who, in fear of fascist terror, deserted the Socialist party en masse

---

[47]To Delesalle (op. cit. in note 39), p. 204.
[48]Ibid., p. 215.

to put themselves under the protection of the blackshirts, came to the conclusion that "the whole of Europe is, without any doubt, fated to experience a new Thermidor...."[49]

The intellectual attitude of Sorel, the social scientist, would have loved nothing better than to accommodate Sorel, the sympathizer with organized labor, by relegating the new phenomenon, fascism, to the camp of counter-revolution. But somehow, it would not work. The thermidorian Mussolini defied the scheme of the **Reflections.** He continued to flout all the rules of the game: by reviling monarchy, by threatening the Church, and in parliament by consistently voting with his enemies against his friends. Was it possible that he, the anti-Socialist, might yet help socialism to win its battle? Not a few Italian radicals thought so at the time. On April 18, 1921, Sorel quoted, without comment, a speculation of his Italian friend, Missiroli[50] to the effect that Socialists and Fascists might arrive at an understanding and unite in a republican front: "The day the call for the republic would be sounded forcefully and taken up in earnest by the Socialists, that day would see the end of all resistance."[51]

Sorel tried very hard to sound detached, even flippant when writing: "You cannot imagine in what a sorry situation the Italian Prolos find themselves.... One has to read, as I do, the Italian press every day in order to understand the magnitude of the disaster."[52]

But if there was any doubt left about Sorel's personal feelings, another letter dispelled it: "The situation of the Italian Socialists is really very discouraging."[53] For a writer of Sorel's reticence, this was as much as an avowal of utter depression. As was his habit when he wanted to say something intensely personal, Sorel borrowed somebody else's voice. This time he copied a postcard in which another Italian friend, Enrico Leone[54] analyzed the route of the Italian left, concluding his report by saying:

"I did not care to register with the Socialist party which has started its crusade against the Communists in order to gain absolution from the Fascists for its past sins. What cowards! But the Communists, with their ideas about a strong state and dictatorship, are even more remote from us than the others. It is the will of destiny that a syndicalist keep aloof from all parties and limit himself to cultural tasks."[55]

---

[49]**Ibid.**, p. 219.

[50]Mario Missiroli, liberal journalist and editor of the **Resto del Carlino,** to which Sorel contributed, fought a duel with Mussolini in May, 1922; later he turned fascist.— About Missiroli, see also above, note 1.

[51]To Delesalle (**op. cit.**, p. 223).

[52]**Ibid.**

[53]**Ibid.** (p. 218), April 9, 1921.

[54]Enrico Leone, co-founder, in 1905, of the periodical **Il Divenire Sociale,** which became Sorel's principal Italian mouthpiece and which published the original **Reflections.**

[55]To Delesalle (**op. cit.,** p. 222), April 9, 1921.

Between fascism and communism, the syndicalist **Candide** had no choice but to turn his back on it all and to "cultivate his garden" in the expectancy of better times. Occasionally he still hoped against hope: so great was Sorel's distaste for fascism that he was ready to forget, for the time being, his older dislike of the ruling bourgeoisie and its liberal state; he came out for a defensive alliance between the Socialists and the government. On July 13, 1921, he wrote about the Socialists: "They know by now they are no longer a match for their enemies. The Italian press thinks the Socialists have become ripe for the government...." And Sorel told Delesalle something he did not tell Benedetto Croce:[56] that he himself had joined his voice to the chorus of Italian newspapers advocating that the Socialist party enter into an anti-fascist government coalition: "A while ago I wrote in the **Carlino** that the Socialist peasants could very well force their leaders to come to an understanding with the government, so as to be able to defend the proletarian institutions against les **fascistes.**"[57]

The enormity of this concession will be clear to anyone who knows that a political deal with the bourgeoisie had been Sorel's "great tabu" ever since he had freed himself from the decisive experience of his youth, the popular-front "illusions" of the Dreyfus revolution.

Now he was willing to sacrifice his dearest principle in order to salvage the institutions of the Italian working class threatened with annihilation by fascist incendiarism.

The correspondence ends on this note, except for one more testimonial Sorel passed on to his friend Delesalle. It comes from Vilfredo Pareto who informed him of a fascist raid on the Bolognese newspaper to which Sorel had contributed many articles: "For reasons of local politics the Fascists became enraged against the **Carlino,** they wanted to kill Missiroli; nothing less would do! Missiroli had to resign as editor precipitously.... The **Carlino,** in order to avoid similar incidents, was forced to adopt a nationalist line...."[58]

Sorel sent no more articles to the **Resto del Carlino.** If he had flirted once with a highly theoretical nationalist movement in France, the brutal reality of fascism stunned him into silence. He would not write for a gagged press. But whatever his feelings as a syndicalist and "disinterested servant of the proletariat," the historian Sorel remained fascinated with the European event that was fascism. As a partisan of the defeated working class, he could not help being resentful and dejected; still, the old engineer and student of the industrial revolution was able to do Mussolini justice. The Duce, harsh taskmaster of his backward, pre-industrial Italians, attained stature in the eyes of the moralist who believed that the machine age, correctly

---

[56]Sorel's last letter to Croce was written six weeks later (see note 45).
[57]To Delesalle (**op. cit.,** p. 236).
[58]**Ibid.** (p. 237), November 8, 1921.

understood, meant more work and not less, an ever greater effort toward a new heroism that was no more that of the battlefield but of the workshop. Seen in this light, the man who tried to bring Italians "up to date" assumed his place by the side of that other founder of a modern industrial society, Lenin. It is in his conversations with Jean Variot[59] that Sorel gave Mussolini, the builder, the recognition he had to withhold from the demagogue and destroyer of free institutions.

His interlocutor had asked him "the" question: Are Lenin and Mussolini disciples of Georges Sorel? The old man was obviously pleased with the question, and his answer was a double, though delighted disclaimer. Did Lenin have to be a reader of Sorel in order to become Lenin? "Frankly, I don't believe it," was Sorel's reply.[60] As to Mussolini, Sorel is reported to have said:

"My works have been more read in Italy than in France . ..It is possible, it is even probable that Benito Mussolini has read me. But, attention! Mussolini is a man no less extraordinary than Lenin. He, too, is a political genius, of a greater reach than all the statesmen of the day, with the only exception of Lenin. ..He is not a Socialist à la sauce bourgeoise; he has never believed in parliamentary socialism; he has an amazing insight into the nature of the Italian masses, and he has invented something not to be found in my books: the union of the national and the social — something I have studied without ever developing the idea. This national-social approach, so characteristic of his method, is Mussolini's exclusive property, and I could not possibly have inspired it, not even from afar."[61]

A moment later, Sorel reconsidered and conceded the possibility that Mussolini might have taken a leaf from the Sorelian theory of violence after all, "violence understood as a mere means to impose certain ends," Sorel said, adding hastily: "But again, all this was in the air...."[62]

Sorel was clearly reluctant to claim his share of Mussolini's work, and he minimized his own influence by confining it to fascist tactics, while denying all responsibility for Mussolini's central concept. But even the merely partial acknowledgment forced Sorel into giving to his original theory of violence a peculiar twist which all but canceled the precise meaning it had possessed in his Reflections. Violence became again the commonplace term it had been before Sorel used it to distinguish the struggle of the labor class that has to rely on its own strength, from bourgeois force that employs the power of the state to impose its class domination. Now it appeared that

[59]See Variot, op. cit., pp. 53-57 and 66-86 passim. The time is March, 1921, and the mood is oddly at variance with the letters so fearful of fascist victory which Sorel wrote in that same month to Benedetto Croce. Cf. also Sorel's statement to Robert Michels in Supplement 2, p. 291.

[60]Variot, op. cit., p. 55.

[61]Ibid., p. 55-56.

[62]Ibid., p. 56.

violence and force had become identical again. Sorel tried in vain to salvage part of his theoretical property by saying: "Violence is, to me, an intellectual doctrine;" when he went on to explain it as "the will of a powerful intellect who knows what he wants."[63] Sorel, it would seem, explained away the unique contribution to modern political theory associated with his name.

Authority and Personality

Why was it that "he spoke of Benito Mussolini with much sympathy?" On the same occasion, he predicted: "Does one know where he will go? At any rate, he will go far."[64]

It must have been that Sorel could no longer convince himself that fascism was identical with thermidorian reaction. As long as he lived, the fascist movement retained its militancy against both proletarian socialism and bourgeois liberalism. It was to retain this ambivalence even afterwards. To be sure, the middle and upper classes, putting themselves wholeheartedly under fascist protection, lost less in the process than did the Italian masses, but the price that had to be paid for the preservation of economic privilege was high. The regime abolished the economic as well as the political autonomy of the capitalist class, and had Mussolini's Social Republic of the last two years after 1943 survived, it might have ended by enslaving the bourgeoisie no less than the workers.[65]

"National Socialism was the peculiar way in which Germany resolved her hesitation between a capitalist past that was far from dead, and a socialist futurism that still had to prove its case. The result of that historic German doubt was a mongrel philosophy and, eventually, a mongrel system which instead of making a choice, or a compromise between capitalism and socialism, was a protest against both. This fact explains, in part, the extreme virulence and viciousness of the two-fronted rejection which it took the conjoined efforts of Western

---

[63]Ibid., p. 55.

[64]Lettere di Georges Sorel a Roberto Michels in Nuovi Studi di diritto, economia e politica (Rome, September, October, 1929), p. 293, note 4.

[65]In the last two years of his life, Mussolini, in order to regain the allegiance of the north Italian masses, reversed to the slogans of his syndicalist beginnings. The First National Assembly of the Republican Fascist Party, which met at Verona on November 14, 1943, adopted a Program Manifesto which introduced, among other "attractions," the so-called consigli di gestione — management production committees — in which organized labor was to play a major role. For details see Muriel Grindrod, The New Italy (London and New York, 1947); the Appendix, pp. 95 ff., gives the text of the neo-fascist Program Manifesto.

Capitalism and Eastern Socialism to defeat."[66] Essentially, the same
was true of Italy. There fascism, while preserving the framework of
capitalism, while tolerating Pareto's "speculators" as individuals,
was destroying their power as a class. The new regime had to do so
in pursuit of its own, corporate interest: only by "terminating" the
class struggle could the Fascists gain a parasitical control over both
Liberals and Socialists, defying both their protest and — their com-
prehension.

It is this nationalist notion of social unity that should have aroused
the suspicion of Sorel, the revolutionary, but it was the social revolutionary, or pseudo-revolutionary character of Mussolini's nationalism
that attracted him. The abjuration of Sorel's past belief becomes fully intelligible only in the light of the new factor, emerging in Europe
after the first World War almost simultaneously in two places as far
distant from each other as Russia and Italy: Sorel blunted his concept
of class violence to the point of pointlessness so as to include the
specific national element which he was one of the very first to discern
in both fascism and bolshevism. He felt no qualms in doing so because he was persuaded that Lenin as well as Mussolini, although both
retained essential characteristics of the past, still signaled an advance beyond the European status quo. If these leaders did not destroy the state once and for all, they did at any rate destroy the democratic state, synonymous, to Sorel, with decadence.

Lenin and Mussolini — these two names occur in Sorel's last pronouncements almost interchangeably, and while he is more eloquent
about the Russian ruler, he never fails to mention Mussolini in the
same breath. As psychologists they rank, in his opinion, even above
a Napoleon who gave plumed hats to his generals and tried to model
a new aristocracy after the old one. In contrast to him, "Lenin and
Mussolini, so different from one another in their social concepts,
meet squarely in being both almost to perfection great conductors of
the people, which they do not use but serve." Sorel was "fully convinced that Mussolini is no less disinterested than is Lenin."[67]

One month after he made this exuberant statement, Georges Sorel
was dead. Two months later, as he had expected, Mussolini, as Prime
Minister of His Italian Majesty, made himself master of the nation.
Lenin's creation proved to be more durable; possibly, Sorel would today reconsider his evaluation of Lenin's Italian counterpart. For,
after all, he was sufficiently aware of the umbilical cord linking
Caesarism to democracy. Remembering that he had once defined the
tendency of class reconciliation as the democratic idée maitresse,
Sorel, were he alive, would probably term il fascismo a perverted
form of mass democracy. Its elite, with all its outward insistence on
the Sorelian virtues of thrift, austerity and heroism, would appear to

---

[66] J. H. Meisel, **"The First Conspiracy against Hitler"** in **Queen's Quarterly,** Vol. LVI, No. 3 (Autumn, 1949), p. 331-332.

[67] Variot, **op. cit.,** p. 86.

be a group of Catilinarian characters rallying around a master demagogue who, in the blackshirt of a twentieth century "little corporal" was imposing on his nation a plebiscitary sham of democratic forms, while adapting the distributive welfare state of our time to the standards of Italian poverty. Nothing was so distasteful to Sorel as the equilitarianism of the dole. Mussolini, he might say, betrayed the revolution of the proletarian aristocracy for the eternal mass rebellion of the poor.

Nor would Sorel have overlooked the fact, obscured by the debris of constitutional guarantees, that the dictatorships of fascist hue always possess a **mass basis** on which to build their pyramid of personal authority — which could claim to be of plebeian origin. But he would add, that Mussolini could establish that authority only by an abject surrender of his social program. In order to become and to remain the Duce, Mussolini had to sell out syndicalism to the bureaucrats; not only did he have to bow to a king he despised but likewise to a church he hated and distrusted. The Fascists were permitted to impose their symbols on the country, on condition that they eschewed real action.

But perhaps Mussolini could afford to drop his program with such ease because it had never really mattered to him. What he **could** do, however was to give the modern mass in his own **image** a vague substitute for their frustrated will to power — in that sense, but in that sense only, one might call a dictator "disinterested." For he is nothing if not our own longing for reintegration and our deadly fears thereof.

Mussolini, Georges Sorel might have concluded, did start out well, only to end as another imitation of Napoleon,[68] and his downfall very likely would have warmed the heart of the old "servant of the people" who recognized power when he saw it and who, on occasion, fell for its pretenders when they promised to use power as a lever to achieve the ends of Georges Sorel. As Benedetto Croce put it: "Had he lived longer, I believe he would have changed his mind, because he was a very honest and profoundly moral man."[69]

---

[68]In the opinion of Edouard Berth, who did not share his master's low opinion of Bonaparte, the Napoleon of our time is Lenin. "Enough of Mussolini's masquerade!" Berth exclaimed in his work, **Du 'Capital' aux 'Reflexions sur la Violence'** (Paris, 1932, p. 246), and in an earlier book he dismissed Mussolini with the contemptuous words: "If Latin civilization cannot find another incarnation than this adventurer and bad comedian, then it is very sick indeed." **(Guerre des Etats ou Guerre des Classes,** Paris, 1924, p. 11).

Robert Louzon expressed himself in a similar vein: "That Mussolini's pretension to a spiritual relationship with Sorel could be taken seriously is an indication of how much we are living in the era of the Great Lie, the lie which is always one of the aspects of decadence." (Sorel, **Lettres a Paul Delesalle,** Introduction, p. 63).

[69]Letter to this writer; see above, p. 225, and note 42.

10. SOREL'S LAST MYTH

The wind bloweth where it listeth, but the spirit's materialization remains a rare feast indeed. Severe injunctions are imposed and have to be met if the word is to be made flesh. As the historic record seems to prove, the tablets are not handed down from any Mount unless a middleman appears to fetch them from on high. Even so, with the radiance of the divine blessing still around his brow, the leader cannot make himself obeyed without a furious struggle. If he succeeds at all it is because his word articulates the as yet unformed thought of other people. The leader may bend them to his will, he may direct them toward new horizons, but he cannot invent their needs, nor can he imbue them with a will that does not, at least, lie asleep in them. He may transform a prehistoric tribe into a nation, as Moses did. He may impose a new creed on nomad animists, as Mohammed did. Or he may, successfully, exploit the breakdown of a late society to lead men back into the cave, as all the Hitlers did. The times in between, the periods of slow, "normal" growth are less propitious to the schemes of test tube revolutionists (Mohammed too had to spend many years in testing out his new religious formula). The case of the Fabian Society is perhaps the unique example of an intellectual "conspiracy" that conquered a whole nation by peaceful, gradual infiltration, by patient day-by-day drudgery, and not by flamboyant thrusts.

Lenin's triumph, to be sure, was of the violent variety, but the story of his struggle is like that of Fabianism in that the element of long delay played a decisive role. For decades, Lenin was cut off, or rather, had cut himself off, from all reality; for many years he was accepted as a leader only by a few, most of them exiles like Lenin himself. Nature had made him not more of a crowd master than Georges Sorel; yet Lenin never sounded too subtle, somehow he could make the driest Marxian test sound simple and intelligible. He could do that because once he had identified his destiny with the Russian working class, or, rather, once he had identified that class with his own person, Lenin never hesitated, never strayed into another camp, as Sorel did almost and Mussolini definitely did. Lenin never doubted that he was the proletariat, even if it was, at times, confined to the one Lenin. Nothing would infuriate Lenin more than "conciliationism": talk of unity. Not that he was at all averse to making deals (he called them "blocks"), — provided they were made on his own terms. While others tried to reconcile whole social groups or even nations, Lenin despised all synthetic compromises. He positively thrived on enmity, positing his narrow dogma of the day as the whole into which the parts would have to fit themselves.

When his hour struck, Lenin, unlike his Italian ex-comrade and pupil, did not enlarge or tone down any of his principles, so as to attract a wider segment of the population. Except for a brief period when he yielded to the remonstrations of his own collaborators, Lenin refused to share power with another party. True to his Marxist precepts, he refused to recognize the Russian nation state. He utterly destroyed it. He did not adjust himself to the grim reality of a defeated nation; he made use of the very fact of that defeat to demonstrate the superiority of his idea over the German conquerors. When he was forced to reconsider and to reconstruct part of the ruined past a few years later, he had already entrenched himself securely on the "commanding heights." He could now afford to use non-party members, bourgeois experts, Tsarist generals — as their master, secure in the knowledge that, whatever the concessions to man's fraility and the country's backwardness, the pattern had been set, and that it would remain his, Lenin's, pattern. Not until a few months before his death did he begin to doubt that this was true.

Those who do not believe in Lenin's way may still, with profit, learn from him as well as from Sorel, Maurras and Mussolini, how the revolutionary mind will shape, or fail to shape, historical reality. In the majority of cases, success is reached only by a lengthy detour. The incubation period of the English Great Rebellion in the seventeenth century lasted about forty years; the ideas of the French Revolution gathered force for roughly thirty years before the pot boiled over. Lenin needed twenty years to achieve his goal, and even Hitler had to fret and fume for fourteen years before he conquered Germany. Or, to turn to a more edifying instance: It was not at Mount Sinai that the wretched fugitives from Egypt were transformed into a nation; only after forty years of far-wandering through the desert did they become, at last, the Lord's chosen people. Successful action, it appears, cannot be improvised; it has to be well timed; it must be single willed, but it must be the action of the many. All these conditions can be met, — it has been done; it will be tried again. And yet, when all is added up, the sum total never seems to vary very much: the revolutionary ledger always shows on one side a net gain, and on the other a net loss. This does of course not make the result zero. Only it seems as if with every advance that promises to set him "free," man stumbles into some new sort of slavery that is as bad as it is unexpected.

Soviets and Syndicates

The ten years between 1909 and 1919 may be called the decade of Sorel's eclipse. For once, though he continued to be a prolific writer, the books and essays which he published after the **Reflections** failed to keep interested the comparatively large audience which that work had created for him. Once more, he relapsed into the oblivion of his pre-**Reflections** period. It only reflected the state of inner isolation and discouragement in which he found himself as the ex-syndicalist and "ex-royalist." It seemed that all he could do was to reassert his old allegiance to the working class, minus the hopes which he once had attached to it.

It was Sorel's time in the desert, and when the new, revolutionary Russia rose over the Eastern horizon, a tired old man believed to see, not a mirage, but an oasis. To be sure, Sorel did not wait for the Red October to recover his old sympathies for the "producers." Of that fact, a book ready for print in 1914, is the evidence.[1] A major purpose of its publication probably was to provide him with the perfect alibi. He merely dramatized his earlier return to the old fold by "coming out" for Lenin at a time when the new Red régime was ridiculed by almost everybody with a claim to being taken seriously, by endorsing the Communist leader in the very book[2] that, to the world, summarized Sorel's pluralistic teachings of proletarian autonomy and self-reliance — concepts which could not by any stretch of imagination be reconciled with Marxist **étatisme** and centralization as practiced in Russia under the name of the "dictatorship of the proletariat."

It seems appropriate, at this point, to restate, if only briefly, the essential difference that separated Georges Sorel from Lenin. The Russian was a man of **politics**: revolutionary action for him was activity within and through the **party.** The Frenchman too believed in revolutionary action, but **his** agent was to be the very economic institution of the proletariat in which Lenin had so little faith that he could write: if left to its own devices, the working class would at best achieve a "trade union consciousness;"[3] it would never start a revolution. In taking that view, Lenin conceded the Revisionist argument, as far as economics was concerned, but he remained a Marxist by reemphasizing what Karl Marx had written about the necessity of generating, in the masses, a **political** class-consciousness as the prerequisite for a successful socio-economic revolution.[4] Sorel agreed

---

[1] **Matériaux d'une théorie du prolétariat** (Paris, 1919).

[2] In the 4. edition of the **Réflexions sur la violence** (Paris, 1919), Appendix III: **Pour Lénine.** (American edition, 1950, pp. 303-311, translated by J. Roth. By including this piece, the publishers (Free Press, Glencoe, Ill.) filled a gap left in the 1941 New York edition.

[3] **What is to be Done** (1902), in Lenin, **Collected Works,** Vol. IV, Bk. II (New York, 1929), p. 115.

[4] "Marx had visualized the conquest of political power as the prerequisite of socialization. The breakdown of capitalism was to be a breakdown of the economic engine from internal causes. Political breakdown of the bourgeois world was to be a mere incident to this. But now the political breakdown had happened, and the political opportunity had occurred, while the economic process was nowhere near maturity as yet. The 'superstructure' had moved more quickly than the propelling mechanism. It was a most un-Marxian situation." Joseph A. Schumpeter, **Capitalism, Socialism, and Democracy**, 2. edition, (New York and London, 1947), p. 364.

with Lenin to the extent that he too was violently anti-Revisionist; but
in his view the battle between revolutionary socialism and reformism
was not an issue between party and trade union: with him, it was the
revolutionary labor union versus the reformist party. In applauding
Lenin's revolutionary denouncements of the socialist parliamentarians, Sorel was apt to ignore that the other one was still talking in
terms of party, not of syndicalist, action.

Or had Sorel, in 1919, reneged on his own doctrine? Had he become in his dotage a convert to the younger revolutionary's creed.

On the contrary. Far from surrendering one iota of his own
views, Sorel approved of Lenin's Bolshevism because, as he saw it,
Lenin had come over to his side and had turned Sorelian. Nothing in
Sorel's last pronouncements permits us to dismiss the appearance of
Sorel's plea "For Lenin" in his syndicalist **chef d'oeuvre** as a mere
act of atonement, as a simple case of "bad social conscience" if not
as sheer sensationalism. To the author of the **Reflections on Violence,** Lenin's state was the final vindication of his own revolt against
The State, the reward, at long last, for decades of frustration, the
fulfilment of a hope almost lost. For Sorel, although he had never
preached the revolution in the conventional meaning of the word, must
nevertheless have thought of himself as the philosopher of a **révolution manquée.** The proletariat seemed to have gone soft, and in the
end, it did go to war for its own enemies. No wonder that the years
following 1914 were the nadir of a life dedicated to a very different
type of war, to a struggle which was to restore, not to destroy civilization.

And then, when Sorel's world seemed to have disappeared in a
bog of blood, there appeared a man who would not be drowned. That
was enough for the old, ailing hermit of suburban Paris to take fresh
courage. And what little news seeped through the thick curtain of
French wartime censorship seemed to corroborate Sorel's great expectations; that novel proletarian parliament called the soviet — was
it not the type of juridical institution Sorel had written about, the
original creation and expression of the proletarian producers? And
so he wrote his endorsement and added it as his aye and amen to his
only "bestseller," thus relegating himself once and for all to the position of the Baptist announcing the socialist Messiah.

It is not difficult for us who can look back on thirty years of the
Soviet Union to dismiss Sorel's Leninism as the last of his many illusions, and this regardless of whether we care to make a distinction
between Lenin and Stalin or prefer to view the evolution of Soviet
Russia as the logical result from premises already present in Lenin's
thought and practice. Sorel's syndicalist interpretation of Bolshevism,
read as of now, will be scorned by any convinced Marxist. It will be
equally useless as a piece of historical analysis for the non-Marxist,
unless he succeeds in projecting himself back into the situation of
Sorel in 1918. In order to understand at all how Sorel could arrive at

his conclusions it is essential to forget what we of 1948 know. Rather
we must find out what Lenin's contemporaries did not and could not
know about him. And, what is even more important, we must try to
assemble the defective or outright faulty information on which Lenin
himself had to rely for his actions. World history may be Hegel's
world court of justice, but its findings are more often than not based
on false evidence and false predictions. Accordingly, our analysis of
any given historic situation ought to include, along with the sum of all
recorded facts and intents, all the ascertainable errors of judgment
which go to form the stuff of historically "correct," meaning successful, solutions. Paradoxical as this seems to be, in the battle with that
factor X, the unknown quantity of facts and acts, the actors are in a
better position than the observing public. A Lenin at least knows what
facts he thinks he knows to be correct, while a Sorel will rarely be
able to gauge correctly the extent to which Lenin would agree with
him in the evaluation of the same evidence.

The recent publication of Sorel's correspondence with his best
friend[5] enables us to study the evolution of historic judgment at close
quarters. We are able to trace, step by step, the weird mental mean-
derings of a man lost in the fog of world history. The contrast between the Sorel who is a frequently inspired student of the past and an
amazingly correct prognosticator of things to come, and Sorel, the
mere contemporary, is indeed impressive.

The first thing that strikes the reader of this correspondence is
the almost total absence of comment during the half year period between March and November, 1917, between the fall of the Tsarist regime and the successful uprising that brought Lenin into power. A
brief suggestion that a study of Proudhon's brochures and articles
would be very helpful at this moment "for an understanding of the
Russian revolution,"[6] and one passing reference to V. M. Chernov,
the Social-Revolutionary leader and minister in the provisional government[7] — these two are the only indications that Sorel was at all
conscious of the great event that was taking place in Russia. However, we will not blame him too harshly, considering the fact that he
was, at the time, far from bombarded Paris, where he would have
been able to receive some information, if not from Frenchmen, then
at least from some of his old friends among the Russian colony who
had remained in touch with developments at home.[8]

---

[5] **Lettres à Paul Delesalle** (Paris, 1947).

[6] To Robert Michels, April 4, 1917, in **Lettere di Georges Sorel a Roberto
Michels**, in **Nuovi Studi di diritto economia e politica** (Rome, September-
October, 1929), p. 291.

[7] To Delesalle (**op. cit.,** p. 115), August 6, 1917.

[8] "In Paris you should be able to find Russians who will have some knowledge of what is going on in their country; the newspapers here distort the sequence of events and mix facts with fancy to such an extent that it has become impossible to get a true picture of Russia." (**Ibid.** p. 161, August 1,
1918.)

But even in the following year, when there could be hardly any doubt left as to the identity and character of the Russian government, Sorel's correspondence with Delesalle still shows him groping in the dark. The very name of Lenin occurs for the first time in a letter dated February 6, 1918. No one ignorant of the world historic cataclysm that had taken place in Russia in the meantime would guess its existence from Sorel's remarks, which on the whole hark back to the dim pre-revolutionary past of the Bolshevik leader. We are told that Lenin had, at one time, opened the columns of his party organ to an attack against the syndicalist theory so dear to Sorel before 1910 and it is with noticeable if restrained satisfaction that the author of the **Reflections** quotes an Italian correspondent as believing that the new Lenin "is being forced by the pressure of events to follow a syndicalist line far removed from his old (Marxist) ideologies, — a development the portent of which Lenin probably does not yet fully realize...."[9]

From then on, Lenin dominates the correspondent's interest, Lenin the man, and Lenin as a movement embodied in one man.[10] Sorel's partiality to the Bolshevik chief has all the ardor of a typical "last love" — a love that has its pathetic aspect inasmuch as it was unrequited.[11]

[9]Ibid., p. 127.

[10]Jean Variot, **Propos de Georges Sorel** (Paris, 1935), pp. 66-86. Sorel calls Lenin **"l'homme-example"** (p. 86), "a man who has become a doctrine in action" (p. 85), and that action "I believe will last" (p. 66), because Lenin succeeded in the "sentiment of mystique which endows people with the strength to suffer for the sake of a goal." (p. 82).

[11]In the Bibliography of Marxism, following his study of Karl Marx, Lenin listed as one of his sources one book of the "Syndicalist" Sorel: the **Insegnamenti sociali della economia contemporanea,** in the Russian translation which appeared in Moscow, 1908. (Lenin, **Collected Works,** Vol. XVIII (New York, 1930), p. 58. But in his **Materialism and Empirio-Criticism,** Lenin had written: "There are people who can give thought to absurdity. To that class belongs the notorious muddlehead, Georges Sorel." (**Collected Works,** Vol. XIII, (New York, 1929), p. 249. — Official Communism saw, however, **some** merit in Sorel's theory of the myth: "Notwithstanding its errors, its exaggerations, and its obscurities, it anticipates with a sure instinct everything that is essential in our agitation and in our program aimed at preparing the soul of the proletariat for revolutionary action...Sorel was neither a Marxist, nor a consistent communist....He reflected the fractured and contradictory social structure of France, with her magnificent revolutionary tradition, her political maturity and her economic backwardness. In Sorel, Proudhon struggles with Marx. He combines a profound and prophetic insight in the soul of the proletariat and its role, with a petty-bourgeois ideology which is naive and absolutely wrong. Sorel assimilated the most heterogeneous currents of modern French philosophy, trying hard to reconcile them ...with the fundamentals of Marxism. One cannot say that he succeeded in that task..." A. Maletzky, **"Georges Sorel"** in **Internationale Communiste** [Organ of the Executive Committee of the Communist International], Petrograd, Smolny, Cabinet de G. Zinoviev, No. 24 (March, 1923), pp. 112, 113.

It is easy for us to ridicule the grand illusion of the old man who had seen revolutionary syndicalism die out in his own France. Could it be that syndicalism would come to life again and, triumphant in Russia, give to the world the Sorelian society of the free producers? Could it be that Lenin was to be the Marxist Balaam, who after having cursed the tribe of Proudhon, would end up by blessing it?

This hope was after all not quite as fanciful as it appears to us today. Russia was actually going through her period of "workers' control;" labor did try to run the factories and was supposed to administer the state through soviet assemblies.

For once, Sorel and Lenin actually meet in the middle, or at least, they seem to meet; they are talking about one and the same thing. Lenin was trying to adjust himself (in his **State and Revolution**) to the new institution of the proletarian assemblies, created by the masses, or, rather, in that work which reamined unknown to Sorel, Lenin is trying to adjust the soviets to his own master instrument, to integrate them with, and to subordinate them, to his party rule. And so he claims the new soviet anti-state for the Bolshevik autocracy, while the spectator from afar claims Lenin for the soviets. While the party chief believes, for a short time, that the principles of proletarian democracy and party heirarchy need not be contradictory, the Syndicalist Sorel sees in Lenin only the chief of the soviets, and ignores the party boss. Lenin is, to him, the proletarian revolt against all party and state machines including that of the Bolsheviks. Their group is labelled, by Sorel, the intellectuals; Lenin will get rid of them, and it will be good riddance.

But while Lenin soon discovers that soviet democracy does not work, that the workers are not able to control and administer production, that they have to be checked, Sorel is less perspicacious; he does not know that Lenin's sovietism, if it had ever been sincere, was an **ad hoc** concession, an improvisation on the improvisation of the masses. Sorel did not know it, and he could not know it, not being on the scene, not being informed, and starting from a premise that was his, not Lenin's.

So, either forgetful, or what is more likely, ignorant, of what Lenin had written about the dependence of the proletarian masses on leaders of bourgeois origin,[12] Sorel notes, on August 26, 1918; "I recall having read somewhere that the Red guards in Russia spontaneously demand 'Death to the intellectuals!' It is beyond doubt that the Russian Intellectuals have done great harm to their country by muddling all ideas. There again one might say that Lenin's friends only have carried Allemanist tendencies to their ultimate conclusion."[13] So much does Sorel cherish this sentence that he repeats it

---

[12] **What is to be Done** in **op. cit.**, p. 115.

[13] To Delesalle, **op. cit.**, p. 170. — "Muddling:" Accidentally or purposely, Sorel employs the very epithet which Lenin had used against him. — "Allemanist tendencies:" See chapter 5, note 4.

in the postscript which he adds to the introduction of his **Matériaux.**
"That shout 'death to the intellectuals!', so often attributed to the Bolsheviks, may yet become the battle-cry of the entire world proletariat."[14]

Producers and Parasites

In letter after letter, Lenin is pitted against his old and new co-
workers, the intellectual lieutenants of the movement. On March 14,
1918, Sorel takes notice of the disagreement between Lenin and Trotzky over the question of accepting or rejecting the harsh German
peace conditions. Sorel has an instinctive dislike for Trotzky, who
wants to fight on and who looks to him like a Russian replica of his
pet enemy, the orating demagogue — "a **parvenu** and bourgeois who
has installed himself, in his new life, like a reveller at a banquet" —
while Lenin remained the ascetic who, in great surroundings, did not
change his style of living in the least. On the other hand, Trotzky's
reported resignation as commissar of foreign affairs seems to indicate his lack of faith in the stability of the Soviet government — is the
rat leaving the sinking ship?[15] Sorel, always a pessimist, believed
at that time, with the overwhelming majority of his contemporaries,
that the Bolshevik regime could not possibly last. "Unfortunately I
am very much afraid that it will all end in an immense disaster," he
writes on February 6, 1918.[16] Sorel's interpretation of the Brest-
Litovsk crisis that rent the Bolshevik Party proved to be wrong for
the time being, but it was a pretty good guess of things to come. To
him, Trotzky's supposed fall from power represented a "happy event
for Russia," for it removed from the political scene the intellectual
who might have attempted to become the red Caesar.[17]
Lenin versus the intellectuals; Russia is shaking off the yoke of
the West. In a letter dated June 23, 1918, Sorel foresees that "Socialism will go down before Bolshevism, although we cannot tell yet
wherein the Russian doctrine consists, nor how the Western mind
could adopt it."[18] Lenin's revolution will consumate the "decomposition of Marxism" as analyzed by Sorel in a book of that title. In a letter not to be found in this correspondence, he writes, "I believe the
Russian events sound the death knell of Socialism." Sorel makes it
very clear that he refers to Marxist socialism: "I am well convinced

[14]**Matériaux** (2. ed., 1921), p. 53. — About Bolshevist concessions to syndicalist **thinking,** as evident in the first constitution of the R. S. F. S. R.
(1918), see Edward Hallett Carr, **The Bolshevik Revolution,** Vol. I (New York,
1951), pp. 127-135
[15]To Delesalle, **op. cit.,** pp. 131-133.
[16]**Ibid.,** p. 128.
[17]**Ibid.,** p. 133.
[18]**Ibid.,** p. 154.

the Russians have been too much beguiled by French literature to understand Marxism; I begin to wonder whether Marxism is not a specifically Germanic product of romanticist infatuation with the middle ages."[19]

This is very Sorelian, and exceedingly amusing. The "impartial" judge reads out of court both the German and the French claimant to the socialist heritage, but we cannot suppress our suspicion that the Frenchman in Sorel was settling accounts with the perennial enemy beyond the Rhine when he explained the advent of Bolshevism as the result of a struggle in the Russian soul of German Marxism with French memories, a struggle in which the older, stronger influence was prevailing. It was, if not a victory for Proudhon, then at any rate revenge for the defeat Proudhon had suffered at the hands of his old enemy, Karl Marx.

In his eagerness to separate the intellectual goats from the bolshevist sheep, Sorel does not refrain from employing that well known device of the despised politician, character defamation. In a passage strangely anticipating the Moscow show-trials of the thirties, he takes notice, in a letter dated June 6, 1918, of the death of Lenin's teacher and rival in the early party struggles, George Plekhanov. Since the great old man of Russian Marxism had lately sided with Kerensky and against Lenin, Sorel wonders whether Plekhanov might not have been a "British agent" after all. In support of that thesis he relates that the leader of Swedish socialism, Branting, had written an obituary praising Plekhanov. As Branting was wax in the hands of the chief editor of the London **Times** who in turn, according to Sorel, had been in charge of anti-German propaganda (Sorel uses a stronger word), and inasmuch as Lenin had just declared that the counter-revolution of the Russian "Whites" was "inspired by London," Plekhanov must have been a traitor.[20] The term, Social Fascist, to characterize democratic Western socialists hostile to Russian communism, was not yet known; otherwise Sorel would have used it.

The Social Revolutionary uprising of July, 1918, heralded by the assassination of the German ambassador, Count Mirbach, and the almost successful attempt on Lenin's life, suggests to Sorel, as a historian, certain parallels from the past when statesmen used to hire thugs in order to eliminate their opponents. And once more Sorel is "convinced that all this blood is shed on orders issued by British diplomacy."[21] This thirst for blood, he insists, is typically bourgeois. The little people are peaceful and generous. It was middle class Jacobinism that unleashed the terror in the French revolution. Has

---

[19]To Croce (**La Critica**, 1930, p. 45), March 15, 1918.
[20]To Delesalle (**op. cit.,** p. 150-151),June 6, 1918.
[21]**Ibid.,** (p. 156), July 10, 1918.

not Drumond[22] recorded the impressive absence of sanguinary excesses in the proletarian uprising in 1848 and 1871?[23]

Against the white terror Lenin, Sorel hopes, will stand firm and give the world the impression of force. In a letter dated August 1, 1918, he even likens Lenin to Robespierre the Incorruptible,[24] forgetting in his ardor that the advocate from Arras had been the man of bourgeois terror. Forgotten are the fine distinctions between proletarian violence and bourgeois force,[25] the glorification of working class militancy that strikes at the enemy in warrior-like fashion, openly and without the hatred, brutal repression, and revenge which are the fighting habits of the ruling class. Now, it seems the syndicalist principle of sportsmanship is reconcilable with the methods of the Cheka.

There is fear in Sorel's shrillness, the fearful expectation of a Bolshevist rout that might turn into wide defeat of the working masses. "It is because of that hatred of the democrats," he confesses on August 18, 1918, "that I have so much sympathy for Lenin and his companions. If he succumbs, Syndicalism all over Europe will be crushed for a long time to come, because it will be made responsible for the Russian events. But I do not believe the Bolsheviks have reached that point yet...."[26]

Daniel Halévy tries to prove that Sorel, a lover of lost causes, made his famous plea for Lenin merely because he was convinced that bolshevism could not last: "...he sees in them the brothers of the Paris Communards of 1871, like them marked for slaughter... Sorel defended a people in revolt, destined to perish in massacre and famine...Sorel is always pleading for the vanquished."[27] But this attempt to detach Georges Sorel from Lenin tells us more about the spirit of the West in 1947, before the Cold War became serious, than about Sorel's view of the revolution that was happening under his very eyes. Halévy's judgment is not wrong, but it obscures the real tragedy that may be called Sorel's Last Hope of Many Hopes:

He has not changed at all; ten years earlier he had attempted to convert the syndicalists of France to Sorelianism. They paid no attention to him whatsoever, and he retaliated by proclaiming the death

---

[22]Edouard Adolphe Drumond, editor of **La Libre Parole**. See Robert F. Byrnes, **Antisemitism in Modern France**, Vol. I (New Brunswick, 1950), p. 137f.

[23]Marxist historiography follows the author of the **Eighteenth Brumaire of Louis Bonaparte** and **The Civil War in France** in maintaining that the White Terror preceded and outdid the Red Terror in both revolutions.

[24]To Delesalle, **op. cit.**, p. 162.

[25]Developed in chapter V, section iv of the **Reflections**.

[26]To Delesalle, **op. cit.**, p. 165.

[27]D. Halévy, **Georges Sorel, Introduction à deux lettres inédites** in **Fédération**, No. 34 (Paris, November, 1947), p. 4.

of socialism.[28]   Now, taking fresh hope, Sorel, while modestly dis-
claiming any direct influence on Lenin's thought,[29] nevertheless sees
in Bolshevism a revived form of syndicalism which will be "made responsible"[30] for Lenin's deeds; it is hardly by accident, even though
perhaps unknowingly, that Sorel chooses the term with the double
meaning of "being saddled with" and "being the cause of" something.
Sorel's concern for Lenin is the feeling of the rejected father for the
prodigal son who must make good.

He still has hesitations. On August 26 of the Year One of the red
calendar, he complains about the lack of available evidence; it is still
impossible to tell what the Bolsheviks really stand for. But, after all,
the revolution is still young; we must withhold judgment. "What would
we say about the French revolution had it ended with the Convention?"
And even at this early date, one thing should be evident to the world,
although the politicians, as usual, understand nothing, or else they
would be for the Soviets. For "the principle of the Bolsheviks is a
principle of Order that ought to please our theorists, if they really
cared for order" as much as they profess.[31] A few months later,
Sorel will write to Benedetto Croce: "It would make me very happy to
hear what you think about the future of Bolshevism as an institution
peculiar to Russia.... The diplomats talk of restoring order in that
country, but they reject the one solution which would make that restoration very easily possible — I mean, the return to monarchy. The
choice is between Tsarism and Bolshevism; there is no third alternative that would guarantee stability. The folly of democratic diplomacy is the secret of Lenin's strength."[32]

And while Lenin continues to "trade space for time," always hoping for the world revolution which would come to his rescue, Sorel
tells Delesalle: "If only the Bolsheviks can hold out long enough, all
social problems will thereafter be posed in new terms. In view of the
almost complete bankruptcy of [Western] socialism, I, for my part,
cling to hope of a socialist renaissance brought about by Bolshevik
vigor."[33] Anxious to convince his friend, Sorel calls in two witnesses
from the country in which Sorel had found more honor than in his own
France, Italy. He cites his good friend, Vilfredo Pareto, "who sees in
Lenin the protagonist of a new era."[34] Coming from the man who
discovered the perennial "circulation of the elites," the statement

---

[28]Edouard Berth in **Guerre des Etats ou Guerre des Classes** (Paris, 1924),
reports that Sorel told him, as early as 1904, "Forget about Socialism, it
has no future; concentrate on the problem of religion."

[29]According to Variot (**op. cit.**) Sorel did not believe that Lenin had ever
read his works (p. 55). "All that was in the air...." (p. 56).

[30]See above, p. 243.

[31]To Delesalle, **op. cit.**, p. 167, 168.

[32]**La Critica**, 1930, p. 50; February 1, 1919.

[33]To Delesalle (**op. cit.**, p. 168), August 26, 1918.

[34]**Ibid.** (p. 175), December 2, 1918.

could hardly have contained the endorsement of a revolution to end all elites which Sorel read into it. Another Italian, the trade-unionist Rigola, gives him equal if not greater pleasure by reminding him of his old prophecy that the proletariat would not be able to fulfill its mission within the framework of democratic institutions; Rigola's belief that "the labor exchanges might take over, in Italy, the role assigned to the Russian soviets by Lenin" is registered by Sorel with distinct satisfaction.[35]

Dissenting opinions are treated with extreme impatience. Guglielmo Ferrero, the famous historian, writes him: "I hear that you have confidence in the Russian revolution. If that is true, I envy you." Ferrero's refusal to share Sorel's faith is "a remarkable confession of weakness for one so conspicuous among the radicals of Italian freemasonry."[36] Then there is Bertrand Russell who published a book, **Bolshevism; Practice and Theory,** in 1920. It seems "the good Englishman" is not as partial to the soviet system as Sorel had expected.[37] If an old friendship gets in the way of his new enthusiasm, the old friendship has to make room. Daniel Halévy, the old companion of the Dreyfus days, editor of the **Reflections** and recipient of the grateful letter that stands in lieu of an introduction, even Daniel Halévy is not exempt from Sorel's vituperation. Delesalle reports that Halévy is uneasy about Sorel's latest development. But Halévy does not deny (or does he?) that "Syndicalism was a slope inclining toward Bolshevism...." Now Halévy "wonders whether he is not guilty of having contributed his faggots to the conflagration which is devouring the world."[38] Sorel does not feel any compunction about his own much larger share; quite the contrary:

For months Sorel had been saying such things privately, but it is not enough, now he will speak out publicly. "I finished the appendix which I must add to the **Reflections.** It will be twelve pages long. I gave it a modest title: 'And the Bolsheviks?' I wonder about another one, 'For Lenin;' unfortunately people may find the piece too short for such a massive title."[39]

As if this were not enough to shock his many enemies and to frighten his last remaining friends, Sorel, one month later, wrote the same plea for Lenin, only in a much more condensed form, into still another of his books — a work first published 16 years earlier and belonging to his pre-syndicalist "democratic" period;[40] it was as if he

---

[35] Ibid. (p. 186), September 6, 1919.

[36] Ibid. (p. 212-213), March 15, 1921.— No longer does he call Ferrero "mon ami" as he had done in his preface to Merlino; see that author's **Formes et essence du socialisme** (Paris, 1898), p. iv (discussed in chapter 4, p. 113f).

[37] To Delesalle, (pp. 226 and 231), May 7 and June 9, 1921.

[38] Ibid. (p. 234), July 7, 1921.

[39] Ibid. (p. 186), September 6, 1919.

[40] Introduction à l'économie moderne (Paris, 1903).

wanted to make sure that posterity would know only one Sorel — Lenin's defender. So he penned a footnote to the old text, saying, "The juridical future of the new socialist society depends on the successful functioning of the soviets...."[41] That reads almost as if Sorel wanted to qualify his general endorsement of Russian socialism. However, if he felt any uneasiness about his Sovereign Producers, his further correspondence with Paul Delesalle shows no trace of it. The story of the withering away of proletarian self-government remained unknown to Sorel and the rest of the world until Trotzky, as the revolution's "bishop in partibus"[42] became free to tell it, years after Sorel's death.

Ultimate Meditations

In the preface to a book that was, however, to remain unpublished,[43] Georges Sorel tried to size up the overall world situation as it looked to him in 1920. It is the inventory of a hopeful pessimist, the only type of man Sorel respected.[44] A curious ambiguity which cannot be resolved, pervades the essay which abounds in declarations of war against Sorel's old and new enemies, while at the same time giving evidence of a judicial attitude toward the very objects of his previous rages. We have already met with the transformed, the mellowed Georges Sorel who, after the world war, would bless what he had, prior to it, cursed so heartily;[45] now he has even a good word for the despised Utopians: "The founders of the early socialist groups abhorred the excesses caused by the class antagonisms...." They wanted to spare the people another "dictatorship of the Jacobin charlatans. They were mistaken in their belief that intelligence was strong enough to...bring about the eradication of an evil, and their error could not be corrected by disciples far too slavishly devoted to the rampant intellectualism, optimism, and humanitarianism of the early nineteenth century."[46]

---

[41] Ibid., 2. ed. (Paris, 1922), p. ix. — Sorel also wrote new "Leninist" chapters for the 2. edition of the Matériaux (pp. 415 ff) in addition to the postscript mentioned before (see above, p. 241); he wrote a new appendix for the 3. edition of his Illusions du progrès (1921), with the ending headed: "Renaissance of socialism under the influence of bolshevist ideas."

[42] Edouard Berth, Du 'Capital' aux 'Réflexions sur la Violence' (Paris, 1932), p. 262.

[43] See chapter 9, note 1.

[44] "So little are we prepared to understand pessimism, that we generally...call pessimists only disappointed optimists." Reflections (1950 ed.), p. 37. For a definition of pessimism see the pages following this quotation.

[45] See Part II, Introduction, p. 174.

[46] "Ultime meditazioni" in Nuova Antologia (September-October, 1928), p. 296.

Such words the earlier Sorel could not have written. Nor could he have said this: "Today, many writers are of the opinion that [the organizations of the proletariat] ought to return to the precepts of the old Utopians," meaning, that they should improve the worker's lot and strengthen his position by developing "cooperatives, mutual help and syndicates," the very organs which the "doctrinarians of social democracy" have always treated with suspicion, as mere "accidents" of history. "It is a fact of singular historic irony that the expectations of so-called scientific socialism have been proven to be dreams, whereas the dreams of the precursors of Marx have found exceedingly significant realizations."[47]

Lest we suspect Sorel of a relapse into "traditionalism" — and we remember how unkindly he reacted to that epithet![48] — he quickly adds that the Utopians had no notion of juridical ideas: "Revolutionary socialism alone is able to promote the evolution of a proletarian right. We can never deplore too much the quasi-complete success which the Marxists had in wrecking Proudhon's tentative explorations in that matter. I, for my part, find that result disastrous, for in the bourgeois world the sense of law is likewise moribund."[49]

It is his old dirge: that all traditions die except the dead traditions. The ambivalence of Sorel's ultimate reflections is not easily resolved; his mind seems to be a house divided between many warring parties: first, he sides with the Utopians in their fight against the Jacobin dictators, only to turn against the allies because of their lack of regard for legal questions, a disregard shared by the Marxist slayers of Proudhon, the great hope of the revolutionary socialist Sorel who deplores the decay of the juridical sense in the bourgeois world — what a bewildering variety of Sic et Non. It comes down to a conflict, within the Sorelian mind, of two main tendencies: there is, on the one hand, the re-emphasized belief in revolutionary action; on the other, also growing in intensity, the conservative concern for the perennial values of the Graeco-Roman-Christian past. One view seems to exclude the other so completely that it is hard to believe one and the same man could hold both, and leave it at that. Many commentators of Sorel, the present writer not excluded, thought they could resolve the great antinomy by showing that it did not really exist: that Sorel's revolution was intent on saving tradition, and that his tradition was, by implication, never static, but the product of incessant revolutionary oscillations — a "struggle for rights." According to this viewpoint, Sorel, far from being inconsistent, would be a slightly more impetuous Edmund Burke: a Conservative Revolutionary.[50]

Unfortunately, we cannot at all be sure that this interpretation would find the assent of the philosopher Sorel, who always preferred

[47]Ibid., p. 300.
[48]See chapter 8, p. 205 - 206.
[49]"Ultime meditazioni," p. 306.
[50]As Michel Freund called Sorel; see chapter 2, note 8.

to assume a world of multiplicity rather than unity.[51] He would have us accept as feasible that two or more trains of thought may run through a human mind and never meet at the same station. "Why speak of contradiction," he would ask, "where there is merely conflict! And why reduce the conflict to one comprehensive system when all we can ascertain, is the clash of a plurality of independent systems?[52] Why insist on a pre-established harmony of human life on earth, which, on its showing, is so ineffective, if it is not altogether spurious? Nor will that modest, modern dodge 'interdependence,' do. There is no half-way house in matters of causality: it must be torn down altogether if we want to unearth harmony. For harmony there is, only it will not be found to be an external order, real even if its law is flaunted. Harmony is not a fact, but an experience of the mind. Your synthesis is death, life is a unity of beliefs gathered up in what I called the myth. It is the myth. But the faith in a myth, in turn, engenders motion, strife, and instability. There is no such thing as a real equilibrium, unless, since humans seem to cherish the idea, it is understood and treated as a counter-myth, or, at best, as the myth to end all myths, because its triumph would eliminate all strife, but its peace would be aimless, listless; it would abolish fear, and destroy hope; and with hatred, love. Did I say, this was death? Let me correct myself: we would be neither fully dead, nor quite alive, but ghostly apparitions walking the earth, no longer even able to feel anything, not even miserable."

To live and think in such an atmosphere of tension and suspense is a feat not accomplished by too many. No wonder, then, Sorel closes his final meditations on a note of supreme agony: "The conclusion I have reached, holds no reassurance for the future of our civilization."[53] But, in the face of all the facts, he still clings to his gallant little hope that not all may be lost: "In conclusion, I do not believe we need despair of law and liberty, because the Russian revolution has given life to institutions which approximate Proudhon rather than the teachings of those who made such poor use of the inheritance of Marx."[54]

The only passage that might be interpreted as defeatist is to be found in a letter Sorel wrote to Croce in the same year;[55] it is a summary of the world situation and it it one of unmitigated despair. "Everything in Europe is rotten. The expectations one might have

---

[51]See **Reflections**, Appendix 1 on "Unity and Multiplicity" (1950 ed., pp. 279-300).

[52]"The heterogeneous, not the homogeneous, is the heart of things." Gabriel Tarde, as cited by Georges Guy-Grand in **La philosophie syndicaliste** (Paris, 1911), p. 139.

[53]"Ultime meditazioni," p. 306.

[54]Ibid., p. 307.

[55]**La Critica**, 1930, p. 193, August 13, 1920.

derived from Vico, the hopes of a truly heroic ricorso must be discounted...." No light pervades this darkness, unusually gloomy even
for such a pessimist as Sorel.[56] Not a word about Russia. But as he
wrote, Russia had ceased to belong to Europe. She had withdrawn into
Asia to lick her wounds. It was precisely because Europe had rejected her that "all was rotten," that Vico was not borne out.

But if Russia was remote, she was not to be counted out forever.
In his last soliloquy, recorded one month before his death,[57] Sorel
predicted: within five or six years the Soviet government will have
solved the peasant problem; by that time those troubles will be "nothing but memories." A fairly accurate guess, for six years later,
Stalin decided to destroy the Kulaks and to collectivize the home-
steads. It seems that Sorel never heard of Stalin; he never mentions
him. But neither are the Soviets mentioned any more. Is their "successful functioning" no longer essential to the success of Russian socialism? Has Sorel lost faith in the self-redeeming "political capacity of the working class?"[58] Rather, Sorel has transferred this faith
to the statesman Lenin; again he calls him, as in that epilogue to the
Reflections, "the greatest Russian since Peter the Great"[59] — a hackneyed statement today, but in 1922 as well as in 1919 still a highly
unorthodox notion. "Lenin, did he or did he not transform a desperate
and hungry people into one that has again confidence in itself?"[60]
Lenin, "the Leader;" Lenin, "the Educator." Nationalization, the rus-
sification of Bolshevism, Sorel has foreseen that trend too, which was
to be discovered at long last ten years later by a world only too eager
to proclaim prematurely the end of the Red International.

Had Sorel lived that long, would he have cooled toward Lenin's
new state, as did the only authentic Sorelian, Edouard Berth?[61]

---

[56]A month later, in September 1920, writing the supplementary chapter
for his Illusions du progrès (see note 41), Sorel quoted from two letters written by Proudhon in 1860: "All traditions are used up, all beliefs abolished;
on the other hand, the new program...has not yet penetrated the conscience
of the masses....We shall not see the new age; we shall fight our battle in
darkest night; we must try to endure this life without too much sadness, per-
severing in our duty...."

[57]By Variot, op. cit. (cf. notes 10 and 29), p. 85.

[58]De la capacité de la classe ouvrière, title of Proudhon's work, published
posthumously in 1865.

[59]Variot, op. cit., p. 82.

[60]Ibid.

[61]In 1931, Edouard Berth added a Post-Scriptum to an essay called "Who
is Lenin, published in 1924 and now included in his book, Du 'Capital' aux
'Réflexions sur la Violence' (cf. note 42). Stalin, we read there, is the "Pha-
raoh of Russian socialist construction — a construction which stresses the
capitalist part of Marxism rather than its working class aspect...." The
truth is that Russia, in order to transform the indolent peasant into a modern

Perhaps, but we cannot be sure. The tired wanderer needed a rest; he could not very well afford another disappointment. We are told that Lenin, who survived the older man by two more years, died unhappy, not certain that his life work would endure.[62]   Sorel, the leader without a mass following, the educator without a school, had certainty accompany him to the grave. We may not want to visit it with flowers, but neither is there any need to desecrate the memory of Georges Sorel's last, hopeful myth. [63]

worker, was forced to make use of the same iron discipline capitalism had found necessary in the past. However, "we have already passed the stage which for Russians and Italians is only now beginning, and that is why Bolshevism and Fascism are not for us. Our problem is not to establish some kind of dictatorship, but, on the contrary...to create the free government of the producers...."

If Berth speaks for Sorel, then the affection the **revolutionary** Sorel did feel for Lenin would leave the **historian** Sorel free to see the limitation of Lenin's significance for the non-Russian world: Bolshevism was to kindle the flame of action in the West, but not to mould its form and content.

[62]In one of his last articles **Selected Works,** Engl. ed., New York, 1943, vol. IX, p. 402 ff.), "Lenin demanded that the Soviet society be built in the main on cooperatives of all producers — an old formula loved by syndicalists and utopian socialists but regarded by the Bolshevik Party as a ridiculous requisite of another century." Ruth Fischer, **Stalin and German Communism** (Cambridge, Mass., 1948), p. 246. — If this interpretation is correct, the dying Lenin turned Sorelian after all.

[63]In the last analysis, it may be said of Sorel what has been written of Anatole France (whom he loathed; see chapter 6, note 113): "He accepted [Lenin's Russia] because he was the prisoner of an attitude. His detestation of the bourgeoisie carried him away." Marcel Le Goff, **Anatole France à la Béchellerie** (Paris, 1947), p. 199.

11. DISCIPLES AND DISSENTERS

Elijah and Elisha

There are the honorable titans of the spirit, the good masters who hold our admiration, whose every word we endorse and file away for reference because it is the truth. But, as the years go by, we find that something has been happening to us. Our esteem of the masters has not changed; we would not dream of casting doubt upon their findings; only, we no longer care. Our integral assent has come embarrassingly close to boredom, whereas lesser figures who are neither sound nor honorable and in no way titans prove to be a lasting source of inspiration. They irritate us, they infuriate us, but they keep us interested. Their premises are unconvincing, their logical transactions dubious, their conclusions impossible. And yet what was at first merely entertaining, keeping us indignantly amused, finally becomes a challenge, serious business. We have a sense of shame, of having sinned because a second-rate mind has gained such a strong hold on us. But there it is; and the inferior and objectionable may yet prove to be the inspiration for a major truth.

Such is perhaps the case of the French thinker, Georges Sorel. The case is complicated further by the fact that he seems to fall between the solid-but-dull thinkers on the one hand and the intellectual gypsies on the other. Both as a person and as a thinker, Sorel is at once intensely honorable and deceptive, elusive and candid, pedestrian and fanciful. If, however, his stature be measured exclusively by the amount of antagonism he aroused in his lifetime and afterwards, Georges Sorel merits the title of greatness.

This is not to say that he lacked ardent friends: if the number of loving disciples that rallied around the "hermit of Boulogne sur Seine" never amounted to more than a small clique, their quality was truly remarkable. Men of the first order such as Benedetto Croce, Vilfredo Pareto, and Henri Bergson treated Sorel as their intellectual equal; and the contemporaries who, calling him their master, were yet distinctly figures in their own right make an impressive list.[1] Although

---

[1] To list them once more: Charles Péguy, the great neo-catholic poet, Daniel Halévy, of the famous dynasty of writers and historians, Paul Bourget, the dramatist, author of the Sorelian play, La barricade, the latter representing the "Right" among Sorel's disciples, as did Georges Valois, René Johannet, Jean Variot, and the brothers, Jérôme and Jean Tharaud, while Edouard Berth eventually returned to the radical camp, like his master. An American disciple is Max Ascoli whose recent work, The Power of Freedom (New York, 1949) proves that the influence of the man to whom he had devoted a youthful study (see below, note 3) may be reconciled with a genuinely liberal outlook.

history will likely never rank Sorel among the Prime Movers, he nevertheless belongs to that select circle of provocative thinkers who do not themselves create a system but assemble the materials for one or even for more than one philosophy. Such men are the indefatigable explorers of the area which is both the meeting place of all the intellectual currents of the time and their Great Divide. No wonder that Sorel, who disliked Socrates, played in his disputations a Socratic role, evoking either love or hatred, but never indifference.

But the study of "reactions to Sorel" is not merely a study in extremes, violent adulation or vitriolic abhorrence; rather it is a study in ambivalence. The enthusiasm of some has an almost hysterical pitch, revealing symptoms of overcompensation or of resentment overcome by a successful effort to love; the opposition to Sorel is often suggestive of a suppressed, frustrated affection that would have preferred to worship but was not quite strong enough to follow the master on his endless and uncertain quest. This intriguing blend of love-hate or hate-love is not merely typical of the past and current estimation of Sorel's work: it reveals something in his own make-up: a contradiction at work in his mental processes. Not that his failure to co-ordinate his thought into a comprehensive system needs to be ascribed to a lack of integrating power.[2] It may be that his refusal to sum up his work was a deliberate act of self-limitation, an abstention reflecting integrity of mind and the modesty of a scholar content to be a sensitive recorder of historic trends. Sorel's questions may be of greater help toward the clarification of contemporary issues than all the answers given by the systematic thinkers. The Sorelian whirlpool of ideas in which idealistic and materialistic currents mingle curiously, in which the diversity of forces obstructs any unity and yet implies it, seems at least well worth exploring.

No one has done more for Sorel's reputation than his disciple, Edouard Berth, though Berth's voice had a tendency to magnify the master's virtues as well as his shortcomings with all the force of a good amplifier.[3] But to call this most authentic of all the Sorelians a mere epigonus would not be fair. He was not Sorel's equal, but neither was he insignificant. If he did not succeed and supersede his tutor as Enfantin eclipsed Henri de St. Simon, he nevertheless had one major advantage over his spiritual father: he was a better, or, at any

---

[2] "He never attempted to elaborate a system or a doctrine." Boris Souvarine in **La Critique Sociale**, March, 1931.

[3] Works of Berth mainly dealing with Sorel: **Les méfaits des Intellectuels** (Paris, 1914), with a preface by Sorel; **Guerre des états ou guerre des classes** (Paris, 1924); **La fin d'une culture** (Paris, 1927); **Du 'Capital' aux 'Réflexions sur la violence'** (Paris, 1932); prefaces to the German translation of the **Reflections** (**Über die Gewalt,** Innsbruck, 1928), to Sorel's **L'ancienne et la nouvelle métaphysique** (**D'Aristote à Marx,** Paris, 1935), and to Max Ascoli's **Georges Sorel** (Paris, 1921).

rate, the more eloquent writer. His work is one long peroration, ex-
hortation, **plaidoyer.** Berth's supercharged style tells all about Berth
and not a little about his master; there was at work behind Sorel's
jolly countenance a palpitating passion, which showed only in his conversation and his correspondence. When he wrote for publication, his
style, as is often the case with people who speak well, became self-
conscious, cramped. Berth is Sorel relaxed and often dangerously
uninhibited. Where Sorel hesitates and ponders, Berth declaims and
lectures with a high, shrill voice While Sorel for a brief period toyed
with the idea of National Syndicalism, only to retract soon after and to
reject firmly the amalgam later known as Fascism, Berth fell for it
hook, line, and sinker, and by vociferously synthesizing Sorel and
Maurras did more to incriminate his old friend as a "premature Mussolini" than all the enemies of Sorel put together.[4]

The record shows that Berth was leading Sorel on rather than
following his lead in the embarrassing episode during which Sorel
permitted himself to become the darling of French monarchists, ac-
tively contributing to their journals though not giving up the essence
of his earlier convictions.[5] The active role was played by Berth, but
he could play it only because Sorel wanted to be led. There is in all
creative natures the yearning to be understood without so many words.
It is a hide-and-seek game which remains a pleasure as long as the
junior partner understands his duty: he must not incriminate the
leader. He is expected to be an interpreter and nothing more But
all interpreters have an urge to overstep that line, to emerge from
the anonymity of service and **to rule the master.**

Berth was not small enough to submerge his own personality in
that of the greater man nor independent enough to break with him as
other disciples did; he remained instead transfixed in an intermediate
position. He sacrificed his intellectual autonomy, but for a consideration: he attempted to be another Sorel, the true Sorel, a better Sorel.
He did not do this consciously. His assertions of indebtedness, of
humble gratitude, abound in dedications, introductions to, and innumerable quotations from Sorel's work; but the impression remains
that the temptation of stepping into the shoes of "Papa Sorel" was too
strong to be resisted. The right of the interpreter seems to include
the duty of **succession,** of fulfilling the unfinished task in Sorel's
name. Always in his name. Yet devotion cannot help becoming ar-
rogation; self-effacement turns into substitution of Berth for Sorel.
It is the human tragedy of the second prophet following the initiator:
Elisha coming after Elijah, the titanic trailblazer for God, the worker
of unprecedented miracles. After him, even the most magnificent feat
cannot be anything but repetitious. On the surface of it, Elisha's

---

[4]Especially in his **Méfaits.** Berth was rather slow to recant, but he finally made a clean break with nationalism and fascism.

[5]See chapter 8.

charismatic powers seem to be even more overpowering, and of more consequence than those of his predecessor. Yet — although the Bible[6] refrains from stating it explicitly — Elisha, who called the wrath of the Lord upon the children heckling him about his baldness, was an angry rather than a blessed prophet. Was he, secretly, an envious man, forever craving to outdo the one Who Came Before Him, to assuage a nagging doubt of insufficiency?[7]

Sorel knew well how fortunate he was in having at his side a friend of Berth's unflinching faith.[8] Had he ever found him presumptuous, he would have told him so, for the old man was as blunt with his friends as he could be kind and considerate, and eventually he quarreled and broke with most of them. We may wonder at the tolerance with which Sorel watched the process of mimicry in Berth's work; we may ask whether he ever felt any uneasiness about the streamlined, monotonously highstrung Sorel as he appears in the writings of the younger man, whether he was not at times a whit nervous about that terrifying loyalty of the disciple who knew him better than he knew himself. It is perhaps no accident that the controversial figure of the Paris Socrates never quite comes to life in Berth's work of possessive devotion. Perhaps we can learn more about Sorel from those who broke away from him.

Socrates and Alcibiades

Georges Valois credits Sorel with having turned his mind in the direction which he ultimately chose: "For a long time, I was hesitating between psychology and political economy; it is he who directed my passion for knowledge toward the study of economic phenomena."[9] But though he "hugely profited" from Sorel's work, Valois refuses to be called Georges Sorel's disciple. The French nationalist in him professes to be repelled by the Germanic element in the intellectual make-up of the master "whom one would classify as an Hegelian, if it were possible to classify him at all." True, Sorel was critical of

---

[6]**Kings** II, 2, 23.

[7]Elisha's own disciple and assistant re-enacts that secret story on a lower, a much lower level and is dreadfully punished by the raging master (**Kings** II, 5, 20-27). The offence in question may be called petty larceny, but what is really at stake is the prophetic prerogative: the monopoly of magic power.

[8]"The reason why I love Edouard Berth is his noblesse of character.... He is the perfect type of the man who serves a cause.... My attachment to him is not that of a master to his disciple. I make no claim whatsoever to be a master....Berth helped me to keep my ideas young...." Jean Variot, **Propos de Georges Sorel** (Paris, 1935), p. 161-162.

[9]Georges Valois (Alfred Georges Gressant), **D'un siècle à l'autre** (Paris, 1921, quotations from the 4. edition, 1924), p. 134-135.

Marx, but "he was always a Marxist." True, Sorel had a sincere affection for Proudhon, but that affection was "sentimental and moral rather than intellectual." And ultimately, in Sorel's mind, "Proudhon lost out to Marx...."[10] Not so with Georges Valois who started being critical of Marxism when he was barely twenty. He remembers, albeit grudgingly, that "it was possibly Sorel himself who started him along that line, Sorel, "destroying with his own hands the very edifice he had been raising...." As early as 1900, Sorel told Valois (who planned to write a book on socialism): "You are wasting your time... socialism is finished."[11]

This acolyte despairs of ever being able to "define" the teacher, but he is ready with a definition just the same: Sorel, he says, took as passionate an interest in the social life of his contemporaries as Fabre did in his insects. "Is that a human attitude?" Valois exclaims, but then he hesitates to answer in the negative, because "I owe too much to **M.** Georges Sorel."[12] Yet, in the end, the debt is cancelled, and the spell is broken. The idol stands exposed as a theoretician with fond illusions about the "ideal proletarian." Georges Valois knows better: the **real** proletarian was no "Spartan hero"[13] — far from it. Taking the **Reflections** as his text, Valois had joined the newly founded printers' union "with the certainty of having entered one of the economic cells of future society." The volunteer was quickly undeceived: "I became convinced that Sorel had failed to interpret the syndicalist movement in accordance with reality...." Not only had revolutionary syndicalism strayed from the path outlined by Proudhon and Pelloutier, — it had turned into a "democratic club" which served the leaders as a pretext for avoiding honest work. The young Sorelian is disgusted: "We [Valois and the union] parted ways, and I went back to my job." He became a man, and finally a writer in his own right, reminiscing about Georges Sorel with the forgiving wistfulness of the adult ashamed and still secretly fond of his shattered teenage dreams.

An altogether different type of disciple is the one who loathes and despises the old mentor and yet lives from him. The only question in **his** mind is whether he ought merely to write Sorel off as scurrilous or expose his viciousness. In most instances he decides that the author of the **Reflections on Violence** is a dangerous character, but in the last end harmless, since the fallacies of the Sorelian argument are so blatantly evident. There is thus no reason to be too indignant with Sorel; in fact, the reasons why Sorel is wrong will easily provide

---

[10]**Ibid.**, p. 135   [11]**Ibid.** (cf. chapter 10, note 28).
[12]**Ibid.**

[13]**Ibid.**, p. 207. — Valois cites Sorel's eloquent lines: "Let us salute the revolutionaries as the Greeks saluted the Spartan heroes who defended Thermopylae and helped to preserve the civilization of the ancient world" (**Reflections**, Am. ed. 1950, p. 113).

the basis for a full-length book of scholarly and highly meritorious refutation.

Wyndham Lewis, no mean author, wrote just such a book.[14] It purports to deal with the predicament of Western society between the two great wars. Our system is on trial, and a great number of the intelligentsia are called upon to testify. The lines between prosecution and defense are so fluid that the same figures may find themselves both on the witness stand and in the dock. From Plato to Shaw, from Swift to Joyce and Bertrand Russell, Rousseau, Proudhon, and, of course, Marx, the panel is illustrious. Sorel is mentioned only twice in the table of contents, but he appears for the first time on page 1 and remains the hero-villain throughout the entire book of 434 pages. Sorel, it seems, is a good man to call upon for definitions. For instance, he "defines so happily the true nature of revolution that I cannot do better than quote him rather fully."[15] Mr. Lewis proceeds to quote almost two pages from **The Dreyfus Revolution.** Soon afterwards, the problem of progress presents itself, and the author finds the "ideology of progress...so admirably exposed by Georges Sorel" that he cites from his **Illusions of Progress** twice and at considerable length.[16] He even uses Sorel instead of consulting the original when he wants to quote somebody else.[17] This is not simply the case of an author pleased to find his views corraborated — Mr. Lewis does not merely end up, he starts with Sorel and, be it added, with Edouard Berth.[18] The whole "intellectual topography" of **The Art of Being Ruled** is extremely familiar to anyone acquainted with the Sorelian and Berthian preoccupation with Marx and, especially, with Proudhon.[19]

Wyndham Lewis, then, may be put down as one who knows his Sorel well and not merely from hearsay — something that cannot be said of many Anglo-Saxon writers in the 1920's. Nor does he fail to acknowledge his debt. Not even Edouard Berth dared to claim, as Mr. Lewis does, that "Georges Sorel is the key to all contemporary political thought."[20] To be exact, he qualifies this judgment by saying that "Sorel is, or was, a highly unstable and equivocal figure," and he defines the Sorelian puzzle with great acuteness: "He seems composed of a crowd of warring personalities, sometimes one being in the ascendant, sometimes another, and which in any case he has not been able, **or has not cared,** to control."[21] The blend of detachment and passion in conjunction with his unquestionable sincerity makes Sorel "a sensitive plate for the confused ideology of his time "

---

[14]**The Art of Being Ruled** (London, 1926).
[15]Ibid., p. 5.   [16]Ibid., pp. 18 and 177.
[17]Ibid., p. 226; the author is Karl Marx.
[18]Ibid., p. 328.   [19]Ibid., p. 322.
[20]Ibid., p. 128.
[21]Emphasis of the present writer.

It does not take long, however, to discover that Wyndham Lewis is not only using Georges Sorel for his own ends, which is his good right; he also puts Sorel on a high pedestal merely to tear him down again with great ferocity. Sorel, we learn, appeals to the worst instincts of the mob, the poor (the same Sorel who actually said that he was interested, not in the perennial, futile rebellion of the slaves against their masters, but in the struggle of the producers against the parasitism of the intelligentsia and the ruling bourgeoisie). Sorel, Mr. Lewis announces, longs for a new caste system (caste is a "bad" word!), and not, as we thought, for a free and self-sufficient proletariat minding its own business and letting the capitalists manage capitalism. Mr. Lewis is occasionally conscious of what he is doing, as when he remarks: "This [the notion of a caste system] is not explicit in the syndicalist doctrine: nor is, I had better add, much of the interpretation I am about to provide." But then he goes on to attribute to the theorist of syndicalism the notion that "the bootmaker must have only bootmaking thoughts. No godlike, éclairé, gentlemanly thoughts must interfere with his pure, sutorial one-sidedness." One who has not read Sorel could never guess from that sentence that Sorel wanted the proletariat to develop its own institutions and disregard everything else for the very purpose of living down the curse of modern specialization. Out of their work — Sorel hoped not quite unnobly — would rise not only the particular morality of the producers but also one which would enclose the broader beliefs of a true community which our civilization has destroyed. If this hope proved to be an illusion, it was at any rate the precise opposite of what Wyndham Lewis made it to appear.

Why all this legerdemain? One of the two chapters of **The Art of Being Ruled,** officially dedicated to Sorel, provides the clue. In this chapter the author strikes terror into the heart of the law-abiding citizen by exposing in blood-curdling words Sorel's philosophy of violence. It is not, as the reader of the **Reflections** is asked to believe, the only effective weapon that enables the proletariat to save its class identity from being swallowed up by Leviathan. Sorel's violence is that thing most contemptible in the opinion of a writer: it is literature: "All the emotional and 'heroic' section of Sorel is deeply romantic....and by that I understand untrue."[22] Sorel, who called himself the "disinterested servant of the proletariat,"[23] is in truth the very prototype of the demagogue, whom he fought all his life: "This crowd-master...takes his revolutionary blessings to them 'whip in hand,' with a girding pedagogic intolerance. Coriolanus could not be more contemptuous asking for their 'voices.' ...His approaches his proletariat with the airs of a missionary among 'natives.'" A

---

[22]Lewis, op. cit., p. 132.

[23]In the dedication of his **Matériaux d'une théorie du prolétariat** (Paris, 1919).

quotation from Sorel is used to prove that he actually despised the proletariat.[24] But that passage obviously is a critique, not of the working class, but of its Marxist leaders, who failed to realize the historic fact that "our nature always tries to escape into decadence"[25] and that mankind will surmount the "law of regression" only under energetic pressure.[26] The point is that Sorel has no faith in a leadership coming from without, from the intellectual class; he set his hopes in a proletarian elite that would be "masterless."

If Wyndham Lewis has no use for such rectifications, it is not because he is separated from Sorel by an abyss. On the contrary, he does not want it to be known, or does not want to admit to himself, how much he owes to the authentic Georges Sorel. Because he wants to use Sorel's pro-labor argument for something else, he has to discredit Sorel as a proletarian thinker; because he wants to impress us with the superiority of his own esoteric creed, he has to depict Sorel as a "vulgarizer of aristocracy," who took his cue from that other vulgarizer, the "vociferous showman," Nietzsche.[27] It is, however, a vulgarized Nietzsche and a vulgarized Sorel who provide the materials for Wyndham Lewis's brand of gentleman authoritarianism.[28] Hence his fury against the original Sorel and the original Nietzsche. We resent nothing so much as to owe the thing we wish to own. Rather than to return a property to the rightful owner, we will turn it upside down and change the paint, hoping prayerfully that we may not be found out.[29]

---

[24]Lewis, op. cit., p. 130. The quotation is taken from Sorel's **Les Illusions du progrès,** 4. edition (Paris, 1927), p. 331: "The transformations that Marxism has undergone illustrate very well the theory of mediocrity.... The great mistake of Marx was to underrate the enormous power of mediocrity displayed throughout history...."

[25]Sorel, **Matériaux,** p. 138.

[26]Sorel, **Illusions,** p. 318.

[27]Lewis, op. cit., pp. 120 and 128.

[28]"That No Man in a No Man's Land, that phantom of democratic enlightenment, is what has to be disposed for good in order to make way for higher human classifications, which, owing to scientific method, men could now attempt." These are the closing lines of Mr. Lewis' work (op. cit., p. 434). And: "Nothing on earth today can overthrow such powers as the soviet or fascismo. ...What they have done...must be the admiration of the world." **Ibid.,** p.75).

[29]Another "renegade" was Julien Benda, (see chapter 7, note 59), who uses Sorel as his whipping boy in **La trahison des clercs** (Paris, 1927). E. g., "We shall be told that the justice denounced by Sorel is the justice of tribunals, which according to him is a false justice.... There is no indication that a justice which was a true justice would receive any more respect from him." (Cited from the English edition, **The Great Betrayal,** London, 1928, p. 91, note 4. Cf. **Ibid.,** pp. 103-105, 117, 119). But occasionally Benda cannot quite suppress his admiration for the former friend and mentor: "He did, indeed, preach class egotism to some extent in a universal manner, but without any explicit preference for the interest of one class rather than that of another. In his preaching of egotism there is a kind of impartiality which does not lack grandeur, a quality not inherited by his disciples." **(Ibid.,** p. 72, note 1).

The Case Against Sorel

The situation that confronts us in **The Art of Being Ruled** is (to paraphrase the famous witticism about the Habsburg monarchy) desperate, but not serious. It is not the Wyndham Lewises that Sorel has to fear, for they share most of his likes and dislikes, rejecting merely his particular conclusions. Their resentment is more that of a competitor than of a genuine opponent. Sharing Sorel's anti-democratic bias, they are unable to dislodge him from his main position. It is quite another thing when a man of the convictions and abilities of Guido de Ruggiero joins the camp of Sorel's critics. His attack, the counterattack of a liberal, commands not only the attention due to the prestige of the author but respect for a feat of great moral courage, since Professor de Ruggiero published his remarks in the year VII of Mussolini's reign — that is, under circumstances which made discretion absolutely imperative.

Another interesting aspect is the place of publication: the essay's appearance in Benedetto Croce's own review.[30] The great historian and philosopher had been linked to Georges Sorel by a friendship lasting more than twenty-five years. Croce had been instrumental in making the French autodidact well known in Italy. His sponsorship of what must be considered one of the severest judgments ever passed on Sorel's work is awkward, but it should not be misinterpreted as a change of mind on the part of the editor toward his late friend. It is more likely that there had always been room for ambivalence in Croce's mind, a last reserve at least against some of Sorel's more extravagant speculations. Even if this were not so, if de Ruggiero's article came to him as a shock, Benedetto Croce must have been pleased with it, nevertheless, for a reason which will become evident in a moment.

In taking as his text and pretext Pierre Lasserre's important study of Sorel's significance,[31] de Ruggiero tones down moderately the angry, bitter tension that pervades that book, while at the same time going far beyond his source in the intransigence of his conclusions.[32] Both the Italian and the Frenchman are agreed on the historic importance of Sorel as a sincere moralist incapable of any Machiavellian "double-talk."[33] Because he was a fundamentally honest thinker, his final nationalism must have been based on something more than intellectual curiosity; it must have been a genuine sympathy.

---

[30] Review of Pierre Lasserre, **Georges Sorel. Le théoricien de l'impérialisme** (Paris, 1928) in **La Critica** (1929), pp. 195-199.

[31] **Georges Sorel. Le théoricien de l'impérialisme ouvrier** (Paris, 1928).

[32] Professor de Ruggiero closes his essay with the slightly apologetic statement: "Seguendo quest' ordine di considerationi, mi sono alquanto discostato dall' esposizione testuale del Lasserre; non credo pero dallo spirito del suo libro" (**loc. cit.**, p. 199).

[33] Ibid., p. 195.

It seems that this particular assertion is to remain a fixture of what may be called "the myth of Sorel," and since a myth, in Sorel's own definition, is the vision of a goal that cannot be refuted by rational argument, the attempt to set Sorel's ideological record straight might well be given up as hopeless. The tradition which has Sorel end his life as a "premature Fascist," and at the same time become a convert to Bolshevism, seems firmly established. We read, in an article written for the centennial of Sorel's birth: "Characteristically, he turned at the end to Charles Maurras and the **Action Française.**"[34] The fact is, that for the last ten years of his life Georges Sorel, having repudiated all relations to that group, firmly reasserted his old faith in the proletariat and died as a leftist, convinced that his syndicalist hopes had come true in Lenin's Russia.

And what are we to think of **M.** Lasserre, who, reputable scholar that he is, informs us in all seriousness that Sorel preached the **lévee en masse** to the workers, who, once victoriously installed in the strong points of the old ruling class, would "impose their will in imperial fashion." Out of that conquest of power were to issue all the juridical and legal institutions of the working class. "It has been said that our epoch is the epoch of imperialism. Sorel has invented proletarian imperialism."[35] Sorel did nothing of the sort. He wrote many hundreds of pages precisely to combat the Marxist thesis of the proletarian dictatorship. Sorel rejected the idea of the "workers' state" even as a transitory necessity. Neither did he believe that the pattern of a new morality and its institutional framework would be set by a victorious revolution; on the contrary, the new morality was, in Sorel's view, the indispensable prerequisite of ultimate "deliverance." Institutions are not the creation of a revolutionary "fiat" (which he called "arbitrary") but the result of the "struggle for rights," the road posts marking the advance toward the "possession of morality." The revolution, if any, only "recognizes" what is an accomplished ethical and social fact.

Lasserre knew all that, of course. Why, then, did he falsify the record? Merely in order to coin a fetching phrase that would provide him with a forceful title for his book? Or was he simply baffled by the almost perverse reticence of a theorist who advocated violence while simultaneously pronouncing a **Gran Rifiuto** of the Will to Power? Lasserre and de Ruggiero decide to reconcile the "nationalist" with the socialist Sorel as well as the man of violence with the man of reflection by discovering Sorel the theorist of the conservative revolu-

---

[34]David Thomson, "Sorel: Apostle of Revolution" in **The Manchester Guardian Weekly,** November 13, 1947, p. 12. — Similarly Bertrand Russell: "In the end...Sorel abandoned syndicalism and became a royalist." (**A History of Western Philosophy,** New York, 1945, p. 791).

[35]Lasserre, **op. cit.,** p. 38.

tion.[36] Thus understood, the use of warlike methods by the working
class was to bring about the regeneration of a decadent mankind.
This conceptual achievement, the critics say, imposed a heavy strain
on Sorel's critical faculty. To build up the proletariat into an "aristocratic elite" which would preserve by violent means the "ancient
heroisms" was not possible without romanticizing and falsifying the
character of a movement which, the historian de Ruggiero insists,
was bound up with its democratic and egalitarian origins. Sorel's
antirationalism, his distaste for democracy are the denial of what is,
to de Ruggiero, the essence of true socialism. No wonder "the philistine reality of the strike" had to undergo, in Sorel's laboratory, "a
fantastic deformation" in order to become the myth of moral rebirth;
no wonder the proletarians and their leaders refused to act out the
sublime precept of the philosopher and continued to wallow in their
democratic swamp. That would have been disastrous for Sorel had he
started out from socialism; but since, according to Ruggiero, he had
been a revolutionary first and was as much influenced by Nietzschean
notions as by Marx, his conversion to nationalism was no self-be-
trayal.

   We are here confronted with another "myth about Sorel." The
intellectual fatherhood of Nietzsche is taken for granted by most students, but it is not borne out by the evidence.[37] In questions involving intellectual paternity the well-known injunction of the Code Napoleon ought to be heeded. Nor is de Ruggiero on safer ground when he
speaks of the revolutionary origins of Sorel's thought. It took the
author of the **Reflections** many years to overcome his initial leanings
toward reformism, the democratic socialism of the Eduard Bernstein
variety. The evidence in Sorel's correspondence with Croce, if not in
Sorel's published early works, should have forewarned de Ruggiero.
At least he does not hold Sorel responsible for fascism. His death
came at a moment when the application of his doctrine to counterrev-
olutionary purposes was still in the experimental stage. Yet the conversion of Sorel's leftist, proletarian myth into the myth of the Italian
nation must be called legitimate: "the revolutionary leaders of both
right and left," Lenin as well as Mussolini, were "fighting Sorel's
battle" against parliamentary liberalism.

   But de Ruggiero is not yet through with his subject. What was it
that transformed that kind and cautious scholar, Georges Sorel, into
the raving enemy of the "intellectual"? Lasserre called Sorel "a

---

[36]Influencing perhaps Michael Freund who gave to his excellent **Georges
Sorel** (Frankfurt a. M., 1932) the subtitle, "Der revolutionaere Konservativismus."

[37]Recent examples are: Hans Barth, **Fluten und Dämme** (Zurich, 1943),
p. 226, and Jean Wanner, **Georges Sorel et la décadence** (Lausanne, 1943),
p. 33.

revolutionary of the brain, not of the heart;" he compared him to Rousseau: both men were rebels against the dominant rationalist spirit of their time, both rose against the cold, arid conventionalism of the enlightenment.[38] Rousseau's tempestuous protest was an isolated phenomenon, while Sorel's impatience with the "Illusions of Progress" not only betrayed its "pale, bookish" origin but also lacked originality.[39] Sorel's voice was only one in a loud chorus of anti-intellectualism led by Henri Bergson and William James, who both influenced Sorel.[40] The growing complexity of our civilization explains their yearning for a new innocence, which is to be found in "pure intuition": the growing depersonalization instills the sentiment for the decisive action, which will break the chain of logical, determined evolution and restore freedom.

At this point Professor de Ruggiero puts in a demurrer: the Bergsonian protest, even as interpreted by Sorel (and that means very freely), was not intended to provide a charter for barbaric instincts. Sorel never intended to go so far as that. His "violence" was the primitivism of a sophisticated mind suffering from intellectual indigestion: the denial of reason was the product of "rationalistic exasperation." But the best reasons and the best intentions of the world cannot prevent that words, once uttered, are misunderstood because they may mean more than they were meant to. Sorel himself knew that only too well.[41] And so, if one is to believe Professor de Ruggiero, the gentle old man was in a way responsible for the return of the barbarians: "Sorel thought to evoke the sublime and unleashed the beast."[42]

---

[38]Lasserre, op. cit., p. 36. The author compares Sorel's Illusions with Rousseau's famous discourse against the arts and sciences. Ruggiero considers the Illusions, not the Reflections to be Sorel's most revealing work. The priority of the comparison Rousseau - Sorel seems to belong to Professor Georges Guy-Grand who made it in his essay, "Georges Sorel et les problemes contemporains" in La Grande Revue, Paris, December, 1922, p. 300. — For Sorel's views on Rousseau, see chapter 6, p.

[39]Lasserre, op. cit., p. 221.

[40]"Those who at the time...hated not so much the economic arrangements of capitalist society as its democratic rationalism were not free to fall back on orthodox socialism which promises still more rationalism. To their intellectual anti-intellectualism — whether Nietzschean or Bergsonian — the syndicalist anti-intellectualism of the fist may well have appealed as the complement — in the world of the masses — of their own creed. Thus a very strange alliance actually came to pass, and syndicalism found its philosopher after all in Georges Sorel." Joseph A. Schumpeter, Capitalism, Socialism and Democracy, 2. edition (New York and London, 1947), p. 340. In a similar vein: W. Y. Elliott, The Pragmatic Revolt in Politics (New York, 1928), chapter IV, pp. 111-141.

[41]See Introductory i, p. 19 and note 18.

[42]De Ruggiero, loc. cit., p. 199. However, he softens the blow by adding that it was "the good-natured, domesticated beast of Xavier de Maistre".

Fortunately, he proceeds, the doctrine of Sorel is neither derived from practice nor meant for it, but is a hothouse flower like Bergson's intuition. To be sure, it is possible to endow such aspects of experience as strikes, acts of violence, dictatorships with Sorelian significance, but the varnish dissolves in the fire of reality. "Contrary to all appearance, Sorelianism, Nietzscheanism, D'Annunzionism...are ideas of the past, ideas dated and depleted, and whatever seems to be enacted in their name, has quite another meaning and releases forces and ideals of a very different order."[43] This enigmatic sentence everyone familiar with the crypto-language used by writers subject to totalitarian censorship will ponder with closest attention. It was impossible for de Ruggiero to list Fascism together with Sorelianism, Nietzscheanism, and D'Annunzionism, having attacked all three. On the other hand, he did not have to dot his i's; the Duce had publicly acknowledged his debt to both the Frenchman and the German, if not to the Duce of Fiume.

But even the Italian reader who preferred to take his de Ruggiero straight could still marvel at those unidentified forces of a "very different order" which had been released in Sorel's name. If it was the Fascist order of the day, Mussolini's censor could be pleased, since Fascism setting wrong Sorelianism right would appear justified. Or perhaps Fascism was merely Sorel's disastrous pipe-dream come true, bound to be defeated by the forces of outraged humanity. There is room for the suspicion that the target was not Sorel, but the dictator himself, by way of Sorel. His argument against Sorel should not be dismissed on that ground, however; it remains a formidable criticism. But it is still far from complete.

"At first sight, religion and rationalism seem to be contradictory. Still, a mind that has intelligence but no religion, is offensive to us, it will strike us as dry, harsh, opaque. In turn, a religious mind which does not endure well the yoke of rational discipline, will repel us as feeble. But lack something, something human." M. Lasserre, continuing, has no doubt that the mark of a fully human intellect is the faculty of "reconciling the demands of reason and the religious sentiment."[44] This reasonably sentimental man is the democratic liberal. Sorel's equation of democracy and abstract intellect leads him astray. As Professor Georges Guy-Grand puts it: "The hatred of abstraction, logic, intellectualism, translates itself for Sorel into hatred of democracy." Still worse, in Sorel's view, "democracy always seeks unity."[45] It always tends "toward equality, toward assimilation, toward the fusion of all classes into a regime of abstract egalitarianism." Because he was convinced that the main reason for the degradation of the modern world was its penchant for unity, Sorel opposed

---

[43] Ibid., p. 199.
[44] Lasserre, op. cit., p. 260.
[45] Guy-Grand, loc. cit., p. 308.

to it his principle of **"scission,"** severance,[46] to the "general will" of mass democracy he opposed the "precise will," or, as Rousseau would call it, the "corporate will" of one class, the proletariat, the only class not yet dissolved in the great democratic melting pot.

The comparison between Sorel and Rousseau breaks down at a crucial point. Yet Professor Guy-Grand remains undisturbed. Rousseau's sovereign community was not meant to obliterate individuality but, on the contrary, to free it from the intervening, petty tyrants of the feudal past. What Sorel confused was the democratic reconciliation of "the wills of all" with their nivellation and destruction. If there is in the present day some evidence of "democratic absolutism," this merely means that "the democratic mechanism is not fully functioning; it only proves that the idea of democracy has not yet become a fact."[47] Democracy, therefore, is not, as Sorel believed, a monistic creed; rather, "the democratic rule of law, a law determined by all, is much less unitarian than are such regimes as absolute monarchies or unilateral dictatorships," which subordinate everything "to the will of one man or one class." Afraid that this allusion to Sorel's pro-Lenin stand might be lost on the reader, Guy-Grand proceeds: "What could be more absolute than Bolshevism, what more abstract than Internationalism, what more opposed to the spirit of Empiricism than a violent revolution?"[48]

Considering Guy-Grand with Lasserre and de Ruggiero, the accusations against Georges Sorel narrow down to two contentions mutually exclusive: (1) that he severed what belongs together, arraigning the forces of instinct, intuition, class, diversity against intellect, democracy, and unity; and (2) that he is himself a rationalist, absolutist, doctrinarian, paying lip service to multiformity but actually meaning unity. But is it possible that one and the same man could be "a foe of progress through reform, and believe in progress through violence; be a foe of the democratic intellectual and exalt the revolutionary intellectual; be the enemy of superannuated notions about the State of Nature and praise the spontaneous virtue of the proletarian; a firebrand against aristocracy who was himself essentially aristocratic, one who denied the absolute but believed in the absolute of the myth?..."[49]

The concept of the myth has likewise been subjected to a severe scrutiny by Guy-Grand.[50] Sorel distinguishes between a social utopia, which is the description of a rational scheme of economic or political organization, and a social **will**, imaginative in origin and expressed in

---

[46]See **Reflections** (Am. ed., 1950), pp. 152, 205, 208 (There translated as "cleavage"). Cf. also chapter 12, p. 275.

[47]Guy-Grand, **loc. cit.**, p. 317.—About Rousseau, cf. chapter 6, p. 153f.

[48]**Ibid.**

[49]**Ibid.**, p. 323.

[50]In his earlier work, **La philosophie syndicaliste** (Paris, 1911), pp. 88-95.

religious or poetical terms — a myth. The particular proletarian, or rather Sorelian myth of the general strike, symbolizes the faith in ultimate liberation, which was in Sorel's view the core of the Marxian doctrine, although Marx had done his best to bury it under an abstract structure far too heavy for the working class to carry. What keeps the proletarian movement alive, then, is the myth; not a blueprint of the socialist future, but an "activating image." readying the proletarian class for battle. The ultimate "napoleanic" finale may never come, and yet the myth will have fulfilled its purpose: to keep morale alive.

But, observes Guy-Grand, if the workers really go into battle without any concrete design, without a program, it is difficult to see why they should want to fight at all. "The movement is everything, the goal nothing" — there is, of course, some truth in Eduard Bernstein's saying, but like all generalizations, this one too exaggerates, for "if the goal were really of no account, the movement would not exist," or it would be mere stupid energy and savagery.[51] What redeems the proletarian dream and makes it, to use Sorel's favorite expression, sublime, is precisely the aim pursued, the ardent vision of a better social order that makes the greatest sacrifices possible and understandable. An intelligent and intelligible plan of social change, blurred as it may be, must and will exist. A myth is, therefore, a utopia that has caught on, that has fired the passionate imagination of the mass mind into action   This sounds like common sense, and once again Sorel seems to be guilty of gross exaggeration. Instead of being content to point out the fallacious overestimation of the rational factor, he went into the opposite extreme of proclaiming irrational will as the sole creative force.

Complete My Work

There remains the possibility that Georges Sorel knew what he was doing and that the extremism of his views was deliberate. He may reply to Guy-Grand that his myth concept alone explains why movements survive even when results are not forthcoming, that it helps to understand the heroic persistence of persistent losers.[52] As an example of a myth sustaining a movement toward a receding goal, Sorel cites the early Christian faith in Christ's second coming. The rationalization of the ends is not the cause but merely a by-product of faith. We may, on the other hand, reject Sorel's notion of the myth altogether on the ground that it forces him to talk intelligently about the unintelligible. But if we do so, Sorel might answer us with Bernard

---

[51]Ibid., p. 97.

[52]Sorel's most telling example of a myth sustaining a movement toward a receding goal is that of the early Christian faith in the Lord's second coming. See **Reflections** (Am. ed., 1950), p. 208.

Shaw: "You could not have Æsop's fables unless the animals
talked."[53] How are we to identify the manifestations of the irrational
unless we apply to them the categories of rational description? Not
able to explain the unexplainable, we may still interpret our awareness
of it. In defining the symptoms of the instinct we should be conscious
of our limitations, of our duty as intellectuals not to interfere but to
remain, in all humility, observers or servants at best of the vital
process.[54]

While paying attention to all nonutilitarian drives, Sorel did not
try to minimize the role of the material factor. He put Marx's methodology to good use without making a fetish out of historic materialism. "There is a force which always leads the mind toward idealism;
one would do well to study the nature of that force and try to find out
whether idealism has not a legitimate place in the intellectual process, but outside of economics and law...."[55] There are "three
great aspects of human activity...." One is that of "free spontaneity
disregarding all material obstacles and replacing reality by the creations of its own imagination...." This is the realm of mythology,
of legend and, on a higher plane, all imaginary abstraction: "man re-
tires into himself and saturates his conscience in the contemplation
of the ideal." Another aspect is "of a social and political nature; it
includes everything that pertains to association and protection" — here
appears "the State, imposing peace by means of penal law." Sorel, it
is plain, was no loyal Marxist, since he did not derive social morality
from economics, which is something else again, "the world of distribution of exchange, amenable to external, abstract manipulation."[56]
It must be distinguished from production proper, the material realization of our creative urge. A society in which distribution ("abstract" intellectualism) dictates to production (Bergson's "intuition")
will be a frustrated society.

, Sorel has been called a relativist. But he said: "First of all, one
ought to distinguish a very small and narrow portion of the human
mind in which thought touches on the absolute; we may call it the domain of science...which reaches its perfection in physical mathematics. At the opposite pole of conscience, there is to be found another very small but equally important sector where we also reach
the absolute. This is the corner in which we conceive ideas freely;
we may call it the corner of morals and religion. Between these two
narrow regions, there extends the immense domain which occupies
almost the entire reach of our consciousness: here the operations of

---

[53]Bernard Shaw, **Sixteen Self Sketches** (New York, 1949), p. 157.

[54]"The intellectual can serve the proletariat only by remaining honestly
an intellectual." Sorel in Variot, **op. cit.**, p. 49.

[55]Sorel, **Introduction à l'économie moderne,** 2. edition (Paris, 1922), p. 392.

[56]Sorel, **Le système historique de Renan** (Paris, 1906), pp. 84-86.

our daily life take place. Here, logic operates very poorly."[57] So-rel's relativism was thus not absolute.

Sorel has been called a pluralist. But in his view diversity and unity were not exclusive:

"Depending on the position we assume, we will have the right of conceiving society as a whole or as a multiplicity of antagonistic forces. There exists in many cases an approximation to economic and juridical uniformity....On the other hand, there are many highly important questions which will not make sense unless we take the view that the activity of class war institutions is the preponderant in-fluence....A great number of organizations are more or less inti-mately integrated into the social ensemble, so whatever unity is re-quired will follow automatically; other organizations, less numerous and sifted out by a severe selective process, conduct the class strug-gle; it is they who create the ideological unity necessary for the pro-letariat to accomplish its revolutionary task...."[58]

If we want to sort out the confused mass of experience, we can do so only at the risk of breaking it up into segments and assigning to the detail full autonomy: "Social philosophy, in order to trace the most important happenings of history, is obliged to practice the method of disruption,[59] to examine certain parts without regard for their con-nection with the whole, and to determine somehow the nature of their activity by pushing them toward independence. Once our understand-ing has reached an optimal point, it is no longer capable of restoring the disrupted unity." The part has become a whole; unjustly so, but the whole from which we broke it loose is not a constant either; it is history in motion. We can never know it until it has become the past, and likewise the philosophic observer "has no right to believe that he can give orders to the future."[60]

---

[57]Sorel, remarks made at a meeting of the **Societé Française de Philoso-phie,** 1907; cited by Georges Goriely in **Fédération,** November 1947, p. 9. — Hermann Heller in his important **Staatslehre** (Leiden, 1934) brands both Pareto and Sorel as advocates of radical relativism (pp. 7 and 9).

[58]Sorel, **Réflexions sur la violence,** 10. edition (Paris, 1946) Appendix I, **"Unité et multiplicité,"** pp. 431-432. (Translated by this writer; a printed translation of that section was not available until very recently: see Am. ed., 1950, pp. 299-300.)

[59]In French: **diremption.** The 1950 American edition gives the French original, and the editor notes: "Not able to find English equivalent — perhaps Sorel coined [the term]" (p. 287).

[60]**Réflexions,** ed. cit., p. 407. — Cf. A. N. Whitehead, **Science and The Modern World** (New York, 1925), p. 66: "The conception of an isolated sys-tem is not the conception of substantial independence from the remainder of things, but of freedom from casual contingent dependence upon detailed items within the rest of the universe. Further, this freedom from casual depend-ence is required only in respect to certain abstract characteristics which at-tach to the isolated system, and not in respect to the system in its full con-creteness."

This means that what at one time or another looks like unity exists only in the mind of the onlooker who takes his partial truth to be the whole. In reality, there is no such thing as a synthesis unless it be, for a fleeting second of history, the equilibrium resulting from the many pulls and hauls of all the social groups each trying to drag all the rest in their direction. What Sorel did was to bring the different group wills into sharper relief, even if that meant patent exaggeration. Not until we clear the ground and fight for our bourgeois or proletarian truths as absolutes, can "the" new truth emerge, and then it will contain whatever valor and validity these absolutes possess, no more, no less. The composite picture of our social world, as Sorel saw it, is at all times the product of a collective workshop in which everyone must exert himself as if he were the only artist. Finally:

"It has been pointed out to me that I wrote without the least concern for any didactic order whatsoever.... Yet, I am convinced that the educational merit of these studies — and that is the only merit they have — would be greater if their primitive form remained unaltered: I am carrying on an intimate conversation with the reader; I submit to him ideas, and I force him to do his own thinking in turn, so that he may correct me and complete my work "[61]

[61]Sorel, La Ruine du monde antique, 3. edition (Paris, 1933), p. xix.

*As this goes to press, the most recent study of our author has just been published. It is Scott H. Lytle's chapter on "Georges Sorel: Apostle of Fanaticism" in Modern France, Problems of the Third and Fourth Republics, edited by Edward Mead Earle (Princeton, 1951), pp. 264 - 290. The very impressive, superbly documented essay is based on Professor Lytle's doctoral dissertation, "Historical Materialism and the Social Myth", an analysis of Sorel's conception of history (typewritten, Cornell University, 1948).

12. THE HERITAGE

If there is, in great leadership, an element of genuine unselfishness, then Georges Sorel was truly a great leader; that he enjoyed his power over young, receptive minds, goes by itself and does not contradict his saying that "there is no service of great causes without great disinterestedness."[1] What puzzles us is not the nature of that power but its distinct limitation: Georges Sorel always remained the master of a Happy Few. Did he disdain mass influence? A partial answer is to be found in the very structure of his mind. It was his intellectual restlessness, his inability to dwell for very long on any one idea, that made Sorel at once so attractive and exasperating. The perpetuum mobile of this potent mind at long last terrified his friend, Péguy: "There, everything that happened in the universe, was weighed and criticized, peeled, analyzed, reduced to pellets, prepared with a thousand diverse sauces...."[2] In the poet's mind, the anti-rationalist becomes, ironically, a logic chopper. For others, he remained a source of mystery — his very intellectual powers seemed to move, like those of Nietzsche's Socrates[3] with effortless, "obscure security" among the noumena which are beyond the grasp of thought, operating in a kind of "permanent reverie."[4] And the same Tharaud who tells of Péguy's exodus from the didactic sawmill of Sorel,[5] also insists that "there was nothing dogmatic about him. An idea was, in his eyes, merely a mirage, a myth (that was his expression), a force of attraction, an agent of excitement. He loathed his own ideas, once they had taken shape and were in danger of becoming common currency."[6]

In his inexhaustible resourcefulness, Sorel could disdain all repose and go on seemingly forever, but in doing so, he also became a source of confusion and frustration. Not only did he disappoint inferior minds desiring certitude — worse, he exemplified, in his own sphere, the great deficiency of all contemporary intellectual élites: their inability, because of overstimulation, to assert and stabilize themselves and their milieu.[7]

---

[1]Jean Variot, Propos de Georges Sorel (Paris, 1935), p. 49 (statement recorded in "January, 1921").

[2]Jérôme et Jean Tharaud, Notre cher Péguy (Paris, 1926), II 138.

[3]See chapter 2, p. 57.

[4]René Johannet, L'évolution de Georges Sorel in Itinéraires d'Intellectuels (Paris, 1921), p. 178.

[5]See chapter 8, p. 209.

[6]Tharaud, op. cit., I 261.

[7]See Karl Mannheim, Man and Society in an Age of Reconstruction (New York, 1940), p. 86 ff.

If Georges Sorel never became a leader of the masses, if the influence of his ideas remained limited and indirect, it was because his own deficiency only reflected an external situation against which even a genius greater than Sorel would have been powerless — a situation in which the contending intellectual forces were so much in balance that they altogether neutralized each other. This is particularly true of Sorel's France. Due to the retarded growth of large scale industry, French socialism suffered from extreme fragmentation: in contrast to the monolithic German social-democratic party, the French labor movement was split into four independent factions: the Dreyfusard and Bernsteinite reformists led by Jean Jaurès; the smaller Marxist Labor Party of Jules Guesde and Paul Lafargue; the Blanquists who, under the leadership of Edouard Vaillant, later merged with the Marxists; and finally, the anti-militarist group around Gustave Hervé. All these parties, with the exception perhaps of the last named, were obnoxious to Sorel who was as hard on Jaurès, "the great orator" and "false prohet" as on the orthodox disciples of Karl Marx, among whom Jules Guesde was his special whipping boy, It is, therefore, not at all surprising to hear from that great authority on modern parties, Robert Michels, that French socialism was "most hostile to Sorel."[8] His correspondence is full of complaints about intriguing fellow socialists: editors are under pressure to reject his contributions; mysterious plots are hatched to force him out. With the years, Sorel develops a strong persecution complex: the death of all those "little mags" which he was affiliated with at one time or another, could have but one reason in his view: "The boycott which official socialism is practicing for the past ten years against everything I write.... The order always was to silence all opinion which is not officially socialist; that is how L'Ere Nouvelle and Le Devenir Social were killed and how Le Mouvement Socialiste is being destroyed now."[9]

Subsequent events in French history, of a character so much more violent than Sorel ever could have anticipated, did not materially affect the virtual deadlock of the social and political dynamics, so uncannily impersonated by Sorel himself.

Today, the author of the Reflections on Violence has achieved text-book stature; even the most casual survey of representative compendia in the field of political theory seems to bear out Sorel's boast that his ideas "ripen in the shade."[10] No doubt that his prestige has grown over the years; it still is on the increase. But whether Sorel's teaching is alive, or a mere paragraph in a closed chapter of past intellectual history — that is another question.

Granted that Sorel had a way of casting his spell over all kinds of

---

[8]Lettere di Georges Sorel a Roberto Michels in Nuovi Studi di diritto, economia e politica (Rome, September — October, 1929), p. 289, note 1.

[9]To Michels (Ibid., p. 289), November 13, 1905.

[10]Matériaux d'une théorie du prolétariat, 2. ed. (Paris, 1921), p. 286.

people who never read him, and on some who, unfortunately, like the late B. Mussolini, did read and misuse him, the attempt to gauge the survival power of Sorel's ideas becomes a melancholy quest. The old guard of Sorelians has passed away; his two closest friends and collaborators, Berth and Paul Delesalle died recently. Daniel Halévy, Sorel's companion in arms in the Dreyfus days and editor of his Reflections, is one of the few main witnesses alive who remember the old sage of Boulogne-sur-Seine with tender respect. But his tenderness and his respect have the wistfulness of nostalgia for something that is irrevocably gone. Also, the venerable M. Halévy is too much a writer in his own right to be called a Sorelian. His love goes out, as did Sorel's, to their common spiritual ancestor, Proudhon, and to that remarkable neo-Catholic, Charles Péguy, but for the rest, if his kindness would permit, he would probably range himself on the side of the critics rather than the worshippers of Sorel. There are a few younger Frenchmen who are writing books about the man they never knew personally, since he died almost thirty years ago, in 1922. Some of these people recently contributed a symposium on the occasion of Sorel's hundredth birthday.[11] How do they feel about him; how does his work appear to them?

Defender of Liberty

It is no accident that the hosts of the centenary celebration, the editors of a review which "belongs neither to the left nor to the right," found it necessary to explain, if not apologize for, Georges Sorel's appearance in their columns. They did not wish it to be said that they were trying to "annex" a revolutionary writer; they refused to be accused of a camouflaged attempt at making up to Marxism. Sorel, they continued, was not a Marxist, but essentially an independent thinker: "No doubt, the author of the Reflections died saluting the nascent Russian revolution. What would he say about the Stalinist tyranny? No doubt, fascism for a time made claims on him. 'The dead do not protest,' as the poet said. No, Sorel cannot be labelled.... He was a bourgeois and created a proletarian myth. He was a socialist, but also an enemy of democracy. He sympathized with Marxism but rejected its materialism.... Like Proudhon, Sorel is fuzzy, disconcerting, contradictory." But also, or, rather, for that reason, "he is thought-provoking, a questioner who gives no respite. Of that we always stand in need, and now more than ever."[12]

This has been quoted, not because it presents a new view of Sorel, but precisely because it repeats so faithfully all that has been written about him for the last forty years. If it has to be said once more at this late date, it is proof that all the attempts made so far to dissociate Georges Sorel from his voluntary attachment to Marx and from his not

---

[11]In Fédération, No. 34 (November, 1947), pp. 1-18.

[12]Ibid., editorial notes, pp. 1-2.

so voluntary identification with fascism have remained unsuccessful.
Of the five contributors to the symposium, four exert themselves in
whitewashing the Marxist and the Leninist Sorel (they disregard the
fascist). "To the extent in which Marxist philosophy and politics conflict with those of Proudhon, Sorel has never been a Marxist,"[13] says
Daniel Halévy, and Pierre Andreu cites Sorel's endorsement of Benedetto Croce's view that Das Kapital is "a bizarre mixture of generalizations, polemics and bitter satire, of historic illustrations and digres-
sions."[14] Sorel was not slow to discover the elements of old-fashioned
idealism in Marx's materialism, Robert Aron informs us: Sorel rejected the rationalist Marx "whose theory of classes he considered to
be an abstraction."[15] Marxism is a bourgeois philosophy. Marx, anxious to be a "scientific socialist," neglected and Sorel added as essential
prerequisites of victory a "metaphysics of mores," discovering as
Halévy puts it,[16] "the epic element" of the class struggle, its "sublime"
quality.[17] Sorel takes to heart Emil Vandervelde's declaration: "If the
workers should triumph without having accomplished the equally indispensable moral evolution, their reign would be abominable and the world
would again be a place of suffering, brutality and injustice as bad as
now."[18]

All this will say that Sorel was not a Marxist. The apologists are
right: Sorel was only temporarily under the spell of Karl Marx, and
even then he was a Marxist very much à la Sorel who used historic
materialism as a "laboratory" for his independent experiments and
was, long before the Russian revolution, "unmasked" and excommunicated by Lenin[19] since he dared to take issue not only with the Marxist
pundits but even with the founding fathers themselves, although he cen-
tered his attacks on Friedrich Engels rather than on Marx.

Still, the marked tendency of these writers to establish Sorel's
autonomy as a social thinker who transcended Marx is significant beyond
the question of accurate interpretation. It indicates an anxiety to salvage from the heritage of socialism that which, these writers hope,[20]

[13]Ibid., p. 12.

[14]Ibid., p. 5. From Sorel's La décomposition du marxisme (Paris, 1908),
p. 5, cited from Croce, Matérialisme historique et économie marxiste, p. 99.

[15]Fédération, p. 15.   [16]Ibid., p. 13.

[17]Ibid., p. 2. Here, in the first of two contributions, Halévy quotes Arnaud
Dandieu (from Anthologie des philosophes contemporains, Paris, 1931), who
holds that Sorel's "heroic syndicalism is the only political doctrine entitled to
the claim of representing a position beyond Marxism." Andreu likewise stresses
Sorel's emphasis on the "sublime" and "heroic" qualities of the proletarian
struggle (Ibid., p. 5).

[18]Robert Aron in Fédération, p. 16.   [19]See chapter 10, note 11.

[20]To this group also belong: Pierre Angel, Essais sur Georges Sorel (Paris,
1936); Jacques Rennes, Georges Sorel et le syndicalisme révolutionnaire (Paris,
1936); S. Beracha, Le Marxisme après Marx (Paris, 1937); Jean Deroo, Le
Renversement du matérialisme historique: L'expérience de Georges Sorel
(Paris, 1939).

is still alive: that which has not been and could not be assimilated by those who claim today to be the true and only heirs of the new dispensation. Thus understood, all recent vindications of Sorel has for its objective the reclamation for the West of its lawful intellectual property, the reassertion of a libertarian tradition that has been discarded by the masters of the East and is severely threatened in the rest of Europe. This tradition is threatened by Stalinist penetration, but endangered likewise by developments within Western society itself.

The vindication of Sorel thus broadens into a defence of freedom in the Western sense, provided two things can be shown conclusively; first, that the Sorel approach means freedom not merely for the one class with which his work is in the main concerned, the proletariat, but freedom for all classes, in distinction to the Marxian approach which likewise aims at freedom for all, but on the condition that there be no classes left; and, secondly, that a trend favouring Sorel's expectations over those of Marx can be shown actually to exist in contemporary Europe.

This is a difficult task, and one in which we shall get little help from Sorel himself because he does his worst to revile democracy. Will the Sorelians prove to be more helpful?

One way to re-establish Sorel as a defender of liberty is to show that his affiliation with Marxism was only part, and not the essence of his work, that he was a moralist first, and a revolutionary only because he was basically a conservative, passionately concerned about the growing symptoms of decadence which bourgeois Europe displayed in his time. His "infatuation" with the proletariat, his conviction that it was the class of the "elect," the chosen instrument of history to save civilization, was due (we must argue) not to any dislike on the part of Sorel for Bourgeois values. On the contrary, because Sorel closely identified all social virtues with the bourgeois virtues of the past, because in his opinion the working class was the only group left in which those "heroisms" which made for greatness were left fairly intact, he elevated the proletariat to the rank of the new aristocracy destined to preserve bourgeois austerity and thrift. While the son of the bourgeoisie, Karl Marx, considered middle-class morality to be expressive of a transitory phase of the industrial revolution, bound to be superseded by a new morality to be created by the proletariat, but not proletarian either since the proletariat would abolish itself in the process, Sorel insisted on proletarian morality as developing under capitalism to be the morality of the future precisely because it was capitalist morality at its best. In contrast to Marx, who believed that the ruling class of his time was doomed together with the capitalist "mode of production," Sorel was satisfied with a blood transfusion which would merely replace the tired old personnel with a new set of "producers." The question of ownership, of private or group enterprise, was secondary for Sorel as long as the vigor, the drive, of industrial civilization was maintained and increased.[21]

---

[21]"Not a single line against capitalism as a régime of production will be found in his works." Pierre Andreu in Fédération, p. 6.

In this light, Sorel's insistence on the need for sharpening the intensity of the class struggle assumes a significance radically different from the Marxist interpretation of that social fact. Marx sees the class struggle as a passing phase, to be resolved in the "higher phase" of socialist, classless society. Sorel, while holding out the hope, like Marx, for a future society of "free producers," is not concerned with the future; the class struggle is, to him, a means not toward the abolition of both capitalist and proletarian social forms and consciousnesses, but the guarantee that both classes will be forced to maintain themselves as they are in top form. Sorel's belief that the proletariat would prove to be more successful in preserving the "morality of the producer" was not always secure from doubt; personally he did not cherish the idea that the middle class would reassert itself because he thought it was past redemption, but he did not exclude the possibility of a bourgeois renaissance.

It was against the threat of bourgeois decadence that Sorel developed the theory which made him famous and infamous: his concept of proletarian "violence." The defensive character of that notion has been curiously neglected by most critics of Sorel. He looked upon violence as the only means that would protect the proletariat from losing its identity as a distinct class. The labor movement had, for Sorel, a sole objective: to remain, or, rather, to become itself. It was, therefore, to scorn all help both from political parties and from the state; least of all was it to become the state. The aggressor was neither the proletariat nor, as Marx saw it, a capitalism torn and driven on by its "inherent contradictions." For Sorel, capitalism (as far as it meant production) and the proletariat were the twin victims of non-productive interest, of parasitic politics sapping the productive energies by arbitrary economic intervention.[22] Because democracy tended to assuage the class struggle, because it "corrupted" the entrepreneurs as well as their workers into mutual appeasement, it became Sorel's arch villain. Paradoxical as it may sound, he was for laissez-faire, and hostile to social legislation because of his proletarian bias.[23]

If these conclusions seem to be arrived at by a rather tortuous road, this is so mainly because of Sorel's view of democracy as a unitary, class-levelling influence will impress many as a faulty interpretation, not of its ultimate objective which is social cooperation, but of its working method. It may easily be argued that the democratic process amounts to an emphatic affirmation of the idea which presupposes

---

[22]Cf. Michael Freund, Georges Sorel (Frankfurt a. Main, 1932): "The two opponents of economic liberalism, protectionism and social legislation, are also Sorel's enemies" (p. 142) and: "Sorel's work is perhaps the most passionate protest of our time against the return of the Welfare State" (p. 143).

[23]"All social legislation is nothing but an element of proletarian decadence." (Sorel, Insegnamenti sociali della economia contemporanea, Palermo, 1907.) In the same work, Sorel rejects the eight-hour working day (p. 278, note.)

discrepancy instead of identity of interests, that in fact democracy requires the very clash of discordant social wills to achieve the balance of power that will ensure harmony, be it ever so precarious.

In this view, the democratic mechanism becomes a transmission belt, driven by the forces engendered by the class struggle, with its conflicting claims being passed on, assembly-line fashion, to emerge as the collective product called the democratic compromise. In so far as the democracies of the West have shown a tendency toward slowing down or even arresting the movement of the transmission belt, in so far as they have become afraid of legalizing the social advances of the working class, Sorel's attack against "democracy" seems consistent with a progressive attitude not necessarily Marxist. However, if we are justified in hoping that democracy has not yet become static, then Sorel's quarrel with it would appear to be incidental rather than basic, a critique of "too little," not of the democratic principle itself. He would have made it easier for us to understand him, if he had annexed the semantics of democracy, as Marx and the Marxists did, instead of exorcizing it.

He could have done so with more right than they and still remained sincere. But precisely because he was sincere, he would not tolerate any confusion between the corrupt democracy of the French politician and his own libertarian beliefs. He would rather be known and reviled as the sinister plotter against law-abiding society than use the terminology of the only system in which his particular type of class struggle was feasible, a system in which both capitalists and proletarians would work out their own destinies separately and thereby fulfill their historic mission, to develop all the forces of industrial production to the limit.

In comparison with Marx's grandiose scheme in which the proletariat figures as the agent but not at all as the primary concern of history, Sorel's preoccupation with the labor movement and its autonomy looks almost petty. If the choice has to be between him and Marx, it is the latter who seems to promise more by focusing on the whole of social evolution and not merely on one class, as Sorel appears to do. This is a second major obstacle that has to be overcome by those who would like to believe that Georges Sorel is a much better guide to freedom than Karl Marx and his disciples.

Withdrawal and Return

The decisive word in Sorel's vocabulary is "scission," schism, severance.[24] The class struggle (in the Marxian scheme of things the phase of "prehistory" after which the proletariat, having abolished itself together with capitalism, will begin to build the new, post-capitalist and post-proletarian society) already contains for Sorel the final solution: it brings into being, while it is going on, and only as long as it is going on, the new institutions which are the new society. The Marxian proletariat, as proletariat, is nothing but one component of a preliminary

[24]Cf. chapter 11, p. 264 and note 46.

process; it poses the question which history will answer. Sorel's proletariat is everything: it is the answer. Marx's working class is the
negation of the old; it is not yet the new, but it will merge into a socialist society. Sorel's proletarian is the new man himself. He is to create
and to bring into existence in the time of capitalism the society of the
producers, not by destroying capitalism but by hollowing it out, not by
"taking it over" but, as it were, in hostile symbiosis. Sorel's class
struggle is combat, to be sure; but beyond and above that it is a withdrawal, a secession within the framework of capitalism, just as the
early Christian Church practiced secession from the Roman world
while growing up in it.

One sees now how radical a transformation the concept of the class
struggle has undergone with Sorel. One also sees why he deliberately
chose as the cadre of the new society the narrow framework of one
class, unlike Marx, who worked on the broadest canvas, drawing into
his design the indissoluble web of all the "productive forces." His
classes were to merge into society by way of a transitory, proletarian
state; in the Sorelian view, all elements of the future world are already
present in the proletarian class as it exists and realizes itself under
the capitalist regime. But before the general may emerge out of the
particular, the small group, conscious of its wider task, must assume
the Archimedean position: the proletarian minority must constitute
itself as a society within society; and it cannot do so unless it has
established its own autonomy, spiritual as well as institutional.

At this point, the question poses itself irrepressibly: But why the
proletariat? Marx nowhere idolized the proletariat qua proletariat;
he saw in it only one of the two prongs of the dialectic pliers. We may
discover within the iron mechanism of the Marxian "science" the motor
of human passion. Marx, no doubt, felt for the proletariat which he
met but little. But if he became its leader it was because he believed
there should not and there would not be a proletariat in the "realm of
freedom." Sorel, the engineer, stressing the technological rather than
the economic role of the working class, believed, on the contrary, the
typical characteristics of the proletarian to be the essence that must
be preserved by the heroic effort of the working class. And he felt that
way not because he was infatuated with some imaginary "sublime proletarian" but because he was under the influence of a new social fact.
An emerging society could be studied prior to its coming into existence:
its chart could be read by the student of historic evolution. This society
would reveal its nature in its institutions. Now, the institution of the
new class, the proletariat, that was coming into its own in Sorel's time
was the professional association of the workers. It was in their syndicates, their trade unions, that he thought that he discovered the unique
organizational principle of his new society. The syndicalist rebellion
against the dominance of political parties, including the parties that
professed to represent the labor interest, was for Sorel an exciting

experience which he translated into the Sorelian theory of revolutionary syndicalism. To quote once more the contributors to the symposium, according to Sorel "the society of the future will grow quite naturally out of the practices of the labor movement. To the degree in which it will be heroic and pure, the society to which it gives birth will attain a more elevated level. Proletarian Right is not the one which the bourgeois legislators, those dillettantes of the social science, are fabricating in their parliament — it is the Right which is being created by syndicalist practice."[25] For, adds Daniel Halévy, "the syndicalist militant, according to Sorel, is a creator of values."[26]

The syndicate, therefore, cannot be merely an agency of economic betterment. Sorel cannot accept Lenin's view that the labor movement, if left to its own devices and lacking proper guidance by a political party, would never attain anything more than trade-union consciousness. For Sorel, the labor union is a moral agency: the intellectual home for the proletariat, its school and church. These new social forms will arise not because the proletarian is endowed with some superior virtue, but one of necessity. They will be wrought by the pressure and counter-pressure of the class struggle. Each proletarian advance will, at the same time, enlarge the sphere of proletarian Right.[27] Socialism will be the sum of the legally recognized institutions of the working class.

The syndicalist movement inspired Sorel to write his **Reflections on Violence.** Has this book in turn been an inspiration to the movement? The general agreement seems to be that it did not exert any practical influence worth speaking of. Yet, even if the work has never been a guide to action, at least not in France, it might still have significance as a correct analysis of syndicalist performance in the past and of its promise for the future. But even this merit of the **Reflections** has been denied by some. Gaétan Pirou, for instance, author of extremely valuable studies of syndicalism, sees "an abyss" between the fighters and the theorist: "While Sorel was concerned with moral culture, the militants were after tangible, material results." They were optimists, envisioning a society of plenty, leisure, and easy morals. Sorel, insists Pirou, was on the contrary a pessimist and a man of austere standards who believed that the society of producers would entail much harder work and, above all, much better morals. He had the traditionally

---

[25]Pierre Andreu in Fédération, p. 6-7. [26]Ibid., p. 13.

[27]Sorel makes a sharp distinction between the struggle for power and the struggle for law; history marks "the passage from a system of obligations to a system of rights" (Les Illusions du progrès, 4. ed., Paris, 1927, p. 316). "The people rebel against duties and insist on obtaining a regime based on Rights. It is proletarian violence alone which makes possible the [successful] development of such a revolt...." From his study of Roman institutions, Sorel draws the conclusion that "the more profound the schism between the subjects of the law, the more perfect the law is held to be" (Ibid., p. 317).

stern notions of the middle class Frenchman concerning family life
and chastity. For these reasons, if there was any agreement of opinion between the syndicalists and Sorel, it was confined to tactics.[28]

Against this negative view, a recent student of syndicalism, who
cannot be called a Sorelian, maintains that Sorel's theory accurately
reflects an important part at any rate of the syndicalist phenomenon,
even if not of its entirety. Robert Goetz-Girey[29] distinguishes three
stages of the movement, lasting from the end of the nineteenth century
to the Second World War, each characterized by a radically different
view of the proper attitude toward the parties and the state. In the first
period the slogan was "Autonomy and Reform." The syndicate was to
strive for piecemeal social advancement. The leaders of the movement
felt confident that they could deal successfully with the representatives
of capital even while relying exclusively on syndicalist strength; they
emphatically rejected all government protection as well as the friendly
guidance of political socialism.

Very soon this gradualism yielded to revolutionary tendencies, and
in the end the trade unions accepted the leadership of the socialist (and
communist) parties to the extent that the alignment of forces could be
expressed by the three words: "Subordination and Revolution."

However, between the first and the third phase a remarkable attempt was made to combine the idea of syndicalist rebellion with the
principle of syndicalist independence: "Autonomy and Revolution." It
is this middle span which corresponds, in Goetz-Girey's opinion, to
Sorel's and his "New School's" Revolutionary Syndicalism, to "Syndicalist Imperialism,"[30] or "Autarchic Imperialism." Between the beginning
which saw syndicalist freedom hampered by the ineffectual precept of
reformism, and the end when the revolution against capitalism was to
be had only at the price of submission to the politicians, between these
two horns of the dilemma, syndicalism for a short while, in the first
decade of this century, tried to solve its problem. This was the time
when "the theoreticians superimposed their systems on the conceptions
of the militants: hence the two syndicalisms, theoretical and militant,
acted and reacted upon one another."[31]

The honeymoon was short, perhaps because only a catastrophe of
at least national dimensions will kindle in the mind of men the moral

---

[28]Gaétan Pirou, Georges Sorel (Paris, 1927), p. 37-38. — See also Alexandre
Zévaès, Histoire du Socialisme et du Communisme en France de 1871 à 1947
(Paris, 1947), pp. 325-327. The author cites Robert Louzon (one of the editors
of Sorel's Letters to Paul Delesalle): "Sorel's influence on the formation and
development of revolutionary syndicalism was nil." (p. 326)

[29]In La Pensée syndicale francaise: Militants et théoriciens (Paris, 1948),
p. 22 ff.

[30]Théoricien de l'impérialisme is the subtitle of Pierre Lasserre's Georges
Sorel (Paris, 1928). About this work, cf. chapter 11, p. 259 f.

[31]Goetz-Girey, op. cit., p. 22.

ardour which was the precondition for Sorel's "labor imperialism" (a not very happy formula because Sorel's proletarian philosophy was one of retrenchment rather than of conquest). Not even the disaster of the first world war stirred French syndicalism into revolutionary action. In despair, Sorel wrote Europe off, although not all of it. For there was now that new provocative force: Lenin's Russia.

Today, we see the element of tragic irony in Sorel's last deception. For, far from bringing to life the society of Sorel's free producers, the success of Bolshevism signalled the death of the syndicalist movement, not in Russia only but everywhere: it meant the triumph of state and party over class, Georges Sorel's independent proletariat.

For a brief moment Georges Sorel seems to have shown to the Left a way out of their predicament: it looked as if he had "reconciled the libertarian tradition of the French, and of Proudhon in particular, with the German school of dialectics."[32] Alas, "a revolutionary effort of this kind cannot retain its vigor forever; there always arrives a time when new routines, new automatisms, sterilize and pervert the forces of renewal."[33] Syndicalism, in which Sorel had seen the wholesome reaction against the gratuitous game of the politicians with their amoralism and penchant for dictatorship, "has once more surrendered to the same old politicians" who, however, have been adding something new to their arsenal of tricks, "the ideas and techniques of the total state."[34] Eloquent words, but they do not tell the full story.

The story may be put into a single sentence: Time has run out on Sorel's proletarian, heroism or no heroism. All his syndicalist hopes were based on the expectation that capitalism was to stay for a long time to come. Impatient as he was with its shortcomings, decrying the vices of the time, always trying to discover the signs of the impending catastrophe, Sorel did not really wish the end to come. The proletariat needed time to build its own society, advancing step by step into its proletarian world. While the Marxist believed a revolution would "shorten and lessen the birthpangs of socialist society," Sorel's syndicalist was, by his revolutionary violence, to ensure the conservation, not the breakdown of capitalist forms. The proletarian quarrel was with the capitalist class, to be sure; but the survival of that class was needed if the proletarian was to remain a proletarian. The quarrel was in the main between workers and owners; the state was considered as a secondary enemy, in so far as it identified itself with the propertied class. Otherwise, the state was relegated to the role of giving its jurisdictional sanction to the slowly emerging forms of the proletarian

---

[32]Robert Aron in **Fédération**, p. 16. — According to J. de Saint-Chamant (**L'actualité de Georges Sorel** in **La Grande Revue**, Paris, January, 1938) a Sorel renaissance occured in Spain where, during the last civil war, "the Anarcho-Syndicalists...borrowed more than one idea from the theoretician of the revolutionary myth and the proletarian elite."

[33]Robert Aron in **Fédération**, p. 16. [34]Ibid.

community. The syndicalist did not much fear the enmity of the state; he did not suspect that the state might become a friend.

Unfortunately for Sorel's scheme, the transformation of European capitalism from a system directed by capitalists, to a system of state control or even state ownership happened much too fast even in Sorel's own industrially trailing country. It happened too early for the French labor movement to develop its full strength. Trade unionism had barely hit its stride in the nineteen-thirties when Léon Blum's "French New Deal" confronted it with an entirely altered situation. The strengthening of organized labor coincided with the enormous strengthening of state power. French dirigisme, Government in Business, seemed to refute the "Sorelian" element within labor. Although Léon Blum had only proposed "to administer capitalism," yet in France no less than in the Russian "Workers' State," a continuation of the class struggle along traditional lines was made difficult, if not impossible. For it was the state through which the labor unions had secured their strong position.

But the whole severity of the syndicalist, Sorelian predicament did not become fully evident until the liberation. The planned economy of the Fourth Republic, as far as it goes, is controlled not primarily by organized labor but by political parties representing the economic groups. What influence over the management of production the syndicates attained through legislation was bought at the expense of syndicalist autonomy: the organs of the workers became state agencies. But the French state in turn — what is it but the battlefield on which massive political machines contend for patronage? It is they who secure to the French masses of all social strata their meager share of the national income. The political organization has triumphed; between state impotence and party mechanism, the classes, bourgeoisie or proletarians, are condemned to impotence. Even though at present Lenin's party is in the opposition, the grand debate between Sorel and Lenin has been, for the time being, decided in favor of the Russian. "As a system, revolutionary syndicalism is finished, even though, after the master's death, one or another of his disciples continue to profess in moving words, their faith and loyalty."[35]

But the funeral oration may be premature. French dirigisme is, at this writing, far from secure against a relapse into what may become not a reversal to the capitalism of the Third Republic but a state of fluidity in which all kinds of social forces, and not last the labor movement, may regain their freedom of action. The symptoms pointing in that direction do not yet constitute what one could call a distinct current, but neither are they to be denied altogether. The great revulsion against party rule is growing;[36] it may well issue in a general

---

[35]Goetz-Girey, op. cit., p. 157.

[36]The withdrawal of the socialist unions from the communist-controlled C. G. T. may be an indication that the idea of syndicalist autonomy is reviving.

flight away from "politics" into the a-political world of professional organization. "If even today socialism has still some chance to escape dictatorship, it is because a path out of the totalitarian impasse reached by Marxism has been traced by Georges Sorel."[37]

Eloquent words, again, and tomorrow they may prove to be not quite as fanciful as they sound to us today.

---

[37]Robert Aron in **Fédération**, p. 16.

SUPPLEMENT: THE GREAT COMPANIONS

1. Benedetto Croce and Sorel

The importance of the great Italian thinker in the life and writings of our author needs no further emphasis. Chapter after chapter of this study witness to the friendship, to the intellectual caméraderie of the two men. There remains the question as to the **why** of their association which was so enduring and so fruitful for both partners. For, at first sight, Sorel and Croce seem to belong to such different intellectual backgrounds, reached such different conclusions, that it is difficult to see what spiritual bond united them for twenty-seven years. When they first got acquainted, both had passed beyond the age in which seniority (Sorel was the older by nineteen years) or superiority (Croce was already famous then) could have played a role in their relationship. No, their association was that of equals. Their mutual admiration was based on conscious self-esteem: it was a friendship between monarchs. But what was it that attracted the neo-idealist and Hegelian, Croce, to the enemy of those who continue "to battle chimeras and to navigate through the empyrean" of idealism?[1] What did the Italian liberal have in common with the French syndicalist? Their tolerance toward each other is all the more remarkable as both men are extremely pugnacious: Benedetto Croce's literary career is as crowded with bitter polemics as that of the notorious scoffer and scolder, Georges Sorel.

There are two possible explanations of the fact that, with one exception, Croce and Sorel never crossed swords. One is, that their spheres of interest were too remote from each other to engender friction. But this is not so: there was Vico, there was Marx; there was the problem treated by Sorel in his **Renan** — all topics about which both men felt as intensely as possible. There is, on Sorel's part an intimation of polite restraint. So, in acknowledging the receipt of one of Croce's books on aesthetics, he would plead non-competence, and this, although he had been publishing not a few works in the same field.[2] But the dominant note in his letters is lavish praise; indeed this praise of all and any of his friend's works would seem a bit on the obsequious side on the part of a man less sincere than Sorel. It may, however, be not disrespectful to assume that Sorel's approval of Croce's oeuvre was in the nature of a blanket endorsement that covered most specifically the work of the historian and political observer Croce; the rest was respect, and an anxiety — not in any way disreputable — to keep the friend in good humor.

---

[1]See chapter 4, p. 99 , and note 40.
[2]See chapter 5, note 12.

Croce's real disposition toward Georges Sorel is even more difficult to appraise. His writings contain various brief, though highly laudatory references to the fellow student of Karl Marx. In his book on Vico, Croce, though silent about Sorel's early study of the **Scienza Nuova,** credits him — and Marx — with having brought to full fruition Vico's "idea of the struggle of classes and the rejuvenation of society, by a return to a primitive state of mind and a new barbarism."[3] Elsewhere, he calls Sorel "the greatest, because most alive, contemporary representative of Marxism."[4] He does not hesitate to place him on a par with the founder, when he speaks of "the only two original thinkers which Socialism has had, Karl Marx and Georges Sorel, both full of a warlike and yet, in a certain sense, conservative spirit."[5] It is, no doubt, this element of "traditionalism" (in a non-Sorelian sense) that attracted Croce to the revolutionary philosophy of the **Reflections.** Another point of contact is Sorel's "strong consciousness of moral problems, a fact not immediately apparent to the superficial reader, for Sorel fights shy of all ostentatious moralizing. He would never make [morality] the title of one of his books...."[6]

But Croce leaves no doubt about the transitory character of his own interest in Sorel's (changing) theoretical convictions: "At one time, I felt enthusiastic about the parliamentary socialism à la Marx, at another time, about the syndicalist socialism à la Sorel; from the one and the other I had expected a regeneration of the present social life. And both times I saw that ideal of labor and justice dissolve and vanish."[7] A lesser man would have turned violently against the protagonist of a disappointed hope. At least, Croce could have turned his back on Sorel, as he had turned his back upon Marx. Yet, he continued to speak of "my venerated friend, Sorel."[8] Was it, because Sorel too had been moving away and beyond his old ideals? Was their friendship then perhaps a fellowship in disappointment? But Sorel, much as he changed, never reneged his anti-democratic, anti-liberal beliefs, while Croce, after having cast off the spell of Marx, developed more and more into a cautious liberal. It is perhaps here that we may discover the other possible reason for Croce's enduring loyalty to Georges Sorel: he admired, and also may have envied him subconsciously, for his own loyalty to an "ideal of labor and justice," however

---

[3]**The Philosophy of Giambattista Vico,** translation by R. G. Collingwood [of **La Filosofia di Giambattista Vico,** Bari, 1911] (London, 1913), p. 243. See also p. 277: "Recently Sorel in France has shown the fruitfulness of certain views of Vico's, especially that of the reflux, by applying them to the history of primitive Christianity and the theory of the modern proletarian movement..."

[4]**Pagine sparse** I (Napoli, 1919), p. 291.

[5]**Pagine sparse** II (Napoli, 1919), p. 227.

[6]**Ibid.,** p. 311.   [7]**Ibid.,** p. 14.

[8]**Ibid.,** p. 15.

nebulous. He could do so without having a bad conscience. For, after all, much as he was and still is vitally concerned in the social and political scene, his own main duty was to literature and philosophy; the Sorel who mattered most to him was, to be sure, a thinker and historian in his own right, but above all a man who tried to keep close to the actual, social and political mass movements of the time. In a vicarious fashion, Croce, by maintaining friendly contacts with Sorel, partook in that experience which was no longer the focal point of his own work, but still an object of his passionate concern as a contemporary. His "veneration" was for a man who, though years his senior, had preserved his own unflagging youthfulness. It is extremely risky to base such speculations on the brief and in-between remarks so far referred to. Fortunately, Croce wrote one comprehensive essay about Georges Sorel, which, although technically a review of **The Historic System of Renan** was considered representative enough of Sorel's entire work to serve later as an introduction to the Italian edition of the **Reflections.** It is in this long essay that we can securely ascertain what Croce really thought of Sorel. It is significant that this piece should reveal, along with the most flattering endorsements,[9] a most fundamental criticism of Sorel's position, in fact the only thorough-going criticism of Sorel which we possess from Croce's pen. Its friendly tone cannot hide that it aims straight at the core of the Sorelian doctrine.

Summing up Sorel's belief that a **modus vivendi** between historic science and theology is possible, Croce states "the only point" in Sorel's book on Renan, "which fills him with the gravest doubts." If Sorel is correct, then "the conflict between scientific history and religious faith cannot occur," since the objective of the former is to study the impact of a certain faith on human institutions, and not to pry into the **causes** of that faith. Sorel's historian is not interested in the factual evidence or lack of evidence which generated the belief in supernatural events: he takes it for granted, as one of the facts of history and proceeds from there. Such a limited concept of the historian's task would indeed make a conflict with theology impossible: the two disciplines could be at peace with one another, as long as history does not attempt a psychological approach. Psychological history, in contrast to scientific history, being as much concerned with the explanation of causes, cannot but clash with theology in fruitless arguments. Hence Sorel's rejection of Renan's method: it attempts what history cannot achieve.[10]

---

[9]Thus, he credits Sorel with having grasped "the problem which Marx did not study: the problem of the **organisation** of the proletariat." (**"Cristianesimo, socialismo e metodo storico"** in **La Critica**, 1907, p. 319. — Croce's emphasis).

[10]Ibid., p. 329.

Now Croce holds "that the comparison of history with physics and the natural sciences [in general] lead Sorel astray." However, the analogy which induced Sorel "to conceive as possible a historiography severed from metaphysics, and hence from all religious determinism" is inacceptable to Croce, "for historiography stands in quite a different relationship to philosophy (and hence to religion) than does physics: all history is an interpretation of reality, conducted, more or less consciously, in terms of philosophical categories...." Croce concludes therefore that "it is impossible to trace limits between history and theology." He defines "all history as a theology in action," regardless of whether that theology is "theistic, pantheistic or atheistic." Sorel deceives himself if he believes that his own "scientific" history is devoid of philosophy: to be sure, that implicit Sorelian philosophy "could not be reconciled with a **transcendentalist** conception of reality," but it is "in perfect accord with an **immanentist** view."[11]

The most dangerous character of this thrust is obvious: Sorel's rejection of psychologic history, on the surface of it a defense of theology, is also, and perhaps primarily, the vindication of his doctrine of the social Myth as a force impervious to all factual inquiry and ratiocination. If religious faith has to "show cause" as to its scientific value, then the secularized faith that mirrors itself in a myth, likewise becomes subject to the pragmatic test; in losing its charmed character it preserves little if anything of its usefulness as a suggestive doctrine of political action. No wonder Sorel did not take the Crocean criticism gently; the unusual tenacity and heat of his rebuttal bespeaks the seriousness of his predicament.[12]

Sorel accepts without reservation Croce's criticism that the boundaries between theology and history can never be defined, because the two fields overlap: "I know well it is impossible to find one or the other method ever applied with exactitude; but in order to explain human activities clearly (which are always more complex than language can convey) it is very useful to resort to types of the uttermost simplicity." In other words, Sorel still holds fast to his principle of **diremption**.[13] However, he is ready to make a concession and to speak henceforth merely of "two tendencies, since they will never confine themselves to their proper spheres." Croce is right: theology and history cannot be separated as distinctly as Sorel had done. "But," he demurs, "could we not try? I am frightened when I read the books of the so-called free-thinkers; the most fanatic priest could not be dominated more by his scholasticism than they are by their own anti-christian theology."

---

[11] **Ibid.**, p. 329-330. — Croce's emphasis.

[12] Letter to Croce (**La Critica**, 1928, p. 100-102), May 6, 1907.

[13] See **Reflections** (1950 Am. ed.), p. 287; cf. chapter 11, p. 267 of this study.

The pleading tone of Sorel's argument is unmistakable. But he is unshaken in his belief that "it is quite immaterial to know for certain whether the great miracles, those generators of great institutions, have ever actually transpired or have merely taken place in the imagination." In particular, the stigmatization of St. Francis continues to fascinate Sorel as an example of human credulity: many natural explanations of that phenomenon are possible, and yet: "What does it matter! The Franciscan history is a fact, and it depends on a miracle . . . . Christ's life after the crucifixion may have been a fact or a mere mental illusion; what does it matter? I try to tell the story without passing judgment upon the correctness of these generating facts; in my view, the generation alone belongs to history."

Does that make Sorel a relativist, disinterested in ascertaining any truth? Not so: "Evidently, it will never be possible to rid oneself of some conception of the world; if we should do so, we would render ourselves deaf and blind; we would no longer understand anything." Even the physicist, Sorel grants Croce, cannot avoid becoming a philosopher of sorts when he is bent on the search for secondary causes; he mentions Faraday as an example, although Faraday never wrote anything about philosophy.

Croce's insinuation that Sorel himself is a "philosopher of sorts" is of course particularly troublesome. Sorel professes not to mind at all being called an "immanentist" if by this Croce wants to characterize his, Sorel's, scientific instinct as well as his historic concept of the class struggle, rather than an actual **Weltanschauung.** If Croce means no more than that, then Sorel is in the best company: "the people who are much concerned with true morality and, above all, with the origin of morals — are they not all, more or less, immanentists?" he exclaims. And, so as to clinch his argument, Sorel brings up a name to conjure with.

"Bergson refrains from ever offering his ultimate conclusions about the [meaning of the] world; in the view of many, he would seem to be a pantheist, but I do not believe he wants to be just that . . . . " Bergson's latest book, **Creative Evolution** could easily be cited, Sorel holds, as "evidence of the attempt to explain . . . pantheism; but to explain it without succumbing to it." All representative contemporary thought is, in Sorel's view, "characterized by the great effort it makes to deal with [philosophic] questions without resorting to the hypothesis of the prime mover."

Did he really expect to convert Croce to his point of view? The argument would probably have died from attrition, had it not been that the two friends decided to use the essay on Renan as an introduction to the Italian edition of the **Reflections.** This gives Sorel an opportunity to reopen the issue and to make the sly suggestion to omit, or at least, shorten the passages in question, as "too special" for the general purpose of a preface.[14] So much do Croce's objections still rankle in Sorel's mind that he could make this awkward proposal with a perfectly straight face. "Rereading the fine article which you have consecrated to my work in **La Critica** — " he writes four days later,[15] ostentatiously to discuss at great length how better to translate a quotation from Tertullian used by him and referred to by Croce. But all this is merely a prelude to bringing up once more the question of the relationship between religion and science:

"It seems more and more certain to me," says Sorel, "that the historian acts much more the part of the philosopher than that of the scientist; as Bergson indicates with regard to biology, so the philosopher is forced to enter a discussion of the facts; he cannot just accept them humbly from the scientist's hands."

This statement contains nothing with which the author of the **Logic**[16] would want to quarrel; but it is, as far as Sorel is concerned, a **volte face** all the more remarkable as he does not seem to be in the least conscious of the fact that his new formula evades the question, if it does not altogether reverse the argument. For the original discussion had not been about the need of the philosopher-historian to inquire into the cause of the beliefs behind the facts — that was precisely the designated activity of what he then had called theology and what he now chooses to call by another name. No, the debate had started with Sorel's assumption that a scientific historiography was excused from looking into the factual evidence on which the man of faith bases both his intellectual systems and his social institutions, which is an altogether different proposition. It is the only one which permits the theorist of the myth to evade not only a critical analysis of the myth-engendering human faculty but also the question as to the validity of a particular myth; once "the philosopher is forced to enter a discussion of the facts," there is nothing left to Sorel but to deny that he is a philosopher — a position which he had just given up as quite untenable.

He must have felt something of embarrassment for, once more, he is forced to arraign his star witness: "I have had occasion to speak to Bergson about [my] extension of his doctrine to the field of history; he found it very satisfactory, and I would not be surprised if he should write something along that line."

Thus fortified, Sorel returns to the assault: "If philosophy is a great complex of historical ports, that recital must no longer be presented as a science, and theology may, without conflicting with science, lean upon a philosophy which has resulted in an account peculiar to the believers."

---

[14]To Croce (**loc. cit.**, p. 190), October 20, 1908.

[15]**Ibid.** (p. 191), October 24, 1908.

[16]Croce, **Logica comme scienza del concetto puro** (Bari, 1909); translated as **Logic as the Science of the Pure Concept** (London, 1917). Cf. R. G. Collingwood, **The Idea of History** (Oxford, 1946), p. 194 ff.

In thus refashioning his previous doctrine, Sorel is at once contrite and firm: "When I wrote my book on Renan, that idea was far from being as clear to me as it is now; reading the **Creative Evolution** helped me a great deal to clarify my own mind about that point. I believe it is of great importance for philosophy and science not to be confounded, as it has been done for so long; it was the fundamental error of rationalism."

On this safe note, Sorel rests his case, not to reopen it again. When Croce's **Logic** appears nine months later, Sorel confines himself to the remark that he went and brought the book to Berthelot.[17] Needless to say, the friendship of the two, Sorel and Croce, remained unaffected by a disagreement which, between other men, not necessarily of lesser stature, might have led to mounting disaffection and eventual estrangement.

2. Sorel and the Elitists

The affinity between our author and the triad of Pareto, Mosca, and Michels has been commented upon sufficiently,[18] although in the main with Fascism in view rather than with the idea of evaluating the four men on their own merits. It would be interesting to investigate to what extent the similarities between the works of Mosca, Michels and Pareto have been exaggerated in the process of establishing the link between them and some other system, Fascism or "Machiavellianism." This leads to the problem whether the agreement between the three "elitists" and the "theorist of syndicalism" went beyond the common rejection of rationalistic and idealistic doctrines. There remains the question to what degree a **positive** agreement exists between the theories of violence and of the myth on the one hand, and Mosca's doctrine of "juridical defense," Michels' "iron law of oligarchy" and Pareto's "circulation of elites" on the other. We believe the answer to this question must take into account the starting points and the ends informing each of the four writers, as well as their intellectual and methodological tools. And then the differences will be found too vast to permit of more than marginal agreement in the conclusions

[17]To Croce (**loc. cit.** p. 197), July 17, 1909. — Rene Berthelot: Son of the famous chemist Pierre-Eugène Marcelin Berthelot; philosopher, author of **Evolutionisme et platonisme** (1908), **Etude sur le mouvement pragmatiste,** Vol. I (Nietzsche), 1911, Vol. II (Bergson), 1913.

[18]**E. G.** James Burnham in his book, **The Machiavellians, Defenders of Freedom** (New York, 1943); G. H Bousquet, **Vilfredo Pareto** (Paris, 1928), p. 200 ff.; F. W. Coker, **Recent Political Thought** (New York, 1934), p. 483 ff.; Ernest Barker, **Reflections on Government** (Oxford, 1942), p. 127-128.

reached.[19] Since the question of the **objective** identity linking the four systems transcends the scope of this study, we shall confine ourselves to the problem of **subjective** identification: What did Pareto, Mosca, Michels think about Sorel, and **vice versa.** Did they feel indebted to each other?

Robert Michels' case is simple. His relation to the older man was that of a now admiring, now rebellious student.[20] His main work abounds with favorable references to Sorel to whom "we owe...the rediscovery of the relationships between democracy in general and absolutism, and their point of intersection in centralization."[21] In his diary he is, as we have seen, much more reserved. Michels could not help but feel a congenital restraint toward the man who "profoundly distrusts the Jews, particularly reproaching them for their capitalistic internationalism." The young German scholar who will soon establish himself, first in Switzerland, and finally in Italy, acutely notes down some of Sorel's more extreme notions: his scorn of moral laxity, of the fops frequenting the **Bal Tabarin,** the woman chasers. "He declares himself strictly in favor of prematrimonial chastity, for men as well as women, because in his view final victory in all social and political struggles always goes to the class with the greatest integrity ...and morality."[22]

Six years later, Michels is still under the old spell: "Saw Sorel again in Rue Sorbonne, at the entrance of Charles Péguy's editorial office. This is perhaps the tenth time I met this forceful thinker. Externally, he has changed little. But in his ideas, he shows a marked tendency in favor of the **camelots du Roy** [sic], a tendency in the main due to their common hatred of the execrated democracy. Complete break with Hubert Lagardelle and his group, with the sole exception of Edouard Berth. Strange, Sorel, essentially a solitary man, cannot endure solitude. Like all theoreticians, he is in need of acolytes...."[23]

Sorel takes Michels seriously enough to criticize one of his works.[24] Writing to Croce, he declares: "The author never understood what is important in Marxism. He presents us Garibaldi, L.

---

[19]This is also the view taken by Arthur Livingston in his introduction to the translation of Mosca's **Elementi di scienza politica (The Ruling Class,** New York and London, 1939, p. xxxvi ff.).

[20]See Part II, Introduction, p. 165. — The tendency to put Michels on a par with Mosca and Pareto is to be resisted.

[21]**Political Parties** (Glencoe, Ill., 1949), p. 222, note 24.

[22]Michels, diary, Paris, April, 1906, **"Lettere di Georges Sorel a Roberto Michels,"** in **Nuovi Studi di Diritto, Economia e Politica,** Rome September-October, 1929, p. 289, note 4.

[23]Diary, Paris, 1913, **ibid.,** p. 290, note 5.

[24]Michels, **"La débâcle de l'Internationale ouvriere et l'avenir"** in Scientia, Milano, May, 1916.

Blanc, Benoît Malon (!!) as the real masters of socialist thought.... "[25]
One may imagine with what feelings the author read that letter when
it appeared in **La Critica** twelve years afterwards. His comment
shows admirable restraint: "There is among the numerous letters
which Sorel wrote to Croce one which incidentally concerns the present writer," he begins. It seems to him that Sorel "evidently did not
understand the plain meaning of the article" (Michels' insistence that
the Marxists, by neglecting the ethical element in the Mazzinian doctrine in favor of the purely economic aspects, had destroyed its socialist content). It is difficult not to sympathize with Michels who "evidently did not understand" in turn that what to him was the main burden of the argument failed to impress Sorel who had said the same
things for many years, and so felt free to pounce on incidentals. But
Sorel's indignation was not serious: "The disagreement," concludes
Michels, "did not in the least affect the good relations with the present writer."[26]

Nor did the good relations prevent Georges Sorel from disagree-
ing once again with Michels: "I received your article on the historic
sphere of Rome," he writes on August 28, 1917, "and almost every
single thesis of it is the opposite of what long studies of the subject
have lead me to believe." There is, Sorel believes, "no country less
Roman than Italy." The very reason that Italy could be conquered by
the Romans is that she had been "as much anarchic as the Barbary
countries; she remained anarchic throughout the Middle Ages, and
her native civilization perished when the Spaniards imposed their administrative regime upon the country." And he puts the finishing
touch to this depressing picture by adding: "Piedmont has concluded
the disastrous work of the Spaniards." Robert Michels is not yet sufficiently Roberto Michels to resent the gallic pride in Sorel's next
statement: "The only Latin country which may lay a claim to the Roman heritage is France where the monarchy has tried to uphold the
[traditions of the Roman] imperial power."[27]

Not only does Michels fail to register his protest, but he notes:
"That thesis...does contain a grain of truth." But since the Fascist
censor is looking over his shoulder, he inserts that Sorel wrote this
"before the rise of Italian Fascism," meaning that afterwards, the
Roman heritage, of course, reverted back to Rome.[28] But Sorel has
not yet shot all his bolts: "As to the Roman genius of assimilation,

[25]To Croce (**La Critica**, 1929, p. 357), May 30, 1916. — Benoît Malon (1841-
1893): Worker, Socialist, Member of the Paris Commune, author of **Histoire
du socialisme et des prolétaires** (1881-84), **La morale sociale** (1887), **Le
Socialisme intégral** (1891-92); founder of **La Revue Socialiste,** to which Sorel
contributed many articles, although its general tendency was too much to the
right for his taste.

[26]Michels, **loc. cit.**

[27]**Ibid.,** p. 292.

[28]**Ibid.,** p. 293, note 1.

what a farce! The Romans destroyed all nationality by suppressing the [native] aristocracies." As Proudhon put it: "the only way to deal with aristocracies is to massacre them."[29] At this point Michels very decently reminds his Italian reader that "Sorel's anti-Roman thesis" was shared by some Italian writers of the Renaissance, for instance by Paolo Paruta who compared his peaceful, commercial Venice favorably with aggressive Rome.

We owe to Robert Michels an account of Sorel in the last year of his life, which shows us the old man scaring the wits out of his chronicler: "Sorel was most affectionate toward me, quite contrary to his habitual grand reserve. He immediately began to talk about the Versailles peace which he condemned severely. The war had ended with the triumph of capitalistic democracy over a democratic oligarchy. Nothing could be more disadvantageous to the interests of syndicalism. Therefore, Sorel believes: "That situation cannot last ...." He goes on to express his confidence in the vitality of the Italians, Russians and "perhaps" the Germans. "He spoke well of Pareto, his old friend, with whom he had had an intensive correspondence during the war years. He spoke of Benito Mussolini with great sympathy: who knows where he will go? At any rate, he will go far."[30]

The conversation then reverts to Russia. How lucky Michels is to teach at Bâle, Sorel exclaims. What a wonderful opportunity of getting information about Bolshevism, not available in censor-ridden France! Michels tries to get in a word of caution: Did Sorel really believe that Europe, exhausted from the war, and longing for peace, stood in need of a propaganda which preached unrest and civil dissension? He immediately regretted his words, for Sorel not only failed to be impressed by Michels' argument, but he revealed "with much heat" his plan — probably improvised on the spur of the moment — to translate, or have translated into French as many writings of Lenin and Trotzky as Michels could hunt up for him in Switzerland! Whether or not Sorel was really serious about it, the effect on Michels was disastrous: "I confess that the prospect appealed to me very little, and using the first opportunity to extricate myself from a conversation which threatened to become painful, I saluted the old friend and master respectfully and took my leave. I never saw him again." And thus the scene ends, with Roberto Michels running fast to save his reputation from the grasp of the fierce old revolutionary whom we may imagine gazing after the escaped disciple with a look of semi-innocence not unmixed with amusement.

*   *   *

---

[29]Ibid., p. 293.
[30]Michels, diary, Paris, March 22, 1922, loc. cit., p. 293, note 4.

There is little to be said about Sorel's relationship to Gaetano Mosca. The two men did not know each other. Sorel never mentions the other although he has a theory of balanced social forces very similar to that developed earlier by Mosca.[31] Sorel's name in turn will not be found in Mosca's **oeuvre maitresse.** In a later, little-known **History of Political Doctrines,**[32] Mosca devotes to Sorel exactly one half of a four page chapter, allotting the other half to — Henri George. One has the impression that he deals with Sorel merely from a sense of duty: not that he treats him harshly or with condescension, but throughout the brief piece one can sense a certain cold restraint, a definite unwillingness to recognize Sorel if only as a poor relation. The reason is not difficult to find: Mosca was an author with that greatest of all grudges: his pioneer work in the study of the ruling class had not found the recognition which he thought his due. It was Pareto who received the credit for ideas which had been expressed by Mosca first. And Pareto had failed to recognize his debt — perhaps because there was no debt to recognize, for it is possible to trace back Mosca's and Pareto's as well as Sorel's conceptions of the ruling class to the influence of Taine and leave it at that.[33] There remained the fact, that Sorel and Pareto were good friends, and Mosca knew it. Possibly his coldness against the hermit of Boulogne sur Seine was a mere by-product of his grievance against the hermit of Celigny: Sorel had to suffer for the failure of his friend to recognize Mosca's priority. This is all the more regrettable as close inspection would bear out much more community of views between the oeuvres of Sorel and Mosca, than between that of Pareto and Sorel.

The author of the great **Trattato di Sociologia Generale** on the other hand shared with the Frenchman two things which may, at least partially, explain their close association. Both were almost exact contemporaries, living an identical amount of years (Sorel: 1847-1922, Pareto: 1848-1923); Mosca was their junior by 10 and 11 years, respectively (1858-1941). More important, both Pareto and Sorel were engineers by training, both were thoroughly grounded in mathematics, and while Sorel neglected that science later on in favor of economics, he remained sufficiently informed to appreciate Pareto's application of the mathematical method to economic problems. However, at this point the likeness ends: Pareto's "logico-experimental method" was

---

[31]Cf. especially their notions on the role of the administrative branch; see chapter 3, p. 89f; chapter 6, p. 151.

[32]**Histoire des doctrines politiques,** introduced and translated by Gaston Bouthoul (Paris, 1936). (Originally published as: **Corso di lezioni di Storia delle dottrine e instituzioni politiche** (Rome, 1933).

[33]"Taine's theory that ruling classes succumb because of neglecting their 'duties' (a theory that Taine may have taken over from Tocqueville)." Arthur Livingston in his introduction to Mosca's **The Ruling Class** (New York, 1939), p. xxxix.

one with which Georges Sorel could sympathize, but it was basically alien to his own philosophy which never could quite rid itself of metaphysics — as Benedetto Croce had shown to the great annoyance of Sorel.

Pareto too was conscious of that "alien" element in his friend's make-up. Much as he quotes and commends him in every one of his works, he very early recognized an element of strain in Sorel thinking, which at first seemed to him to be a tendency to go too far. Being the more systematic of the two, Pareto frequently accompanied his laudatory references with small notes of caution. Here are two examples: Commenting on Sorel's rejection of "soft," democratic and "humanitarian" socialism, Pareto writes "There is much truth in what G. Sorel says, but there is also exaggeration. In trying to avoid the vagaries of Tolstoyianism, we must not go to the opposite extreme."[34] Sorel is right in exposing the insincerity of contemporary European pacifism which pins its hopes on the International Court of Justice newly set up at the Hague, but he is on dubious ground when he insists that the strong pacifistic movement in England is closely bound with the continuous intellectual decadence of that country. Pareto is unable to discover any symptoms of English decadence in comparison with other parts of Europe. Sorel is likewise wrong in attributing the fanatic pacifism of contemporary Italy to the same reasons which are causing her great economic backwardness. "If that were true," remarks Pareto, "the pacifist fanaticism should be even greater in Spain, a country certainly more backward than Italy." Finally, if it is utopian to believe that all international conflicts are susceptible of peaceful arbitration, "it is incontestable that in our time it has been possible to resolve by that method conflicts which, in the past, would almost certainly have lead to war."[35]

Again, Sorel is right to hold the "idealists" of all times responsible for a great deal of misery, and to fear that the rationalist attempt "to change the world by propagating convictions," will once more lead to an "immense destruction of forces."[36] Sorel is wrong in hoping that the working class would remain immune against the ideologies of the "new Saint Simonians." What Sorel does not see is that "the workers too possess an ideology.... The Marxist religion is of the same nature as all other religions." To a certain extent, humanitarian sentiments are indispensable to the conservation and progress of human societies. Even if one would deny the usefulness of these humanitarian sentiments, "it would not do to deny their existence, nor the fact that ideology is an integral part of civilized man's character."[37]

[34]Pareto, Les systèmes socialistes [1902], 2. edition, (Paris, 1926), Tome II, p. 408-409.

[35]Ibid., p. 410.

[36]Ibid., p. 410-412.

[37]Ibid., p. 412-413.

In thus opposing his own theory of residues to the "errors of people who imagine man could rid himself entirely of religion and replace it by simple scientific notions,"[38] Pareto, without naming him explicitly, has put his finger on the element of strain in the Sorelian work. It is Sorel who, trying to rid himself of non-scientific notions, projects his internal conflict on the social plane, by positing a sharp and absolute dichotomy between the ideologists (utopians) and the "class of the producers" (who possess a myth). In rejecting this dichotomy, Pareto protects Sorel from himself: in finding fault with his analysis, he emphasizes the importance of his synthesis. For if the work of Sorel will survive it will not be on account of his "scientific" method, but precisely because he did violence to it. His concept of the myth is the very vindication of Pareto's thought. But whereas Sorel remained unable to square his new, important insight with his "scientific" heritage, we find, in Pareto's work, "non-scientific sentiments" securely reconciled with a persistently, if not always consistently used scientific method.

The admiration which the system builder felt for the inspired extravaganza of "his very good friend, G. Sorel"[39] thus remained unencumbered by any feelings of indebtedness. Musing about the "strange case of how Sorel and I, starting from opposite points, have reached identical conclusions," Pareto snarls at "G. and R., who, in their stupid **History of Political Economy,** say that Sorel got his ideas from me. That is not true; those fellows just don't understand. We did our work independently from one another...and if we happen to agree in our results, that only demonstrates the logic of the facts."[41]

Noting "that in France, a theatre play, Bourget's **La Barricade,** has drawn attention to the scientific thought of Sorel," he adds, "Poor science that needs literature in order to make itself known!"[40] He is most anxious to assert his own, historical importance: "Bourget knows only Sorel, and so he says that he had been inspired by him, but without knowing it, he was even closer to [the ideas of] my **Manuale.**"[42] And there is more than patriotic wistfulness in his concluding

————————

[38]Ibid., p. 413.

[39]Pareto, letter to his editor, Guido Sensini, November 14, 1907, in Guido Sensini, **Corrispondenza di Vilfredo Pareto** (Padova, 1948), p. 38.

[40]To Sensini (**op. cit.,** p. 47), January 16, 1910. — G. and R.: Gide and Rist.

[41]Ibid.

[42]Ibid. — In the last-named work Pareto wrote of Sorel's **Reflections:** "This is the most remarkable scientific work in sociology to appear in a great many years. We are all the more happy to find in it the conformation of several theories advanced in the Italian edition of this Manual, published in 1906. G. Sorel arrived at his conclusions by an independent and different way...." (Cited from the 2. French edition: **Manuel d'économie politique** (Paris, 1927), p. 480, note 1. (Originally published as: **Manuale di economia politica** (Milano, 1906).

words: "In a few years, people in Italy will talk about...Sorel. We always trail a few years behind France...."[43]

When Sorel died in 1922, Pareto, who was to follow him only a year later, took leave from his friend in moving words: "I got to know Sorel in 1897, and since then to this day, for more than twenty-five years, no cloud has even darkened the sky of our friendship."[44] In retrospect, Pareto once more marvels at the fact how it was possible that such a friendship could grow and endure between one who was "a man of faith," and a practitioner of the "purely experimental method." His explanation is a candid criticism and, at the same time, a noble vindication of Sorel.

Why, asks Pareto, was Sorel so much resented by so many people? His answer is that, man being a mixture of both sentiment and reason, faith and skepticism, the differences between people are in the main due to the various proportions in each of them of the two opposite characteristics. Between those with the same beliefs, there will be unity; between those of opposing faiths, a more or less acute dissension; frequently not, as it would seem natural, in a direct ratio to the difference in creeds, but in an inverse ratio: the orthodox detests the heretic more violently than the atheist. Hence "the incurable aversion that existed between the admirer of the Demos and the worshipper of the divine proletarian" — between the democrats and the humanitarians on the one hand, and Georges Sorel on the other.[45]

But while his enemies used against him "almost exclusively the weapons of sentiment," Sorel employs against them "logico-experimental reasoning to demonstrate the emptiness of the democratic and humanitarian dogmas," lifting the veil behind which his opponents tried to hide reality.[46]

In labelling them "intellectuals" Sorel caused, for himself and others, some semantic trouble. If by "intellectual" we mean a man with intellect, then Sorel surely was no anti-intellectual; he "could not have been without becoming his own enemy, he, who was provided with that gift to such a large degree." What Sorel understood and wanted understood by "intellectual" was the type of man who is convinced that in social action "reason prevails over sentiment," or at least, that it **could** prevail. It is this "pseudo-scientific attitude" which Sorel exposed with such merciless and masterful consistency.[47]

"Hence our consensus, hence our common enterprise." Thus it was possible for Pareto "to treat as a special aspect of his theory of **Residues** the celebrated doctrine of the **Myth,** which Sorel had arrived at independently by using logico-experimental means."[48]

---

[43]Sensini, op. cit., p. 47.

[44]"Georges Sorel" in La Ronda 1922, p. 541.

[45]Ibid., p. 542.   [46]Ibid.

[47]Ibid., p. 546. — Pareto's emphasis.

[48]Ibid., p. 542. — Pareto's emphasis.

For that achievement, Sorel was of course detested by his victims, but he also found "approval among a few people who, although far from sharing all his sentiments, would gladly welcome some as helpful arguments."[49] Thus the Italian Fascists, Pareto holds, could detach Sorel's theory of violence from his belief in "the Producers" without being unfair to his work, for the two notions are indeed not conjoined by any intrinsic logic; it was therefore possible for the Fascists to "confirm in a splendid way the uniformity of the empirical laws observed by Sorel, without endorsing in the least his admiration for the Proletariat."[50]

If this sounds like the statement of a Fascist sympathizer, that does not disturb Pareto. It does not interest him that he is labelled "the theorist of nationalism" in distinction from Sorel, "the theorist of syndicalism."[51] He prefers to discuss this issue in a wider context: if there is a real argument between him and Sorel, it consists in the fact that Pareto thinks of himself as a scientist and nothing else, whereas in Sorel science is marred by his "inclination toward metaphysics."[52]

If this is so, then how could he, one of his friends inquired, afford to speak so well of Sorel's work? Pareto replies that, if Sorel was guilty of metaphysical leanings, so was Newton, in his main work, the Principia. The proper question to ask of a man is not: does he indulge in metaphysics? For no writer will be found free from that blemish. But: does that element prevail, or not prevail? In Sorel, both the metaphysical and logico-experimental method are found side by side, often in one and the same work: Pareto mentions Renan's System of History, in which the Introduction represents, in his view, the work of a metaphysician, while all the rest is dominated by Pareto's favorite method.[53]

The same is true of the Reflections. In that work, Sorel combines a certain faith with a study of the way facts are related. The scientist is concerned merely with the latter. We must distinguish between the Sorel who voices certain social desiderata, and Sorel, the student of "experimental uniformity." We are free "to choose the former and to reject the latter, or vice versa, or else to accept both together, as our sentiments and reasoning commands us."[54]

Now, in Pareto's view, the logico-experimental test would not let Sorel seem to be correct when he assigned such a constructive role to violence in human history. To that extent, Pareto would feel tempted to side with Sorel's detractors. But since they do not offer anything in turn but "sentimental and dogmatic arguments and a priori judgments," since "they do not treat of that which is, but of what ought to be or will be," Pareto comes to the conclusion, that, all his

49Ibid., p. 546.
51Ibid., p. 545.
53Ibid., p. 544.
50Ibid., p. 544-545.
52Ibid., p. 541.
54Ibid., p. 545.

objections notwithstanding, "Sorel is much superior to his critics who are neither willing nor able to understand him."[55]

Even though it will not stand close scrutiny as an historic "law," the theory of violence may have its value as an indication of the extent to which the rationalistic and humanitarian credo, perfectly valid and of great use in the early nineteenth century, has become discredited today. Sorel's work would thus indicate the violent recoil from democratic principles, a swing of the pendulum so extreme that it may, by virtue of its own excess, revert to a position where democracy would again prove its worth. In that case, Sorel would have made a "profitable contribution to a useful social transformation."[56] It seems, Pareto took the view that Sorel represented the antithesis required, in the Hegelian-Marxian dialectic, to bring forth another synthesis of Western humanism.....

He concludes: "Of the man I shall say little. He was upright, he possessed integrity, nobility and dignity of character....If he had chosen to be pliable and to serve those in power, with his genius, he could have collected riches, honors and official recognition. Instead he died in poverty, ignored by the Academies...passed over by official science. He did not care, and he was right in that....For, after all, we cannot have everything, and he who searches for the truth only, must not complain if he finds no material rewards."[57]

---

[55]Ibid., p. 543. — Pareto's emphasis.
[56]Ibid., p. 547.
[57]Ibid., p. 547-548

SELECTIVE BIBLIOGRAPHICAL CHRONOLOGY[1]

I. Books and Brochures by Sorel

Contribution à l'étude profane de la Bible (Paris, 1889), pp. 339.

Le procès de Socrate (Paris, 1889), pp. 396.

L'Avenir socialiste des syndicats (Paris, 1901), pp. 88.

La ruine du monde antique (Paris, 1902), pp. 281. - 2. ed., 1925. - 3. ed. 1933. - Spanish ed. 1912.

Introduction à l'économie moderne (Paris, 1903), pp. 385. - 2. ed., 1922. - Russian transl., 1908.

Saggi di critica del Marxismo (Palermo, 1903), pp. xlviii + 401.

Insegnamenti sociali della economia contemporanea (Milano, 1906), pp. xxii + 398. - Russian ed., 1908.

Le système historique de Renan (Paris, 1906), pp. 475.

Degenerazione capitalista e degenerazione socialista (Milano, Palermo, 1907).

La décomposition du Marxisme (Paris, 1908), pp. 64. - 2. ed., 1910. - Japanese, 1929; German transl., 1930.

Les illusions du progrès (Paris, 1908), pp. 282. - 2. ed., 1911, 3. ed., 1922, 4. ed., 1927, 5. ed., 1947. - Spanish transl., 1909.

Réflexions sur la violence (Paris, 1908), pp. 257. - 2. ed., 1910, 3. ed., 1913, 4. ed., 1919, 5. ed., 1921, 6 ed., 1925, 7. ed., 1930, 8. ed., 1935, 9. ed., 19 , 10, ed., 1946, 11. ed., 1951. - Russian ed., 1907; Italian, 1909; English and American editions, 1914; Spanish, 1915; German and Japanese translations, 1928. - For further details, see Introductory i, note 2.

La révolution dreyfusienne (Paris, 1909), pp. 64. - 2. ed., 1911.

Le confessioni. Comme divenni sindicalista (Rome, 1910), pp. 38. Included in the

Matériaux d'une théorie du prolétariat (Paris, 1919), pp. 414. - 2. ed., 1921, 3. ed., 1929.

De l'utilité du pragmatisme (Paris, 1921), pp. 471. - 2. ed., 1928.

D'Aristote à Marx [L'ancienne et la nouvelle métaphysique] with an introduction by Edouard Berth (Paris, 1935); pp. 275.

---

[1]This writer is greatly indebted to the **"Bibliographie Sorélienne,"** edited by Paul Delesalle (International Review for Social History, Vol. IV, Leiden, 1939, pp. 463-487), the most complete catalogue of **Soreliana** in existence, listing more than 550 items, ending, however, with 1938. The present bibliography is a sketchy attempt to bring the record up to date.

<u>Selections</u>

El sindicalismo expuesto por Sorel, edited and introduced by Edmundo Gonzales Blanco (Madrid, 1931). Excerpts.

Giorgio Sorel, **L'Europa sotto la tormenta,** edited and introduced by Mario Missiroli [1932] 2. ed., Milano, 1941, pp. 308. Thirty brief articles contributed by Sorel to the Bolognese journal, **Il Resto del Carlino,** between 1910 and 1921 (1910: 1, 1919: 23, 1920: 3, 1921: 3).

Georges Sorel, **Der falsche Sieg** [False Victory]. Selected Sayings, edited and introduced by Michael Freund (Berlin, 1944); pp. 119.

II. Articles and Prefaces by Sorel

"Essai sur la philosophie de Proudhon" in Revue philosophique, Tomes XXXIII and XXXIV, June, July, 1892.

"Science et socialisme" in Revue philosophique, Tome XXXV, May, 1893.

"L'Ancienne et la nouvelle métaphysique" in L'Ere nouvelle, March - June, 1894. As a book, under the title **D'Aristote à Marx,** with a preface by Edouard Berth (Paris, 1935).

"La fin du paganisme"in L'Ere nouvelle, August - October, 1894. As a book, under the title La ruine du monde antique (Paris, 1902).

"Les théories de M. Durkheim" in Le Devenir Social, April, May, 1895.

"La métaphysique évolutioniste de M. Brunetière" in Le Devenir Social, September, 1895.

"Les théories pénales de MM.Durkheim et Tarde" in Archivio di Psichiatria, Vol. XVI, 1895.

"Superstition socialiste" in Le Devenir social, November, 1895.

"Progrès et développement"in Le Devenir Social, March, 1896.

"L'idéalisme de M. Brunetière" in Le Devenir Social, May, 1896.

"Les sentiments sociaux" in Le Devenir Social, August - September, 1896.

"Economie sociale catholique" in Le Devenir Social, October, 1896.

"Etude sur Vico" inLe Devenir Social, October - December, 1896.

Preface to Antonio Labriola, Essais sur la conception matérialiste de l'histoire (Paris, 1897).

"Contre une critique anarchiste" in Le Devenir Social, May, 1897.

"Sur la théorie marxiste de la valeur" in Le Journal des Economistes, May, 1897.

"Die Entwicklung des Kapitalismus"in Sozialistische Monatshefte, Oktober, 1897.

"Pro e contro il socialismo"(on Saverio Merlino's book of that title) in Le Devenir Social, October, 1897.

"Der Ursprung des Staatssozialismus in Deutschland" in Sozialistische Monatshefte, November, 1897.

"L'avenir socialiste des syndicats" in L'Humanité nouvelle, March - May, 1898 - Separate, enlarged edition, Paris, 1901. - Included in the Matériaux d'une théorie du proletariat (Paris, 1919)

"Was man von Vico lernt" in Sozialistische Monatshefte, June, 1898

"Betrachtungen über die materialistische Geschichtsauffassung" in Sozialistische Monatshefte, July - September, 1898.

Preface to Saverio Merlino, Formes et essence du socialisme (Paris, 1898).

"La necessità e il fatalismo del Marxismo" in La Riforma sociale, August, 1898.

"La Crisi del socialismo" in La Riforma sociale, October, 1898 - Also as "La crise du socialisme" in La Revue politique et parlementaire, December, 1898.

"Der amerikanische Kapitalismus" in Sozialistische Monatshefte, December, 1898.

"Y-a-t-il de l'utopie dans le Marxisme?" in La Revue de métaphysique et de Morale, March, 1899.

"Morale et socialisme"in Le Mouvement socialiste," March, 1899.

"Il vangelo, la Chiesa e il socialismo" in Rivista critica des Socialismo, April, May, 1899. - Incorporated into La ruine du monde antique.

"L'éthique du socialisme" in La Revue de Métaphysique et de Morale, May, 1899.

"L'evoluzione del socialismo in Francia" in Riforma sociale, June, 1899.

"Le Idee giuridiche del marxismo" in Rivista di storia e filosofia del diritto, August, 1899. Also as "Les aspects juridiques du socialisme" in Revue Socialiste, October - November, 1900.

"Dove va il Marxismo?" Separate edition, La Rivista critica del socialismo, 1899.

"Über die kapitalistische Konzentration" in Sozialistische Monatshefte, February - March, 1900.

"   "Les polemiques pour l'interprétation du marxisme" in La Revue Internationale de Sociologie, April, May, 1900.

"Les Dissensions de la socialdémocratie allemande à propos des écrits de M. Bernstein" in La Revue politique et parlementaire, July, 1900.

"Le système des mathématiques" in Revue de Métaphysique et de Morale, July, 1900.

"Les grèves. Les théories contrariées par les faits" in La science sociale, October, November, 1900. Included in the Matériaux d'une théorie du prolétariat.

"Les facteurs moraux de l'évolution" in Questions de morale (Paris, 1900).

"La science et la morale," ibid.

Preface to N. Colajanni, Le socialisme (Paris, 1900) - Included in the Matériaux.

"Economie et l'agriculture" in Revue socialiste, March, April, 1901.

"La valeur sociale de l'art" in Revue de Métaphysique et de Morale, May, 1901.

"Quelques mots sur Proudhon" in Cahiers de la Quinzaine, 13. cahier de la 2. série, June 1901.

"L'église et l'état" in La Revue socialiste, August - October, 1901.

"De l'église et de l'état. Fragments" in Cahiers de la Quinzaine, 3. cahier de la 3. série, October, 1901.

Preface to G. Gatti, Le Socialisme et l'agriculture (Paris, 1901). - Incorporated into the Máteriaux. Also published as "Socialismes Nationaux" by Cahiers de la Quinzaine, 14. cahier de la 3. série, April, 1902.

"Idées socialistes et faits économiques au XIXe siècle" in La Revue socialiste, March - May, 1902.

"Les syndicats industriels et leur signification" in La Revue socialiste, July - August, 1902.

"La crise de la pensée catholique" in Revue de Métaphysique et de Morale, September, 1902.

Preface to Fernand Pelloutier, L'histoire des bourses du travail (Paris, 1902).

"Sur divers aspects de la mécanique" in Revue de Métaphysique et de Morale, November, 1903.

"A propos de l'anticléricalisme" in Etudes socialistes (Paris, 1903).

"Léon XIII," ibid.

"Nouveaux réquisitoires de M. Brunetière," ibid.

"La lotta di Classi e la violenza" in Divenire sociale, October 1 and 15, 1905.

"Le syndicalisme révolutionnaire" in Le Mouvement socialiste, November 1 and 15, 1905. Included in the Matériaux.

"Les préoccupations métaphysiques des physiciens modernes" (with Julien Benda) in Revue de Métaphysique et de Morale, November, 1905.

"Lo sciopero generale" in Divenire sociale, December, 1905.

Preface to Georges Castex, La douleur physique (Paris, 1905). Included in the 2. ed. of Introduction à l'économie moderne as an appendix entitled "L'humanité contre la douleur."

"Réflexions sur la violence" in Le Mouvement socialiste, January 15 - June 15, 1906.

"Les droits acquis de Lassalle" in Le Mouvement socialiste, April 15, 1906.

"Grandeur et décadence de Rome" (on G. Ferrero's work) in Le Mouvement socialiste, July 15, 1906, February, 1907 and July 15, 1908.

"Les illusions du progrès" in Le Mouvement socialiste, August - December, 1906.

"Le caractère religieux du socialisme" in Le Mouvement socialiste, November, 1906. - Included in the Matériaux.

"L'Organizzazione della democrazia"in Divenire sociale, November 16, 1906. Also as "De l'esprit du gouvernement démocratique" in Le Mouvement socialiste, November, 1906. As "L'organisation de la démocratie" included in the Matériaux.

"Le prétendu socialisme juridique" in Le Mouvement socialiste, April, 1907.

"Les Cahiers de jeunesse de Renan" in Le Mouvement socialiste, May, 1907.

"Jean Jacques Rousseau" in Le Mouvement socialiste, June, 1907.

"La crise morale et religieuse"in Le Mouvement socialiste, July, 1907.

"Lettre à M. Daniel Halévy" (which became the introduction to the Reflections on Violence) in Le Mouvement socialiste, August 15 and September 15, 1907.

"L'évolution créatice" (a propos of Henri Bergson's work) in Le Mouvement socialiste, October 15, December 15, 1907, January 15 and April 15, 1908.

"Apologie de la violence" in Le Matin, May 18, 1908. Became appendix ii of the 3. ed. of the Reflections (Paris, 1913).

"La politique américaine" in Le Mouvement socialiste, June 15, 1908.

"Les intellectuels à Athènes" in Le Mouvement socialiste, September 15, 1908.

"Le modernisme dans la Religion et dans le socialisme" in Revue critique des livres et des idées, 1908.

"La religion d'aujourd'hui" in Revue de Métaphysique et de Morale, March and May, 1909.

"Evoluzione e decadenza" in Divenire sociale, December, 1909. - March, 1910. Became the appendix of the 2. ed. of Les Illusions du progrès (Paris, 1911).

Preface to V. Griffuelhes and L. Niel, Les objectifs de nos luttes de classe (Paris, 1909).

Preface to Arturo Labriola, Karl Marx: L'économiste, Le socialiste (Paris, 1910).

"Le mystère de la Charité de Jeanne d'Arc de Charles Péguy" in L'Action française, April 14, 1910.

"La Cité française," prospectus of a revue that did not appear (Paris, 1910).

"Vues sur les problèmes de la philosophie" in Revue de Métaphysique et de Morale," September, 1910, and January, 1911.

"Le monument de Jules Ferry" in L'Indépendance, March 1, 1911.

"L'Abandon de la revanche" in L'Indépendance, April 1, 1911.

"Lyripipi sorbonici moralisationes" in L'Indépendance, April 15, 1911.

"Les responsabilités de 1870" in L'Indépendance, May 1, 1911.

"Si les dogmes évoluent" in L'Indépendance, September 15, 1911.

"A la mémoire de Cournot" in L'Indépendance, October 15, 1911.

Preface to E. R. A. Seligman, L'Interprétation économique de l'histoire (Paris, 1911).

"Urbain Gohier" in L'Indépendance, January, 1912.

"D'un écrivain prolétarien" in L'Indépendance, March 1, 1912. (Included in the Matériaux.)

"Quelques prétensions juives" in L'Indépendance, May 1, and 15, June 1, 1912.

Preface to Edouard Berth, Les méfaits des intellectuels (Paris, 1913).

Preface to Mario Missiroli, Il papa in guerra (Bologna, 1915).

"Germanesimo e storicismo di Ernesto Renan," written 1915, published in La Critica, 1931 (see chapter 8, note 8).

"Violence et folies de la ploutocratie" in Resto del Carlino, May 26, 1917.

"Charles Péguy" in La Ronda, April 1, 1919.

"Proudhon" in La Ronda, September 5, 1919.

"Ultime meditazione," written 1920, published in Nuova Antologia, September - October, 1928.

"La Chine" in La Revue Communiste," July, 1920.

"Le Bolchévisme en Egypte" in La Revue Communiste, September, 1920.

"Lénine d'après Gorki" in La Revue Communiste, January 1921.

"Le Génie du Rhin" (on Barrès' book of that title) in La Revue Communiste, April, 1921.

"Jeremy Bentham et l'indépendance de l'Egypte" (with L. Auriant) in Le Mercure de France, April 15, 1922.

III. Letters by Sorel

343 letters to Benedetto Croce (La Critica, 1927 - 1930).

65 letters to Paul Delesalle (Lettres à Paul Delesalle, Paris, 1947, pp. 238).

5 letters to Robert Michels ("Lettre di Georges Sorel a Roberto Michels" in Nuovi studi di diritto, economia e politica, Rome, September - October, 1929, pp. 288 - 294).

To Hubert Lagardelle, July 25 and August 10, 1898, in L'Homme Réel, Nos. 2 and 3, February, 1934.

To Daniel Halévy, July 7, 1907 and October 16, 1917, in **Fédération,** No. 34, (November, 1947), pp. 2 - 4.

To Agostino Lanzillo, February 20 and November 20, 1910, in **Johannet, Itinéraires d'Intellectuels** (Paris, 1921), pp. 216 and 227.

To Edouard Dolléans, October 13, 1912, in **Revue d'histoire économique et sociale,** Vol. XXVI, No. 2 (1940 - 1947), pp. 106 - 107.

To Edouard Berth [1913] in **Cahiers du Cercle Proudhon,** No. 5-6 (1913), p. 263 - 265.

To Guido Castellano, February 9, 1919, in Croce, **Pagine sparse II** (Napoli, 1919), p. 300 - 302.

IV. Books or Brochures on Sorel

Agostino Lanzillo, **Giorgio Sorel** (Rome, 1910), pp. 120.

Frederic D. Cheydleur, **Essai sur l'évolution des doctrines de M. Georges Sorel** (Grenoble, 1914), pp. 174.

F. Aguilanti, **Georges Sorel** (Rome, 1916).

Max Ascoli, **Georges Sorel** (Paris, 1921), pp. 48.

Enrico Leone, **Il néomarxismo. Sorel e Marx** (Milano, 1922).

Paul Perrin, **Les idées sociales de Georges Sorel** (Alger, 1925).

Gaétan Pirou, **Georges Sorel** (Paris, 1927), pp. 67.

Pierre Lasserre, **Georges Sorel. Le théoricien de l'impérialisme ouvrier** (Paris, 1928), pp. 268.

G. La Ferla, **Introduzione allo studio delle opere di Georges Sorel,** (Assisi, 1929).

Michael Freund, **Georges Sorel. Der revolutionäre Konservativismus** (Frankfurt a. M., 1932), pp. 366.

Jean Deroo, **Le renversement du matérialisme historique. L'expérience de Georges Sorel** (Paris, 1933), pp. 253.

G. La Ferla, **Ritratto di Georges Sorel** (Milano, 1934).

Jean Variot, **Propos de Georges Sorel** (Paris, 1935), pp. 270.

Jacques Rennes, **Georges Sorel et le syndicalisme révolutionnaire** (Paris, 1936), pp. 187.

Pierre Angel, **Essais sur Georges Sorel** (Paris, 1937), pp. 352.

Victor Sartre, **S. J., Georges Sorel. Elites syndicalistes et révolution prolétarienne** (Paris, 1937), pp. 307

Jean Wanner, **Georges Sorel et la décadence** (Lausanne, 1943). pp. 90.

Fernand Rossignol, **La pensée de Georges Sorel** (Paris, 1948), pp. 282.

V. Prefaces, chapters or articles about Sorel

Benedetto Croce, "Cristianesimo, socialismo e metodo storico" in La Critica, July 1907, pp. 317 - 330; also published, under the title, "Il pensiero di Georges Sorel" as the preface to Considerazioni sulla violenza, the Italian edition of the Refleçtions (Baris, 1909).

Edouard Berth, "Le système historique de Renan" in Le Mouvement Socialiste, August - September, 1907, pp. 179 - 196.

G. Prezzolini, chapter I, "Notre maître Sorel"in La teoria sindicalista (Napoli, 1909).

Henri Massis, "Les idées sociales de Georges Sorel" in Le Mercure de France, February 16, 1910.

Georges Guy-Grand, Le procès de la démocratie (Paris, 1911), throughout, especially chapter II, pp. 71 - 86.

Gilbert Maire, "La philosophie de Georges Sorel" in Cahiers du Cercle Proudhon, No. 2 (March - April, 1912), pp. 57 - 81.

Georges Valois, "Sorel et l'architecture sociale" in Cahiers du Cercle Proudhon, No. 3 - 4 (May - August, 1912), p. 111 - 116.

René de Marans, "Grandes rectifications soréliennes," ibid., p. 117 - 124.

Henri Lagrange, "L'oeuvre de Sorel et le Cercle Proudhon," ibid., p. 125 - 133.

H. du Passage, "G. Sorel, E. Berth et les antidémocrates de gauche" in Etudes, February 20, 1913. "M. G. Sorel et la 'morale des producteurs,'" ibid., March 5, 1913.

Paul Seippel, "Sur l'influence possible des 'Réflexions sur la violence' sur Lénine et Trotzky" in La Journal de Genève, February 4, 1918. - Evoked Sorel's reply in "Pour Lénine" (appendix iii of the Reflections).

René Johannet, "L'évolution de Georges Sorel"in Itinéraires d'Intellectuels (Paris, 1921).

Edouard Berth, Preface to Max Ascoli, Georges Sorel (Paris, 1921).

Vilfredo Pareto, "Georges Sorel"in La Ronda, 1922, p. 541 - 548.

R. Narsy, "Georges Sorel" in Journal des Débats, September 1, 1922.

Emile Buré, "Péguy et Sorel" in Eclair, September 7, 1922.

Georges Guy-Grand, "Georges Sorel et les problèmes contemporains" in La Grande Revue, December, 1922, p. 293 - 324.

A. Lalande, On Sorel's De l'utilité du pragmatisme in Revue philosophique, 1922, p. 485 - 486.

(Unsigned): Necrology in Special Supplement of the Revue de Métaphysique et de Morale, October - December, 1922.

R. Salomé, "Le lyrisme de M. Georges Sorel" in La Revue des Jeunes, February 10, 1923.

A. Maletzky, "Georges Sorel" in Internationale Communiste, IV, No. 24 (March, 1923), p. 86 - 113.

Edouard Berth, Chapter III ("Proudhon, Marx, Georges Sorel") and Appendix ("Le Tertullien du socialisme") in Guerre des Etats ou Guerre des Classes (Paris, 1924).

T. E. Hulme, Speculations (London, 1924), Appendix A.

René Johannet, "Adieu à Georges Sorel" in Eloge du bourgeois français (Paris, 1924).

G. Michael, "Qu'est-ce-que fut le sorélisme" in Clarté, January 1, 1925. "Sorélisme ou léninisme" in Clarté, March 1, 1925.

Jérôme and Jean Tharaud, Notre cher Péguy (Paris, 1926), I. 255 - 262; II, 137 - 142.

Edouard Berth, Post-Script to Ueber die Gewalt (German ed. of the Reflections), 1928.

William Yandall Elliott, The Pragmatic Revolt in Politics (New York, 1928), chapter IV, pp. 111 - 141.

Gottfried Salomon, Preface to the German edition of the Reflections, 1928.

Ernst H. Posse, Preface to Die Aufloesung des Marxismus (German ed. of La décomposition du marxisme, 1930.

Waldemar Gurian, "Georges Sorel" in Staatslexikon, 1930.

Marcel Péguy, "La rupture de Charles Péguy et de Georges Sorel d'après des documents inédits" in Les Cahiers de la Quinzaine, Paris, 1930.

Boris Souvarine, Introduction to a selection from Sorel's correspondence with Croce, in La Critique Sociale, March, 1931.

Edouard Berth, Du "Capital" aux "Réflexions sur la Violence" (Paris, 1932): the chapter of the same title, pp. 169 - 204.

Sigmund Neumann, "Sorel" in Encyclopaedia of the Social Sciences, Vol. XIV (New York, 1934), pp. 262 - 263.

Thomas Niederreuther, Georges Sorels Betrachtungen ueber die Wirtschaft (doctoral thesis, Muenchen, 1934).

Edouard Berth, Preface to Sorel, D'Aristote à Marx [L'ancienne et la nouvelle métaphysique] (Paris, 1935), pp. 8 - 92.

Gaetano Mosca, Histoire des doctrines politiques (Paris, 1936) pp. 298 - 300.

Sammy Beracha, Le Marxisme après Marx (Paris, 1937), chapter VII, pp. 169 - 196.

Rainer Heyne, "Georges Sorel und der autoritaere Staat des 20. Jahrhunderts" in Archiv des oeffentlichen Rechts, Bd. 29 (Tuebingen, 1938), Heft 1 und 2.

Gaudens Megaro, Mussolini in the Making (Boston and New York, 1938), chapter 7, pp. 228 - 245.

V. E. Michelet, "Georges Sorel" in Le Mercure de France, June 15, 1938.

J. de Saint-Chamant, "L'actualité de Georges Sorel" in La Grande Revue, January, 1938, pp. 308 - 322.

James Burnham, The Machiavellians, Defenders of Freedom (New York, 1943), Part IV, pp. 119 - 132.

Pierre Andreu, "Le socialisme de Sorel" in Fédération No. 34, November, 1947), pp. 5 - 7.

Robert Aron, "De Marx à Sorel," ibid., pp. 15 - 16.

Georges Goriély, "Georges Sorel, pluraliste," ibid., pp. 8 - 9.

Daniel Halévy, "Introduction à deux lettres inédites," ibid., pp. 1 - 4. "Proudhon, Sorel, Péguy," ibid.,pp. 10 - 14.

Gilbert Maire, "Le bergsonisme dans la pensée sorélienne," ibid., pp. 17 - 18.

David Thomson, "Sorel: Apostle of Revolution" in The Manchester Guardian Weekly, November 13, 1947, p. 12.

Pierre Andreu, "Du nouveau sur Georges Sorel" in Le Figaro Littéraire, July 10, 1948, p. 6.

Jean-Jacques Chevalier, Les grandes oeuvres politiques. De Machiavel à nos jours(Paris, 1949), Part IV, chapter iii, pp. 313 - 332.

E. H. Carr, Studies in Revolution (London, 1950), chapter 10, pp. 152 - 165

"Sorel, Georges" in Philosophen — Lexikon by Werner Ziegenfuss and Gertrud Jung, Vol. II (Berlin, 1950), pp. 565 - 567.

Scott H. Lytle, "Georges Sorel: Apostle of Fanaticism" in Modern France, Problems of the Third and Fourth Republics, ed. by Edward Mead Earle (Princeton, 1951), pp. 264 - 290.

VI. References to Sorel or Sorelian Themes[2]

Vilfredo Pareto, Les systèmes socialistes [1902-3] (Paris, 1926), Vol. II, pp. 408 - 413.

Antonio Labriola, Discorrendo di socialismo e di filosofia (Rome, 1898), transl. as Socialisme et philosophie, Lettres à Georges Sorel (Paris, 1899), Am. ed.: Socialism and Philosophy by Ernest Untermann (Chicago, 1907), transl. from the 3. Italian ed.

Benedetto Croce, Historical Materialism and the Economics of Karl Marx [1900] New York, 1914), pp. 55, 131 - 138.

Vilfredo Pareto, Manuel d'économie politique [1906] (Paris, 1927), pp. 20 - 21, 115 - 116, 134, 480 - 483, 499.

Edouard Berth, "Marchands, Intellectuels et Politiciens" in Le Mouvement Socialiste, July 15, October 15, November 15, 1907.

C. Bouglé, Syndicalisme et démocratie (Paris, 1908).

Leon Duguit, "Le syndicalisme" in Revue Parlementaire, June 10, 1908.

Hubert Lagardelle, Syndicalisme et socialisme (Paris, 1908).

G. Weill, Le syndicalisme en France, in Revue d'Economie internationale, January, 1908.

---

[2]Year of original publication in [ ]

F. Challeye, Syndicalisme réformiste et syndicalisme révolution-naire (Paris, 1909).

Yves Guyot, "Les interêts économiques et l'oeuvre socialiste. Conférence faite 2. April, 1909." (Labadie Collection, Ann Arbor, Michigan).

Gaétan Pirou, Proudhonisme et syndicalisme révolutionnaire (Paris, 1910).

Benedetto Croce, The Philosophy of Giambattista Vico [1911] (London, 1913), pp. 243, 247.

Georges Guy-Grand, La philosophie syndicaliste (Paris, 1911), pp. 88 - 95.

Hubert Lagardelle, "Monarchistes et syndicalistes" in Le Mouve-ment Socialiste, January, 1911.

Arthur D. Lewis, Syndicalism and the General Strike (London, 1912).

Gaston Serbos, Une philosophie nouvelle de la production (Aix et Paris, 1913).

Vladimir G. Simkhovitch, Marxism versus Socialism (New York, 1913), p. 293.

Edouard Berth, Les méfaits des intellectuels (Paris, 1914).

Robert Hunter, Violence and the Labor Movement (New York, 1914), p. 264.

Robert Michels, Political Parties [1915] (Glencoe, Ill., 1949), pp. 142, 222, 264, 346, 381, 385.

Vilfredo Pareto, Mind and Society [1916] (New York, 1935), §§538, 541, 663, 671, 765, 997, 1101, 1627, 1638, 1668, 2193, 2450.

Bertrand Russell, Roads to Freedom (London, 1918), pp. 46, 80.

Benedetto Croce, Pagine sparse (Napoli, 1919), I 291, II 14, 15, 227, 311.

Georges Valois [Alfred Georges Gressent], D'un siècle à l'autre (Paris, 1921), pp. 131 - 135, 207, 256.

Gide et Rist, Histoire des doctrines économiques (Paris, 1922), pp. 565 - 567.

P. Gorgolini, Les Fascismes [Prefaces by B. Mussolini and J. Bainville] (Paris, 1923).

Werner Sombart, Der proletarische Sozialismus (Jena, 1924-25), I 222f., 414f., II 180, 257, 298, 311.

G. Moreau, Essai sur les théories et l'histoire du syndicalisme ouvrier en France (Paris, 1925).

Wyndham Lewis, The Art of Being Ruled (London, 1926), pp. 5, 18, 128, 130, 132, 177.

Franz Oppenheimer, System der Soziologie II (Jena, 1926), pp. 139, 681, 729.

Erwin von Beckerath, Wesen und Werden des Fascistischen Staates (Berlin, 1927), pp. 24, 26, 27, 31 - 33.

Carl Schmitt, Der Begriff des Politischen [1927] (Hamburg, 1933), p. 23.

Julien Benda, The Great Betrayal [1927] (London, 1928), pp. 91, 103 - 105, 117, 119.

Edouard Berth, La fin d'une culture (Paris, 1927).

Max Eastman, Marx, Lenin and the Science of Revolution (New York, 1927), pp. 137 - 139.

Henri Moysset, Introduction to La Guerre et la Paix in Oeuvres complètes de P.-J. Proudhon, Vol. VI (Paris, 1927), p. xciv.

Henri Sée, Matérialisme historique et interprétation économique de l'histoire (Paris, 1927), p. 87, n. 1.

Pitirim Sorokin, Contemporary Sociological Theories (New York and London, 1928), pp. 54, 58, 60, 464, 662, 669, 671, 688.

Karl Mannheim, Ideology and Utopia [1929] (New York, 1946), pp. 119 - 123, 125, 129.

Peter M. Riccio, On The Threshold of Fascism (New York, 1929), pp. 107, 162 - 163.

Morris R. Cohen, "Belief" in Encyclopaedia of the Social Sciences, Vol. II (New York, 1930), p. 501.

Georges Guy-Grand, Introduction to De la justice in Oeuvres complètes de P.-J. Proudhon, Vol. VIII, Pt. 1 (Paris, 1930), p. 7.

Roger Soltau, French Political Thought in the 19 Century (New Haven, 1931), pp. 435 - 436, 444 ff., 146, 156, 298, 228, 276, 351, 357.

Leon Dandieu, Anthologie des philosophes français (Paris, 1932).

Sidney Hook, Toward the Understanding of Karl Marx, (New York, 1933), pp. 45 - 46, 53.

Francis W. Coker, Recent Political Thought (New York, 1934), pp. 233, 234, 235, 238 - 239, 241, 242, 243, 245 - 246, 484.

Hermann Heller, Staatslehre (Leiden, 1934), pp. 7, 9, 206.

Charles E. Merriam, Political Power [1934] in A Study of Power (Glencoe, Ill., 1950), pp. 170, 299.

R. Palme Dutt, Fascism and Social Revolution (New York, 1935), p. 176.

Leo Strauss, The Political Philosophy of Hobbes (London and New York, 1936), p. 165.

George H. Sabine, A History of Political Theory [1937] (New York, 1950), pp. 871 - 872, 794, 873.

Albert Weisbord, The Conquest of Power (New York, 1937), I 180, 306 - 307, 584, 586 - 587, 665.

William J. Blake, Elements of Marxian Economic Theory and its Criticism (New York, 1939), pp. 576 - 577.

Alfred Cobban, Dictatorship (New York, 1939), pp. 120 - 121, 123.

Diana Spearman, Modern Dictatorship (New York, 1939), pp. 12, 143, 145, 147, 149.

Veit Valentin, Weltgeschichte II (Amsterdam, 1939), pp. 560, 627, 694, 698.

D. W. Brogan, France Under the Republic (New York and London, 1940), pp. 345, 421f., 643.

Emil Lederer, **The State of the Masses** (New York, 1940), p. 49.

W. M. McGovern, **From Luther to Hitler** (Boston and New York, 1941), pp. 427 - 434, 438, 546, 548, 625f.

Ernest Barker, **Reflections on Government** (London and New York, 1942), pp. 127 - 128, 129.

Franz L. Neumann, **Behemoth** [1942] (New York, 1944), p. 194.

Joseph A. Schumpeter, **Capitalism, Socialism and Democracy** [1942] (New York and London, 1947), p. 340.

R. A. Tsanoff, **The Moral Ideas of our Civilization** (New York, 1942), p. 547 f.

Hans Barth, **Fluten und Daemme** (Zuerich, 1943), pp. 176 - 177, 223 - 232.

Jacob P. Mayer, **Political Thought in France** [1943] (London, 1949), pp. 115 - 120, 59, 80, 97, 111.

Ludwig von Mises, **Omnipotent Government** (New Haven,1944), p. 126.

Henri de Lubac, **The Unmarxian Socialist** [1945] (New York, 1948), p. 56.

Bertrand Russell, **A History of Western Philosophy** (New York, 1945), p. 791.

Alfred Weber, **Farewell to European History** [1945] (New Haven, 1948), pp. 148-149.

Alexandre Zévaès, **Histoire du Socialisme et du Communisme en France de 1871 à 1947** (Paris, 1947), pp. 325 - 327.

Carl Brinkmann, **Soziologische Theorie der Revolution** (Goettingen, 1948), p. 82.

Robert Goetz-Girey, **La pensée syndicale française. Militants et théoriciens** (Paris, 1948), pp. 60 - 75, 38, 39, 156 - 158.

Chester C. Maxey, **Political Philosophies** (New York, 1948), pp. 591, 627, 629, 646.

Max Nomad, "The Sorel Interlude" in **European Ideologies**, ed. Feliks Gross (New York, 1948), pp. 334 - 338; see also pp. 776, 789, 1946.

Harold D. Lasswell, **The Analysis of Political Behaviour** (London, 1949), p. 197.

Robert K. Merton, **Social Theory and Social Structure** (Glencoe, Ill., 1949), p. 392.

Henri Peyre, "Literature and Philosophy in Contemporary France" in **Ideological Differences and World Order**, ed. F. S. C. Northrup (New Haven, 1949), pp. 270 - 271, 278.

David Spitz, **Patterns of Anti-Democratic Thought** (New York, 1949), pp. 76, 83 f, 97, 192.

Crane Brinton, **Ideas and Men** (New York, 1950), pp. 429 - 430.

Robert F. Byrnes, **Antisemitism in Modern France**, Vol. I (New Brunswick, 1950), p. 68 - 69.

John H. Ballowell, **Main Currents in Modern Political Thought** (New York, 1950), pp. 458 - 463, 604.

R. N. Carew Hunt, **The Theory and Practice of Communism** (London, 1950), pp. 74, 110.

Harold D. Lasswell and Abraham Kaplan, **Power and Society** (New Haven, 1950), pp. 24, 117, 267, 280.

J. R. Pennock, **Liberal Democracy** (New York, 1950), pp. 128 - 129.

Hannah Arendt, **The Origins of Totalitarianism** (New York, 1951), pp. 110, 318, 320. - Cf. also the chapter on the Dreyfus Affair, pp. 89 - 120.

Herbert Spiegelberg, **Case Socrates Resumed** [scheduled for publication in New York, 1951].

Robert J. Niess, **Julien Benda** [in preparation].

INDEX